Post-Pandemic Pedagogy

Post-Pandemic Pedagogy

A Paradigm Shift

Edited by
Joseph M. Valenzano III

LEXINGTON BOOKS
Lanham • Boulder • New York • London

Published by Lexington Books
An imprint of The Rowman & Littlefield Publishing Group, Inc.
4501 Forbes Boulevard, Suite 200, Lanham, Maryland 20706
www.rowman.com

6 Tinworth Street, London SE11 5AL, United Kingdom

Copyright © 2021 The Rowman & Littlefield Publishing Group, Inc.

All rights reserved. No part of this book may be reproduced in any form or by any electronic or mechanical means, including information storage and retrieval systems, without written permission from the publisher, except by a reviewer who may quote passages in a review.

British Library Cataloguing in Publication Information Available

Library of Congress Cataloging-in-Publication Data

Names: Valenzano, Joseph M., III, 1978- editor.
Title: Post-pandemic pedagogy : a paradigm shift / edited by Joseph M. Valenzano III.
Description: Lanham : Lexington Books, [2021] | Includes bibliographical references and index. | Summary: "Post-Pandemic Pedagogy: A Paradigm Shift discusses how COVID-19 upended the college and university pedagogical paradigm. This collection looks at what we thought we knew about good teaching, how those notions changed during the pandemic, and speculates on where we will go from here in our classrooms and on our campuses"—Provided by publisher.
Identifiers: LCCN 2021033917 (print) | LCCN 2021033918 (ebook) |
  ISBN 9781793652218 (Cloth) | ISBN 9781793652225 (ePub)
Subjects: LCSH: College teaching. | Flipped classrooms. | Educational change. |
  Critical pedagogy. | COVID-19 Pandemic, 2020-
Classification: LCC LB2331 .P65 2021 (print) | LCC LB2331 (ebook) |
  DDC 378.1/25—dc23
LC record available at https://lccn.loc.gov/2021033917
LC ebook record available at https://lccn.loc.gov/2021033918

This project is dedicated to all the faculty, staff, administrators, and students who persevered through professional and personal challenges during the COVID-19 pandemic. Even through the sense of loss that pervaded your work and lives, your ability to remain focused on student learning and respond to adversity inspired many.

Contents

Acknowledgments		ix
Introduction: The COVID-19 Classroom *Joseph M. Valenzano III*		1
1	Teaching in the Midst of COVID-19: Teaching Effectiveness as a Function of Student Preferences for Instructional Behaviors *Scott A. Myers and Casey M. Stratton*	17
2	From Novel to Necessary: COVID-19 and the *Kairos* of Bringing Technology into the Communication Classroom *Ashley A. Hanna Edwards*	37
3	Post-Pandemic Pedagogy: Compassionate and Caring Course Curriculum in the Digital University *Linda Carozza and Steve Gennaro*	57
4	Reimagining Engagement for (Post)Pandemic Teaching: A Multileveled Approach *Lindsey B. Anderson, Raphael Mazzone, and Melissa A. Lucas*	73
5	Teaching Communication in a Pandemic and Post-Pandemic World *Brad Mello and Cyndi Grobmeier*	91
6	Networked Family Spirit: Paradox and Dialectical Tensions in Moving a Small, Liberal Arts University Online *Katherine Hampsten and Amanda Hill*	109

7	Post-Pandemic Anxiety: Teaching and Learning for Student Mental Wellness in Communication *Lori Blewett and Maureen Ebben*	129
8	The Pandemic and Disability Inclusive Pedagogy: Examining the Response to COVID-19 in Higher Education *Brittany N. Lash*	149
9	Landscape of Service Learning Courses: Post-Pandemic Evolution of Community Partnerships and Service Learning Projects *Sharon Storch*	167
10	Navigating Uncertainty Together: Pandemic Lessons Learned from Training New GTAs in Teaching Public Speaking *Anne C. Kretsinger-Harries, Elizabeth Helmick, Kate Challis, and Ali Garib*	185
11	A Case for Teaching Public Speaking without Live Audiences *Matt McGarrity*	203
12	Progressing through Tuckman's Phases in a Virtual College Classroom: Using Online Tools to Support Student Group Development *Angela M. McGowan-Kirsch and Amanda Lohiser*	219
13	Post-Pandemic Pedagogy in Intercollegiate Academic Debate: Performing Civic Life in Hybrid, Virtual, and In-Person Environments *John J. Rief*	239

Conclusion: Predicting the New Pedagogical Paradigm	259
Index	265
About the Contributors	277

Acknowledgments

During the fall 2020 semester I found myself teaching Political Communication. I am not a technologically adept instructor, and so I typically avoid using the course management system for anything beyond posting readings and grades. COVID-19 and the ensuing adjustments to classes on my campus necessitated that standard approach change. Due to social distancing my Tuesday/Thursday class split so that half my students came one day and the remaining students came the other day. That's not enough in-person time to teach the course. So, I found myself designing a class that relied heavily on discussion posts through the course platform, as well as announcements and posts to keep students on track with what was due. I had no expectations, but halfway through the term I found that the students were referencing the discussion posts for the week that each of them made when we met in-person. I also was able to dive deeper into material during our meetings and cover things they felt they needed more information to understand. It was a tremendous teaching experience in the craziest semester of my life. That group of students and how they handled my class inspired the ideas and approach to this volume. COVID changed how I taught, and some of the changes it forced will continue in classes I teach in the future. Could that be the same for other instructors? How did what we thought we knew about teaching and learning change as a result of COVID? And so began this volume.

No achievement—especially editing a book—comes without the help of others. This project is a testament to that truism. It would not have come to fruition without the hard work of the contributors to this volume. When I issued the call for proposals in fall 2020, I had no idea what would happen because I knew everyone was underwater just trying to get through the COVID-year. I was humbled and gratified by the sheer volume of proposals, and even more so by those whose contributions appear here. These individuals worked hard to deliver meaningful and thoughtful discussions about this past year and the teaching innovations and adjustments all faculties made. They did this while also tending to their own students and lives—I am forever grateful to them for their dedication to this project.

These contributors, and in fact faculty, staff, administrators, and students around the world deserve thanks. As the dedication indicates, your hard work, adaptability, and compassion for each other inspired me and others to deliver the best year we could under COVID-19 conditions. One cannot think about the last year and feel a sense of loss, but as I hope this book shows, we also will have gained much in the long run. Thank you for not giving up on each other.

I also would have never even conceptualized this volume if not for a perfectly timed email from Nicolette Amstusz of Rowman and Littlefield. Her inquiry about what I was working on spurred me to think beyond the day-to-day tasks I was checking off just to stay the course during a challenging semester. *Kairos* is all, as the ancient Greeks would say, and her timing could not have been better. Thank you for thinking of me and encouraging me to pursue new ideas that had purpose and meaning.

As a department chair, even in a good year, research can be a difficult thing to maintain. I would not be able to do so without the best group of faculty and staff around. I owe my department a deep debt of gratitude for their grace, effort, understanding, and support for both me, but in particular our students. In particular, I am grateful to Sam Wallace and Jon Hess who helped me think through elements of this project in a way that made its argument and purpose clear. They never said "no," and always were there with a careful read and thoughtful response. I am indebted to both of them. Staff such as Amy Droege, Mark Hillman, Pat Enright and Heather Parsons also deserve my thanks for their ability to be there with an ear, but also their dedication to the department that makes my job so much easier and more enjoyable.

During the pandemic lockdowns when much of this project took place, external support was difficult to find. That said, my friend and colleague Lee Dixon of the UD Psychology department did more than he will ever know to keep me sane and focused. His kindness is without peer, and his ability to say the right thing at the right moment is simply uncanny. I am thankful God blessed our paths so they might cross, as I likely would have had a much more challenging time during the pandemic had they not. Thank you for your support, encouragement, and always kind but honest perspective.

Finally, and without question, the people who instilled in me the confidence I could complete this project and the desire to do so were my family. My wife Lauren is my rock, and an ever-present source of encouragement and support. She keeps me on task, believes in me, and is the source of all my energy. Whether it is a gentle nudge, or her willingness to let me work on this book into the evening, she has never wavered in her support. My son Connor and his boundless enthusiasm and curiosity inspired me daily. In fact, watching him navigate school and see how his teachers responded—and how he, in turn, did as well—provided the kernel of this book's central idea. His smile, laugh and jokes always kept my grounded on the things in life that are important. My nephew Chris, who endured half of his first year and all of his second in less than optimal conditions in college while living with us, reinforced me when I needed it. If he could get up and work hard during the pandemic, changing course modalities and adapting how he learned, I knew I could do the same. And finally, my in-laws, Lisa and Bill Mack, whose constant support and familial dedication opened up time for me to write and encouraged me to pursue my ideas. I know I am beyond blessed to have them in my life, and will be eternally grateful to them for helping us navigate the pandemic.

There are others I know who need thanks and helped make this project a reality. To Anne Crecelius, Andy Horner, Eric Spina, Paul Benson, Danielle Poe, Kevin Gray, Jackson Goodnight, Brad Balser, Mary Buchwalder, Deb Bickford, Tom Skill, Carolyn Phelps, Katherine Cleaver, Robin Oldfield, Bill Fischer, Ryan Allen and the UD E-Learning team, Jason Edwards, Tim French, and many others I know I am forgetting; to my family back in New Jersey—Matt, Andy, Mike, Pete, my mother and father, my late Uncle Ron who passed during the pandemic, Rita Chacon, my Uncle Don, Aunt Roseanne and all my cousins, and my nieces and nephews (Nick, Alexis, Ava, Bella, MJ, David, Teddy and Esme) who will benefit from the lessons offered in this volume when they go to college: Know that you are in my heart and that you provided support and meaning when I needed it most, whether you were aware of it or not. Thank you.

Introduction

The COVID-19 Classroom

Joseph M. Valenzano III

In the summer of 2019, students traveled around the world, taking classes in foreign countries, seeing and learning about history, and practicing their language skills. spring college sports concluded, while fall sports made plans for their seasons. Universities prepared budgets, recruited students for the upcoming academic year, and improved campus infrastructure. Faculty conducted research, updated course materials, and planned experiential learning opportunities for the fall. Everything functioned as it had for decades.

Little did students, university administrators, and faculty know, fall 2019 would be the last semester that would function "normally."

Sometime in fall 2019, unbeknownst to anyone, a silent, invisible force emerged that soon upended the world. The first reported cases of a deadly pathogen emerged in Wuhan, China, and in the first few weeks of December 2019, six symptomatic cases were tested and confirmed at a regional hospital (Huang et al. 2020). By the end of December doctors identified a new viral pathogen, similar in effect to influenza or pneumonia, which they believed was a novel, or new, coronavirus (Huang et al. 2020). By the end of December, an international alert was issued regarding this new infectious disease (Stone 2020). On December 31, the United States provided its first acknowledgment of 27 cases of what the novel coronavirus located in Wuhan, China (Taylor 2020), but a later study found that 41 cases appeared between mid-December and January 2 (Huang 2020). Despite the occurrence of this new pathogen as the new year approached, the world continued to turn as normal.

Things would quickly change, however. On January 1, United States Deputy National Security Advisor, Matthew Pottinger, was informed of a new outbreak that appeared similar to SARS and, according to the *Chicago Tribune*, this left him "rattled" (Lipton et al. 2020). On January 3, the Chinese government notified the United States of an outbreak (Harris et al.

2020). Of the 44 cases now reported, 11 were seriously ill, and doctors had ruled out common respiratory diseases (Branswell 2020). On January 7, they announced the discovery of a new coronavirus—labeled COVID-19—and consequently, the United States issued a travel advisory for Wuhan, China (Khan 2020). Two days later the first person died of COVID-19.

By mid-January, when most college and university students returned to classes, the disease had spread even further than Wuhan. The first evidence of human-human spread of COVID-19 outside of China occurred in Singapore, among a group of travelers who attended a business meeting in Singapore (Geddie 2020). Numerous countries on multiple continents, including the United States, reported their first cases by the end of January. The disease had not been contained. On January 30, the World Health Organization declared COVID-19 a Public Health Emergency of International Concern and asked, "All countries should be prepared for containment, including active surveillance, early detection, isolation and case management, contact tracing and prevention of onward spread of 2019-nCoV infection, and to share full data with WHO" ("Statement" 2020). On January 31, the United States banned anyone from entering who had visited China in the previous 14 days (Kennedy 2020). Within a month into the new year the world faced a significant health crisis, but the United States seemed—at least outwardly—optimistic it would not impact normal operations.

Throughout February cases exploded, and the travel and tourism industry began to experience disruptions. The *Diamond Princess* cruise ship spent several days trying to find a port that would receive it as hundreds of passengers came down with coronavirus (Thompson and Yasharoff 2020). Cases exploded throughout Asia, and countries began to impose travel restrictions in the hopes it would keep individuals from spreading the virus across borders and continents. Unfortunately, by late February, these measures clearly were shown to be ineffective, and the ripple effects of the virus spread from tourism and travel to other areas as well.

On February 21, despite the virus being largely contained to Asia with nominal cases popping up elsewhere, signs pointed toward a worldwide spread of the disease. Italy confirmed 16 cases in the affluent Lombardy region, a significant increase over the prior day, bringing their total to 20 ("Coronavirus: outbreak grows" 2020). Iran added 13 cases to its total, while other countries such as Israel reported their first case (Newey et al. 2020). The United States also leapt from 15 to 35 confirmed cases, mostly situated on the West Coast (Johnson 2020). It was clear that travel restrictions did not stop the spread of the virus around the globe.

Over the course of the next two weeks, Italy became a major hot spot for the virus as it quickly overtook the country. By the end of February it totaled 1,128 cases with 29 deaths (Borghese 2020). The rate of spread was exponential and began to put a strain on the healthcare system of the country. Additionally, universities in the United States began to recall students who were studying abroad from Italy and other countries (Fischer 2020). The impact of the virus had now reached higher education in the United States, despite the American total of the virus sitting only at 68 (Hernandez 2020). These moves proved prescient, however, because in March, things would escalate quickly.

As cases increased across the globe and in the United States, it became clear one of the major areas of concern was community living areas, like nursing homes, hospitals, and college dormitories. It stands to reason given that the virus "landed" on the West Coast that the first university to take action on their campus would be located there. On March 6, the University of Washington—with an enrollment of 50,000+ students—announced it would send students home on March 9 to finish the quarter (which ended on March 20) ("Beginning March 9" 2020). Such began what universities thought to be a temporary trend, one that picked up when, on March 11, the World Health Organization declared COVID-19 a pandemic (Gumbrecht and Howard 2020). In fact, by that date, over 100 universities canceled in-person instruction and moved courses online for at least a few weeks (Quintana 2020).

Thankfully, for many schools this timing coincided with the end of quarters or spring breaks for their campuses, allowing a little time for faculty and IT staff to pivot to the now immediate demand for online instruction ("The coronavirus is upending higher ed." 2020). Many schools had to act quickly to expand wireless hotspots, supply students with laptops, ensure access to software programs, and triage instruction for faculty, many of whom never taught online before ("The coronavirus is upending higher ed." 2020). Faculty needed the time to adjust syllabi, assignments, and even prep digital lectures in lieu of normal in-class learning. Students—as well as faculty and staff—were left to hope this change was temporary, but worried it might be more lasting.

Unfortunately, the pivot to online learning was anything but short. By the end of March universities and colleges suspended in-person instruction for the entire term and moved traditional end-of-semester festivities like graduation online as well. The pandemic continued to rage into the summer with little signs of abatement. This, in conjunction with changes to the university admission cycle due to modifications in federal guidance,[1] dramatically impacted schools' ability to recruit, enroll, and budget for the fall semester. Now, in addition to uncertainty over the ability to deliver in-person learning, there was uncertainty over budgets and funding for the necessary training and staffing to teach classes come fall.

Numerous schools, several of whom who were financially strapped already, felt the sting of the pandemic most acutely. Several small liberal arts schools, like MacMurry College and Urbana University, announced their closures due to financial stresses exacerbated by the pandemic (Bauman 2021). Major public university systems, such as the University of Massachusetts, California State University, Ohio University, University of Arizona, and Boston University, large regional schools like the University of Akron, and even private universities like Canisius College all announced severe austerity measures that included faculty and staff layoffs and furloughs due to the strains the pandemic created for higher education budgets ("Outrage as coronavirus" 2020). Even with federal stimulus money approved in spring 2020, some schools just could not survive, or radically altered their operations to stay afloat. COVID-19 created a dual pandemic of sorts for universities and colleges. They had to find ways to financially survive in uncertain times while weathering financial hardships due to losing significant room and board revenue from spring term, and they were unable to model or recruit effectively for fall 2020, all while keeping everyone safe from a virus circulating out of control.

As the summer of 2020 moved along, it became apparent that colleges and universities would be forced to adapt how they educated their students. The idea of bringing back thousands of students to live in close quarters with each other created a significant challenge for universities, many of which relied heavily on revenue driven from room and board from returning students. There were varied approaches, with only a handful of schools able to welcome students back to fully in-person courses for fall 2020. Some large systems, like the California State University system, opted for announcing early that all classes would be online for the year and nothing would be in-person (Hubler 2020). Many schools, however, decided to do a modified approach where students were welcomed back to campus and taught in socially distanced classrooms. These courses asked students to attend class once a week with half of their class, while the other half met on another day, with much of the work and even lectures taking place asynchronously through a course management system. As is clear, these approaches, regardless of which, necessitated changes to pedagogy for university and college students on a scale and with a speed never before seen in higher education.

THE PANDEMIC INDUCED PARADIGMATIC MOMENT

Higher education is no stranger to change, but that change often comes slowly and after much time, consideration, and thought. In fact, the hallmarks of the educational experience at a college, like lectures, have stood the test of centuries. Disciplinary boundaries have evolved slowly over time, with new disciplines emerging every decade or so, but the core of a college or university education has remained constant. Not even two world wars and a worldwide flu pandemic in 1918 forced the type of change made in the last 15 months. There have been changes in terms of access, structure, emphasis, and even campus life to be sure, but these emerged over the course of decades and not all at once (Thomas, 1962). In point of fact, scholars have been suggesting for some time that online pedagogy is both realistic and effective (see: Shwartzman 2007; Westwick, Hunter, and Haleta 2018; Broeckelman-Post et al. 2019). Not even they could have predicted the marked shift brought on by the response to COVID-19.

Over the course of a spring break faculty were forced to adapt classes that were not meant to be delivered online, for just that mode. They jury-rigged assignments, leveraged video lectures, Zoom, and Microsoft Teams, and spent more time checking in with students for their mental health than lecturing and teaching. The spring shift was abrupt and everyone, from faculty and administrators to students, recognized people were doing their best under unprecedented conditions filled with stress, uncertainty, and, in many instances, unstable WiFi connections. Then the summer came, and faculty often were asked to prepare to teach their classes in multiple modalities depending on where the conditions on the ground would let them go. This was a tremendous amount of work for faculty over a summer time when they typically rested and researched. Unlike the spring, however, students who entered the fall had higher expectations for their educational experience than they did when faculty only had one week to prepare in spring.

COVID-19 disrupted the work life of academics, upending traditional approaches to preparing classes, conducting research and participating in service. summers normally spent doing research and slowly prepping courses for fall became an intensive workshop on how to deliver effective online courses for fall. Many faculty lost access to research subjects or field sites stymying the development of their research agendas, and forced many schools to provide extensions or adjustments to tenure clocks. Service suddenly became a requirement of many faculty during a period when they typically would do next to none. Faculty at schools across the country provided feedback on committees tasked with getting campuses ready for pandemic move-in, and helped educate colleagues who had less experience with teaching online or using course management software.

Despite the disruptions, the pandemic forced faculty to rethink teaching and course design on a large scale. There are a number of ways instructors adapted to the pandemic both in advance of fall semester and in between fall and spring 2021. In some cases, they tapped into existing research and best practices for teaching online, and in other instances simply winged it, trying new methods and adapting to new challenges. The end result was that faculty learned a lot about what they thought they knew about teaching, what actually works, and what they should pay attention to going forward. There will be no returning to the way things were wholesale when the pandemic recedes, but rather it will be a changed environment in higher education in ways we can foresee and others we may not. It is, as Thomas Kuhn (1962) would say, a "paradigm shift" for higher education.

Faculty have long differed in their approaches to things like attendance, for example. With in-person instruction, attendance policies ranged from no expectation whatsoever to stiff penalties for absences that exceeded a defined number of days. During the pandemic, video conferencing software (i.e., Zoom) allowed students to attend even when they could not be in the same physical space, and even when they were ill (to a degree). This facilitated changes to attendance policies across the board. Students, however, quickly adapted by realizing they could join class but turn their videos off, thus calling into question whether they were actually attending class or simply signing on because they were required to do so.

Related to attendance, we saw a dramatic change in the pedagogical concepts of immediacy and engagement. Traditionally, instructors have employed a variety of tactics to facilitate student engagement and participation, but one tried and true method is silence in the classroom. Typically, when the instructor pauses and waits long enough, social pressure sets in and a student will speak. Not so on Zoom, where students don't have to feel the social pressure as they are by themselves in their own rooms, and can even stop looking at the screen to eliminate the pressure. Additionally, it is hard to get to know students and allow them to know you in the online environment. Some faculty became more adept at using virtual video conferencing programs like Zoom and were able to incorporate breakout rooms for classes, which mimicked small group work in class and mitigated some of the reluctance to engage by students. Nevertheless, engagement and immediacy were extraordinarily difficult to navigate and facilitate in a "Zoom" classroom.

Another area that changed was the rapid embrace of flipped learning. To be clear, flipped learning is nothing new, having been used by faculty in varying degrees for the last two decades with the increase in prevalence of e-learning (Fanguy and Costley 2021). It is an offshoot of active learning, which asks students to engage in course material through learning activities and not simply require them to take notes (Prince 2004). In flipped classes, lecture, or instruction, is largely done through posting prerecorded videos of the content to a course management system where students watch it before coming to class. In addition, students are also often asked to engage in discussion through posts in the same system to help build connections with each other and demonstrate deeper thinking on the material. During class, time is often spent on student-centered activities that apply material from the online portion of the class in ways students can learn through application (Fanguy and Costley 2021). With the challenges presented by COVID-19 to classroom, some faculty developed their classes for fall 2020 in a flipped format, where students would engage with online lectures and discussions, while their once-a-week in-person class meeting was focused on activity-based learning.

The idea of prerecorded lectures also had an application for classes that met entirely through Zoom or some other software. The software allowed faculty to record virtual class meetings and post them in perpetuity online for students to view over and over again. In theory, this would allow for greater access to course content by students and improve note-taking as well. This was not really feasible for most classes before the pandemic when they met in-person. Either classes were not equipped with the video equipment to record lectures in many cases or faculty bristled at allowing people to record their lectures in the event something embarrassing happened whereby it would then be made available more broadly or potentially used against them.

Some courses, particularly in the sciences and arts, were experientially based before the pandemic and encountered even more significant challenges due to the pandemic because of their design. Lab classes, production classes, music classes, courses with fieldwork requirements, and internships all needed to substantially course-correct due to the pandemic as the classes had to run so students could continue to matriculate toward graduation; however, with social distancing, mask wearing, and lockdowns in effect in the community designing these types of courses and experiences was not as simple as moving content into a virtual atmosphere. Faculty did the best they could to find creative solutions under the circumstances, but for these courses even the solutions were suboptimal.

These are just a handful of the common challenges to teaching presented by the pandemic, none of which were anticipated even at the start of 2020 when the virus began to spread in other areas of the globe. Even in the midst of doing the work of adapting their pedagogical styles and approaches under pandemic conditions, faculty also reflected upon the experience and began to take lessons away from the changes they made. Some of these changes will stay, others will not, but college instruction will never be the same as it was in early 2020. The higher education pedagogical paradigm has substantially shifted from where it was, and it is more than simply moving classes online from in-person. The real questions remaining are what changes will endure and how will they improve student learning?

PREDICTING THE POST-PANDEMIC PEDAGOGICAL PARADIGM

Faculty have explored teaching and learning for a long time, and there have been changes and adaptations, but none of them came as fast as they have in the wake of COVID-19. This produced a seismic shift in pedagogy for faculty. We went from a model of teaching which we gradually changed through adaptation, experimentation and study, to one forced by circumstance. In both April 2020 and May 2021, *The Chronicle of Higher Education* ran pieces that pushed the notion remote work and remote classes would remain even after the pandemic recedes ("How will the pandemic change" 2020; Ellis 2021), but the changes made to higher education, and specifically our teaching paradigm, will be more varied and complex. Contributors to this book take stock of concepts and practices we believed were best before the pandemic arrived, but then speculate on how those things may change in the coming years based on what we learned during the pandemic.

Scott A. Myers and Casey M. Stratton begin the volume with an examination of student perceived effectiveness, and its relationship to student learning and satisfaction. Teaching effectiveness is a primary focus on research in instructional communication, grounded in work by Scott and Nussbaum (1981), and so it makes sense this would be a logical starting point for exploring the pedagogy paradigm shift. They emphasize the need for instructor resilience and offer suggestions for how to incorporate it in a way so that, going forward, students and faculty both improve cognitive learning in online courses, but also inoculate against future disruptions to courses such as the one experienced with COVID-19.

In chapter 2 Ashley A. Hanna Edwards proposes that the pandemic presented higher education with a *kairotic* moment, where the embrace between technology and teaching moved from being optional to required. For Edwards, this *kairotic* moment represents even more than just a time to shift pedagogy, but also a time where communication scholars—specifically those who are experts in computer-mediated communication—are needed to help debunk myths about the practice, and export their knowledge across other disciplines to elevate pedagogy across the academic spectrum. As Edwards argues, the technological upheavals of the last year are here to stay, and we should embrace the moment in our classes and in our discipline to share our own expertise with colleagues across academe.

Linda Carozza and Steve Genaro use chapter 3 to address how the pandemic underscored the importance of incorporating ethics of care into teaching. They use critical theory to argue some of the pitfalls of online teaching, which include increased surveillance of students, increase discomfort in the online classroom and should be replaced with an approach grounded in humanity and care for each other. They argue that the online space remains a communal and social space despite the fact students are not in physical proximity to each other. Online teaching, if it is to remain in the same way as part of our educational system moving forward, must consider ways to establish trust, build positive relationships, and adopt structures of course design that best facilitate those ends.

In chapter 4 Lindsey Anderson, Raphael Mazzone, and Melissa A. Lucas take a deep dive into student engagement in the online environment. They look at each of the major ways in which engagement manifests in a classroom: instructor to instructor, student to instructor, student to student, and administration to instructor. Drawing on their own experience with a large multi-section basic course, as well as experiences elsewhere, they offer some guiding principles for fostering engagement in an online environment post-pandemic. They also suggest how the discipline should orient research on engagement moving forward.

In chapter 5 Brad Mello and Cyndi Grobmeier illustrate how a student-centered approach to teaching during the pandemic allowed for a greater understanding of the challenges and limitations faced by everyone in the learning process, and offer ways those challenges might be mitigated in the future. Specifically, they address the technological needs and challenge of access faced by students—particularly first-generation college students— and the need for ongoing professional development for faculty on how best to employ the technological tools at their disposal to maximize learning. They present this through a case study of their experience with the basic public speaking course at their urban private institution.

Chapter 6 brings a unique perspective by Katherine Hampsten and Amanda Hill that suggests COVID-19 was the great equalizer in higher education in that all universities, big and small, suddenly found themselves in the same uncertain economic and pedagogical boat. They offer a case study from an institution grounded in a Marianist and Catholic philosophy that emphasizes the importance of community that suddenly had to pivot from an in-person environment to an online one. They suggest that although teaching changed, and will continue to as a result of the pandemic, that does not mean community needs to disappear. Their examination of how the tensions between a university's mission and identity and the realities of the crisis open an important conversation about how to advance, not just implement, online learning for universities both large and small, and private or public universities.

Chapter 7 extends the well-being argument as Lori Blewett and Maureen Ebben discuss the importance of teaching and learning for student mental health. They discuss the prevailing pre-pandemic literature surrounding student mental health and pedagogy, before discussing the shift in mental health and pedagogy that necessarily occurred during the pandemic as administrators and faculty alike recognized the immediate need for self-care by faculty for themselves and their students. They ultimately offer thoughts on how communication teaching and learning could, and perhaps should, change in the post-pandemic era. As they adroitly point out, mental health is now front and center in how faculty teach.

In chapter 8 Brittany Lash looks at the literature surrounding disability and pedagogy. She explores how students with disabilities have traditionally faced significant challenges in higher education classrooms, and suggests that the pandemic created both new challenges and some remediation for existing obstacles faced by this growing student population. She identifies the ways the pandemic exacerbated existing difficulties for students with disabilities, but also suggests ways in which the pandemic also made classes more flexible and accessible to them as well. She proposes that some of these adaptations during COVID-19 should remain moving forward to further advance efforts around inclusivity.

Sharon Storch, in chapter 9, takes a specific look at how the COVID-19 pandemic forced significant alterations to the way in which service learning was implemented in college classrooms. Using a case study of how a Midwestern public university with a strong track record of supporting service learning adapted during the pandemic to ensure these pedagogical opportunities remained, Storch offers ways in which service learning can evolve in the future and perhaps increase in use. In this way, she suggests that the pandemic and service learning's adaptations during it illustrate how universities benefit from strong community partnerships and how those relationships are vital moving into the future.

A key element of instructional training in communication is work done as a graduate teaching assistant, and in chapter 10 Anne C. Kretsinger Harries, Kate Challis, Ali Garib, and Elizabeth Helmick address how the pandemic dramatically impacted this important developmental pipeline for future faculty. They discuss the prevailing pre-pandemic literature regarding GTA training, before spending time exploring the experiences of a "pandemic cohort" of GTAs and how their experiences can help inform improvements to future GTA training efforts. They describe how graduate pedagogy training changed as a result of the pandemic, and specifically examine the most substantial challenges faced by the GTAs, including building credibility with students, developing their own communication skills, teaching with empathy, and navigating the shifting structure of the sometimes chaotic pandemic classroom.

Chapter 11 turns to the public speaking course and the specific disruptions brought to that performance class. Matt McGarrity argues that, although long struggling for acceptance, online delivery of public speaking courses should be here to stay. In many cases COVID-19 forced an embrace of online public speaking pedagogy that diminished, or even eliminated, the need for in-person audiences—a move McGarrity suggests has been long overdue. His argument is grounded in the skill-based approach to the class, and he proposes that the goals of such a class can be achieved through video submission of presentations just as well as it can with in-person speeches. For him, the public speaking instructional paradigm was permanently shifted as a result of COVID-19.

In chapter 12, Angela McGowan-Kirsch and Amanda Lohiser look at the changes brought to communication courses that teach transferable group communication skills. Using Tuckman's model of group formation (1965), they identify specific digital tools that can facilitate effective group work, and how those tools can be used to engage students in both teacher-student and student-student online learning. They argue that the sudden move to online instruction shifted practices, student perceptions, and expectations for such work. This rapid adoption of online tools to help small group communication classes represents, for them, a more permanent change to pedagogy resulting from the pandemic.

In chapter 13, the final chapter, John Reif provides an in-depth examination of how one of the most popular cocurricular programs in communication, intercollegiate forensics (debate), was forced to pivot during the pandemic, and suggests that elements of how it changed should remain in the future. Reif explores how the shift to a virtual debate environment opened the door for things like interactivity between different programs, even when not formally debating, creating an opportunity for a new virtual "associative pedagogy" (Hawhee 2004, pp. 150, 159–161). He also suggests how in a post-pandemic world schools may continue to use the virtual platform for debating as it is less expensive and time-pressured than having to travel to regional tournaments. He also sees opportunity for advancing interest in debate through the audience expansion offered by virtual debate platforms. All of these represent seismic shifts for the way the activity could, should, and may evolve when the pandemic recedes.

Following the chapter contributions, I return to offer some concluding thoughts about the way in which the pandemic has changed the pedagogical paradigm for university life. These changes may be at the macro-level, such as budgeting and staffing, but also on the more-micro-level of how instructors design courses for their students. No matter how you slice it, pedagogy has changed more in a 15-month period due to the pandemic that it has at any other similar period in its history.

NOTE

1. The National Association for College Admissions Counseling, under pressure from the federal government changed their code of ethics to allow for recruitment

and competition for high school graduate commitments throughout the year. This was in response to antitrust challenges from the federal government. See Scott Jaschik, "NACAC agrees to change its code of ethics," *Insidehighered.com* (September 30, 2019). https://www.insidehighered.com/admissions/article/2019/09/30/nacac-agrees-change-its-code-ethics

REFERENCES

Bauman, Dan. 2021. "Becker College May Close as Officials Cite Pandemic's Toll." *The Chronicle of Higher Education,* March 3, 2021. https://www.chronicle.com/blogs/live-coronavirus-updates/becker-college-may-close-as-officials-cite-pandemics-toll

"Beginning March 9, Classes and Finals Will Not be Held In-Person (Message to Students)." 2020. *University of Washington,* March 6, 2020. https://www.washington.edu/coronavirus/2020/03/06/beginning-march-9-classes-and-finals-will-not-be-held-in-person-message-to-students/

Borghese, Livia. 2020. "Italy Confirms 1,128 Cases of Coronavirus." *CNN.com,* February 29, 2020. https://www.cnn.com/asia/live-news/coronavirus-outbreak-02-29-20-intl-hnk/h_6af8ab045650c56261e4a9f42c2f95b8

Branswell, Helen. 2020. "Experts Search for Answers in Limited Information About Mystery Pneumonia Outbreak in China." *STAT,* January 4, 2020. https://web.archive.org/web/20200128223237/https://www.statnews.com/2020/01/04/mystery-pneumonia-outbreak-china/

Broeckelman-Post, Melissa A., Katherine E. Hyatt Hawkins, Anthony R. Arciero, and Andie S. Malterud. 2019. "Online Versus Face-to-Face Public Speaking Outcomes: A Comprehensive Assessment." *Basic Communication Course Annual 31,* art. 10. https://ecommons.udayton.edu/cgi/viewcontent.cgi?article=1569&context=bcca

"Coronavirus: Outbreak Grows in Northern Italy, 16 Cases Reported in One Day." 2020. *The Straits Times,* February 22, 2020. https://www.straitstimes.com/world/europe/italian-national-tests-positive-for-coronavirus-in-italy-lombardy-region

Ellis, Lindsay. 2021. "At Some Colleges, Remote Work Could be Here to Stay." *Chronicle of Higher Education,* May 5, 2021. https://www.chronicle.com/article/at-some-colleges-remote-work-could-be-here-to-stay

Fanguy, Mik and Jamie Costley. 2021. "Creating a Framework for Understanding and Defining Flipped Learning." *Journal of Educators Online 18,* no.1. https://www.thejeo.com/archive/archive/2021_181/fanguy__costleypdf~1

Fischer, Karin. 2020. "CDC Warns Colleges to 'Consider' Canceling Study Abroad Trips." *Chronicle of Higher Education,* March 4, 2020. https://www.chronicle.com/newsletter/global/2020-03-04

Geddie, John. 2020. "WHO Probes Singapore Meet Linked to Spread of Virus." *Reuters,* February 5, 2020. https://www.reuters.com/article/us-china-health-singapore-summit-idUSKBN2000C7

Gumbrecht, Jamie, and Jacqueline Howard. 2020. "WHO Declares Novel Coronavirus Outbreak a Pandemic." *CNN.com,* March 11, 2020. https://www.cnn.com/2020/03/11/health/coronavirus-pandemic-world-health-organization/index.html

Harris, Shane, Greg Miller, Josh Dawsey and Ellen Nakashima. 2020. "U.S. Intelligence Reports from January and February Warned About a Likely Pandemic." *The Washington Post,* March 20, 2020. https://www.washingtonpost.com/national-security/us-intelligence-reports-from-january-and-february-warned-about-a-likely-pandemic/2020/03/20/299d8cda-6ad5-11ea-b5f1-a5a804158597_story.html

Hawhee, Debra. 2004. *Bodily Arts: Rhetoric and Athletics in Ancient Greece.* Austin, TX: University of Texas Press.

Hernandez, Salvador. 2020. "Officials Have Confirmed the First Death from Coronavirus in the US." *Buzzfeed News,* February 29, 2020. https://www.buzzfeednews.com/article/salvadorhernandez/washington-state-coronavirus-death-us

"How Will the Pandemic Change Higher Education?" 2020. *Chronicle of Higher Education,* April 10, 2020. https://www.chronicle.com/article/how-will-the-pandemic-change-higher-education/

Huang, Chaolin, Yeming Wang, Xingwang Li, Lili Ren, Jinaping Zhao, Yi Hu, Li Zhang, Guohui Fan, Jiuyang Xu, Zhenshun Cheng, Ting Yu, Jiaan Xia, Yuan Wei, Wenjuan Wu, Xuelei Xie, Wen Yin, Hui Li, Min Liu, Yan Ziao, Hong Gao, Li Guo, Jungang Xei, Guangfa Wang, Rongmeng Jiang, Zhancheng Gao, Qi Jin, Jianwei Wang, and Bin Cao. 2020. "Clinical Features of Patients Infected With 2019 Novel Coronavirus in Wuhan, China." *The Lancet* 395 (February): 497–506. doi:10.1016/S0140-6736(20)30183-5.

Hubler, Shawn. 2020. "Fearing a Second Wave, Cal State Will Keep Classes Online in the Fall." *The New York Times,* May 12, 2020. https://www.nytimes.com/2020/05/12/us/cal-state-online-classes.html

Johnson, Carla K. 2020. "US Virus Cases Climb to 35 with Return of Cruise Passengers." *ABC News,* February 21, 2020. https://abcnews.go.com/Health/wireStory/us-virus-cases-climb-35-return-cruise-passengers-69133712

Kennedy, Merrit. 2020. "WHO Declares Coronavirus Outbreak a Global Health Emergency." *NPR,* January 30, 2020. https://www.npr.org/sections/goatsandsoda/2020/01/30/798894428/who-declares-coronavirus-outbreak-a-global-health-emergency

Khan, Natasha. 2020. "New Virus Discovered by Chinese Scientists Investigating Pneumonia Outbreak." *The Wall Street Journal,* January 9, 2020. https://www.wsj.com/articles/new-virus-discovered-by-chinese-scientists-investigating-pneumonia-outbreak-11578485668

Kuhn, Thomas. 1970. *The Structure of Scientific Revolutions.* Chicago, IL: University of Chicago Press.

Lipton, Eric, David E. Sanger, Maggie Haberman, Michael D. Shear, Mark Mazzetti and Julian E. Barnes. 2020. "They Saw It Coming: Inside the Trump Administration's Failures on Coronavirus." *Chicago Tribune,* April 11, 2020. https://www.chicagotribune.com/coronavirus/ct-nw-nyt-trump-early-warnings-ignored-timeline-20200411-dmyrwzmmanhajptjnqlwqfees4-story.html

Newey, Sarah, Jordan Kelly-Linden, LaToya Harding and Global Health Security Team. 2020. "Coronavirus: Chance to Contain Outbreak is 'Narrowing' Says WHO." *The Telegraph,* February 21, 2020. https://www.telegraph.co.uk/global-health/science-and-disease/coronavirus-uk-news-china-wuhan-deaths-latest/

"Outrage as Coronavirus Prompts US Universities and Colleges to Shed Staff." 2020. *The Guardian,* August 12, 2020. https://www.theguardian.com/us-news/2020/aug/12/us-universities-colleges-job-losses-coronavirus

Prince, Michael. 2013. "Does Active Learning Work? A Review of the Research." *Journal of Engineering Education 93,* no. 3. doi:10.1002/j.2168-9830.2004.tb00809.x.

Quintana, Chris. 2020. "College Closings: More Than 100 Colleges Cancel In-Person Classes and Move Online." *USA Today,* March 11, 2020. https://www.usatoday.com/story/news/education/2020/03/11/coronavirus-college-closings-list-online-classes/5022256002/

Schwartzman, Roy. 2007. "Refining the Question: How Can Online Instruction Maximize Opportunities for All Students?" *Communication Education 56,* no. 1: 113–117.

Scott, Michael D., and Jon F. Nussbaum. 1981. "Student Perceptions of Instructor Communication Behaviors and Their Relationship to Student Evaluation." *Communication Education* 30, no.1: 45–32. doi:10.1080/03634528109378452.

Shear, Michael D., Abby Goodnough, Sheila Kaplan, Sheri Fink, Katie Thomas, and Noah Weiland. 2020. "The Lost Month: How a Failure to Test Blinded the U.S. to COVID-19." *The New York Times,* March 28, 2020. https://www.nytimes.com/2020/03/28/us/testing-coronavirus-pandemic.html

"Statement on the Second Meeting of the International Health Regulations (2005) Emergency Committee Regarding the Outbreak of Novel Coronavirus (2019-nCOV)." 2020. *World Health Organization,* January 30, 2020. https://www.who.int/news/item/30-01-2020-statement-on-the-second-meeting-of-the-international-health-regulations-(2005)-emergency-committee-regarding-the-outbreak-of-novel-coronavirus-(2019-ncov)

Stone, Judy. 2020. "Wuhan Coronavirus Outbreak Shows the Importance of Sound Science, Sleuthing, and Cooperation." *Forbes,* January 11, 2020. https://www.forbes.com/sites/judystone/2020/01/11/wuhan-coronavirus-outbreak-shows-the-importance-of-sound-science-sleuthing-and-cooperation/?sh=7fa09d931add

Taylor, Marisa. 2020. "Exclusive: U.S. Axed CDC Expert Job in China Months Before Virus Outbreak." *Reuters,* March 22, 2020. https://www.reuters.com/article/us-health-coronavirus-china-cdc-exclusiv/exclusive-u-s-axed-cdc-expert-job-in-china-months-before-virus-outbreak-idUSKBN21910S

"The Coronavirus is Upending Higher Ed." 2020. *Chronicle of Higher Education,* March 3, 2020. https://www.chronicle.com/article/the-coronavirus-is-upending-higher-ed-here-are-the-latest-developments/

Thomas, Russell. 1962. *The Search for a Common Learning: General Education, 1800-1960.* New York: McGraw Hill.

Thompson, Julia, and Hannah Yasharoff. 2020. "Coronavirus Cases on Diamond Princess Soar Past 500, Site of Most Infections Outside China." *USA Today,*

February 18, 2020. https://www.usatoday.com/story/travel/cruises/2020/02/18/coronavirus-jose-andres-provides-meals-diamond-princess-passengers/4788804002/

Tuckman, Bruce W. 1965. "Developmental Sequence in Small Groups." *Psychological Bulletin* 63, no. 6: 384–399. doi:10.1037/h0022100.

Westwick, Joshua N., Karla M. Hunter and Laurie L. Haleta. 2016. "A Digital Divide?: Assessing Self-perceived Communication Competency in an Online and Face-to-Face Basic Public Speaking Course." *Basic Communication Course Annual 28*, art. 11. https://ecommons.udayton.edu/cgi/viewcontent.cgi?article=1502&context=bcca

Chapter 1

Teaching in the Midst of COVID-19
Teaching Effectiveness as a Function of Student Preferences for Instructional Behaviors

Scott A. Myers and Casey M. Stratton

Instructional communication researchers traditionally have posited that teaching effectiveness is linked directly with student learning; that is, when instructors engage in prosocial communication with their students, these students should report gains in their affective, behavioral, and cognitive learning (Scott and Nussbaum 1981) as well as increases in their state motivation, communication satisfaction, and perceived relevance of course content (Goodboy and Myers 2008; Knoster and Myers 2020). For several decades, these researchers have directed their scholarly efforts toward (a) identifying the behaviors that they believe constitute prosocial instructor-student communication and (b) examining the effects that these behaviors have on student learning outcomes. As a result, instructional communication researchers have investigated numerous in-class communication behaviors that are considered to be effective teaching behaviors (see Houser and Hosek 2018; Mottet, Richmond, and McCroskey 2006; Witt, 2016 for reviews of these behaviors).

To create a cohesive and organizing framework of effective teaching behaviors, Myers (2020) identified three frames through which teaching effectiveness can be viewed. These frames are *teaching effectiveness as rhetorical*, *teaching effectiveness as relational*, and *teaching effectiveness as presentational*. Two additional frames—*teaching effectiveness as nonaggressive* and *teaching effectiveness as managerial*—are presented in this chapter. The premise behind this framework is that when instructors teach from any, several, or all of these frames, they are doing so with the intent of positively influencing student affect for the course and the subject matter, student cognitive learning (whether measured indirectly through student self-reports or directly through assignment or exam scores), and student classroom engagement. Moreover, this framework follows previous recommendations that effective teaching requires instructors to be content specialists, communication pedagogy experts, and competent communicators (Myers 2018; Staton 1989).

It should be noted that while the behaviors encapsulated within each of these five frames have been applied to or studied in almost exclusively face-to-face instructional settings, these behaviors and frames are equally applicable to the hybrid, online synchronous, and online asynchronous teaching modalities that instructors transitioned to during the COVID-19 pandemic. Regardless of the teaching modality used during the pandemic, teaching from both the rhetorical and relational frames is essential as the behaviors contained within each frame act directly as predictors of student learning outcomes (Myers et al. 2014) and are linked specifically to student impressions of instructor credibility (Myers et al. 2018a). Teaching from the presentational, nonaggressive, and managerial frames, however, is likely more challenging due to the lack of face-to-face contact between instructors and students, which can result in increased misinterpretation, misunderstanding, or frustration, among other feelings. Moreover, when teaching through mediated channels, instructors have to become more aware of the verbal and nonverbal behaviors they use to establish *social presence*, which refers to the personnel connection students associate with their classmates and instructors despite their physical separation (Sellnow and Kaufmann 2018). Socially present instructors are respectful of their students' time and identity, solicit and acknowledge students' contributions, and encourage students' expressions of their emotions, thoughts, and feelings (Sung and Mayer 2012). By establishing social presence, instructors can become more mindful of the ways in which they present themselves, avoid communicating in ways that could be perceived by students as aggressive, and manage or respond to student expectations, compliance, and needs in both a timely and responsive manner.

TEACHING EFFECTIVENESS AS RHETORICAL

The teaching effectiveness as rhetorical frame is based on the notion that teaching effectiveness occurs when instructors engage in efficient and strategic message design and dissemination (Myers et al. 2018b). That is, instructors who embrace a rhetorical approach to teaching pay particular attention to how they construct and deliver their in-class instruction, realizing that the purpose behind it is to act as an information source through which their students can learn. Two instructional communication behaviors typically associated with the rhetorical frame are clarity and humor.

Clarity refers to the verbal and nonverbal behaviors that instructors use to facilitate student selection, understanding, and retention of information (Titsworth and Mazer 2016). Whether presented orally or written, clear instructors are verbally and nonverbally fluent, incorporate structural tools (e.g., preview, review, and transition statements; relevant examples; visual organizers) into their messages, and are straightforward in their presentation and explanation of course policies, assignments, grading rubrics, and expectations (Chesebro 2003; Simonds 1997). *Humor* refers to the verbal and nonverbal messages that instructors incorporate into their teaching to make learning enjoyable, pleasant, or delightful (Booth-Butterfield and Booth-Butterfield 1991). While instructor humor can take the form of statements or comments, jokes, anecdotes, and narratives, among others (Gorham and Christophel 1990), for humor to be considered an effective tool, students must view these forms as appropriate and relevant to the course content (Frymier, Wanzer, and Wojtaszczyk 2008).

Two other rhetorical behaviors include self-disclosure and justice (i.e., fairness). *Self-disclosure* refers to instructor information about themselves that they share with students as a way to purposefully clarify or illustrate the relevance and salience of course content (Downs, Javidi, and Nussbaum 1998; Sorensen 1989). Considered to be information that students would not otherwise know or be able to obtain from other sources, effective instructors ensure that the information they elect to disclose in the classroom is intentional, honest, and positive (Sorensen 1989). Justice refers to those behaviors that instructors use to elicit student perceptions of fairness regarding classroom practices and interactions across three types: distributive, which occurs when instructors grade all students in the same manner so that some students are not at an advantage over other students; procedural, which occurs when instructors apply classroom-related procures and policies equally to all students; and *interactional*, which occurs when instructors communicate with all students respectfully and politely (Chory 2007).

TEACHING EFFECTIVENESS AS RELATIONAL

The teaching effectiveness as relational frame is centered on the idea that instructors engage in interpersonal behaviors with their students to create a professional working relationship with them (Myers 2020). Instructors who embrace a relational approach to teaching focus on achieving relational growth with their students as a way to facilitate student learning (Myers et al. 2018b). Three instructional communication behaviors typically associated with the relational frame are immediacy, affinity seeking, and confirmation. *Immediacy* refers to the verbal and nonverbal behaviors that instructors use to reduce the psychological or physical distance that students often perceive as a barrier to effective instruction (Witt, Wheeless, and Allen 2004). By engaging in immediacy, instructors implicitly inform their students that they are approachable while simultaneously inviting them to engage in classroom activities and discussion. Verbal immediacy behaviors include initiating conversations with students before or after class, asking questions that are not school-related, and praising student work (Gorham 1988), whereas nonverbal immediacy behaviors include moving around the classroom (rather than remaining behind a lectern or desk), engaging in eye contact and affirming facial expressions with students when talking with them, using vocal variety, and having a relaxed body position (McCroskey et al. 1995).

Affinity seeking refers to instructor use of verbal messages that are intended to increase or enhance student liking for the course, the subject matter, or even the instructor (Gorham, Kelley, and McCroskey 1989). Although there are multiple affinity-seeking strategies from which instructors can choose, Frymier and Wanzer (2006) identified several strategies that are more effective for use with college students as these strategies suggest to students that their instructors care and are concerned about them. These strategies include assuming equality with, listening to, and behaving altruistically toward students; engaging in conversational rule-keeping when speaking with students; and facilitating student enjoyment in the classroom. *Confirmation* refers to instructor recognition, endorsement, and acknowledgment that students are valuable and significant contributors to the classroom environment (Ellis 2000), which is conveyed through instructor use of verbal and nonverbal messages with their students. Instructors who communicate with their students in a confirming manner do so by adopting an interactive teaching style, demonstrating an interest in student learning, and taking the time to process and respond to student questions (Ellis 2000).

TEACHING EFFECTIVENESS AS PRESENTATIONAL

The teaching effectiveness as presentational frame revolves around Infante, Rancer, and Womack's (2003) identification of presentational communication traits. According to Infante and his colleagues, presentational traits are the ways in which individuals portray themselves to a conversational partner. In essence, what this means is that instructors create a presentational style that acts as a filter for instructor-student interaction; that is, it is through presentational style that (a) instructors create a unique style through which they engage in verbal and nonverbal communication with their students and (b) once students recognize and accept this style, they then verbally and nonverbally respond, react, or interact accordingly with them.

Two presentational styles associated with this frame are communicator style and socio-communicative style. Norton (1977) conceptualized *communicator style* as referring to an instructor's unique use of verbal and nonverbal behaviors that indicate to students how literal they should take or attach meaning to these behaviors. With communicator style, the focus is on *how* an instructor communicates a message rather than on *what* is communicated in the message (Norton 1983). To do this, instructors create a communicator style cluster that consists of any combination of several of 10 communicator style attributes (see Norton 1983 for a review); this cluster represents a unique, personable, and habitual way of communicating with students, which then establishes expectations and boundaries for instructor-student interaction. *Socio-communicative style* encompasses two general sets of communication behaviors—assertiveness and responsiveness—that are desirable in effective instructor-student exchanges (Martin 2008). Assertive instructors are self-oriented and strong in their conversational rule-keeping and interaction management skills; they possess the ability to competently initiate, maintain, and terminate conversations or interactions with others by speaking in a forthright manner, remaining goal-oriented, and being forceful as needed. Responsive instructors, too, are strong in their communicative skills, but instead are other-oriented and take into consideration their students' feelings when interacting with them. Responsive instructors display compassion, helpfulness, and friendliness when communicating with their students (Richmond and McCroskey 1990).

TEACHING EFFECTIVENESS AS NONAGGRESSIVE

The teaching effectiveness as nonaggressive frame considers Infante's (1987) model of aggressive communication, which posits that an individual's use of aggressive communication traits interacts with situational factors that then influence message behavior. From this model, two communication traits—instructor argumentativeness and instructor verbal aggressiveness—are particularly salient to student learning. *Argumentativeness* is considered to be a constructive trait in which instructors are able to verbally defend their position on a given topic while refuting those opposing positions advanced by students, whereas *verbal aggressiveness* is considered to be a destructive trait in which instructors verbally attack the self-concept of students as a way to inflict psychological hurt (Infante and Rancer 1982; Infante and Wigley 1986). While both traits are aggressive in nature, the primary distinction lies in their locus of attack: for argumentativeness, it is a student's position on an issue; for verbal aggressiveness, it is a student's self-concept (Infante 1988).

When teaching from the nonaggressive frame, engaging in argumentativeness is an acceptable behavior because its intent is beneficial to student learning. Argumentativeness is a way in which instructors can stimulate student curiosity, improve social perspective-taking, and decrease egocentric thinking, all of which contribute to student learning (Infante 1988). Conversely, instructor verbal aggressiveness is a behavior that should be avoided due to its deleterious learning and motivational effect on students. While the rate at which instructors direct verbally aggressive messages toward their students usually is low, when they do engage in verbal aggressiveness, it often is to attack students' competence (i.e., comments about intelligence or ability) or work ethic (Myers, Brann, and Martin 2013).

Instructor misbehaviors can be perceived as aggressive due to the fact that when instructors engage in incompetent, indolent, or offensive misbehaviors, they disrupt classroom instruction and student learning (Kearney et al. 1991). Vallade and Myers (2014) suggested that (a) incompetent instructors engage in behaviors (e.g., unfair testing or grading, lack of subject matter expertise) that imply that they do not possess the pedagogical skills necessary for effective teaching, (b) indolent instructors use behaviors (e.g., inaccessible to students, keeping students overtime) that imply that they do not possess the procedural skills necessary for effective teaching, and (c) offensive instructors utilize behaviors (e.g., sarcasm, impatience) that imply that they do not possess the interpersonal skills necessary for effective teaching. Similar to instructor verbal aggressiveness, while the rate at which instructors misbehave in the classroom is relatively low, when they do misbehave, these misbehaviors take the form of engaging in ineffective teaching behaviors (i.e., those behaviors that impede student learning), deviating from the syllabus, presenting boring lectures, and grading unfairly (Goodboy and Myers 2015).

TEACHING EFFECTIVENESS AS MANAGERIAL

Galvin (1999) identified learning management as one of five instructor role functions, which serves as the foundation of the teaching effectiveness as managerial frame. She proposed that instructors who teach from this frame understand that to facilitate student learning, they must create a classroom climate in which students feel safe and supported through the establishment of rules, policies, and procedures that enable students to take risks, ask questions, seek assistance, and share thoughts and opinions. Three behaviors included in this frame are power, behavior alteration techniques, and feedback.

Power refers to an instructor's ability to affect or influence, in some way, student in-class behavior (Richmond and McCroskey 1984); in essence, power allows instructors to gain compliance from their students. For student behavior to be affected or influenced, however, students must believe that their instructors possess power, which is revealed through five power bases: reward, coercive, legitimate, expert, and referent (McCroskey and Richmond 1983). According to Schrodt, Witt, and Turman (2006), instructors who possess *reward power* can provide students with tangible or intangible rewards, prizes, or benefits, whereas instructors who possess *coercive power* can enforce student punishment or impose negative consequences for undesirable student behavior. Instructors who depend on *legitimate power* use the authority vested in them by virtue of their teaching role while instructors who use *expert power* rely on their knowledge, experience, and education to gain student compliance.

While these four power bases are grounded in the role and functions that instructors play and serve, the fifth power base—referent power—is grounded in instructor liking and affiliativeness. Instructors who possess *referent power* gain compliance because students perceive them to be approachable, relatable, or likeable. *Behavior alteration techniques*, more commonly referred to as BATs, refers to a typology of 22 strategies from which instructors can choose to directly gain compliance from their students with each BAT considered to be a specific strategy emanating from one of the five aforementioned instructor power bases (McCroskey, Richmond, and McCroskey 2006).

While not centered on student compliance per se, the extent to which instructors provide feedback to their students is another way in which they manage the learning expectations they have established. Known as *instructional feedback*, the purpose behind an instructor's provision of feedback is to inform students about the discrepancy that exists between their current and their desired academic performance (Kluger and DeNisi 1996). For instructional feedback to be the most informative and useful, Lizzio and Wilson (2008) recommend that feedback be fair, encouraging, and developmental. At the same time, it is essential to recognize that student ability to accept instructional feedback in the manner in which it was intended is influenced by four orientations: whether the feedback was perceived as useful for improving academic performance, the ability to recall and apply the feedback to the assignment for which it was intended, the setting in which the feedback was provided (e.g., in front of peers, in an instructor's office), and the extent to which the feedback was considered to be threatening or intimidating (King, Schrodt, and Weisel 2009).

TEACHING EFFECTIVENESS IN THE TIME OF COVID-19

For many colleges and universities, the emergence of COVID-19 in March 2020 across the United States necessitated the move from face-to-face instruction to online instruction, which continued well into the fall 2020 and spring 2021 semesters. For example, across these three semesters at West Virginia University, the majority of instruction utilized some form of online modality, with less than 30 percent of courses meeting entirely face-to-face during this time and the remaining courses being taught via hybrid, online synchronous, or online asynchronous modalities. Those courses that were taught entirely face-to-face were subjected to a host of new instructional requirements and guidelines, including mandated mask-wearing, social distancing, seating arrangements, and cancellation of most face-to-face out-of-class communication (e.g., office hours, review sessions).

Because we were curious as to how this shift in instructional modality affected students' perceptions of effective teaching, we used the Build-A-Professor methodology (Senko, Belmonte, and Yakhind 2012) to ask undergraduate students about their preferences for effective instruction by directing them to "buy" those behaviors that they believed contributed the most toward their cognitive learning in online courses. Following Institutional Review Board approval and recruiting students enrolled in several introductory communication courses to participate in this study, 156 students[1] were provided with a link to a Qualtrics survey. The survey contained a cover letter and the following instructions:

> *Listed below are 10 behaviors[2] that college instructors are known to use with their students in the classroom. We are interested in your perceptions of how these behaviors generally contribute to college students and their cognitive learning, which is conceptualized as student comprehension and retention of knowledge.*
>
> *Now, using these 10 behaviors, we would like you to create your preferred instructor for an online course by assigning monetary values to those behaviors that you believe contribute to your cognitive learning. You have a $20.00 budget to "buy" those behaviors that—when instructors who teach an online course use them—contribute to your cognitive learning. Here are the criteria for your "purchases:"*
>
> - *You have a budget of $20.00, all of which must be spent in some way in $1.00 increments.*
> - *You can spend anywhere from $0.00 to $10.00 on each behavior, but the maximum amount you can spend on any one behavior is $10.00.*
> - *You are not required to "spend" money on any behavior that you do not consider contributing to your cognitive learning.*
> - *The more money you spend on a behavior, the more valuable you consider it to be contributing toward your cognitive learning. For instance, if you spend $6 on assertiveness and $2 on justice, you are essentially saying that when*

it comes to your cognitive learning, you value instructor assertiveness much more than instructor justice.

Remember, your "purchases" of instructor behaviors should equal—but not exceed—your $20.00 budget.

We then asked participants to indicate the extent [using a five-point rating scale ranging from (1) *To no extent* to (5) *To a very great extent*] to which each of the same 10 behaviors contributes to their cognitive learning in an online course.

FINDINGS

Two sets of findings emerged from our data, which are contained in table 1.1. First, in terms of the preferred instructor behaviors used in an online course, participants indicated a preference for clarity, feedback, and responsiveness, followed by confirmation, assertiveness, humor, justice, verbal immediacy, self-disclosure, and nonverbal immediacy. Second, in terms of the extent to which these behaviors contributed to their cognitive learning, students identified clarity as the largest contributor, followed by feedback, justice, confirmation, assertiveness, responsiveness, verbal immediacy, humor, nonverbal immediacy, and self-disclosure. Interestingly, these findings are similar to prior research studies conducted on students enrolled in face-to-face instruction. Goldman et al. (2017) reported that undergraduate students indicated a preference for clarity, competence, and relevance, whereas Knoster et al. (2021) discovered that medical school students indicated a preference for clarity, relevance, and competence. In both studies, nonverbal immediacy

Table 1.1 Instructor Teaching Behaviors

Behavior	Preferred/Purchased			Contributing to Learning	
	M ($)	SD ($)	Range ($)	M	SD
Clarity	4.28	2.09	0–10.00	4.12	1.01
Feedback	3.06	1.64	0–10.00	3.97	1.04
Responsiveness	2.65	1.73	0–10.00	3.58	1.06
Confirmation	1.98	1.60	0–10.00	3.70	1.12
Assertiveness	1.89	1.97	0–10.00	3.69	0.98
Humor	1.69	1.40	0–7.00	3.28	1.11
Justice	1.65	1.42	0–5.00	3.85	1.01
Verbal immediacy	1.44	1.35	0–6.00	3.53	1.07
Self-disclosure	0.79	1.26	0–6.00	2.58	1.09
Nonverbal immediacy	0.77	1.02	0–5.00	2.99	1.01

and self-disclosure were rated as being among the least preferred instructor behaviors.

A post-hoc Spearman's Rho correlation coefficient was conducted between the two sets of findings, with the results ($r_s = .83, p < .01$) indicating that a strong relationship exists between them. What this correlation suggests is that those behaviors that students prefer their instructors to use while teaching an online course generally mirror the same behaviors they report as contributing the most to their cognitive learning in online courses.

RECOMMENDATIONS

The COVID-19 pandemic catalyzed a new frontier for researchers and instructors navigating post-pandemic pedagogy (Rudick and Dannels 2020) as pandemic pandemonium caused unanticipated challenges with online learning, thus illuminating the need for flexibility (Huber 2020). This pandemic acted as a crossroads where many instructors were forced to increase their *instructional resilience* by adopting strategies that would prepare them for future (un)anticipated academic interruptions, similar to the notion of universal design (King-Sears 2009). We suggest that the greatest way for instructors to improve their instructional resilience is by implementing instructional communication behaviors that complement any instructional context, be it face-to-face, online synchronous, online asynchronous or a mix (e.g., hybrid, hybrid-flex). Certain behaviors—as demonstrated in our data and discussed in this section—serve as *instructional inoculations*, or strategies that can thoughtfully be used to enhance instructional resilience. Dutifully noted, these behaviors—namely clarity, feedback, confirmation, and responsiveness—have been recognized as important influencers on student cognitive learning (see Houser and Hosek 2018 or Mottet, Richmond, and McCroskey 2006). As such, it comes as no surprise that the participants in this study deemed these instructional behaviors necessary for online learning. To this end, we offer four instructional inoculation recommendations that instructors should consider regardless of instructional modality to increase their instructional resiliency, although in this section we focus specifically on online teaching.

Our first instructional inoculation recommendation centers on instructor clarity. As our participants indicated, an instructor's use of clarity—or presenting information in an organized manner at an appropriate pace—proved to be the most desired online teaching behavior. This finding comes as no surprise, considering a prior meta-analysis that supports the important role that instructor clarity plays in student cognitive learning (Titsworth et al. 2015) regardless of instructional modality. Though instructors may use a variety of structural tools to increase their verbal and nonverbal fluency (e.g., providing skeleton outlines, communicating succinctly, focusing instruction around learning outcomes, using summary statements), these attempts at increased fluency could be suppressed by students' unnecessary stress from online learning as the online environment presents additional learning barriers for those students unskilled with technology. These stressors include student ability to navigate the learning management system, participate in online discussions via breakout groups, submit assignments online, or log into systems for the first time. Online instructors can circumvent these stressors by providing students with resources such as recorded how-to videos, allocating time during the first class meeting to demonstrate how to use required technology, or showcasing resources that learners can consult (e.g., learning management system job aids, helpdesk website). By anticipating these stressors, instructors can reduce extraneous student cognitive load, thus promoting deeper cognitive learning (Bolkan 2016).

Asynchronous courses likewise present a unique terrain for instructor clarity. Without the presence of instructors to explain course material and answer questions, students could experience frustration which, in turn, could affect their motivation to learn. Bolkan, Goodboy, and Kelsey (2016) found that students scored higher on a test in conditions of high instructor clarity and high student motivation to elaborate on course material. That is, when student motivation to process course material is high, this motivation interacts with high instructor clarity, which results in increased student test scores. Without considering student motivation to process course material, test scores did not increase even in the presence of clear instruction. Of course, although motivation to learn at a deeper level is at the mercy of students, instructors can create a clear course design that neither hampers nor frustrates student motivation. To this end, both online and face-to-face instructors should scrutinize their syllabi and course learning outcomes for problematic ambiguity, explain how each learning activity exemplifies the course learning outcomes and objectives, and include detailed rubrics so that students understand assignment expectations. Likewise, since the asynchronous experience more often is managed by students, providing a suggested study schedule encourages a steady learning pace. Overall, with events like COVID-19 causing uncertainty, clarity remains an integral, resilient behavior that promotes certainty.

The second instructional inoculation recommendation is that instructors should recognize the integral role of instructor feedback on student academic performance. While some instructors may communicate collective feedback directed toward all students enrolled in a course, we recommend that instructors provide personalized feedback to each student due to its positive impact on academic performance and satisfaction (Gallien and Oomen-Early 2008). We acknowledge that while personalized feedback can be time-consuming, online instructors can utilize technology to their advantage when providing it. For instance, rather than having to type feedback to each student, some course learning management systems allow instructors to record their voice directly to an assignment, thus saving time and providing students with valuable nonverbal cues. For some assignments, because instructors can anticipate assignment feedback that they will need to provide, they can generate templated feedback (i.e., "stock" responses, "commonplaces"), which can then be stored in a "feedback bank" (e.g., computer document, excel file) to save time when grading.

Instructors also should consider the tone of their feedback. Clark-Gordon et al. (2018) suggested that written feedback should be thoughtfully written, typed, or recorded using language or nonverbal behaviors that mitigate student face-threat, particularly if students are unable to rely upon instructor nonverbal cues to interpret feedback. They further suggested that instructors should use straightforward, welcoming language and refrain from using peripheral tactics such as emoticons or pictures. By mitigating any possible face threat, it is likely that students will be able to focus on their cognitive learning and engage collaboratively with their online instructors. As the COVID-19 pandemic taught, peripheral distractions—such as face-threatening feedback—should be controlled rather than spread to promote greater resilience to other uncontrollable classroom factors.

The third instructional inoculation recommendation is for instructors to create a positive learning environment in their online teaching by taking into consideration their use of confirming and responsive teaching behaviors with their students. To do so, instructors must recognize that relational and presentational teaching behaviors—all of which are necessary to make students feel welcomed, valued, and needed—take priority over rhetorical, aggressive, or managerial behaviors. When teaching online, instructors should pay particular attention to the ways in which they are perceived by their students as being understanding and approachable, demonstrating respect, and showing support (Kaufmann, Frisby, and Sellnow 2016). Instructors also need to consider that when they express interest in their students, they will have students who become excited and energized by the course material; view the course, the instructor, and their classmates positively; and perceive the instructor as being a source of emotional support about both course- and non-course related topics (Goldman and Goodboy 2014). Of course, it may not always be possible, relevant, or even practical for instructors to always engage in confirming and responsive interaction with students. What is possible, however, is that instructors create a stable and predictable learning environment that students perceive as generally confirming and responsive. As Teven and McCroskey (1996) posited in their study on instructor caring, "it is not the caring that counts; it is the perception of caring that is critical"

(p. 1). Their position is likely true for instructor confirmation and responsiveness. As a way to further behave in a confirming and responsive manner, we recommend that instructors take the time to express interest in their students and get to know them—even if it is relegated to obtaining surface-level or demographic information (e.g., favorite sports team, hometown)—and reference this information during their in-class and out-of-class interactions. To this end, perhaps the greatest remedy to instructional maladies is generating a positive atmosphere of caring where instructional resiliency can be nurtured rather than weakened.

The fourth instructional inoculation recommendation is that because it is all too easy for students to misconstrue instructor behavior in an online format, particularly if students are unfamiliar with an instructor, instructors should strive toward presenting their authentic self. While students identify clarity, feedback, confirmation, and responsiveness as preferential teaching behaviors—and to a lesser degree, assertiveness, justice, humor, immediacy, and self-disclosure—it is vital to recognize that there is more to effective teaching than simply engaging in these behaviors frequently and consistently. Rather, effective online teaching demands that instructors create an authentic self through which their use of these aforementioned behaviors can emerge. Instructors who demonstrate authenticity communicate with their students in a way that not only is genuine and self-aware but also brings parts of themselves into an interaction and "impacts the communicative and relational processes that occur between them and students" (Johnson and LaBelle 2017, p. 425). To capitalize on this, we suggest that instructors actively reflect on their use of these teaching behaviors and think about how their use of these behaviors can operate in tandem with the five indicators— approachable, passionate, attentive, capable, knowledgeable—of teaching authenticity (Johnson and LaBelle 2017). Though being the authentic self may promote vulnerability, being honest about potential weaknesses creates a baseline for instructional resiliency toward which instructors and students can work together.

CONCLUSION

Instructors can learn from the difficulties wrought by COVID-19 by building instructional resiliency through the four recommendations presented in this chapter. That said, there are numerous lessons still to be learned, particularly because teaching effectiveness encompasses numerous behaviors (Myers et al. 2014). As such, an organizing framework that instructors can use—via the five frames detailed in this chapter—acts as a starting point to prepare for and prevent future classroom interruptions. While each instructional behavior has its place, in our study, the participants indicated their preference for instructor clarity, feedback, confirmation, and responsiveness in the online classroom. We conclude that these teaching behaviors not only aid cognitive learning in the online context, but with enough practice, they also inoculate against future (un)anticipated classroom interruptions. By embracing these instructional inoculation recommendations, instructors can overcome the difficulties manifested by the COVID-19 pandemic and build instructional resiliency for future academic uncertainties.

NOTES

1. Participants were 50 male and 106 female undergraduate students whose ages ranged from 18 to 33 years ($M = 20.04$, $SD = 2.07$). Sixty-two ($n = 62$) participants were first year students, 32 participants were sophomores, 37 participants were juniors, and 25 participants were seniors. The majority (87 percent; $n = 135$) of participants reported their ethnicity as White/Caucasian, followed by Black/African American ($n = 7$), Middle Eastern ($n = 5$), Asian/Asian American ($n = 4$), Hispanic ($n = 4$), and Biracial ($n = 1$). At the time of data collection, participants reported that they were enrolled, on average, in 15 credit hours ($M = 15.62$, $SD = 2.12$, range = 9–21 hours) across four modalities: face-to-face ($n = 69$), hybrid ($n = 55$), online synchronous ($n = 131$), and online asynchronous ($n = 114$).

2. Students were provided with a list of 10 behaviors and a brief description of each behavior. These behaviors were taken from Myers et al. (2018b), who found that college students identified these 10 behaviors as having a direct effect on whether instructors were able to able to meet their academic and relational classroom needs. These behaviors are assertiveness (initiates communication with students that is direct and to the point), clarity (presents information at an appropriate pace and in an organized manner that makes it easy for students to understand and to follow), confirmation (recognizes and acknowledges that students are valuable and important contributors to the classroom environment), feedback (provides feedback that is valuable and useful for improving students' academic performance), humor (incorporates humorous stories, examples, and jokes into class lectures that may or may not be related to the course content), justice (applies classroom-related procedures, policies, and grading practices fairly to all students), nonverbal immediacy (uses nonverbal behaviors such as vocal variety, smiling, leaning toward students, sustaining eye contact, and walking around the classroom as a way to increase psychological closeness with students), responsiveness (initiates communication with students that is empathic, caring, and sincere), self-disclosure (discloses personal information about themselves that students otherwise would not know or would not be able to obtain), and verbal immediacy (uses verbal behaviors such as asking questions, addressing students by name, and engaging in conversations with students as a way to increase psychological closeness with students).

REFERENCES

Bolkan, San. 2016. "The Importance of Instructor Clarity and its Effect on Student Learning: Facilitating Elaboration by Reducing Cognitive Load." *Communication Reports* 29, no. 3: 152–162. doi:10.1080/08934215.2015.1067708

Bolkan, San, Alan K. Goodboy, and Dawn M. Kelsey. 2016. "Instructor Clarity and Student Motivation: Academic Performance as a Product of Students' Ability and Motivation to Process Instructional Material." *Communication Education* 65, no. 3: 129–148. doi:10.1080/03634523.2015.1079328

Booth-Butterfield, Steven, and Booth-Butterfield, Melanie. 1991. "Individual Differences in the Communication of Humorous Messages." *Southern Communication Journal* 56, no. 3: 205–218. doi:10.1080/10417949109372831

Chesebro, Joseph L. 2003. "Effects of Teacher Clarity and Nonverbal Immediacy on Student Learning, Receiver Apprehension, and Affect." *Communication Education* 52, no. 2: 135–147. doi:10.1080/0363452032000085108

Chory, Rebecca M. 2007. "Enhancing Student Perceptions of Fairness: The Relationship Between Instructor Credibility and Classroom Justice." *Communication Education* 56, no.1: 89–105. doi:10.1080/03634520600994300

Clark-Gordon, Cathlin V., Nicholas David Bowman, Evan R. Watts, Jaime Banks, and Jennifer Knight. 2018. "'As Good as Your Word': Face-Threat Mitigation and the Use of Instructor Nonverbal Cues on Students' Perceptions of Digital Feedback." *Communication Education* 67, no. 2: 206–225. doi:10.1080/03634523.2018.1428759

Downs, Valerie C., Manoochehr "Mitch" Javidi, and Jon F. Nussbaum. 1988. "An Analysis of Teachers' Verbal Communication Within the College Classroom: Use of Humor, Self-Disclosure, and Narratives." *Communication Education* 37, no. 2: 127–141. doi:10.1080/03634528809378710

Ellis, Kathleen. 2000. "Perceived Teacher Confirmation: The Development and Validation of an Instrument and Two Studies of the Relationship to Cognitive and Affective Learning." *Human Communication Research* 26, no. 2: 264–291. doi:10.1111/j.1468-2958.2000.tb00758x

Frymier, Ann Bainbridge, and Melissa Bekelja Wanzer. 2006. "Teacher and Student Affinity-Seeking in the Classroom." In *Handbook of Instruction: Rhetorical and Relational Perspectives*, edited by Timothy P. Mottet, Virginia P. Richmond, and James C. McCroskey, 195–211. Boston, MA: Pearson.

Frymier, Ann Bainbridge, Melissa Bekelja Wanzer, and Ann M. Wojtaszczyk. 2008. "Assessing Students' Perceptions of Inappropriate and Appropriate Teacher Humor." *Communication Education* 57, no. 2: 266–288. doi:10.1080/03634520701687183

Gallien, Tara, and Jody Oomen-Early. 2008. "Personalized Versus Collective Instructor Feedback in the Online Classroom: Does Type of Feedback Affect Student Satisfaction, Academic Performance, and Perceived Connectedness with the Instructor?" *International Journal of E-Learning* 7, no. 3: 463–476.

Galvin, Kathleen M. 1999. "Classroom Roles of the Teacher." In *Teaching Communication: Theory, Research, and Methods*, 2nd edition, edited by Anita

L. Vangelisti, John A. Daly, and Gustav W. Friedrich, 243–255. Mahwah, NJ: Erlbaum.

Goldman, Zachary W., Gregory A. Cranmer, Michael Sollitto, Sara LaBelle, and Alexander L. Lancaster. 2017. "What do College Students Want?: A Prioritization of Instructional Behaviors and Characteristics. *Communication Education* 66, no. 3: 280–298. doi:10.1080/03634523.2016.1265135

Goldman, Zachary W., and Alan K. Goodboy. 2014. "Making Students Feel Better: Examining the Relationships Between Teacher Confirmation and College Students' Emotional Outcomes." *Communication Education 63,* no. 3: 259–277. doi: 10.1080/03634523.2014.920091

Goodboy, Alan K., and Scott A. Myers. 2008. "The Effect of Teacher Confirmation on Student Communication and Learning Outcomes." *Communication Education* 57, no. 2: 153–179. doi:10.1080/03634520701787777

Goodboy, Alan K., and Scott A. Myers. 2015. "Revisiting Instructor Misbehaviors: A Revised Typology and Development of a Measure." *Communication Education* 64, no. 2: 133–153. doi:10.1080/03634523.2014.978798

Gorham, Joan. 1988. "The Relationship Between Verbal Teacher Immediacy Behaviors and Student Learning." *Communication Education* 37, no. 1: 40–53. doi:10.1080/03634528809378702

Gorham, Joan, and Diane M. Christophel. 1990. "The Relationship of Teachers' Use of Humor in the Classroom to Immediacy and Student Learning." *Communication Education* 39, no. 1: 46–62. doi:10.1080/03634529009378786

Gorham, Joan, Derek H. Kelley, and James C. McCroskey. 1989. "The Affinity-Seeking of Classroom Teachers: A Second Perspective." *Communication Quarterly* 37, no. 1: 16–26. doi:10.1080/01463378909385522

Houser, Marian L., and Angela M. Hosek, eds. 2018. *Handbook of Instructional Communication: Rhetorical and Relational Perspectives*, 2nd edition. Boston, MA: Pearson.

Huber, Aubrey A. 2020. "Failing at the Help Desk: Performing Online Teacher." *Communication Education* 69, no. 4: 464–479. doi:10.1080/03634523.2020.1803379

Infante, Dominic A. 1987. Aggressiveness. In *Personality and Interpersonal Communication*, edited by James C. McCroskey and John A. Daly, 157–192. Newbury Park, CA: Sage.

Infante, Dominic A. 1988. *Arguing Constructively*. Prospect Heights, IL: Waveland Press.

Infante, Dominic A., and Andrew S. Rancer. 1982. "A Conceptualization and Measure of Argumentativeness." *Journal of Personality Assessment* 46, no. 1: 72–80. doi:10.1207/s15327752jpa4601_13

Infante, Dominic A., Andrew S. Rancer, and Deanna F. Womack. 2003. *Building Communication Theory*, 4th edition. Prospect Heights, IL: Waveland Press.

Infante, Dominic A., and Charles J. Wigley, III. 1986. "Verbal Aggressiveness: An Interpersonal Model and Measure." *Communication Monographs* 53, no. 1: 61–69. doi:10.1080/03637758609376126

Johnson, Zac D., and Sara LaBelle. 2017. "An Examination of Teacher Authenticity in the College Classroom." *Communication Education* 66, no. 4: 423–439. doi:10.1080/03634523.2017.1324167

Kaufmann, Renee, Deanna D. Sellnow, and Brandi N. Frisby. 2016. "The Development and Validation of the Online Learning Climate Scale (OLCS)." *Communication Education* 65, no. 3: 307–321. doi:10.1080/03634523.2015.1101778

Kearney, Patricia, Timothy G. Plax, Ellis R. Hays, and Marilyn J. Ivey. 1991. "College Teacher Misbehaviors: What Students Don't Like About What Teachers Say and Do." *Communication Quarterly* 39, no. 4: 309–324. doi:10.1080/01463379109369808

King, Paul E., Paul Schrodt, and Jessica J. Weisel. 2009. "The Instructional Feedback Orientation Scale: Conceptualizing and Validating a New Measure for Assessing Perceptions of Instructional Feedback." *Communication Education* 58, no. 2: 235–261. doi:10.1080/03634520802515705

King-Sears, Margaret. 2009. "Universal Design for Learning: Technology and Pedagogy." *Learning Disability Quarterly* 32, no. 4: 199–201. doi:10.2307/27740372

Kluger, Avrahan N., and Angelo DeNisi. 1996. "The Effects of Feedback Interventions on Performance: A Historical Review, A Meta-Analysis, and A Preliminary Feedback Intervention Theory." *Psychological Bulletin* 119, no. 2: 254–284. doi:10.1037/0033-2909.119.2.254

Knoster, Kevin C., Alan K. Goodboy, Matthew M. Martin, and Alan Thomay. 2021. "What Matters Most: A Prioritization of Medical Students' Preferences for Effective Teaching." *Communication Education* 70, no. 2: 183–200. doi:10.1080/03634523.2020.1841254

Knoster, Kevin C., and Scott A. Myers. 2020. "College Student Perceptions of Frequency and Effectiveness of Use of Relevance Strategies: A Replication and Extension." *Communication Studies* 71, no. 2: 280–294. doi:10.1080/10510974.2020.1720260

Lizzio, Alf, and Keithia Wilson. 2008. "Feedback on Assessment: Students' Perceptions of Quality and Effectiveness." *Assessment & Evaluation in Higher Education* 33, no. 3: 263–275. doi:10/1080/0260293071292548

Martin, Matthew M. 2008. "Teacher Socio-Communicative Style." In *The International Encyclopedia of Communication*, edited by Wolfgang Donsbach, Vol. 11, 4994–4996. Malden, MA: Blackwell.

McCroskey, James C., and Virginia P. Richmond. 1983. "Power in the Classroom I: Teacher and Student Perceptions." *Communication Education* 32, no. 2: 175–184. doi:10.1080/03634528309378527

McCroskey, James C., Virginia P. Richmond, and Linda L. McCroskey. 2006. *An Introduction to Communication in the Classroom: The Role of Communication in Teaching and Training*. Boston, MA: Pearson.

McCroskey, James C., Virginia P. Richmond, Aino Sallinen, Joan M. Fayer, and Robert A. Barraclough. 1995. "A Cross-Cultural and Multi-Behavioral Analysis of the Relationship Between Nonverbal Immediacy and Teacher Evaluation." *Communication Education* 44, no. 4: 281–291. doi:10.1080/03634529509379019

Mottet, Timothy P., Virginia P. Richmond, and James C. McCroskey, eds. 2006. *Handbook of Instructional Communication: Rhetorical and Relational Perspectives*. Boston, MA: Pearson.

Myers, Scott A. 2018. "Making a Difference: The Launch of the *Journal of Communication Pedagogy*." *Journal of Communication Pedagogy* 28, no. 1: 1–2. doi:10.31446/jcp.2018.1

Myers, Scott A. 2020. "Learning the Three C's: Becoming a Competent Classroom Communicator." Webinar from National Communication Association, Washington, DC, June 1–5, 2020. https://www.natcom.org/convention-events/nca-sponsored-events/nca-speaker-events-developing-ideas-teaching-and-research

Myers, Scott A., Alan K. Goodboy, and Members of COMM 600. 2014. "College Student Learning, Motivation, and Satisfaction as a Function of Effective Instructor Communication Behaviors." *Southern Communication Journal* 79, no. 1: 14–26. doi: 10.1080/1041794X.2013.815266

Myers, Scott A., James P. Baker, Heather Barone, Stephen M. Kromka, and Sara Pitts. (2018a). "Using Rhetorical/Relational Goal Theory to Examine College Students' Impressions of Their Instructors". *Communication Research Reports* 35, no. 2: 131–140. doi:10.1080/08824096.207.1406848

Myers, Scott A, Kathryn T. Garlitz, Stephen M. Kromka, Andrew L. Nicholson, Andrew L. Sutherland, and Matthew J. Thomas. (2018b). "Using Rhetorical/Relational Goal Theory to Examine Millennial Students' Academic and Relational Needs." In *Millennial Culture and Communication Pedagogies: Narratives from the Classroom and Higher Education*, edited by Ahmet Atay & Mary Z. Ashlock, 121–141. Lanham, MD: Lexington Books.

Myers, Scott A., Maria Brann, and Matthew M. Martin. 2013. "Identifying the Content and Topics of Instructor Use of Verbally Aggressive Messages." *Communication Research Reports* 30, no. 3: 252–258. doi:10/1080/08824096.2013.806260

Norton, Robert W. 1977. "Foundation of a Communicator Style Construct." *Human Communication Research* 4, no. 2: 99–112. doi:10.1111/j.1468-2958.1978.tb00600.x

Norton, Robert. 1983. *Communicator Style: Theory, Applications, and Measures*. Beverly Hills, CA: Sage.

Richmond, Virgina P., and James C. McCroskey. 1984. "Power in the Classroom II: Power and Learning." *Communication Education* 33, no. 2: 125–136. doi:10.1080/03634528409384729

Richmond, Virginia P., and James C. McCroskey. 1990. "Reliability and Separation of Factors on the Assertiveness-Responsiveness Measure." *Psychological Reports* 67, no. 2: 449–450.

Rudick, C. Kyle, and Deanna P. Dannels. 2020. "Yes, and . . .': Continuing the Scholarly Conversation About Pandemic Pedagogy." *Communication Education* 69, no. 4: 540–544. doi:10.1080/03634523.2020.1809167

Schrodt, Paul, Paul L. Witt, and Paul D. Turman. 2007. "Reconsidering the Measurement of Teacher Power Use in the College Classroom." *Communication Education* 56, no. 3: 308–332. doi:10.1080/03634520701256062

Scott, Michael D., and Jon F. Nussbaum. 1981. "Student Perceptions of Instructor Communication Behaviors and Their Relationship to Student Evaluation." *Communication Education* 30, no. 1: 45–32. doi:10.1080/03634528109378452

Sellnow, Deanna D., and Renee Kaufmann. 2018. "Instructional Communication and the Online Learning Environment: Then, Now, and Next." In *Handbook of Instructional Communication: Rhetorical and Relational Perspectives*, 2nd edition, edited by Marian L. Houser & Angela M. Hosek, 195–206. Boston, MA: Pearson.

Senko, Corwin, Kimberly Belmonte, and Anastasyia Yakhind. 2012. "How Students' Achievement Goals Shape Their Beliefs About Effective Teaching: A 'Build-a-Professor' Study." *British Journal of Educational Psychology* 82, no. 3: 420–435. doi:10.1111/j.2044-8279.2011.02036.x

Simonds, Cheri J. 1997. "Classroom Understanding: An Expanded Notion of Teacher Clarity." *Communication Research Reports* 14, no. 3: 279–290. doi:10.1080/08824099709388671

Sorensen, Gail. 1989. "The Relationships Among Teachers' Self-Disclosive Statements, Students' Perceptions, and Affective Learning." *Communication Education* 38, no. 3: 259–276. doi:10.1080/0363452, 8909378762

Staton, Ann Q. 1989. "The Interface of Communication and Instruction: Conceptual Considerations and Programmatic Manifestations." *Communication Education* 38, no. 4: 364–371. doi:10.1080/03634528909378777

Sung, Eunmo, and Richard E. Mayer. 2012. "Five Facets of Social Presence in Online Distance Education." *Computers in Human Behavior* 28, no. 5: 1738–1747. doi:10.1016/j.chb.2012.04.014

Teven, Jason J., and James C. McCroskey. (1996). "The Relationship of Perceived Teacher Caring with Student Learning and Teacher Evaluation." *Communication Education* 46, no. 1: 1–9. doi:10.1080/03634529709379069

Titsworth, Scott, and Joseph P. Mazer. 2016. "Teacher Clarity: An Analysis of Current Research and Future Directions." In *Handbooks of Communication and Science: Communication and Learning*, vol. 16 edited by Paul L. Witt, 105–128. Berlin, Germany: DeGruyter/Mouton.

Titsworth, Scott, Joseph P. Mazer, Alan K. Goodboy, San Bolkan, and Scott A. Myers. 2015. "Two Meta-Analyses Exploring the Relationship Between Teacher Clarity and Student Learning." *Communication Education* 64, no. 4: 385–418. doi:10.1080/03634523.2015.1041998

Vallade, Jessalyn I., and Scott A. Myers. 2014. "Student Forgiveness in the College Classroom: Perceived Instructor Misbehaviors as Relational Transgressions." *Communication Quarterly* 62, no. 3: 342–356. doi:10.1080/01463373.2014.911767

Witt, Paul L., ed. 2016. *Handbooks of Communication and Science: Communication and Learning*, vol 16. Berlin, Germany: DeGruyter/Mouton.

Witt, Paul L., Lawrence R. Wheeless, and Mike Allen. 2004. "A Meta-Analytical Review of the Relationship Between Teacher Immediacy and Student Learning." *Communication Monographs* 71, no. 2: 184–207. doi:10.1080/036452042000228054

Chapter 2

From Novel to Necessary

COVID-19 and the Kairos of Bringing Technology into the Communication Classroom[1]

Ashley A. Hanna Edwards

In early 2021, there was a TikTok trend set to part of Lady Gaga's song *Bad Romance* (2009). Creators would use a sound by @theofficialgracegroski (Groski 2020) that repeated the line "Oh, caught in a bad romance" seven times with growing intensity to tell an escalating story where each new revelation is more startling. The escalation of the song fits well as a representation of the ways the COVID-19 pandemic disrupted higher education: *Ohhhhhhhh, caught in a bad romance . . .* Early March 2020: Higher education is aflutter with anxiety about COVID-19. *Ohhhhhhhh, caught in a bad romance . . .* Mid-March: Campuses go from "don't worry" to "let's extend spring break" in 24 hours. *Ohhhhhhhh, caught in a bad romance . . .* Late March: Colleges and universities move the rest of spring semester online. *Ohhhhhhhh, caught in a bad romance . . .* June: fall 2020 looks suspect. Choose your modality and cross your fingers! *Ohhhhhhhh, caught in a bad romance . . .* Four days into fall semester: Cases are rising exponentially. Pivot online immediately! *Ohhhhhhhh, caught in a bad romance . . .* 2020–2021 Academic Year: Teach your class in every modality and have lots of grace! *Ohhhhhhhh, caught in a bad romance . . .* March 2021: No matter that cases are still rising, it's safe to return to normal next fall!

The COVID-19 pandemic illuminated many problems that existed long before the crisis, but were magnified by a highly contagious airborne virus (Shin and Hickey 2020). In addition to societal issues, the pandemic highlighted problems within higher education and our communication pedagogy. The post-pandemic classroom represents an important opportunity to reconsider the ways that we teach and build community within our courses (Schwartzman 2020).

Post-pandemic, communication instructors should shift our pedagogy in ways that are influenced by communication scholarship, especially theories of computer-mediated communication. Pre-pandemic, using technology in instruction, was often a novelty, not a requirement. Instructors might use learning management software (LMS) to host course readings or a copy of the syllabus. Instructors might use email to communicate with students or slide decks as visual aids in the classroom. Still, instructors held onto reservations about the quality and rigor of online education, including ableist bans on technology use in the classroom.[2] But the COVID-19 pandemic challenged all of these assumptions and practices and made technology necessary.

Although communication scholars were not immune to the chaos and stress of emergency remote teaching (ERT), our foundational knowledge about human communication and technology gave us an advantage over many disciplines. In this chapter, I argue that the COVID-19 pandemic provides a kairotic moment for the communication studies discipline to thoughtfully integrate technology and technology-mediated communication into our curriculum and pedagogy. Integrating technology in a multitude of ways that are informed by our scholarship can enhance student learning and export communication studies expertise to other disciplines. This chapter overviews instructional use of technology in pedagogy before and during the pandemic, then provides a rationale and recommendations for integrating technology into our classrooms as we move forward.

THE BEFORE TIME: TECHNOLOGY AS NOVEL (AND SOMETIMES DANGEROUS)

Pre-pandemic, many viewed technology as a novelty. Instructors engaged in a wide range of technology-mediated behaviors, including prevalent email use, university-hosted LMS or external applications to connect with students, screening movies or online videos in the classroom for engagement, the use of online textbooks to cut costs, and classroom clickers to gamify learning. Disagreements about how to integrate technology in the classroom go back to the mid-1990s (Koehler, Mishra, and Yahya 2007). Over the decades, instructors have increased the integration of technology into the classroom. Integrating hardware has evolved from overheard transparencies and television carts with a VCR to clickers and classroom computers. Additionally, student access to personal computers has increased dramatically. There has also been a shift in how we integrate software into higher education spaces. Educational technology is a profitable industry, estimated to be worth $104B

(Grand View Research, 2021). New software is continuously developed for application in higher education classrooms, from open source quiz games to tools like Jamboard, VoiceThread, and GoReact. Instructors and students have expanded the classroom into social media spaces, from instructor-managed Facebook pages, to student work groups communicating on Snapchat. Often, integration of technology into higher education classrooms is met with mixed responses, ranging from praise for innovation and student-centered pedagogy to cautions about using tools that are too flashy or diminish the rigor of student learning outcomes.

Those responses reveal that people don't just see technology as novel; some consider technology to be dangerous. Catfishing and trolling represent online interpersonal dangers, but the threat of technology extends to more widespread concerns. Research from Safiya Umoja Noble and others on algorithms of oppression document the ways that technology is often discriminatory (Noble 2018). Popular culture pieces like the documentary *The Social Dilemma* (2020) highlight the control and surveillance nature of social media. Facebook's Cambridge Analytica scandal demonstrates the ways social media data is harvested without user consent for advertising (Lapowsky 2019). The rise of QAnon draws attention to the contagion of misinformation, how easily it spreads online, and the off-line consequences (Tollefson 2021).

Technology also threatens higher education via access to online, for-profit colleges and massive open online courses (MOOCs), which have the potential to decrease enrollment putting brick and mortar institutions into increasingly perilous financial conditions. Beyond technology increasing the competition for higher education's market share, many are skeptical of the use of technology for learning. Scholars have warned that bringing technology into the classroom, or the classroom into virtual space decreases learning, social and academic integration, motivation, and belonging (Allen 2006; Chametzky 2021). Educators and students alike perceive technology as potentially distracting, and support some technology-restrictive policies, like cell phone restrictions (Campbell 2006). Some even fear that machines might replace instructors (Marcus 2020) and textbooks (Economist Intelligence Unit 2008) in efforts to reduce the costs of higher education.

However, the belief that students learn less online is at odds with research. Multiple studies have found that students in fully online public speaking classes have comparable learning outcomes to students in fully face-to-face public speaking classes (Broeckelman-Post et al.. 2019). Additionally, online students perceive that their public speaking has improved the same amount or more than it would have in a face-to-face course (Linardopoulos 2010). There is some data that online students have higher rates of anxiety (Chametzky 2021); however, some suggest that this might be an issue of self-selection by anxious students into online courses (Hanson and Teven 2004). Beyond fully online courses, disciplinary journals like *Communication Teacher*, *Communication Education*, and the *Basic Communication Course Annual* share ideas of ways instructors can successfully integrate technology into their pedagogy.

Although the fear that technology diminishes student learning outcomes is largely unsubstantiated (Westwick, Hunter, and Haleta 2016), there is little doubt it has influenced the ways we use technology in higher education. However, instructors were required to collectively pivot when a global pandemic forced everyone to social distance and move the majority of our interactions online.

THE COVID-19 PANDEMIC: TECHNOLOGY AS NECESSARY

The COVID-19 pandemic paused our conversations about whether or not to use technology because public health recommendations for social and physical distancing required us to use technology for ERT. As many others have pointed out, there is a difference between ERT, or "crisis pedagogy," and critical technological pedagogy (Morreale, Thorpe, and Westwick 2021). The collective pivot higher education made in March 2020 to virtual learning temporarily diminished the agency instructors had to control how technology is integrated into instruction. All professors, from innovators to laggards, were required to quickly adapt to a new reality. Many instructors completely redesigned courses within a week or two. Technology was no longer novel, it was necessary.

The COVID-19 pandemic changed the language we use to describe our classes. Communication descriptors like "synchronous" and "asynchronous" went from technical to colloquial. Today, modality is a common term understood by all, as are a host of modality descriptors, like "hybrid" and "hyflex." Many jokes have been made about Zoom University, as virtual videoconferencing platforms have become commonplace in academic, professional, and social environments. Colleges and universities were required to invest in new and expensive software to facilitate virtual instruction, as well as in professional development opportunities for instructors to learn more about integrating technology into the classroom.

As spring semester came to a close, institutions needed to finalize decisions about the 2020–2021 academic year. Some entire systems, like California State University, committed to remaining fully virtual (Burke 2020). Some institutions mandated that faculty and students return to in-person learning, but with face masks and reduced classroom capacity to aid social distancing. Some institutions allowed instructors to make pedagogical and personal choices about the modality of their classes. However, instructors and institutions alike made modality decisions for fall 2020 without much information. One article about the ways that college could look different for fall 2020 offered every possible alternative: fully virtual, delayed start, blended format, shortened semesters, only some students permitted to be on campus, or a full return to campus with public health-related changes (Nadworny 2020). Students, faculty, and administrators all spoke of concerns that college students would not follow social distancing recommendations (Wong 2020). Additionally, rumors abounded about other possibilities: lecture as the only option for face-to-face classes to minimize spread, reduced classroom capacities that required students to only attend every other session, and mask mandates. Some instructors elected to teach virtually because of the increased certainty it afforded, a choice which was affirmed when many institutions pivoted back to virtual learning as soon as four days into the semester ("UWL Puts All Residence Halls" 2020) when COVID-19 spiked across the country as students returned to campus. The uncertainty and related need to continuously pivot was taxing.

Although there is limited research to date on the ways that technology and COVID-19 crisis pedagogy impacted students and faculty, the current research makes clear that the outcomes are mixed. Many have overtly questioned whether the quality of education was worth its high price tag. Lawsuits allege that online education is inferior to learning on campus and demand the return of tuition and student fees (Van Voris and Lorin 2020). Most institutions have done little to advocate for the value of online education. Faculty are burned out (Gewin 2021).

Research also finds that students are dissatisfied with the emergency remote learning they've received. Students report reduced learning, a loss of motivation, a lack of communication and feedback, a struggle to foster creativity, insufficient workload adjustment, and the amplification of existing educational and social inequities (Shin and Hickey 2020). Another study found that ERT resulted in inefficient education with students lacking feedback and attention, as well as an increase in academic integrity issues (Mukhtar et al., 2020). Concerns about academic integrity during the pandemic influenced many instructors and institutions to adopt plagiarism software and online proctoring technology (Harwell 2020a). Many students were uncomfortable, irritated, and deeply upset with the increased surveillance (Harwell 2020b) and there has been substantial backlash from others concerned about institutional overreach and invasions of privacy (Hubler 2020). The technology we choose to integrate into our classes communicates our beliefs about technology and students to the class. The choice to rely heavily on surveillance technology communicates a lack of trust for both students and the uses of technology that may run counter to many of our intended pedagogical messages.

However, researchers find that students have also experienced positive outcomes of ERT. Students in Pakistan, for instance, indicated that flexibility and accessibility were advantages of virtual learning and that they benefited from being asynchronous and self-directed (Mukhtar et al.. 2020). Other research focused on ERT in response to a natural disaster found students had increased resilience as a result of their ERT experience (Ayebi-Arthur 2017). There's also early evidence to suggest that black students with access to technology are thriving in remote learning,[3] likely due to a decrease in the daily experience of microaggressions (Miller 2021), raising important questions about the ways that technology can be used as a tool for social justice.

Instructors report some silver linings, too. Many institutions offered and encouraged faculty to engage in professional development to enhance their online teaching skills. Faculty reported an increased willingness to ask for help and to share resources (Lederman 2020). Instructors have innovated, found ways to make connections, and used virtual space to access resources usually out of reach, like guest speakers (McMurtrie 2021). ERT reduced spontaneous, face-to-face conversations, but provided an opportunity to think critically about teaching practices and dialogue about pedagogy. Instructors have learned to use new technologies and think creatively about student engagement in synchronous and asynchronous spaces. While many instructors are eager to return to campus, we should also strive to be bringing these lessons and innovations back to campus with us.

There will be decades of research on the impact of virtual, emergency remote learning during the COVID-19 pandemic on students and instructors. However, instructors cannot wait for this research to plan our next steps, as many institutions are promoting a return to "normal" as soon as fall 2021. This is a kairotic moment for communication studies and other academic disciplines: We must use what we've learned about communication and technology to inform our post-pandemic pedagogy.

THE AFTER TIME: A KAIROTIC MOMENT

There is strong rationale for post-pandemic pedagogy to continue to view technology as a pedagogical necessity, especially for those of us who teach in communication studies. Pandemic and post-pandemic pedagogy is an opportunity for the discipline to consider the ways that our scholarship informs our pedagogy (Morreale, Thorpe, and Westwick 2021) and to export those lessons to others in higher education (Schwartzman 2020). I argue there is a strong rationale for integrating technology into our pedagogy in ways that are informed by communication scholarship and the lessons gleaned from the COVID-19 pandemic.

First, technology is pervasive and communication scholars agree that digital communication is important (Frisby 2017; Lind 2012). Most students are avid users of technology, with 45 percent of Gen Z reporting they use the Internet "almost constantly" in a pre-pandemic Pew survey (Parker and Igielnik 2020). Millennials, and now Gen Z, are often referred to as "digital natives" (Prensky 2001, 1) although the label can blur the distinction between those comfortable consuming digital content and those comfortable producing digital content (Gradim 2009). Employers want and expect students to have technological skills (National Association of Colleges and Employers 2020) and it benefits students and the discipline to provide that training (Edwards 2021). Additionally, students may expect technology use in their education due to its pervasiveness in their daily lives (Grauer 2019). Integrating technology in the classroom increases students' agency, especially when using technology they are already using outside of class. Incorporating forms of technology students regularly use also helps them to connect course content to their daily lived experiences.

Second, technology is already a part of the communication model we teach to all of our students as a part of communication channel, so integrating technology into our pedagogy is consistent with our discipline's foundations. Most students in communication classes learn multiple iterations of the communication model. Each of those models, from the Shannon–Weaver Model (Shannon and Weaver 1964) to the transactional model of communication (Barnlund 1970), includes the concept of the communication channel. To integrate technology and discussions about technology-mediated communication into our courses is merely to increase the focus and attention we give to part of our existing models of communication. We can help students to understand technology or communication modality as a tool, rather than an inherently positive or negative communication environment. We can help to contextualize the overly simplified, falsely dichotomous perspectives represented in popular culture about social media being dangerous and responsible for our social ills or as a utopia that connects and democratizes the world. Learning to see technology as a communication tool will enhance students' critical thinking skills and communication competence.

Third, technology and pedagogy provide an opportunity for communication studies to share our expertise and maintain credibility with our students. When we share unnuanced beliefs about technology being novel, dangerous, or *less than* face-to-face communication with our students, we diminish our credibility and expertise as a field. Instead, instructors should draw on decades of computer-mediated communication scholarship for insight on how to integrate technology into our pedagogy and then share those insights with other educators. According to instructional communication scholarship, students expect technology use in the classroom and when used effectively it enhances instructor credibility (Schrodt and Witt 2006), extends students' learning experience beyond the walls of the classroom, and increases the perceptions an instructor cares about their students (McComb 1994). Technology can also be a bridge to help students see the interconnectedness of our field (Oh and Owlett 2017), since technology touches all the areas of our discipline, from rhetoric to mass media, and from interpersonal to organizational communication.

Fourth, technology can enhance the diversity, equity, and inclusion of our courses. When we pivoted to ERT, many of us engaged in technology practices disabled and chronically ill students have been requesting long before the pandemic: offering lecture materials in multiple modalities, archiving lectures, using closed captioning for all resources, being mindful to add alternate image descriptions, and so on. Many instructors incorporated elements of universal design for learning (Burgstahler and Cory 2010) without even being familiar with the approach. Students in hybrid courses were able to choose their class modality for the day based on their physical or mental health, without concern that they would miss critical learning or be penalized for being absent. Moreover, those early findings that virtual learning can improve the educational experience of Black students (Miller 2021) suggest that multimodality or modal flexibility might have anti-racist impacts. Continuing to use technology in these ways can make learning accessible to more students in ways that match institutional goals for inclusion. Marginalized communities would be further marginalized by returning to pre-pandemic pedagogy, with no consideration for how ERT measures offered resources and benefits to students in ways that are regularly overlooked. Mindfully incorporating technology into the classrooms may welcome students who wouldn't attend otherwise (Schwartzman 2007).

Fifth, technology provides opportunities to enhance students' communication skills. In 2021, media literacy is a communication skill that is salient and essential to public dialogue. Work by Sam Wineburg and Sarah McGrew (2019) refers to these skills as "civic online reasoning" (38) and provides Internet specific strategies for evaluating information like lateral reading, where you open multiple browser tabs to judge the credibility of sources by comparing them to each other. In a later study, they demonstrated that students' media literacy can be improved through instruction (McGrew et al.. 2019). Instructors can help our students to develop media literacy by incorporating technology into our courses and educating them on strategies for assessing source credibility. Beyond media literacy, instructors can incorporate the Internet in our courses as a way of equipping our students for deliberation in the public sphere (Papacharissi 2002). By moving classroom communication environments into the public sphere, instructors can help students to access new audiences for civic engagement. As an example, students assigned to propose a policy that will help their community can present that work synchronously or asynchronously online to an audience of community members, rather than exclusively relying on their classmates as a convenient audience. Encouraging students to engage in the public sphere and giving them opportunities to practice can increase their agency for making changes that matter to them (Martin and Bollinger 2018).

Sixth, technology can help our discipline to prepare for the known and unknown challenges that lie ahead. For years, higher education has been warned about the looming demographic enrollment cliff resulting from a low birth rate during the Great Recession (Seltzer 2020). Using technology to create hybrid and fully virtual learning communities might offer institutions a wider pool of students. Beyond the predictable challenges, infusing technology into our pedagogy can help us to better manage unexpected situations, from extreme weather and natural disasters related to climate change (Herring et al. 2018) to future pandemics or crises related to gun violence. Communication instructors met in November 2019 at the National Communication Association convention for a panel discussion on surviving shortened semesters with no clue how useful that conversation would soon be (Edwards et al. 2019). The panelists shared many ideas for coping included using technology to build in flexibility. For example, in the future a snowstorm might result in a virtual class session rather than a class cancellation or snow day. As Todorova and Bjorn-Andersen (2011) said: "The key lesson for others may be to embrace e-learning technology before disaster strikes!" (599).

RECOMMENDATIONS FOR INCORPORATING TECHNOLOGY INTO OUR PEDAGOGY

Communication scholarship, especially from the computer-mediated and instructional areas of our discipline, offers insights into ways of integrating technology into our pedagogy.

Consider Reduced Processing Speed when Communicating Through Technology

Early research on communicating through technology demonstrated that social information processing is slowed when communication occurs through computer-mediated channels (Walther 1992). According to social information processing theory, it takes longer for us to send messages, longer to decode messages, and as such, communication through these channels is both more effortful and more time-consuming. Thus, one important consideration for incorporating technology into our pedagogy is budgeting for the longer processing time it will take for both instructors and students to communicate.

When ERT started in March 2020, many instructors replaced synchronous in-person discussions with synchronous videoconferencing and asynchronous virtual discussion boards. However, most instructors failed to account for the added communication processing time and cost these shifts required. Consequently, students and instructors experienced burn out (not to mention the extensive emotional and physical toll of a global pandemic and social distancing). As a result, in many instances the communication labor of spring 2020 was more costly of time and cognitive resources with reduced outcomes than we could have expected from a similar length of face-to-face instruction.

For many, fall 2020 and spring 2021 yielded similar outcomes. Ongoing, and sometimes unplanned, modality shifts increased faculty labor as instructors created new plans and were then required to make adjustments. Faculty were more exhausted, and expending more resources than they are accustomed to, but often with reduced benefits. When we consider that technology-mediated communication requires more processing time, it makes sense to cut back on the number of assignments and to budget more time for virtual activities than would be required if the activity were off-line.

Draw on the Known Advantages of Communication Technologies

Learning that incorporating technology into your course might require more time and fewer activities may feel discouraging, but computer-mediated communication research also shows virtual communication can surpass the outcomes of face-to-face communication. The hyperpersonal model argues that sender effects, receiver effects, asynchronous channel effects, and feedback can all coalesce to make computer-mediated communication hyperpersonal, or more rewarding than face-to-face communication (Walther 1996). Sender effects allow us to curate our identities and messages, receiver effects idealize the messages we receive, the asynchronous channel allows us to communicate on our own time, and the feedback loop demonstrates that these combined effects are more than additive.

By understanding the advantages of technology-mediated channels, instructors can integrate technology in instances that might benefit both communicators. For example, students indicate that using email for regular announcements or reminders is helpful (Martin and Bollinger 2018). This may be because an instructor can carefully craft those messages, double-checking to share correct deadlines (sender effect), the student can perceive the email as having a warm tone and thus, the instructor as caring (receiver effects), and the student can benefit from mode of communication by reading it in their own time with the option to reread (asynchronous channel effects). In combination, all of these factors may result in the student feeling an increased connection to the class and submitting better quality work, which results in higher quality feedback from the instructor (feedback loop).

The social identity model of deindividuation effects (SIDE) (Lea and Spears 1991) is another model of computer-mediated communication from which we can draw insight. SIDE tells us that the limiting of nonverbal cues online can amplify group identity over individual identity. Although the model is often used to explain online polarization and trolling, in the classroom it may operate in prosocial ways. Students from marginalized groups often feel pressure to be "native informants" (hooks 1994) and to feel tokenized (Cooper Stoll 2019). In virtual spaces, these students can benefit from the pseudo-anonymity afforded by a reduced cue environment as a way of blending into the crowd. This provides a strong rationale for not requiring students to appear on camera in virtual class. Research demonstrates that turning off cameras can reduce emotional labor (Shlossberg and Cunningham 2016). Requiring cameras to be on during class creates equity issues related to sex, gender, and class as well (Finders and Muñoz 2021).

Be Flexible

The beauty of a missive like "incorporate technology into your pedagogy" is that there are many directions instructors can personalize their approach: Instructors can teach full courses or individual class sessions in an entirely virtual format. Instructors can integrate computer-mediated scholarship into larger discussions about theory. Instructors can share relevant viral media in the classroom and virtual class space. Researchers recommend using varied instructional material, including content you create, online resources, book chapters, and instructional videos (Martin and Bolliger 2018). Instructors should not feel the pressure to adopt all technology at once, but instead should educate themselves on the multitude of options and opportunities, then adopt technology incrementally based on pedagogy and comfort.

One starting point is to create multimodal discussion opportunities for students. Even pre-pandemic, not all students were comfortable participating in the same communication format. As an alternative, instructors can award discussion points for a wider variety of participation activities: sharing synchronously in-person, posting asynchronously to the LMS discussion forum, in-person nonverbal engagement (e.g., immediacy cues), and sharing resources with the instructor by email to bring into class discussion. Some of the students who might initially appear quiet may simply prefer to prepare what they were going to say before sharing. The same affordances that enable hyperpersonal communication, like an asynchronous channel and sender effects, can empower students to share with classmates they also see in person. Moreover, research shows that asynchronous discussion boards may result in more sustained self-reflection as students are able to return to the conversation (Shlossberg and Cunningham 2016).

Another advantage of flexible, multimodal pedagogy is that it empowers students to make their own communication decisions. Instructors should not to require students to use or download specific applications that are not university-affiliated. External software or applications can create information security issues. Moreover, students make individual choices about what social media applications and platforms to support in accordance with their personal values and goals. Those choices represent critical decision making about communication channel, which instructors should encourage.

Consider Student Uncertainty and Develop Clear Policies about Technology

Uncertainty is one of the reasons adopting technology can be so intimidating, for instructors and for students. Communication scholarship on uncertainty management highlights the multitude of ways that uncertainty can impact our communication, from asking more questions in order to reduce uncertainty (Berger and Calabrese 1975) to avoiding messages in order to preserve uncertainty (Afifi and Weiner 2004). For instance, students might seek to reduce uncertainty around classroom expectations. Clear policies about technology use may help to manage student uncertainty. Instructors can include lists of required technology, as well as guidance about how to access the LMS and what students can expect to find there. Instructors should also be clear with students about how the instructor might use the digital data available by adopting a digital surveillance policy, which might state:

> Online learning provides an abundance of surveillance tools (e.g., TurnItIn, Panopticon). I promise to never use these tools from a place of mistrust of students. I will occasionally use [LMS]'s tools for seeing which students have viewed course content, but ONLY for the purposes of supporting your success in the course. Please let me know if you have any privacy concerns related to the technology use in this course.

Instructors might also add policies to address student retention, which research shows is more of a problem in virtual learning spaces (Allen 2006). A student retention or "ghosting" policy might read:

> Online learning also makes it easier for absences to go unnoticed. Some absence is normal, even during typical times, but certainly during a pandemic. At the

same time, our collective learning is better when we are all present—you matter! So, if you ghost us, here's what you can expect from me:

1. I will check in with you by email just to make sure you're doing alright. It will be perfectly acceptable for you to say you are (no other detail needed) and that you're pacing coursework in a way that works best for you. It will also be an opportunity for you to ask me for support.
2. If I don't hear from you, I will message you using [campus-specific tool].
3. If I still don't get a response and more than a week has passed since my attempts, I will reach out to [office on campus that focuses on supporting students]. These folks have even more access to resources for supporting students.

   Any of these follow-ups DO NOT mean you are in trouble or that your course grade is necessarily at risk. Rather, these follow-ups are designed to make sure you know how much your presence is valued and to be sure you have what you need (within my power) to be successful and engage with this class.

Sharing clear policies about how and when instructors will use technology for student interaction can reduce the uncertainty and anxiety that students experience. Instructors should tell students how the class will use technology and share the rationale so that students can understand how and why instructors make decisions. Instructors can also link resources for the campus technology help desk and the help hotline for the LMS in the syllabus.

Model Thoughtful Criticism of Technology for Communication

It is time for instructors to acknowledge the multifaceted nature of technology and social media for education: Technology can both help and harm student learning. Communication scholars should familiarize ourselves with the basics of computer-mediated communication (CMC), or at least defer to CMC scholars' judgment. Communication scholars have been studying the ways that digital technology operates as a communication channel for over three decades. When instructors offer unnuanced criticism of technology, we diminish the scholarship of our peers and exacerbate the challenges of getting students to competently communicate through technology. Instead of offering simplified judgments, instructors should model thoughtful criticism of communication channel.

In viewing technology as a tool, we must acknowledge its limitations. Tools can be used for prosocial and antisocial ends. The same way computer-mediated channels can enable a long-distance couple to maintain their relationship, social media can provide information access to abusers. Social media can be a tool for public advocacy, like the use of Twitter for Arab spring, but it can also be used to silence already marginalized groups (Botella 2019), or the ways TikTok has shadow-banned Black creators (Gassam Asare 2020). Digital communication in the workplace can be used to empower folks to work from home, but it can also be used to make employees accessible outside of contracted hours. It is important to have these critical conversations with students so they begin to see technology as a rich tool with important implications for communication.

Unfortunately, not all students or faculty have access to reliable technology (Schwartzman 2020) and broadband Internet. Access is a heightened issue for students and faculty from marginalized communities (McKenzie 2021). Technology failures are another issue when incorporating technology into our pedagogy. Additionally, there are times when technology creates archival concerns. Students may self-censor their disclosures when discussions are being recorded, especially due to power, difference, or inequality (Shlossberg and Cunningham 2016). Research also shows that fully virtual classes can struggle with student retention, likely the result of increased social distance (Allen 2006). Moreover, there is substantial faculty concern about the ways that technology can facilitate academic dishonesty. The invasive technological tools for identifying dishonesty raise additional ethical concerns (Wintrup 2017). As educators and as a discipline, it is incumbent on us to continue having these conversations with our students and with each other. We must advocate for increased access to technology and the Internet as public infrastructure. We must have difficult conversations about whether the ethical trade-offs of surveilling students are worth the substantiated cases of academic dishonesty. We need to develop mindful classroom practices that help frame technology use for our students and to be conscientious that we are choosing the right technologies for the right learning tasks.

CONCLUSION

The COVID-19 pandemic fundamentally changed higher education. Technology has gone from novel to necessary. This is a kairotic moment: the time to take these actions is now. Students are already learning about digital communication through their own experiences and popular culture. Yet communication scholars who have studied technology-mediated communication for decades are rarely highlighted as experts in these conversations. Moreover, popular dialogue about technology and communication rarely deals in the nuance of when the modality or tool is effective versus ineffective. Predominantly negative judgments of technology-mediated communication, especially uninformed by communication scholarship, put us in jeopardy by undermining the value of virtual education, technology in the classroom, and the ability of our discipline to add to substantive public dialogue about technology and communication. We do this by drawing on the expertise of our field, sharing resources, and continuing a dialogue about the challenges and issues we face. Post-pandemic pedagogy must be multimodal because technology is now necessary.

NOTES

1. *Acknowledgements:* Special thanks to Dr. M. Elizabeth Thorpe for introducing me to the concept of kairos through her Kairoticast podcast and for answering my many questions about Chicago-style citation and to Jessica M. Peterson for feedback on a chapter draft and endless conversations about communication pedagogy.

2. Sincere thanks to #AcademicTwitter for helping me to understand!

3. It is important to note that emergency remote learning has also widened racial disparities in higher education, related to issues like technology access and financial status. However, these issues are not new, but are rooted in larger systemic issues. Moving forward, we must work to reduce those racial disparities in higher education and consider the ways that technology is a tool of both oppression and liberation.

REFERENCES

Afifi, Walid A., and Judith L. Weiner. 2004. "Toward a Theory of Motivated Information Management." *Communication Theory* 14, no. 2: 167–190.

Allen, Terre H. 2006. "Is the Rush to Provide On-Line Instruction Setting Our Students Up For Failure?" *Communication Education* 55, no. 1: 122–126.

Ayebi-Arthur, Kofi. 2017. "E-learning, Resilience and Change in Higher Education: Helping a University Cope After a Natural Disaster." *E-Learning and Digital Media* 14, no. 5: 259–274.

Barnlund, Dean C. 1970. "A Transactional Model of Communication." In *Language Behavior: A Book of Readings*, edited by Johnnye Akin, Alvin Goldberg, Gail Myers, and Joseph Stewart, 43–61. The Hague: Mouton.

Berger, Charles R., and Richard J. Calabrese. 1975. "Some Explorations in Initial Interaction and Beyond: Toward a Developmental Theory of Interpersonal Communication." *Human Communication Research* 1, no. 2: 99–112.

Botella, Elena. 2019. "TikTok Admits It Suppressed Videos by Disabled, Queer, and Fat Creators." *Slate Online.* December 4, 2019. https://www.slate.com/technology/2019/12/tiktok-disabled-users-videos-suppressed.html

Broeckelman-Post, Melissa A., Katherine E. Hyatt Hawkins, Anthony R. Arciero, and Andie S. Malterud. 2019. "Online versus Face-to-Face Public Speaking Outcomes:

A Comprehensive Assessment" *Basic Communication Course Annual* 31, article 10: 144–170.

Burgstahler, Sheryl, and Rebecca C. Cory. 2010. *Universal Design in Higher Education: From Principles to Practice.* Cambridge, MA: Harvard Education Press.

Burke, Lilah. 2020. "Cal State Stands Alone." *Inside Higher Ed.* May 14, 2020. https://www.insidehighered.com/news/2020/05/14/cal-state-pursuing-online-fall

Campbell, Scott W. 2006. "Perceptions of Mobile Phones in College Classrooms: Ringing, Cheating, and Classroom Policies." *Communication Education* 55, no. 3: 280–294.

Chametzky, Barry. 2021. "Chapter 58: Communication in Online Learning: Being Meaningful and Reducing Isolation." In *Research Anthology on Developing Effective Online Learning Courses.* 1184–1205. Hershey, PA: IGI Global.

Cooper Stoll, Laurie. 2019. *Should Schools Be Colorblind?* Cambridge: Polity.

Economist Intelligence Unit, 2008. "The future of higher education: How Technology Will Shape Learning." *The Economist.* https://files.eric.ed.gov/fulltext/ED505103.pdf

Edwards, Ashley A. Hanna. 2021. "From TED Talks to TikTok: Teaching Digital Communication to Match Student Skills with Employer Desires." *Basic Communication Course Annual 33*, article 17: 336–341.

Edwards, Ashley A. Hanna, Angela M. Hosek, Shawna Malvini Redden, George F. McHendry, Jr., and R. Brandon Anderson. 2019. "Surviving Shortened Semesters: Best Practices for Extended Class Cancellations [discussion panel]." *National Communication Association*, November 14, 2019.

Finders, Margaret, and Joaquin Muñoz. 2021. "Cameras On: Surveillance in the Time of COVID-19." *Inside Higher Ed.* March 3, 2021. https://www.insidehighered.com/advice/2021/03/03/why-its-wrong-require-students-keep-their-cameras-online-classes-opinion

Frisby, Brandi N. 2017. "Capitalizing on the Inevitable: Adapting to Mobile Technology in the Basic Communication Course." *Basic Communication Course Annual* 29, article 8: 76–82.

Gassam Asare, Janice. 2020. "Does TikTok Have a Race Problem?" *Forbes.* April 14, 2020. https://www.forbes.com/sites/janicegassam/2020/04/14/does-tiktok-have-a-race-problem/

Gewin, Virginia. 2021. "Pandemic Burnout is Rampant in Academia." *Nature.* March 15, 2021. https://www.nature.com/articles/d41586-021-00663-2

Gradim, Anabela. 2009. "Digital Natives and Virtual Communities: Towards a New Paradigm of Mediated Communication." *Estudos em Comunicação* 5: 53–73.

Grand View Research. "Education Technology Market Size, Share, & Trends Analysis Report By Sector (Preschool, K-12, Higher Education), By End User (Business, Consumer), By Type (Hardware, Software), By Region, and Segment Forecasts, 2021-2028." April 2021.

Grauer, Don. 2019. "7 Technology Trends in Higher Education." *Educause Review.* November 11, 2019. https://er.educause.edu/blogs/sponsored/2019/11/7-technology-trends-in-higher-education

Groski, Grace 2020. @theofficialgracegroski, "Original Sound." TikTok, November 12, 2020.

Hanson, Trudy L. and Jason J. Teven. 2004. "Lessons Learned from Public Speaking Online." *Online Cl@ssroom.* August 2004: 1–8.

Harwell, Drew. 2020a. "Mass School Closures in the Wake of the Coronavirus are Driving a New Wave of Student Surveillance." *The Washington Post.* April 1, 2020. https://www.washingtonpost.com/technology/2020/04/01/online-proctoring-college-exams-coronavirus/

Harwell, Drew. 2020b. "Cheating Detection Companies Made Millions During the Pandemic. Now Students are Fighting Back." *The Washington Post.* November 12, 2020. https://www.washingtonpost.com/technology/2020/11/12/test-monitoring-student-revolt/

Herring, Stephanie C., Nikolaos Christidis, Andrew Hoell, James P. Kossin, Carl J. Schreck III, and Peter A. Stott. 2018. "Explaining Extreme Events of 2016 from a Climate Perspective." *Bulletin of American Meteorological Society* 99, no. 1: 1–157.

hooks, bell. 1994. *Teaching to Transgress: Education as the Practice of Freedom.* New York: Routledge.

Hubler, Shawn. 2020. "Keeping Online Testing Honest? Or an Orwellian Overreach?" *The New York Times.* May 10, 2020. https://www.nytimes.com/2020/05/10/us/online-testing-cheating-universities-coronavirus.html

Koehler, Matthew J., Punya Mishra, and Kurnia Yahya. 2007. "Tracing the Development of Teacher Knowledge in a Design Seminar: Integrating Content, Pedagogy and Technology." *Computers & Education* 49, no. 3: 740–762.

Lady Gaga. 2009. "Bad Romance." October 23, 2009, track 1 on *The Fame Monster*, Interscope: digital download.

Lapowsky, Issie. 2019. "How Cambridge Analytica Sparked the Great Privacy Awakening." *Wired.* March 17, 2019. https://www.wired.com/story/cambridge-analytica-facebook-privacy-awakening/

Lea, Martin, and Russell Spears. 1991. "Computer-Mediated Communication, De-Individuation and Group Decision-Making." *International Journal of Man Machine Studies* 34, no. 2: 283–301.

Lederman, Doug. 2020. "'We're All in This Together.'" *Inside Higher Ed.* June 17, 2020. https://www.insidehighered.com/digital-learning/article/2020/06/17/pandemic-driven-teaching-pivot-drives-surge-sharing-among

Linardopoulos, Nick. 2010. "Teaching and Learning Public Speaking Online." *MERLOT Journal of Online Learning and Teaching* 6, no. 1: 198–209.

Lind, Stephen J. 2012. "Teaching Digital Oratory: Public Speaking 2.0." *Communication Teacher* 26, no. 3: 163–169.

Marcus, Jon. 2020. "How Technology is Changing the Future of Higher Education." *The New York Times.* February 20, 2020. https://www.nytimes.com/2020/02/20/education/learning/education-technology.html

Martin, Florence and Doris U. Bolliger, 2018. "Engagement Matters: Student Perceptions on the Importance of Engagement Strategies in the Online Learning Environment." *Online Learning* 22, no. 1: 205–222.

McComb, Mary. 1994. "Benefits of Computer-Mediated Communication in College Courses." *Communication Education* 43, no. 2: 159–170.

McGrew, Sarah, Mark Smith, Joel Breakstone, Teresa Ortega, and Sam Wineburg. 2019. "Improving University Students' Web Savvy: An Intervention Study." *The British Psychological Society* 89, no. 3: 485–500.

McKenzie, Lindsay. 2021. "Bridging the Digital Divide: Lessons from COVID-19." *Inside Higher Ed*. February 2, 2021. https://www.insidehighered.com/content/bridging-digital-divide-lessons-covid-19

McMurtrie, Beth. 2021. "Teaching: After the Pandemic, What Innovations Are Worth Keeping?" *The Chronicle of Higher Education*. April 1, 2021. https://www.chronicle.com/newsletter/teaching/2021-04-01

Miller, Elizabeth. 2021. "For Some Black Students, Remote Learning Has Offered a Chance to Thrive." *National Public Radio*. March 1, 2021. https://www.npr.org/2021/03/01/963282430/for-some-black-students-remote-learning-has-offered-a-chance-to-thrive

Morreale, Sherwyn P., Janice Thorpe, and Joshua N. Westwick. 2021. "Online Teaching: Challenge or Opportunity for Communication Education Scholars?" *Communication Education* 70, no. 1: 117–119.

Mukhtar, Khadijah, Kainat Javed, Mahwish Arooj, and Ahsan Sethi. 2020. "Advantages, Limitations and Recommendations for Online Learning During COVID-19 Pandemic Era." *Pakistan Journal of Medical Sciences* 36, no. 4: 27–31.

Nadworny, Elissa. 2020. "6 Ways College Might Look Different In The Fall." *National Public Radio*. May 5, 2020. https://www.npr.org/2020/05/05/848033805/6-ways-college-might-look-different-in-the-fall

National Association of Colleges and Employers. 2020. "Key Attributes Employers Want to See on Students' Resumes." January 13, 2020. https://www.naceweb.org/talent-acquisition/candidate-selection/key-attributes-employers-want-to-see-on-student-resumes/

Noble, Safiya Umoja. 2018. *Algorithms of Oppression*. New York: NYU Press.

Oh, Soo-Kwang, and Jennifer S. Owlett. 2017. "Embracing Social Media in the Basic Communication Course: Recommendations for the Digital Age." *Basic Communication Course Annual* 29, article 11: 98–108.

Papacharissi, Zizi. 2002. "The Virtual Sphere: The Internet as a Public Sphere." *New Media & Society* 4, no. 1: 9–27.

Parker, Kim, and Ruth Igielnik. 2020. "On the Cusp of Adulthood and Facing an Uncertain Future: What We Know About Gen Z So Far." *Pew Research*, May 14, 2020. https://www.pewresearch.org/social-trends/2020/05/14/on-the-cusp-of-adulthood-and-facing-an-uncertain-future-what-we-know-about-gen-z-so-far-2/

Prensky, Marc. 2001. "Digital Natives, Digital Immigrants." *On the Horizon*, MCB University Press, Vol. 9, No. 5: 1–6.

Schrodt, Paul, and Paul L. Witt. 2006. "Students' Attributions of Instructor Credibility as a Function of Students' Expectations of Instructional Technology Use and Nonverbal Immediacy." *Communication Education* 55, no. 1: 1–20.

Schwartzman, Roy. 2020. "Performing Pandemic Pedagogy." *Communication Education* 69, no. 4: 502–517.

Schwartzman, Roy. 2007. "Refining the Question: How Can Online Instruction Maximize Opportunities for All Students?" *Communication Education* 56, no. 1: 113–117.

Seltzer, Rick. 2020. "What Do Demographic Projections Mean for Colleges?" *Inside Higher Ed*. December 15, 2020. https://www.insidehighered.com/news/2020/12/15/what-do-new-projections-high-school-graduates-mean-colleges-and-universities

Shannon, Claude E. and Warren Weaver. 1964. *The Mathematical Theory of Communication*. Champaign, IL: The University of Illinois Press (1964).

Shlossberg, Pavel, and Carolyn Cunningham. 2016. "Diversity, Instructional Research, and Online Education." *Communication Education* 65, no. 2: 229–232.

Shin, Minsun, and Kasey Hickey. 2020. "Needs a Little TLC: Examining College Students' Emergency Remote Teaching and Learning Experiences During COVID-19." *Journal of Further and Higher Education* 3. doi:10.1080/0309877X.2020.1847261

The Social Dilemma, directed by Jeff Orlowski. 2020. United States, Exposure Labs, streaming on Netflix.

Todorova, Nelly, and Niels Bjorn-Andersen. 2011."University Learning in Times of Crisis: The Role of IT." *Accounting Education* 20, no. 6: 597–599.

Tollefson, Jeff. 2021. "Tracking QAnon: How Trump Turned Conspiracy-Theory Research Upside Down." *Nature*. February 4, 2021. https://www.nature.com/articles/d41586-021-00257-y

"UWL Puts All Residence Halls on Lockdown, Suspends In-Person Classes." 2020. *La Crosse Independent*. September 13, 2020. https://lacrosseindependent.com/2020/09/13/uwl-puts-all-residence-halls-on-lockdown-suspends-in-person-classes/

Van Voris, Bob, and Janet Lorin. 2020. "Angry Undergrads Are Suing Colleges for Billions in Refunds." *Bloomberg*. May 1, 2020. https://www.bloomberg.com/news/articles/2020-05-01/angry-undergrads-studying-online-sue-for-billions-in-refunds

Walther, Joseph B. 1996. "Computer-Mediated Communication: Impersonal, Interpersonal, and Hyperpersonal Interaction." *Communication Research* 23, no. 3: 3–43.

Walther, Joseph B. 1992. "Interpersonal Effects in Computer-Mediated Interaction: A Relational Perspective." *Communication Research* 19, no. 1: 52–90.

Westwick, Joshua N., Karla M. Hunter, and Laurie L. Haleta. 2016. "A Digital Divide? Assessing Self-Perceived Communication Competency in an Online and Face-to-Face Basic Public Speaking Course." *Basic Communication Course Annual* 28: 1–39.

Wineburg, Sam and Sarah McGrew. 2019. "Lateral Reading and the Nature of Expertise: Reading Less and Learning More When Evaluating Digital Information." *Teachers College Record* 121, no. 11: 1–55.

Wintrup, Julie. 2017. "Higher Education's Panopticon? Learning Analytics, Ethics and Student Engagement." *Higher Education Policy* 30: 87–103.

Wong, Wilson. 2020. "College Students Are Preparing to Return To Campus In The Fall. Is It Worth It?" *NBC News*. July 6, 2020. https://www.nbc.com/news/us-news/college-students-are-preparing-return-campus-fall-it-worth-it-n1232879

Chapter 3

Post-Pandemic Pedagogy

Compassionate and Caring Course Curriculum in the Digital University

Linda Carozza and Steve Gennaro

In the spring of 2020 educators across higher education in North America and around the world were forced to pivot to fully online teaching and learning practices as a result of COVID-19. Initially the responses were short term and temporary, more about triage measures than pedagogically informed practices. However, as the summer months of 2020 continued with no vaccine in sight, it became clear that COVID-19's impact on higher education would be profound. In the short term, classes would remain online for at least two more semesters, or quarters, into the winter of 2021. Long term, a collective of employees in the education sector were forced by circumstance to learn an entirely different set of skills immediately or leave the workforce; and they were forced to learn these skills while on the job and with very little margin for error. As we write this paper in the spring of 2021 in Toronto, Canada, the University remains digital, and it will continue to exist entirely online through the summer across much of North America.

There are now preparations for many institutions to reopen campuses for the fall of 2021, but after a 15-month hiatus from face-to-face teaching and learning, we contemplate what has changed, what will change, and what must change as we reassemble on campuses. More specifically we are curious about what has changed in our approach to teaching and learning since pre-pandemic, face-to-face, classrooms and lecture halls. With necessary training for many of us, it is likely that we have learned from the various workshops and lived experiences in the last year (both successes and failures). After 15 months of forum posts and breakout rooms the pedagogical landscape has likely been augmented for many. This paper explores the potential transformations that the pandemic has compelled as we reflect on our experiences inside our virtual classrooms, and we posit ideas for the future of higher learning.

With a critical lens toward digital pedagogy, we reflect on what happened before the pandemic, what happened during the pandemic, and then speculate about what is to come from our collective experiences. We do so with a particular focus on online invigilation and surveillance technologies, and also with a discussion about types of assignments and their deadlines. What is abundantly clear is that the emphasis to teach with a pedagogy of compassion that surfaced as a "suggested" practice inside digital COVID-19 classrooms must be the foundation of post-COVID-19 teaching and learning. There is no going backward on this. Furthermore, as we have been striving to make the digital more "humane," it is apparent that "ethics of care" in course design and delivery is essential to creating transformative learning experiences for our students. In part, we want to reveal the systemic constructs that have hijacked our pedagogical practice, and in part we want to highlight how the pandemic has made obvious to all of us the value of teaching with compassion and care ethics. What we suggest moving forward is antithetical to institutionalized teaching practices (in a neoliberal institution of higher learning), yet it highlights what digital pedagogy will look like post-pandemic for an engaged student body in online courses.

[COVID-19] ONLINE PEDAGOGY AND CRITICAL THEORY

One of the immediate *obviousnesses* of pandemic teaching was how flawed some of our notions of teaching and learning were pre-pandemic. Algerian philosopher and critical theorist Louis Althusser (1970) argued that ideology is most dangerous when it becomes so deeply ingrained in our collective consciousness and everyday practices that we no longer question the power imbalances they perpetuate. He referred to these embedded ideologies of normalcy as *obviousnesses*. These *obviousnesses* are what we today acknowledge as the structural components of institutionalized racism, misogyny, heterosexism, classism, and white supremacy. An example of these *obviousnesses* in higher education practice can be seen in our procedures for examination invigilation and the need to surveil our students' activities online. In terms of everyday teaching, the pandemic highlighted structural problems that already existed. Pandemic responses to pedagogy made visible a teacher-to-student transmission model that Paulo Freire (2008) called the "banking method of education" and exposed the inequity of access, opportunity, and agency across class, gender, and racial lines in our student body and our ingrained need to police these.

Whereas, in its earlier Gramcian definition, ideology referred more to a collection of ideas, Althusser's work explored not only the ideas themselves but also the material structures of practices, rituals, and power relations inside the construction of these ideas. According to Althusser, "[a hu]man is an ideological animal by nature," therefore ideologies exist in and around everything (1970). Here Althusser makes the distinction between two types of ideologies, those that are obvious and those that are hidden, or what he terms explicit and implicit ideologies. The surveillance of students' online activities, and in particular online examination invigilation, during COVID-19 pedagogy displays an explicit ideology of academic honesty and university integrity concerns, but implicitly it suggests that the University suspects its students to be cheaters and liars as a default. The data demonstrates that this is magnified along racial lines.

Multiple stories, such as Shea Swauger's op-ed in the August 2020 *MIT Technology Review*, noted concerns about the racial profiling of students using Proctor Track and similar types of online proctoring technology (2020). Students of color were more likely to be flagged for inappropriate and suspicious behavior and this increased with the darkness of the students' skin tones. The initial response of many universities in Canada to this information was to ignore the data, despite a strong student uprising. One change.org petition (2020) at the University of Western Ontario, Canada, received more than 10,000 signatures in protest. It took a security breach during student examinations in the fall 2020 term, and the resulting news coverage of the security breach on the invigilation software, before there was any response from Western University administrators. Even as we worked in leading sessions for faculty professional development at York University in Toronto, Canada during the summer 2020 session, and while some faculty continued to stress the problems with online proctoring technology, the University continued to pay its institutional license to Proctor Track and professors and course instructors could make requests to use it for midterm and final exams in their courses.

For Althusser, ideology is most dangerous not when it is seen as an ideology but rather when it is dismissed as "normal" and a regular part of everyday life. Ruha Bejamin's *Race After Technology* and Safiya Noble's *Algorithms of Oppression* provide clear examples for how technology, including the recent issues of online proctoring technology, creates a false sense of equity, justice, and representation. The technologies themselves are constructed in a human world, by human coders, builders, and computer scientists, each of whom grows up with a worldview that implicitly gets embedded in the technologies they create. De-gendering S.T.E.M. education (science, technology, engineering, and mathematics) has only recently emerged as an area of priority in education (Lucht 2015). Nonprofit organizations such as Black

Girls Code (2011) and Girls Who Code (2012), among others, even offer free classes and courses outside of the industry of government-run education systems. However, an institutional and structural bias still remains. A March 25, 2021, tweet from Black Girls Code notes, "Did you know that Black women account for a mere 2.5% of the #STEM workforce? We're on a mission to change the narrative." Only two weeks earlier, on March 7, UNESCO had posted to LinkedIn "only 22% of Artificial Intelligence professionals globally are women. Evidence suggests that by 2022, 85% of AI projects will deliver erroneous outcomes due to bias." This is the same AI technology used in facial recognition of online proctoring software. Reminiscent of Althusser, on the topic of online teaching Siân Bayne, Peter Evans, et al. write, "As teachers, we need to confront the negative ethical and pedagogic aspects of creeping surveillance on campus and resist the uncritical assumption that the intensification of monitoring and tracking of students is somehow inevitable" (2020, 180). The technological surveillance tools we subscribe to and use across higher education normalize a culture of distrust. When we focus on available "technologies" for teaching online, we worry that technology trumps pedagogy for many making decisions about course assessments. Strong pedagogy would guide instructors to focus on prompting a community of trust first and foremost, and from there a course dynamic where students are motivated to learn (Deacon 2012; Darby and Lang 2019).

For Althusser, these are the *obviousnesses* of everyday life, or the depoliticization of ideology in material actions, which gets explored not by examining discourse (what is said)—but instead by examining structure (how it is said and by whom). Althusser (1970) defines ideology as "an imaginary relation to real relations" because it "always exists in apparatus and its practice or practices." Apparatus are what make the imaginary (ideologies), material or real. It is through the state apparatus of the lived experiences of individuals (or what Althusser calls subjects) that inequality gets legitimated, or what his former student Michel Foucault would call "crystalized" in society as normal. In the case of online proctoring technology, what is being normalized is the ongoing systemic racism, misogyny, heterosexism, classism, and white supremacy of the higher education industry. Foucault (1980) discusses the relationship between institutionalized structures of power and self-fulfilling ideologies in Volume I of his work *History of Sexuality*.

> It seems to me that first what needs to be understood is the multiplicity of relations of force that are immanent to the domain wherein they are exercised, and that are constitutive of its organization; the game that through incessant struggle and confrontation transforms them, reinforces them, inverts them; the supports these relations of force find in each other, so as to form a chain or system, or, on the other hand, the gaps, the contradictions that isolate them from each other; in

the end, the strategies in which they take effect, and whose general pattern or institutional crystallization is embodied in the mechanisms of the state, in the formulation of the law, in social hegemonies. (121–122)

At the time of the writing of this article, despite significant student protest and well-documented concerns about surveillance, data collection, and racist AI infrastructure, online proctoring technology remains a regular component for many North American universities, and the use of Turnitin is an even more normalized surveillance tool for assignment submissions. The rapid emergence of COVID-19 made visible many of the implicit ideologies embedded into pre-pandemic teaching practices.

At the structural level, the pandemic highlighted how the neoliberal model of higher education required radical change if it was to survive the seismic environmental shift that COVID-19 created. Online proctoring and assignment surveillance are just some examples of the previous misgivings and the need for radical change. We should be concerned that "there is a problem of leadership in digital education when significant decisions about technology practices are made on the basis that they are technical rather than pedagogical, cultural, or ethical" (Bayne et al. 2020, 194). When institutions and their faculty members utilize tools like Turnitin, a culture of distrust affects the community, and typically in a harmful manner. Plagiarism, though, is not a failure of technology, but rather it has been argued as a failure of "community" (Townley and Parsell 2004). If it is not obvious, pedagogy needs to inform technology, and not vice versa. In *Race, Politics, and Pandemic Pedagogy: Education in a Time of Crisis*, critical theorist Henry Giroux notes that "critical pedagogy makes visible the struggle over those public and private spaces in which people's everyday lives are aligned with particular narratives, identities, cultural practices, and political values. As such, pedagogy is the essential scaffolding of social interaction and the foundation of the public sphere" (2021, xv). What is required then is a focus on pedagogy, not simply as the tool that we use as teachers, but instead as the *pathway* to access, agency, citizenship, and democracy. Critical pedagogy must inform the policy decisions of higher education after COVID-19.

A PEDAGOGY OF COMPASSION

There is little debate as to how quickly the pandemic destabilized the entire industry of education. Everyone was exposed: teachers, administrators, staff, and students. Pandemic pedagogy exposed all of us for the teachers *that we are* (e.g., decent lecturers, conversationalists) and not necessarily for the teachers that we envision ourselves as (e.g., adaptive), nor for the teachers that we want to be (e.g., innovative). As an emergency response to COVID-19 many of us were forced to immediately move to 100 percent online teaching with minimal institutional support, and often without the technology, or skill base required. This sudden paradigm shift in educational practice highlighted not just the weaknesses of us as individuals, but the weaknesses of us as an entire system. From the ashes of the system's disarray, we witnessed great moments of opportunity for real, systemic change in the teaching practices of many of our colleagues who responded to the challenges of COVID-19 digital classrooms with a *pedagogy of compassion*.

As we have already described in earlier publications (Carozza and Gennaro forthcoming), to teach with compassion is to: (1) design a course where the learning environment is built to be inclusive to all students, (2) structure a course where modes of assessment provide all students multiple opportunities to achieve success, and (3) teach a course with a genuine feeling of concern for others. To teach with compassion is to communicate through radical dialogue. This communication is radical because it forces educators to think about what makes us human *and* to recognize the humanity (and therefore dignity and subjectivity) of each and every one of our students. The United Nations estimates over 1.6 billion learners in more than 190 countries were displaced from traditional classrooms due to COVID-19 (UNESCO, 2021). Radical dialogue as communication also fosters a pedagogy of compassion by reintroducing the humane into an inhumane structure—online learning platforms that are technical, virtual, and digital.

As educators, we need to bring the humane to the technical to compensate for the loss of community and opportunity being experienced by our students. Even still, this only accounts for a portion of the student body. As of March 2021, when we write this, UNESCO notes that more than half the world's student population, which is more than 800 million young people, are still removed from traditional classrooms because of COVID-19, and 1 in 3 students globally do not have the appropriate connectivity, device, or digital skills required to learn online. This is not a phenomenon that exists in *other* countries. Even in the Western world, there are issues with stable internet connectivity and digital literacy challenges that students and instructors face. For example, a September 2020 news report by the Canadian Broadcasting Company noted how the CRTC (the governing regulatory agency in Canada) recognizes that 1 in 10 Canadians had no broadband access and more than 60 percent of students and families in rural areas lacked broadband access with speeds and capacity of at least 50 Mbps download and 10 Mbps upload—a minimum requirement for participation in online learning (2020). Responding to students' needs with dignity requires radical dialogue and a pedagogy of compassion in our digital classrooms.

One component of understanding why the communication process in a pedagogy of compassion is radical is in noting that the response to COVID-19, which forced educators online, was not endorsed by all teachers. In fact, many faculty kicked and screamed because they did not want to move to online teaching. However, everyone was placed in a position where they had to let go, since the only options due to COVID-19 were to teach online or not to teach at all. Ironically, a new tension arose between those who stringently defended what they believed to be the authenticity of the institution, and the management (above them at the institution that they were defending) who advised: you have to be willing to extend deadlines; you have to provide multiple means of learning (universal design for learning); you have to caption your lectures; you have to provide asynchronous lectures for students who cannot attend synchronous ones; you have to allow students the right to turn their cameras off; you have to infuse multimodalities for the types of assignments that you have (McGill University, Dartmouth, UMassAmherst, York University Teaching Commons). These types of mandates, and likely others, came from a governance structure that was also forced to adapt. Again, ironically, the neoliberal University found itself forced to respond to the consumer needs of its "widget-students" as competition for student enrollments in digital learning spaces fueled concern about the survival of the university. So, in responding to market demands, the university was forced to adapt a model that ensured all students had access to digital learning materials. As teachers we must not create barriers for students. We were/are being asked to be compassionate. The mandates above are examples of some changes to our course design and delivery that even the most strident defenders of the neoliberal education system were forced to incorporate during the pandemic. They are also examples of teaching with compassion.

Prior to the pandemic there were many educators who were adamant in their desire to defend the institution or their teaching practices. Prior to the pandemic, there was a clear and obvious narrative to defend the rigidity and the values of the institution, which were often couched in language such as "this is what it means to be a university" and masqueraded around using words like "standards." This rigidity was used not only to defend the institution but also to attack our students by positioning them as lazy, unwilling to work, and even as criminals who prefer to cheat than to learn. This discourse lines the pages of policy across the sector of higher education pre COVID-19 around examination invigilation, student accommodations, forms of assessment, and deadline policies. When we defend the institution so rigidly we are actually defending capitalism, white supremacy, misogyny, and a history that is exclusive and violent (hooks 2000; Hill Collins and Bilge 2016; Kellner and Share 2019; Giroux 2020). However, what we have learned from pandemic pedagogy, and what we have written about elsewhere, is that COVID-19 has exposed the entire sector of higher education and that the resolution to our conflict lies in the need for a pedagogy of compassion.

Paulo Freire, in chapter two of *Pedagogy of the Oppressed*, discusses the dichotomy between a banking method of education and a problem-posing method of education (2008). Whereas, the current banking model of education positions students as empty vessels into which educators deposit information to withdraw from students when they regurgitate the information on a test or in an essay for evaluation. A problem-posing method of education engages students critically in their own real lives by igniting a critical consciousness of the injustice of their social surroundings. It invites them as co-constructors of their learning to engage in answering the questions of the very problems they pose. A problem-posing method of radical dialogue features communication between teacher-to-students and students-to-teacher. This communication is not linear, or top down, but instead is multidirectional and places emphasis on the value of each student as human, as worthy, and as an equal partner to the teacher in the learning space. Another example of the emphasis on the banking method in practice can be seen in our methods and policies surrounding student deadlines and assignment submission.

Going forward, we argue that higher education can never go back to the rigidity of the standardized banking model pre COVID-19 and that we must fight against those who seek to hold on to an antiquated model of higher education for political reasons that provide access to some and deny access to others, while couching these politics in *obviousnesses* such as invigilation software (Proctortrack). We believe that COVID-19 has forced the entire sector of higher education to reexamine its core principles for course delivery and that this is not a temporary moment. Rather, it is a social movement toward inclusivity, equity, and social justice. Each of these are spokes on the wheel of a pedagogy of compassion. The wheel moves forward. As a result of COVID-19, we are seeking out the learning styles, value judgments, and lived experiences of our students, and then we are trying to use those as tools to engage our students. That is radical dialogue. We recognize the movement made to date as positive social change. Even educators who did not see themselves as part of this movement prior to the pandemic are now active members in it. We have moved the critical mass, and the proof is in our teaching. However, there remain obstacles and challenges going forward. What is needed is a pedagogy of compassion that destabilizes the traditional "teacher knows best" methodology and decenters the power imbalance within the classroom.

CARE ETHICS

Teaching with compassion, communicating via radical dialogue, and abiding by an ethics of care—each of these is at work simultaneously to foster an engaged and accessible online course. Psychologist Carol Gilligan (1982) described a moral theory called "ethics of care" in a feminist challenge to the moral development theory made famous by her mentor Lawrence Kohlberg (1981). Kohlberg's argument that women remain stagnant in the interpersonal stage of moral development, unable to reach full moral development, was challenged by Gilligan. Her research demonstrated how subjects used different ethical approaches and subsequently challenged Kohlberg's moral development theory because it was limited, prioritizing a morality of rights as universalized and principled thinking. By valorizing a rights-based morality and independence over a morality of responsibility and relationship-centered dispositions, Kohlberg's work did not account for an empathetic approach, which values particular knowledge, context, and relationships. Nel Noddings (1982) theorized an ethics of care as a preferable feminist moral theory. The crux of care ethics is that it stems from a disposition of interconnectivity. In making decisions, a normative parameter of care ethics is that decisions are based on context (situation, agents, location, etc.), rather than *universal* principles. We introduce the ethics of care as a means of "practicing" or "implementing" care pedagogy in academe.

Tammy Shel (2006) discusses a pedagogy of caring in education, demonstrating how it aligns with Herbert Marcuse's critique of standardized education. Shel states that Marcuse promoted a pedagogy of caring (52), which fosters a relationship between instructors and students that requires the *humanization* of students (54). Since caring has been established as an ingredient for humans' growth (morally, socially, emotionally, and intellectually), it follows that caring should be a component in education and recognized as an integral aspect of the relationship between teacher and student. A compassionate mindset and a caring practice can impact student autonomy in a *nurturing* environment and facilitate a student's individual growth and intellectual autonomy.

Extending this concept of caring pedagogy into the online classroom, we have noted that it can succeed in cultivating more equitable spaces for students to learn. A care ethics in education provides students with more accessible ways to engage—with course material, with each other, with the instructor—and it encourages students to actualize their authentic selves. A concentration on relationships, a philosophy of nonviolence, and an awareness of unique circumstances lead to a more "relational way of being" in the online classroom. For many individuals new to online learning, teachers and learners alike, the discourse of resistance was strong and felt immediately. Resistance often unfolded through a series of narratives such as: "face-to-face learning is better"; "face-to-face learning can allow for experiential education, deeper learning, social contact"; "online learning privileges those with adequate access"; or, "online learning makes it challenging to invigilate student assessments." We are not denying these challenges, which are very real when adapting to virtual classrooms. However, if we assume a one-size-fits-all approach to digital pedagogy, if we try and implement "best practices," we run the risk of creating the standardized practices that Marcuse critiqued. Compassionate and caring course curricula involve the compassionate spirit of course development and delivery with the continual practice of care ethics that allows for revisions, malleability, and flexibility as concerns and issues arise in an unpredictable time. This becomes most obvious when exploring the practices of educators surrounding student deadlines and assignment submissions.

FORMS OF ASSESSMENT AND DEADLINE POLICIES

In this section we refer to assignments within a large general education class one of the authors teaches. Prior to COIVD-19, assignment and test deadlines in this course were developed in adherence with some principles of UDL (Universal Design for Learning guidelines) related to student engagement. For example, a typical assignment would include "choices" for students. Students were offered choices such as the topic for a writing assignment, the medium to present a project, or the option to work independently or with partners. Often students were given some combination of these choices in the same assignment. The pedagogical thinking behind this design was to empower students with autonomy in deciding what to focus on, how to present their ideas, and whether their learning experience would be better served by working independently or with another student(s). In addition, students were coached to reflect on their experiences of such choices—the meaningfulness of assignments and how it felt to work independently, with a partner, or with a small team are examples of such reflections.

Although choice was provided to students in the design of the assignment, choice was not provided with the timelines for assignment submission. Prior to COVID-19, assignments had nonnegotiable due dates for students (note: exceptions were granted for students who had documented accommodations provided to the instructor at the outset of the course). This approach to assignment submission was justified with a "tough love" rationale—students need to get used to having and abiding by deadlines. After all, students need to have awareness of what it is like in the "real world." Since students entered into an implicit contract at the outset of a course (i.e., the syllabus), it is essential that the service-provider (instructor of the institution) and client (student enrolled in course) engage in their contract's details accordingly. This "real world" rationale is falsifiable, of course. There are circumstances where deadlines are malleable and adapted based on context. Imposing unwavering deadlines is an instance of the implicit ideologies that structure inequality into the pedagogy of higher education. This tough love approach to assignment deadlines pre-COVID-19 mirrors Shel's description of standardized tests—emphasizing, prioritizing, and rationalizing the quantitative over the qualitative (Shel 2006). Grades and profits are prioritized over authentic learning. Arbitrary calendar dates are prioritized over students' situations, agencies, and locations. There are some dangers in emphasizing the normalization of accepted standards in education, at least from a pedagogical perspective. Students as individuals get blurred, or become invisible even, when instructors are primarily concerned with due dates, grades, word counts, and so on, all of which can detract from authentic teaching and learning. While this criticism of teaching practices is applicable to pre-pandemic classrooms, it was precisely the experience of higher education during the COVID-19 pandemic that highlighted inequities and hardships that these types of common teaching protocols perpetuated—so much so that administrators were providing guidance for addressing the unique situations students would be facing (as summarized above).

In response to COVID-19, changes were made to the online general education course introduced above. The course was reorganized to implement a new assignment deadline policy. It was a test pilot during the early days of the pandemic. Each assignment was given an original due date, a preferred submission window, and, finally, an open-ended submission timeline. In the syllabus these new policies were explained. Each assignment instruction file included descriptions of the different due date options. Students were encouraged to stay on track and meet the original deadline, to avoid having an unbalanced workload. This was followed by a preferred/extended submission window, typically one to two weeks, which students could decide autonomously, based on their own circumstances, situations, and mental health, whether they needed to make use of that extension to meet their personal goals and the assignment's goals. Furthermore, they did not need to justify the later assignment submission. Students who submitted their assignments during the preferred submission window, given the delay, received minimal written feedback from the instructor. When students took advantage of extension periods, they did so knowing there would be less time to provide feedback, and with the knowledge that they could attend the instructor's office hours instead to discuss any concerns. Students expressed relief that they could take the extra time needed to complete the assignment to their satisfaction.

Finally, there was a third option—a student could submit work by the end of the course, but the assignment would be assessed only using a pass/fail rubric.

Throughout the summer term, and even during the fall term of 2020 when these submission options were in place, many students struggled with COVID-19 in their nonacademic lives. Students took advantage of the extension offered by the preferred submission window and submitted work of good quality. Very few students took the option of the pass/fail assignment submission. What became clear to us by implementing this variation of an assignment deadline was how it humanized the teacher-student relationship. It used a compassionate and caring course curriculum to accommodate students' individual circumstances *without* judgment.

In the post-COVID-19 world of higher education, when we return to the face-to-face classroom, we will take this approach to assignment deadlines with us. It has taken a pandemic to realize that students are humans with lives and circumstances that are out of their control. The same unpredictability with life happens for us as instructors, and at least in the classes that we teach there is no strong rationale for penalizing students when they do not, or cannot, adhere to a deadline. In fact, this approach helps students build reflective skills, time management skills, and it guides them to be autonomous decision-makers. With reference to UDL, this relates to promoting student self-regulation as it provides strategies for students to reflect and regulate. Assignments do not disappear, deadlines do not disappear, but they are much more flexible within the contexts of our classes. In part this revised deadline policy deteriorates the hierarchical relationship between instructor and student. Care ethics would expect teachers to empathize with student perspectives, it would expect everyone to benefit from the course experience, and it would expect us to care about each other's welfare.

CONCLUSION: COMPASSIONATE AND CARING COURSE CURRICULUM

MOOCs (massive online open courses) have been described as sites of "data colonialism" (Knox 2016). In an effort to open education to all, to make it accessible, MOOCs actually change education, rather than augment pedagogy. For example, they rely heavily on algorithms and absent teachers (i.e., actionable intelligence on behalf of a "teacher"). We are not arguing that automation is the problem when it comes to online pedagogy, but we have shown that without knowledge of pedagogy, of teaching and learning dynamics in an online atmosphere in context with discipline, teachers, and students, decisions around available technology run the risk of MOOCs—creating impoverished spaces for learning. We hope it is obvious that a concentration on technical applications over students and teachers is a problem. The online course environment, like a face-to-face context, is still a social and communal space. As such, the compassionate and caring course curriculum we have discussed acknowledges the humanity in digital pedagogy. We are at a point in history where the direction of online pedagogy is anyone's guess—to scale back after the pandemic, to make use of all the technological applications and stay on the course of online teaching and learning, and so on. What we have learned is that with most things, reflexivity is necessary for successful implementation and experiences in online learning. Online teaching is a balancing act involving careful consideration of meeting a course's learning objectives, delivering an accessible course, and cultivating a community. Online courses are not just spaces of digital correspondence; they are extensions of lively humans. As Darby and Lang write, "With careful thinking about your course and your learning outcomes, you can implement strategies that will build relationships, establish trust, and help your students realize their full cognitive potential" (2019, 105). There are many ways to get this "right," including considering class size, teaching team, and other contexts in addition to learning goals. Above all these structural considerations, when we act in accordance with a pedagogy of compassion and care ethics magic occurs.

We leave readers with several subjects and issues for reflection that stem from this paper. Within our own community we have discussed and problematized the structures that institutions, or instructors, establish and their impacts on teaching and learning, on teachers and learners. We question whether they all need to be adhered to, and we encourage other instructors to engage in similar dialogues with colleagues that can yield reflection.

We urge other instructors to consider who gets "left out" when a course is designed and delivered online. Soliciting feedback from students in the form of a survey may help in this endeavor. This can shed light on where instructors need assistance in providing a more diverse and accessible course.

For instructors who rely on surveillance tools (e.g., course analytics, Turnitin, Proctortrack, etc.), whether this is a decision made at the instructor or institutional level, it is important to consider the culture such technologies cultivate within courses. Where a culture of distrust is detected, perhaps transparent discussions with students can mitigate this potential cultural dynamic.

As instructors or students, consider whether you have been quantitatively focused, qualitatively focused, or a unique combination of the two. It is plausible that a rule-driven approach, or grades-focused participation, can detract from an authentic learning journey.

We think it is important when developing assignments to expand choices for student discretion and exploration. There may be different paths to fulfilling learning objectives within a given course—allowing students to engage in course assessments according to their preferences may facilitate student autonomy and reflection.

Regarding *inflexible* assignment deadlines, consider their impacts on teachers and students. We have not suggested to do away with deadlines, but rather to challenge how important they *really* are, and whether there are ways to support students by adapting to a less rigid approach to assignment submissions.

Generally, we are intuitive. If you were ever dissatisfied with the delivery and/or experience of a course, try and pinpoint some of the problems that contributed to the sense of course dissatisfaction you experienced.

Finally, during moments of magic that you have experienced in a course—reflect on what was happening, with who, how, and why. If you can determine what contributed to the energy in those spaces, you may have a special ingredient that you can add to courses.

This paper was written with the goal of prompting reflexive thinking when it comes to teachers' (and perhaps even students') comforts and habits with teaching and learning. If online courses are something you will continue to hone in the future—post-pandemic, then this paper's critical analysis can influence decisions that you will have to make. For everyone's sake, whether we return to the online classroom or a lecture hall when the pandemic is behind us, we hope the critical nature of widespread teaching online due to the global pandemic and the "emergency" teaching measures that were employed have been an eye-opening experience. For some instructors, learning that their administrators would not support student penalties meant that instructors had to shift to less quantitatively rule–driven teaching. This shift, if we were open to it, brought humanity back to our teaching. It returned us to "quality" engagements and considerations and pedagogy. By extending compassion to students in unprecedented situations, and by exercising care with unique situations, the last year of teaching for many of us was a truly engaging experience, a cathartic teaching experience, and in turn we hope it led to transformative learning experiences for our students as well. There is no turning back—the post-COVID-19 classroom must adopt a compassionate and caring course curriculum.

REFERENCES

Althusser, Louis. 1970. "Ideology and the Ideological State Apparatus (Notes Towards an Investigation)." *Marxists.org*. https://www.marxists.org/reference/archive/althusser/1970/ideology.htm Date accessed: 26 Mar. 2021

Bayne, Siân, Peter Evans, Rory Ewins, Jeremy Knox, James Lamb, et al. 2020. *The Manifesto for Teaching Online*. Cambridge, MA: MIT Press.

Benjamin, Ruha. 2019. *Race After Technology: Abolitionist Tools for the New Jim Code*. Medford, MA: Polity.

Black Girls Code (@BlackGirlsCode). 2021. "Did You Know that Black Women Account for a Mere 2.5% of the #STEM Workforce? We're on a Mission to Change the Narrative." Twitter, March 25, 2021. https://twitter.com/BlackGirlsCode/status/1375056650785148931?ref_src=twsrc%5Egoogle%7Ctwcamp%5Eserp%7Ctwgr%5Etweet

Canadian Radio-Television and Telecommunications Commission. 2020. "Communications Monitoring Report 2019." https://crtc.gc.ca/pubs/cmr2019-en.pdf

Carozza, Linda & Steve Gennaro (forthcoming). "Reflections on Best Practices for Online Teaching: Ethnographies from the Front Lines." In *Teaching Online: Passion, Purpose, Practice*. Cambridge: Cambridge Scholars Press.

change.org. 2020. "Growing Fast! Share This Petition And Be Heard!" Last modified October 27, 2020. https://www.change.org/p/alan-shepard-stop-the-use-of-proctortrack-at-western-university

Darby, Flower, and James M. Lang. 2019. *Small Teaching Online: Applying Learning Science in Online Classes*. San Francisco, CA: John Wiley & Sons.

Dartmouth. 2020. "Remote Teaching Good Practices: Beyond the Tech." Accessed June 2, 2021. https://sites.dartmouth.edu/teachremote/remote-teaching-good-practices/

Deacon, Andrea. 2012. "Creating a Context of Care in the Online Classroom." *The Journal of Faculty Development* 26, no. 1: 5.Freire, Paulo. 2008. *Pedagogy of the Oppressed*. NY: Continuum International Publishing Group.

Foucault, Michel. 1980. *The History of Sexuality: An Introduction, Vol. I*. Translated by Robert Hurley. New York: Vintage.

Freire, Paolo. 2008. *Pedagogy of the Oppressed*. New York: The Continuum International Publishing Group.

Girls who Code (@Girlswhocode). 2021. Twitter. https://twitter.com/girlswhocode

Giroux, Henry. 2020. "Racist Violence Can't Be Separated From the Violence of Neoliberal Capitalism." *Truthout*, June 9, 2020. https://truthout.org/articles/racist-violence-cant-be-separated-from-the-violence-of-neoliberal-capitalism/

Giroux, Henry. 2021. *Race, Politics, and Pandemic Pedagogy: Education in a Time of Crisis*. New York, NY: Bloomsbury.

Gilligan, Carol. 1982. *In a Different Voice: Psychological Theory and Women's Development*. Cambridge, MA: Harvard University Press.

Hill Collins, Patricia, and Sirma Bilge. 2016. *Intersectionality*. Cambridge, UK: Polity Press. hooks, bell. 2000. *Feminist theory: From margin to center*. London, England: Pluto Press.

Kellner, Douglas, and Jeff Share. 2019. *The Critical Media Literacy Guide: Engaging Media and Transforming Education*. Leiden: Brill Sense.

Knox, Jeremy. 2014. "Digital Culture Clash: 'Massive' Education in the E-learning and Digital Cultures MOOC." *Distance Education* 35, no. 2: 164–177. https://www.tandfonline.com/doi/pdf/10.1080/01587919.2014.917704

Kohlberg, Lawrence. 1981. *The Philosophy of Moral Development*. San Francisco, CA: Harper & Row.

Lucht, Petra. 2015. "De-Gendering STEM - Lessons Learned From an Ethnographic Study of a Physics Laboratory." *International Journal of Gender, Science and Technology*, 8, no. 1: 67–81. http://genderandset.open.ac.uk/index.php/genderandset/article/view/408/760

McGill University Teaching and Learning Services. 2020. "Guidelines for Instructors and Students on Remote Teaching, Learning, and Assessment." Accessed June 2, 2021. https://www.mcgill.ca/tls/instructors/class-disruption/guidelines-remote-s2021

Noble, Safiya Umoja. 2018. *Algorithms of Oppression: How Search Engines Reinforce Racism*. NY: NYU Press.

Noddings, Nel. 1982. *Caring: A Feminine Approach to Ethics and Moral Education*. Oakland, CA: University of California Press.

Shel, Tammy. 2006. "On Marcuse and Caring in Education." *Policy Futures in Education* 4, no. 1: 52–60.

Swauger, Shea. 2020. "Software that Monitors Students During Tests Perpetuates Inequality and Violates Their Privacy." *MIT Technology Review*, August 7, 2020. https://www.technologyreview.com/2020/08/07/1006132/software-algorithms-proctoring-online-tests-ai-ethics/

Townley, Cynthia, and Mitch Parsell. 2004. "Technology and Academic Virtue: Student Plagiarism Through the Looking Glass." *Ethics and Information Technology* 6, no. 4: 271–277.

UMass Amherst. n.d. "Should We Require Students to Turn on Their Cameras During Synchronous Sessions (e.g., Zoom)?" Accessed June 2, 2021. https://www.umass.edu/ctl/should-we-require-students-turn-their-cameras-during-synchronous-sessions-eg-zoom

UNESCO. 2021. "One Year into Covid Disruption Where Do We Stand." *LinkedIn*. March 7, 2021. https://en.unesco.org/news/one-year-covid-19-education-disruption-where-do-we-stand York University Teaching Commons. 2020. "YorkU Guide to Teaching Remotely." Accessed June 2, 2021. https://teachingcommons.yorku.ca/wp-content/uploads/2020/05/YorkU-Guide-to-Teaching-Remotely.pdf

Chapter 4

Reimagining Engagement for (Post)Pandemic Teaching

A Multileveled Approach

Lindsey B. Anderson, Raphael Mazzone, and Melissa A. Lucas

The speed at which classes were moved online during spring 2020—a result of the coronavirus (COVID-19) pandemic—created a high level of uncertainty about how to effectively restructure in-person communication courses for an online setting. As course administrators, we were tasked with assisting almost 50 instructors in the transition of over 90 sections to an online format in less than 2 weeks. The process of shifting the course online highlighted expected challenges, such as accounting for varied instructor technological literacy levels and supplementing the lack of instructor experience with online teaching. It also made visible an unexpected challenge: how to foster engagement for both students and instructors in the online setting. The importance of engagement was amplified given the isolation of the pandemic, and the fact that online teaching and learning can be a lonely experience for both instructors and students (Kaufmann and Vallade 2020).

Engagement is situated as a goal of higher education (McKinnon and Vos 2015). However, it is a difficult term to define given that engagement has been broadly conceptualized as a form of participation (Frymier and Houser 2015; Livingstone 2013), presence (Kaufmann and Vallade 2020), and collaboration (Dixson 2010). We argue that engagement is constitutive of the communicative interactions that take place inside and outside of the classroom at multiple levels—including instructor to instructor, student to instructor, student to student, and administration to instructor.

Online teaching presents different challenges than the traditional in-person setting in terms of how to create engagement (Chatham-Carpenter 2017). However, reflecting on engagement during this era of pandemic teaching provides us with the opportunity to problematize the term, and take a different approach to supporting instructors as they engage with their students and each other. This chapter explicates the challenges we faced fostering multileveled engagement, and puts forth principles for facilitating engagement based on our administrative experience.

CHALLENGE: FOSTERING MULTILEVEL ENGAGEMENT IN ONLINE SETTINGS

Student engagement research dates to the 1930s and continues to be studied in a variety of disciplines. One of the first definitions of engagement can be found in the work of American psychologist Ralph Tyler (1949), where he described learning as taking place through the actions of the student. In the 1970s, C. Robert Pace developed The College Student Experience Questionnaire (CSEQ) focusing on the relationship between effort and time on tasks (Pace 1984, 1990). Building off this, researchers such as Astin (1999) and organizations such as the National Institute of Education and Education Commission of the States highlighted the role and influence of involvement on student achievement (Groccia 2018). Naturally, scholars have built upon this construct to understand the college experience (Pascarella and Terenzini 2005) as well as refine the definition of engagement (Pike and Kuh 2005).

Although the phrase "student engagement" originally focused on quantitative measures such as effort and time, it has evolved and now reflects the relationship between student interest in their own learning and their connection to the content, the instructor, the institution, and their peers (Axelson and Flick 2011). In addition to the CESQ, student engagement is also measured by the National Survey of Student Engagement (NSSE), in an effort to document conditions and activities that promote student learning (Kuh 2001) and educational outcomes (Pascarella, Seifert, and Blaich 2010). These educationally purposive activities correlate with student success and development, including satisfaction, persistence, academic achievement, and social engagement (Trowler 2010). The ability of the institution to provide the students with the opportunities to engage is seen as a marker of educational excellence and is the single best predictor of learning and personal development (Kuh 2003). Moving away from a primarily institutional focus, researchers began to operationalize engagement from a student perspective (Mazer 2012).

Engagement

Engagement, although similar to the idea of participation (Frymier and Houser 2015), takes a more holistic view as it calls on emotional (e.g., interest, enjoyment, motivation), cognitive (e.g., mental processing), and behavioral dimensions (e.g., participation and effort in learning) (Appleton, Christenson, and Furlong 2008; Groccia 2018). As a result, engagement is both a precondition of participation and an outcome of student learning (Dahlgren 2011). Engaged students exhibit many common behaviors: they listen attentively; they verbally contribute during discussions; they take notes; and they ask questions of instructors (Mazer 2012). Engagement matters because it has been connected to positive outcomes related to achievement (Carini, Kuh, and Klein 2006; Frymier and Houser 2015), motivation (Liem and Martin 2012), and performance (Fredricks, Blumenfeld, and Paris 2004). In terms of increasing a sense of engagement, Kaufmann, Sellnow, and Frisby (2016) argued that instructors need to, "encourage positive peer interaction and engagement" in the online classroom by building a supportive classroom climate (307). Past communication research has illustrated that engagement is facilitated through collaboration (Dixson 2010), participation (Frymier and Houser 2015), and presence (Kaufmann and Vallade 2020). These ideas (collaboration, participation, and presence) highlight the communicative nature of engagement.

Traditional conceptualizations of engagement prioritize face-to-face interactions that occur between instructors and students. However, the communicative dimensions of engagement can be enacted through various means (e.g., virtual classrooms, online Zoom meetings, discussion boards) and occur at multiple levels with different constituents (e.g., instructors, students, administrators). As such, we argue the communication education and instructional communication scholars need to problematize the concept of engagement beyond the traditional understanding of instructor-student interactions to include how instructor-instructor and administration-instructor interactions foster a sense of engagement in the online teaching and learning process. This diversity of interactions highlights the complexity of the term as well as its communicative function.

The question then becomes how to build multilevel engagement in the online context during an ongoing pandemic. Adding to the complexity involved in addressing this question is the role context (Ryan and Deci 2000). It is important to look at the online environment, especially during the uncertain times of post-pandemic teaching (Swerzenski 2021). Although technology has created novel avenues to facilitate the communications that foster engagement, principles to guide its integration still need to be developed.

Active Learning

Active learning is one way to encourage engagement (Dixson 2010) and serves as a guiding principle for many communication courses. An active learning approach to higher education encourages both instructors and students to apply course concepts in a collaborative way (Chickering and Gamson 1987; Stearns 2017) and, as such, is one way to foster engagement. However, taking an active learning approach in an online context requires instructors and students to reimagine what it looks like, which is a challenging task.

The resulting rapid course redesigns due to the pandemic created a variety of ways that communication courses were delivered that fell on a continuum from low-level engagement that limited—and sometimes completely omitted—active learning opportunities (e.g., emails explaining assignments, slide decks in lieu of a class meetings) to high-level engagement that incorporated active learning in some form (e.g., biweekly synchronous sessions, discussion boards, peer reviews). This disparate student experience was problematic given the need for consistency to meet course-wide learning objectives—especially in multi-section communication classes (Anderson et al. 2016). The shift to online instruction illuminated the need to reimagine instructor training to facilitate engagement in the online setting in a consistent manner, especially during this challenging and uncertain time.

Context: Background

The need to reimagine engagement in a multilevel and mediated way was reflected in published reports that appeared in popular higher education outlets (e.g., *The Chronicle of Higher Education* and *Inside Higher Education*) as well as traditional academic journals focused on communication pedagogy (e.g., *Communication Education* and *Communication Teacher*). We reviewed these outlets to aggregate the experiences of other faculty and captured some of the prevailing strategies they employed to encourage online engagement. These data informed the principles we developed that guided the course we administered.

The course we administer is a large, multi-section presentational speaking course that is housed in a department of communication at the University of Maryland (COMM107). The course fulfills the oral communication component for the general education program at the university for 3,800–4,000 undergraduate students per academic year. Over 50 instructors—including professional track faculty and graduate teaching assistants—teach the class. Given the sheer size of the course, there is a leadership team in place that manages administrative tasks. The team is composed of an executive director (tenured faculty member), two managing directors (two professional-track faculty members with doctoral degrees), and a graduate assistant. This team develops the common curriculum, creates instructor resources, trains new instructors, and responds to student questions/concerns.

The course is designed to facilitate active learning and we train instructors to adopt this format as they are hired/assigned to teach. In addition, we provide resources (e.g., sample activities and lesson plans) to support this pedagogical approach to instruction. The active learning structure is predicated on traditional conceptualizations of engagement whereby students interacted with their instructors through participation in a physical classroom. However, the shift to completely online instruction during spring 2020 and the reality that virtual learning will be a part of higher education in some form for the foreseeable future forced a reexamination of our conceptualizations of engagement in a way that frames the changes as an opportunity to improve the course.

OPPORTUNITIES: PRINCIPLES FOR FACILITATING MULTILEVEL ENGAGEMENT IN ONLINE TEACHING

Communication scholars have the opportunity to prepare for the future of higher education, which will undoubtedly include versions of in-person, blended, and online instruction (Morreale, Thorpe, and Ward 2019). To do so, we reflected on our experience responding to the need to foster engagement at multiple levels of the teaching-learning process. As previously stated, we started by searching peer-reviewed journals focused on communication pedagogy (e.g., *Communication Education, Communication Teacher*) and popular academic outlets (e.g., *The Chronicle of Higher Education, Inside Higher Education*) to develop a set of principles that then guided our response to the challenges that emerged from teaching during the pandemic. We then detail our experience enacting these principles as a way to illustrate how they can be used in communication courses. Through the integration of the published reports and our experience, we put forth several propositions for the future of engagement in higher education.

Principle 1: Establish Teaching Standards that Provide Opportunities for Engagement

Course administrators and department leadership should encourage practices that facilitate engagement by developing common standards for online instruction that make use of design features that can facilitate student engagement (Swan 2001). Besides providing clarity about expectations, these standards should also be co-constructed with key constituents in the teaching and learning process—from administrators to graduate teaching assistants. This step—cocreating standards and expectations—serves as a way to encourage multilevel engagement. As such, this process should focus on finding ways to infuse student and instructor participation, presence, and collaboration, all of which are hallmarks of engagement, into online teaching standards.

Rationale. This principle can take various forms depending on the unique characteristics of the course/program/university. For example, in his account of the shift to online instruction, Schwartzman (2020) found that up to 40 percent of the faculty on his campus were not using the university's learning management system before being asked to move their courses online. This gap in knowledge underscores the need to establish common teaching standards to help the transition. The first question is what format the online courses should take. Indeed, during the pandemic, communication scholars compared the delivery of both synchronous and asynchronous online courses (507). Past research has suggested that synchronous online classes can help to reduce the feelings of distance felt between student-student and instructor-student (Lang 2020). Schwartzman (2020, 507) explained that synchronous live sessions were "a closer approximation of face-to-face interactions" that often exceeded the scheduled class time given that students continued classroom conversations.

Establishing a consistent schedule was an important component of the live sessions (Scutelnicu et al. 2019). Schwartzman (2020) emphasized this point as he noted that "the regularity of synchronous class meetings also maintains structure and ritual that could aid in time management, induce self-discipline to complete assignments, and increase commitment to the course by providing more vibrant means of relationship renewal" (507). We argue that these benefits are extended not only to the students but also to instructors—thus contributing a sense of engagement in the virtual settings.

The need for consistency also included class communication. Students and instructors alike needed to know when to expect messages. The online format also allowed for the messages other than emails to be delivered. Recording videos and using the other forms of available multimedia forms of communication (e.g., discussion board, Voice Thread) available on learning management systems are also a means to create opportunities for engagement between students as well as with instructors.

Application. While enacting this principle we focused on the student-instructor and student-student level of engagement and emphasized the need to integrate an active learning approach. For example, we set the expectation that online classes should hold a minimum of one synchronous class—or what we termed, live session—per week. These live sessions would include a mini-lecture that highlights key material, an interactive activity that students would complete collaboratively (e.g., using breakout rooms), and discussion that allows students to interact with their peers and instructor in real time (Moore and Hodges 2020).

We also recognized the importance of consistency from the student's perspective and encouraged instructors to set up that consistency in both time (e.g., day of the week) and space (e.g., course content). The standardization of the weekly structure throughout the semester allowed for students to prepare accordingly and provided instructors with some semblance of normal routine. If a course met on Monday/Wednesday and Tuesday/Thursday, instructors selected which of the days would be asynchronous and which of the days would be synchronous. For example, an instructor would assign an asynchronous activity for students to complete by the end of scheduled class time on Tuesdays and then hold synchronous sessions on Thursdays. This schedule would then remain consistent throughout the semester. To support this consistency, we also provided guidance for how to structure activities within Canvas, the learning management system used at our university, so in that system this is achieved through the use of pages and modules and determined best practices for not only what to publish on the course site but when and how to notify the students.

To that end, we discussed with our instructors the need to provide consistent and patterned correspondence in campus email, Canvas messaging, and course space announcements. Setting the expectations for when to receive messages, similarly to how to organize information, provides students with a blueprint for success in the course and allows them to interact with the messaging and the instructor in a more consistent manner. We found that some instructors unintentionally overloaded students with messages across platforms with little regard to consistency. For example, instructors would send instructions to students a message through Canvas the night before a live session and then would send an email to students the morning of the live session with slightly different instructions. The result confused and frustrated students that only had a piece of the intended message, an outdated message, or conflicting messages altogether. Informing students of when to expect correspondence and in what form helps to create a more engaging virtual learning experience. In our program we guided instructors to provide an early week announcement with updates on the schedule and any modifications to assignments or meetings as well as a post-live-session wrap-up summary with information looking ahead to the next week. In fact, students reported through mid-semester and end of the semester evaluations that the twice-weekly announcements provided them with structure and reassurance during a time of great uncertainty.

We also wanted to create a greater sense of instructor presence when developing the common standards for teaching a multi-section online class, so we asked instructors to record a short video at the beginning of each week that highlights course concepts, provides information about the class, and reminds students of upcoming assignments. These videos helped to produce a feeling of presence as well as model the type of presentations expected in the course.

We found that we needed to explicitly communicate these standards to establish consistency between sections. To do so, we held additional orientation sessions that specifically addressed online teaching and explained these standards in terms of fostering student engagement. The enactment of this principle also created the need to develop resources that would support instructors with varying degrees of online teaching experience. Course directors must consider how to bridge the digital divide between instructors who have advanced technology literacy skills and those with little technology experience.

Principle 2: Develop a Robust Virtual Space for Instructors

The rapid shift to online instruction magnified the need for robust interactive spaces for instructors to share ideas and resources to enact active learning online that could encourage engagement between students. This site would not only serve as a repository of resources that would facilitate engagement with their students but also provide a co-constructed space where instructors could communicate with one another; thus, addressing the need for instructor-instructor engagement.

Rationale. Virtual spaces were created outside of departments to help instructors make the shift to completely online teaching. For instance, Roy Schwartzman started the Pandemic Pedagogy group on Facebook in March 2020 to serve as a place that allowed instructors to easily pose questions and share resources/information. The need for this virtual space where instructors could connect was evident by the influx of members, which topped 30,000 by the end of 2020 (Schwartzman 2020).

Application. We created a virtual space that we termed instructor resource site (IRS) to serve as a co-constructed virtual repository for our program. This space enabled instructors to collaborate and share resources across courses and course sections (Lowell and Exeter 2017). Our pre-pandemic IRS featured lesson plans, test banks, active learning best practices, and forums for instructors to seek and give advice. However, it was designed for in-person classes and did not encourage collaboration between instructors, thus completely ignoring ways to foster instructor-instructor and administration-instructor engagement. We redesigned the new IRS to emphasize pedagogical flexibility for instructors as they envisioned what online teaching looked like for them in a collaborative way.

To develop this virtual space, we worked with a diverse group of instructors who ranged from graduate teaching assistants to tenured faculty members to adjust and create lesson plans using a common template that explained how activities could be adjusted for different instructional modalities (e.g., in-person, asynchronous online, synchronous online). The adaptability of the IRS is vital given the remaining uncertainty surrounding the future delivery method of classes. We encourage communication educators to collaborate with instructors and administrators to cocreate digital repositories where instructors can find and contribute ideas for online student engagement.

Furthermore, we propose that communication scholars explore the ways in which co-constructed virtual sites that represent voices from multiple constituencies facilitate "collaborative consistency" in multi-section courses (Anderson et al. 2016). The challenges many instructors faced during the shift to online instruction illustrated the need to create clear standards and instructions for online engagement. Through these virtual spaces, instructors receive communication about course standards and, at the same time, are able to contribute to what these standards look like in practice.

In practice, the standards are not just related to student engagement or clarity of message, but include standards pertaining to student evaluation and assessment. Historically, two approaches (i.e., rating scales and descriptive rubrics) have been used to assess public speaking proficiency for both expert and nonexpert evaluators (Schreiber, Paul, and Shibley 2012). After the transition to the online environment, the leadership team revised the rubrics to remove much of the assessment criteria and competencies related to physical, in-person presentational speaking. During the summer, we completely overhauled the rubrics, adding in elements of virtual presentations, updating language for verbal and nonverbal communication in a mediated setting, and clarified specifics on technology integration. The standardization provided by the updated rubrics provided clear and consistent expectations for instructors as well as the students.

Principle 3: Facilitate Formal Training and Informal Connections

Instructors who expressed feelings of isolation and loneliness teaching online and responding to the pandemic also struggled to create community in their virtual classrooms (Kaufmann and Vallade 2020). To combat these feelings, we attempted to create more engaging online interactions. Specifically, we scheduled recurring formal training in a shared digital space to develop technical literacy skills and promote online active learning techniques. During these training sessions, instructors engaged in pandemic sensemaking efforts that occupied the majority of the allotted time.

Rationale. The importance of the everyday workplace interactions, or maintenance communication (Meisenbach and McMillan 2006), was highlighted during the shift to remote instruction as people lost the opportunity to talk to one another during informal, just-in-time moments. Meisenbach and McMillan (2006) posit that maintenance communication sustains the workplace/classroom. Sell (2021) noted that the virtual environments can facilitate maintenance communication, which contribute to morale—ultimately starting a virtual book club to build community. We can see how maintenance communication occurs between instructors as they highlight their shared work experiences as well as with instructors and students in terms of their shared class experiences.

Online office hours also serve as a virtual space where students and instructors can connect and engage in maintenance communication activities. Brinkley (2021) highlighted this reality as she reminisced that traditional, in-person office hours were routinely underutilized; but argued that the online environment opened new possibilities for instructor-student meetings that were not necessarily constrained by physical space and predetermined times.

Application. Without physical shared offices, we soon recognized the need to create online spaces where informal maintenance communication could take place (Meisenbach and McMillan 2006). As the pandemic progressed, instructors expressed feelings of isolation and loneliness in an online setting without the everyday interactions of shared office spaces. We responded to this need by starting "conversation hours" that occur one or two times per month and center on a timely topic (e.g., "Giving Effective, Timely, and Accessible Outline Feedback" and "Working with and Facilitating Group Presentations"), but are open, agenda-free meetings for instructors to talk about their experiences.

Although the primary purpose of these conversation hours was to provide structured space for maintenance communication between instructors (e.g., instructor to instructor), we quickly found out these informal meetings also provided multilevel engagement opportunities between administrators and instructors. During the shift to online instruction, only two members of the leadership team were COMM107 instructors, so these conversation hours provided valuable insight into how the instructors created and maintained relationships with administrators. Furthermore, the ability to have administrators share their experiences outside of COMM107 allowed for a deeper understanding of course expectations, student engagement, and the process of handling the pandemic at the individual level. These virtual water cooler moments encapsulated the shared struggle and the shared success of everyone involved with the program.

Another unexpected by-product of these informal conversation hours was the development of new course policy pertaining to instructor presence—this time in the form of online office hours. It flows logically that if instructors and administrators benefited from these shared virtual spaces by engaging in pandemic sensemaking efforts, then students would benefit from the same opportunities. During the week before classes resumed, while our university was still away from campus, the leadership team developed a guide for instructors on providing office hours in both form (e.g., virtual platform specifications and recommendations) and function (e.g., presentation topic brainstorming sessions, opportunities for informal oral feedback).

This practice guidance focused on how to set up and facilitate virtual office hours. Virtual office hours have been identified as a tool that can increase student engagement and interaction with faculty (Li and Pitts 2009). However, virtual office hours were not the norm at our university, so we had to train instructors on the use of a new platform. First, we explained to instructors how to choose the best virtual platform that meets their needs and university requirements. Next, instructors needed to identify how to schedule their office hours with students. Some instructors utilized an open Zoom Personal Meeting Room available during their specified office hours while others set up short five-minute appointment times in their Google calendars or through Calendly. Open office hours have the benefit of facilitating more informal conversations and allow for maintenance communication to organically occur. However, open office hours also pose student privacy concerns. For example, any student could join office hours while another student was discussing accommodations or grades with their instructor. As a result, we made sure to provide instructions about how to ensure student privacy during open office hours. Specific applications include using a breakout room to have a sensitive discussion with a student instead of having the discussion in the main Zoom room or inviting students to schedule one-on-one meetings outside of the open office hours.

We propose that communication scholars explore how informal online meetings enable and inhibit maintenance communication that creates and sustains teaching/learning communities in higher education. We also instituted practices that would encourage maintenance communication between instructors and students, such as open online office hours and workshops. We also ensured that communication about the class was especially clear by utilizing weekly messages and videos that previewed the upcoming deadline and tasks/content for the week. These efforts can help mitigate the loss of presence between students, instructors, and administrators by providing an alternative shared space while encouraging communication.

Principle 4: Evaluate Online Engagement Strategies

Finally, we must critically examine the ways students, instructors, and administrators engage with one another in online and hybrid settings to develop best practices and educational structures that are effective in the new teaching and learning era that has been ushered in by the coronavirus pandemic. These examinations should occur in an iterative and purposeful way. To this end, we developed a mid-semester evaluation assignment that is built into the course structure. This assignment enables instructors to ask students about their experiences in the online classroom, assess the responses, and adjust their teaching strategies during the semester in an effort to create a more engaging learning environment for students (Sozer, Zeybekoglu, and Kaya 2019).

Rationale. The shift to online instruction led to questions about how to best evaluate teaching/learning in virtual settings. Greene (2020) highlighted the need to conduct regular check-ins with the students to see how the course is going and to incorporate their feedback. These check-ins can take many forms, such as polls, questionnaires, exit tickets; however, they share some commonalities—transparency and purpose—and are modeled after midterm evaluations (McGrath 2014). Pre-pandemic, mid-semester evaluations were used to assess how the course was going at one point in time, but the pandemic has illuminated the necessity of offering paths for student feedback more frequently as students and instructors were forced into the virtual classroom.

Application. We adapted survey questions from the Mid-Semester Evaluation of College Teaching and added the anonymous survey to the course space as an ungraded quiz (Teaching and Learning Transformation Center n.d.). The survey included three open-ended questions: (1) What's going right for you in this course? (2) What should change in the course? and (3) What would help you get more out of the course? This provided the instructors with an opportunity to provide substantive feedback and adjust the course structure in real time. Not only did this provide more engagement between the instructor and the student, but it provided definitive proof the instructors were willing to listen to the students. Each section is different, but there is one such interaction we can discuss in detail and that is the establishment of specific due dates for weekly assignments. During the initial transition to online instruction, students expressed confusion over hard deadlines and penalties for late assignments. It was through this feedback where the instructor and the students agreed to a more appealing submission time—which was based on the student input on the mid-semester evaluation—and was used as a talking point during the next live session. In addition, the instructor was then able to communicate this experience to other instructors and administrators at the next conversation hour on the schedule. If an instructor agreed to provide the results, we collected the surveys and used the information to develop changes to the curriculum for future semesters.

Communication pedagogy scholars should explore how to use communication assessment techniques in an online environment in order to supplement midterm evaluations in a recurring and iterative manner (e.g., weekly). These tools can capture the online teaching/learning experience in real time, thus giving instructors and administrators information to enact changes as needed that can lead to engagement throughout the semester. Additionally, as course administrators, we will capture and evaluate instructor perceptions of engagement using qualitative methods (e.g., open-ended qualitative questionnaires). This approach would prioritize instructor voice as they reflect on their teaching experiences in the online classroom and could produce insights into how engagement was/was not fostered.

ENGAGEMENT IN THE FUTURE

Engagement will look different as courses are offered in a variety of formats. The traditional conceptualization of engagement as face-to-face interactions between student and instructor will need to evolve to be more inclusive of means (i.e., online, written), and levels (e.g., instructor-instructor). Ultimately, the reconceptualization of what engagement looks like will better account for the varied ways that students, instructors, and administrators communicate collaboration, presence, and participation in online, hybrid, and in-person classes of the future.

We expect this future to look like a pendulum—where universities will attempt to swing back to the way things were (predominately in-person instruction/engagement) before settling somewhere in the middle that integrates the best aspects of both in-person and online instruction. With that being said, we argue for the development of integrated models of teaching and learning in higher education in general, and communication specifically. For instance, Miller and colleagues (2021) advocated for the development of new instructional formats, such as HyFlex (a combination of hybrid and flexible) and BlendFlex (blended and flexible) as ways to meet student learning needs following the pandemic and integrate the lessons we learned during the shift to completely online learning.

Given the important role of technology in finding a comfortable more static spot in the pendulum swing, we predict that instructor engagement will expand to include additional outside platforms, such as social media groups. Once example that emerged during 2020 was the *Pandemic Pedagogy* group on Facebook (Schwartzman 2020). Platforms like this could serve as another space where instructors can pose questions, contribute to conversations, build relationships, and learn about new teaching/learning ideas that adapt instructor-instructor engagement to the uncertain future of higher education.

In a similar vein, we posit that virtual office hours (Brinkley 2020) will become one norm for instructor-student engagement. This mediated form of office hours addresses student needs in terms of accessibility and flexibility. Indeed, virtual office hours may facilitate more instructor-student interaction while also minimizing the number of student emails that have taken the place of traditional in-person office hours.

Given the changed teaching/learning environment, we argue for the inclusion of more holistic means of teaching evaluations. Specifically, we posit that a move from traditional metrics measured by Likert-type scales to narrative evaluations that include student accounts of learning and instructor reflections (Greene 2020) could better capture the classrooms experience (regardless of if it in-online, in-person, or hybrid).

In all, the use of the four principles that we created will allow our community of educators to continue to develop innovative and flexible curricula that respond to the context-based needs of both students and instructors. The establishment of teaching standards can provide opportunities for multilevel engagement in the online communication classroom. The development of a robust virtual space can lead to more collaborative consistency between instructors (Anderson et al. 2016). Creation of regular training sessions can provide a discursive space for both formal and informal interactions between instructors and with administrators. Finally, the evaluation of online engagement strategies can gauge which ones are more or less effective in the online context. Within this new worldview of teaching and learning, the exigence for transforming what engagement looks like across communication contexts requires an adaptable approach—one that encourages presence, participation, and collaboration and, in doing so, supports multilevel engagement in a (post) pandemic world.

REFERENCES

Anderson, Lindsey B., Elizabeth E. Gardner, Andrew D. Wolvin, Rowie Kirby-Straker, Ben Bederson, and Mehmet A. Yalcin. 2016. "Incorporating Learning Analytics into Basic Course Administration: How to Embrace the Opportunity to Identify Inconsistencies and Inform Responses." *Journal of the Association for Communication Administration* 35, no. 1: 2–13. https://drvinitaagarwal.files.wordpress.com/2017/02/jaca-35-12.pdf

Appleton, James J., Christenson, Sandra L., and Michael J. Furlong. 2008. "Student Engagement with School: Critical, Conceptual, and Methodological Issues of the Construct." *Psychology in the Schools* 45, no. 5: 369–386. doi: 10.1002/pits.20303

Astin, Alexander W. 1999. "Student Involvement: A Development Theory for Higher Education." *Journal of College Student Development* 40, no. 5: 518–529. https://www.researchgate.net/publication/220017441

Axelson, Rick D., and Arend Flick. 2011. "Defining Student Engagement." *Change: The Magazine of Higher Learning* 43, no. 1: 38–43. doi: 10.1080/00091383.2011.533096

Brinkley, J. (2020). Should We Do Away with Office Hours? *Inside Higher Education.* https://www.insidehighered.com/advice/2020/06/17/professor-questions-value-set-office-hours-students-opinion

Carini, Robert M., George D. Kuh, and Stephen P. Klein. 2006. "Student Engagement and Student Learning: Testing the Linkages." *Research in Higher Education* 47: 1–32. doi: 10.1007/s11162-005-8150-9

Chatham-Carpenter, April. 2017. "The Future Online: Instructional Communication Scholars Taking the Lead." *Communication Education* 66, no. 4: 492–494. doi: 10.1080/03634523.2017.1349916

Chickering, Arthur W., and Zelda F. Gamson. 1987. "Seven Principles for Good Practice in Undergraduate Education." *AAHE Bulletin* 39: 3–7. https://files.eric.ed.gov/fulltext/ED282491.pdf

Dahlgren, Peter. 2011. "Parameters of Online Participation: Conceptualizing Civic Contingencies." *Communication Management Quarterly* 6: 87–109.

Dixson, Marcia D. 2010. "Creating Effective Student Engagement in Online Courses: What do Students Find Engaging?" *Journal of the Scholarship of Teaching and Learning* 10, no. 2: 1–13. https://files.eric.ed.gov/fulltext/EJ890707.pdf

Fredricks, Jennifer A., Phyllis C. Blumenfeld, and Alison H. Paris. 2004. "School Engagement: Potential of the Concept, State of the Evidence." *Review of Educational Research* 74, no. 1: 59–109. doi: 10.3102/00346543074001059

Frymier, Ann B., and Marian L. Houser. 2016. "The Role of Oral Participation in Student Engagement." *Communication Education* 65, no. 1: 83–104. doi: 10.1080/03634523.2015.1066019

Greene, Jody (2020). How (Not) to Evaluate Teaching During a Pandemic. *The Chronicle of Higher Education.* https://www.chronicle.com/article/how-not-to-evaluate-teaching-during-a-pandemic/

Groccia, James E. 2018. "What Is Student Engagement?" *New Directions for Teaching and Learning* no. 154: 11–20. doi: 10.1002/tl.20287

Kaufmann, Renee, Deanna D. Sellnow, and Brandi N. Frisby. 2016. "The Development and Validation of the Online Learning Climate Scale (OLCS)." *Communication Education* 65, no. 3: 307–321. doi: 10.1080/03634523.2015.1101778

Kaufmann, Renee, and Jessalyn I. Vallade. 2020. "Exploring Connections in the Online Learning Environment: Student Perceptions of Rapport, Climate, and Loneliness." *Interactive Learning Environments.* doi: 10.1080/10494820.2020.1749670

Kuh, George D. 2001. "Assessing What Really Matters to Student Learning: Inside the National Survey of Student Engagement." *Change: The Magazine of Higher Learning* 33, no. 3: 10–17. doi: 10.1080/00091380109601795

Kuh, George D. 2003. "What We're Learning about Student Engagement from NSSE." *Change: The Magazine of Higher Learning* 35, no. 2: 24–32. doi: 10.1080/00091380309604090

Kuh, George D. 2009. "The National Survey of Student Engagement: Conceptual and Empirical Foundations." *New Directions for Institutional Research* 2009, no. 141: 5–20. doi: 10.1002/ir.283

Lang, J. M. (2020, May 18). On Now Drawing Conclusions About Online Teaching Now—Or Next Fall. *Chronicle of Higher Education.* https://community.chronicle

.com/news/2353-on-not-drawing-conclusions-about-online-teaching-now-or-next-fall?cid=VTEVPMSED1

Li, Lei, and Jennifer P. Pitts. 2009. "Does it really matter? Using virtual office hours to enhance student-faculty interaction." *Journal of Information Systems Education* 20, no. 2: 175–185. http://jise.org/Volume20/n2/JISEv20n2p175.html

Liem, Gregory. A. D., and Andrew J. Martin. 2012. "The Motivation and Engagement Scale: Theoretical Framework, Psychometric Properties, and Applied Yields." *Australian Psychologist* 47, no. 1: 3–13. doi: 10.1111/j.1742-9544.2011.00049.x

Livingstone, Sonia. 2013. "The Participation Paradigm in Audience Research." *The Communication Review* 16, no. 1–2: 21–30. doi: 10.1080/10714421.2013.757174

Lowell, Victoria, and Marisa Exeter. 2017. "Leading a Collaborative Effort: Providing Effective Training and Support for Online Adjunct Instructors." *International Journal of Designs for Learning* 8, no. 2: 59–79. doi: 10.14434/ijdl.v8i2.21160

Mazer, Joseph P. 2012. "Development and Validation of the Student Interest and Engagement Scales." *Communication Methods and Measures* 6, no. 2: 99–125. doi: 10.1080/19312458.2012.679244

Mazer, Joseph P. 2013. "Validity of the Student Interest and Engagement Scales: Associations with Student Learning Outcomes." *Communication Studies* 62, no. 2: 125–140. doi: 10.1080/10510974.2012.727943

McGrath, Lauren, B. 2014. Mid-Semester Evaluation. *Inside Higher Education.* https://www.insidehighered.com/blogs/gradhacker/mid-semester-evaluations

McKinnon, Merryn, and Judith Vos. 2015. Engagement as a Threshold Concept for Science Education and Science Communication. *International Journal of Science Education* 5, no. 4: 297–318. doi: 10.1080/21548455.2014.986770

Meisenbach, Rebecca J., and Jill J. McMillan. 2006. "Blurring the Boundaries: Historical Developments and Future Directions in Organizational Rhetoric." *Annals of the International Communication Association* 30, no. 1: 99–141. doi: 10.1080/23808985.2006.11679056

Miller, Ann Neville, Deanna D. Sellnow, and Michael G. Strawser. 2021. "Pandemic Pedagogy Challenges and Opportunities: Instruction Communication in Remote, HyFlex, and BlendFlex Courses." *Communication Education* 70, no. 2: 202–204. doi: 10.1080/03634523.2020.1857418

Moore, Stephanie, and Charles B. Hodges. 2020. So You Want to Temporarily Teach Online? *Inside Higher Education*, March 11, 2020. https://www.insidehighered.com/advice/2020/03/11/practical-advice-Instructors-faced-abrupt-move-online-teaching-opinion

Morreale, Sherwyn, Janice Thorpe, and Susan Ward. 2019. Teaching Public Speaking Online—Not a Problem but an Opportunity! *Journal of Communication Pedagogy* 2, no. 1: 76–82. doi: 10.31446/JCP.2019.15

Pace, C. Robert. 1984. "Measuring the Quality of College Student Experiences." Los Angeles, CA: University of California Center for the Study of Evaluation.

Pace, C. Robert. 1990. *"The Undergraduates: A Report of Their Activities and Progress in College in the 1980's."* Los Angeles, CA: University of California Center for the Study of Evaluation.

Pascarella, Ernest T., and Patrick T. Terenzini. 2005. *How College Affects Students: A Third Decade of Research.* San Francisco, CA: Jossey-Bass.

Pascarellea, Ernest T., Seifert, Tricia A., and Charles Blaich. 2010. "How Effective are the NSSE Benchmarks in Predicting Important Educational Outcomes." *Change: The Magazine of Higher Learning* 42, no. 1: 16–22. doi: 10.1080/00091380903449060

Pike, Gary R., and George D. Kuh. 2005. "A Typology of Student Engagement for American College and Universities." *Research in Higher Education* 46, no. 1: 185–209. doi: 10.1007/s11162-004-1599-0

Ryan, Richard M., and Edward L. Deci. 2000. Self-Determination Theory and the Facilitation of Intrinsic Motivation, Social Development, and Well-Being. *American Psychologist* 55, no. 1: 68–78. doi: 10.1037//0003-066x.55.1.68

Schreiber, Lisa M., Gregory D. Paul, and Lisa R. Shibley. 2012. "The Development and Test of the Public Speaking Competence Rubric." *Communication Education* 61, no. 3: 205–233. doi: 10.1080/03634523.2012.670709

Scutelnicu, Gina, Rebecca Tekula, Beth Gordon, and Hillary J. Knepper. 2019. "Consistency is Key in Online Learning: Evaluating Student and Instructor Perceptions of a Collaborative Online-Course Template. *Teaching Public Administration* 37, no. 3: 274–292. 10.1177/0144739419852759

Sell, A. J. 2021. "The Somewhat Surprising Benefits of Book Groups." *Inside Higher Education*, May 5, 2021. https://www.insidehighered.com/advice/2021/05/07/f orming-book-group-can-create-online-community-faculty-opinion

Sozer, E. Murat, Zuhal Zeybekoglu, and Mustafa Kaya. 2019. Using Mid-Semester Course Evaluation as a Feedback Tool for Improving Learning and Teaching in Higher Education. *Assessment & Evaluation in Higher Education* 44, no. 7: 1003–1016. 10.1080/02602938.2018.1564810

Stearns, Susan. 2017. "What is the Place of Lecture in Student Learning Today?" *Communication Education* 66, no. 2: 243–245. doi: 10.1080/03634523.2016.1275723

Schwartzman, Roy. 2020. "Performing Pandemic Pedagogy." *Communication Education* 69, no. 4: 502–517. doi: 10.1080/03634523.2020.1804602

Swan, Karen. 2001. "Virtual Interaction: Design Factors Affecting Student Satisfaction and Perceived Learning in Asynchronous Online Courses." *Distance Education* 22, no. 2: 306–331. doi:10.1080/0158791010220208

Swerzenski, J. D. 2021. "Why Teaching Technology Must Adapt to Our Teaching." *Communication Education* 70, no. 2: 211–213. doi: 10.1080/03634523.2020.1857414

Teaching and Learning Transformation Center. n.d. "Mid-Semester Evaluation of College Teaching." Last Modified May 2019. https://tltc.umd.edu/mid-semester-e valuation-college-teaching

Trowler, Vicki. 2010. "Student Engagement Literature Review." *The Higher Education Academy* 11, no. 1: 1–15.

Tyler, Ralph W. 1949. *Basic Principles of Curriculum and Instruction.* Chicago, IL: The University of Chicago Press.

Chapter 5

Teaching Communication in a Pandemic and Post-Pandemic World

Brad Mello and Cyndi Grobmeier

Nothing illustrates the teaching and learning challenges faced during the COVID-19 pandemic better than an experience one of the authors had early on in the transition to remote learning. The author had a student who, along with her mom, became homeless during the pandemic. The instructor shared her phone number so the student could text every day to check-in, since she didn't know when she'd have access to the internet, and the two connected daily by sharing Minion GIFs. Although such dire situations are not the norm, the student body we serve is very diverse. Not only are we officially a Hispanic Serving Institution with a large number of first-generation college students but, as the opening anecdote illustrates, many students come to us with significant financial barriers.

Our students were not unique in this regard, as Katz, Jordan, and Ognyanova (2021) point out, "The pivot to remote learning in the spring of 2020 quickly brought digital inequality to the forefront for undergraduate college students" (para. 3). The lived experiences of our students illustrated this consistently as we encountered students competing for bandwidth, literally and figuratively—whether they balanced caring for younger siblings and helping them with their schooling or were students like the one in the opening example who became homeless because of the pandemic.

The abrupt transition to remote learning presented challenges for teachers, learners, and departmental administrators that taxed everyone's ability to support students. As administrators and teachers, the authors focused their energies on determining what must be done to ensure that our students learn what they need to in our introductory course, which is required of all students via general education, and what must be done to ensure our majors continue to progress to an on-time graduation. Westwick and Morreale support this concern,

Clearly, we need to understand why the rapid shift to online teaching was disquieting for faculty and students alike. Furthermore, we have a responsibility to establish frameworks for managing this and other future crises we in the academy may encounter. The present situation, the pandemic, and the rush to entirely online and remote teaching and learning are useful cases in point for considering challenges and opportunities for individual members of the communication professoriate, their departments, and our discipline. (Westwick and Morreale 2020, 219–220)

We learned many important lessons through this process—many that will stay with us long after this pandemic. While we look forward to the day when we can teach in person without masks, we will remain focused on being more aware of the technological needs of students, the constant need for professional development for instructors to ensure they can use the plethora of technology-based teaching tools well, and the importance of effectively utilizing all learning formats to serve students on their learning journey—all while remaining cognizant that the socio-emotional well-being of our students and faculty alike is at the forefront of everything we do.

In this chapter we discuss how we managed to quiet the disquiet and grapple with the challenges. We took a student-centered approach, and we learned that we needed to focus on the following issues: technological access, as well as physical, mental, and emotional well-being for students; technological ability for both instructors and students; optimal designs for educational experiences in multiple formats (online, hybrid, and face-to-face) that best meet the needs of students; and support for the overall health of everyone, particularly adjuncts and students, during the crisis. We begin by discussing the importance of starting with the basics: supporting students.

SUPPORTING STUDENTS IN A CRISIS: TECHNOLOGICAL ACCESS AND ABILITIES, AND SOCIO-EMOTIONAL WELL-BEING

There has been much research surrounding the broad implications of the "Digital Divide," but little research on concerns with undergraduate students being under-connected exists because it has not been seen as an issue—until COVID-19. Katz, Jordon, and Ognyanova explain, "In large part, this is because, under normal (non-pandemic) circumstances, on-campus resources help to mitigate digital inequality by providing students with Wi-Fi access and devices in campus libraries and computer labs" (Katz, Jordan and Ogynaova 2021, para. 7). As Handel et al. (2020) argue, based on their research on German college students, the more students were technologically equipped, the better the learning, and the more joy the students experienced. They also conclude that the more that is done to build a community among learners, even in a remote learning environment, the better the learning outcomes. When learners struggle with basic technological access, community building becomes challenging, and a secondary focus.

So, surveying students to determine their technological situation was an important first step in the process of addressing the basics of technological access. We created a survey within our learning management system (LMS) that was shared with all faculty to quickly assess what technological challenges our students had in the immediate future, how their personal and working lives may have changed, and what other immediate concerns they had. The questions on the survey included these four areas:

- A checklist to indicate computer equipment available (laptops, smart phones, tablets), software availability (MS Word, PowerPoint), and internet type (broadband or not)
- A drop-down menu survey question asking their comfort level with working with various tech platforms (Zoom, Google Hangout, Google Docs, video/audio recording, presentation software)
- A Yes/No question asking if they were available to log on to Zoom meetings during regularly scheduled class time
- An open-ended question asking for times students weren't available to connect live.

The survey also allowed instructors to assess which students were still engaged so appropriate campus services could be notified to intervene with students who seemed to have fallen off the radar. Learning what technology our students had access to helped us plan for the switch to remote learning, but we have come to recognize that an understanding of student's access to technology is something we need to reassess and plan for every year moving forward, which might range from creating more technological infrastructure on campus, to providing alternative options for completing assignments, providing more workshops, or administering more on-demand instructional videos on navigating an LMS for our students. In hindsight, having all instructors use an open-source e-textbook and requiring all our basic course instructors, every semester, to fully utilize our LMS in their courses to help students become comfortable and familiar with it early on in their academic career proved vital to helping students shift to fully remote learning.

Student technological access issues encountered included bandwidth limitations, equipment availability and quality, and the availability of general technological infrastructure. We start with the most important, lack of bandwidth to access course materials and mediated instruction. Not all students had access to high-speed internet, or even if they did, they were competing with multiple people in their home for use. Lack of reliable, fast internet led to students not being able to share Google slides while having their camera on in Zoom, audio breaks up due to low bandwidth, and difficulty hearing due to activity in the household and the inability of students to find a quiet space. We determined that we need to be flexible and, particularly for student presentations, accept audio as more important than video.

We also encountered significant variance in terms of available technology. Some students worked on phones, not laptops, and were thus limited in what is available in apps and on mobile. Lack of student access to a good laptop with a working camera made it difficult to deliver speeches remotely. Our institution provided laptops to some students based on need and availability, but quantities were limited and not all needs could be met. Students could come to campus and utilize a limited number of computers that were socially distanced and sanitized after each use. Students could also reserve space on campus and access campus Wi-Fi if they did not have access at home, but space was limited due to social-distancing guidelines. These strategies worked for participating in class, but students could not deliver speeches in either situation because they would disturb other students in the room, even if they were socially distanced.

Technology infrastructure issues with campus systems made the ability to hold real-time classes unreliable, at best, requiring a significant secondary shift to predominately asynchronous instruction. Even campus Wi-Fi could be unreliable because of such high demand on the system. Often our LMS synchronous video system could not handle the demand and would simply shut down. In response all faculty were given professional Zoom accounts which solved the immediate problem, but spotty student access to high-speed bandwidth and adequate technology as mentioned above could not be overcome simply by switching to the Zoom platform. Fortunately, the record feature on Zoom at least provided a way for students to listen to lectures and discussion at a time when there was not as much competition for bandwidth and family computer time.

These were just the initial issues that needed to be addressed—there are ongoing issues that can arise anytime, including service being cut-off for nonpayment, running out of data on cell phone plans, or devices breaking down and needing repairs—all of which can cause tremendous financial hardship. These concerns exemplify first-level digital inequalities but did not even begin to address the second-level digital inequalities experienced by many of our students. According to Katz, Jordon, and Ognyanova,

> An expansive body of research shows how unequal digital access (first-level digital inequality) affects individuals' likelihood of developing the necessary

skills to fully engage in digital environments (second-level digital inequality). For example, children and adults who have daily internet access are more likely to develop capabilities to successfully locate online information and assess its quality, as well as to engage in digital content production (as opposed to consumption, which requires a much more limited digital skillset). (Katz, Jordon and Ognyanova 2021, para. 9)

We, as a program, worked hard to ensure that first-level digital inequality issues were solved as best as possible through a variety of strategies discussed above, in order to ensure our students obtained a sophisticated level of digital information literacy in order to avoid a second-level digital inequality that could impede progress in future courses and career paths.

The most important concern for every section of the public speaking course, all of which had been face-to-face classes, was how students were going to deliver speeches virtually, particularly given the first- and second-level digital inequalities many of our students experience. Taking a scaffolded learning approach, instructors began with a simple video blog assignment to familiarize students with speaking on camera. This assignment also gave instructors an opportunity to assess their students' mental and emotional well-being in this crisis situation, as they were given this first video blog prompt:

- What are your thoughts and feelings about your rapid transition to being an online student (You might talk about some of the communication challenges you've faced this week and how you worked through them; what positive experiences you've seen come out of this transition; and what concerns you have moving forward this semester)?
- What are your thoughts and feelings in general about this situation for you, your family, your friends, your community, your university, your country, and your world?

Not only did this give students and instructors a trial-run opportunity for delivering speeches in a low-stakes assignment, the informal format of the video blog assignments encouraged students to speak authentically about what they were experiencing. One student spoke about how she had to pick up more hours at work because her dad's workplace shut down due to the pandemic; she said, "So, I have to bring the money home now, and it feels kind of weird and exhausting." Katz, Jordon, and Ognyanova (2021) also found that student financial insecurity, as well as their family's financial insecurities resulting from the pandemic, led to increased anxiety. In their video blogs, many students discussed the overwhelming stress they felt with the shift to online learning, with one student talking about how, because she was only able to do her online schoolwork from her bedroom, that "It almost feels like there is no separation, that I don't get a break," and another student shared similar thoughts, saying, "Being a college student on quarantine converted to online classes really suck. I hate not seeing my teachers, and I hate not seeing my friends." Lischer, Safi, and Dickson (2021) also found that students missed daily communication exchanges with classmates and that this was a contributing factor to increased stress and anxiety.

In student video blogs, many students also talked about the overwhelming workload that they felt was being "piled on them," as one student described, as a result of the shift to online learning. Our students were not alone in this assessment, as Lischer, Safi, and Dickson (2021) found, students self-reported increased anxiety levels that they attributed to several factors: the added stress of a perceived increased workload, unclear communication from faculty and administration, and the need for extensive self-study without mechanisms for further explanation or the ability to ask questions. Katz, Jordon, and Ognyanova (2021) found some similar results in their survey of 2,913 undergraduates from 30 U.S. colleges and universities, with challenges faced when communicating with instructors and teaching assistants as well as connectivity and device challenges having a significant negative effect on their Remote Learning Proficiency (RLP). In their study, RLP was measured based on student perceptions of three elements of the remote learning environment: understanding instructor expectations, staying on top of deadlines and due dates, and figuring out how to use the technological programs, such as Zoom, to complete their coursework. RLP was one of four endogenous variables in their study—the other variables included communication challenges, connectivity challenges, and device challenges—all of which we saw in our students as well.

With so many new concerns to address, student technological access, while complicated, was a more easily solvable issue than others. So, as we were addressing student issues we also had to turn our attention to a learning curve in the technological ability and professional development among our faculty.

TECHNOLOGICAL ABILITY AND PROFESSIONAL DEVELOPMENT

In the sudden pivot to remote learning, we had to rapidly assess our instructors' comfort level with teaching online. While our full-time faculty had considerable online teaching experience, most of the adjunct faculty had only basic experience using the LMS for assignment submissions and quizzes; however, all faculty were familiar with having students submit recorded speeches for our common final assignment that is used for assessment. Having at least this basic working knowledge of the LMS, as well as having basic working knowledge of how students can record and submit speeches proved vital. Working with our Center for Instructional Design and Academic Technology, our public speaking coordinator came up with a quick menu of options for instructors to choose from to have students deliver speeches, ranging from videotaped submissions to using the LMS conferences feature, to using third-party platforms, such as Zoom and Power of Public Speaking, both of which offered free access to everyone during the initial pandemic shutdown.

This menu included full-text submission instructions for students that instructors could simply cut-and-paste or adapt to fit their needs. Not only did we offer some quick pedagogical tips to translate what instructors tacitly knew how to do in the classroom to the online environment, following Jones-Bodie, Anderson, and Hall's (2020) research on what resources students found particularly valuable to turn to when they need assistance. We encouraged our faculty to be as responsive to student emails as possible, offer personalized feedback—especially on speeches, make sure assignment instructions were clear, provide rubrics ahead of due dates, and try to model assignments using video examples whenever possible. Providing as many plug-and-play tools as possible and engaging in frequent communication through emails and Zoom conferences prepared instructors to shift classes designed for in-person delivery to a fully online format in less than two weeks.

We encouraged faculty to be creative in how they engaged with students, and many took to recording weekly preview videos so students could continue to feel connected to their faculty by seeing and hearing them; by recording and posting the videos, it also allowed students to view them as many times as they needed to, when they could, and on their phones or other devices. In short, it provided connection in a more accessible manner. Not only were faculty encouraged to communicate frequently with their students, but the public speaking coordinator also sent frequent—as often as daily at the beginning of the pandemic shift, communication to faculty. Toward the end of the semester, one adjunct emailed, thanking everyone for the level of communication because they hadn't even heard from anyone at other schools where they taught. Another adjunct noted that they took some of the tools, tips, and best practices that we shared among our faculty and provided them to colleagues at other schools who were struggling to figure things out on their own. One final move that provided an extra sense of support was that adjuncts added full-time faculty as additional instructors on all of their courses just in case someone fell ill—this is a practice that will most likely remain permanent. This gave adjuncts a much-needed sense of support in this crisis situation.

Jones, Saulnier, and Fulick-Jagiela (2020) found that a sense of being supported in a crisis moderated the effect of feeling overwhelmed by an increased workload among faculty and staff and had a positive impact on mental well-being. They indicated that students, when feeling overwhelmed by their workload, could also benefit mentally from feelings of being supported.

As a department, we made every effort to make sure all our faculty felt supported and encouraged them to routinely offer students opportunities to get assistance, not just from the faculty themselves, but also through other campus support mechanisms such as the Learning to Center. Others have found that providing resources students can turn to supplement the support they seek from their instructor to be beneficial (Jones-Bodie, Anderson, and Hall 2020). For example, students who utilize speaking centers have reported reduced anxiety and increased confidence (Dwyer and Davidson 2012), so since our institution didn't have a formal speaking center, we worked with our Learning Center to hire a communication major to serve as an online tutor for public speaking students. The counseling center began meeting with students via Zoom, and other campus personnel who, when their regular daily responsibilities were disrupted, began serving other newly needed roles to support students and faculty.

Joshua Kim (2021), in an interview with assistant provost Derek Bruff of Vanderbilt, confirms many of the important strategies discussed above. When asked what lessons were learned during the pandemic he said,

> There are so many lessons! The first one that occurred to me last year, as we worked with hundreds of faculty in our Online Course Design Institute, is that faculty now have so many more tools in their teaching toolboxes. And by "tools" I mean educational technologies, but also teaching strategies. The last 15 months of teaching required faculty to step outside of their comfort zones, and many of them have found new approaches to teaching that they'll continue to use in the future, regardless of their teaching contexts. (para. 10)

He also mentions how faculty adopted new forms of assessment, turning away from high-stakes assessments like final exams and moving toward lower-stakes assessments such as the video blog mentioned earlier.

PLANNING FOR A HYBRID ACADEMIC YEAR IN 2020–2021

After surviving the quick pivot to remote learning in March of 2020, we began to plan for an uncertain fall semester. The benefit of having an entire summer to plan was essential. We wanted to move from surviving mode to thriving mode. We followed a plan similar to what Miller, Sellnow, and Strawser (2020) term a "hyflex model," where much of the content was delivered online, but students would come to class in smaller groups to allow for social distancing and to deliver speeches. At this writing, we only have anecdotal data about the success of this model; however, previous research with similar course design models showed that students found the course material stimulating, but noted issues with understanding directions and staying on schedule (Preston, Giglio, and English 2008). We support Miller, Sellnow, and Strawser's call for more research on this hyflex model and plan to conduct an assessment of how well the model worked in terms of producing desired student learning outcomes.

One vital action taken by our institution to plan for a fall semester still rooted in a global pandemic proved essential. Our university used CARES Act funds to offer a summer stipend to all faculty, including adjuncts, to complete an abbreviated version of our in-house online pedagogy course. All four members of our department faculty had completed the full version of the training course, but our adjuncts had not. After some discussion about the unique needs of our courses, particularly public speaking, we came together as a department and offered the full version of the course for our adjuncts rather than the abbreviated self-paced version created by our instructional design services. Full-time faculty took turns running each week of the six-week course. Although labor and time intensive, this ensured that our adjuncts were fully prepared, both in terms of technological skills and, perhaps more importantly, in sound online teaching pedagogy, to be prepared to be fully online for the entire academic year of 2020–2021 if need be.

Essentially, we heeded the call Westwick and Morreale (2021) made to departments to reimagine professional development for a pandemic world. Our department, and our discipline, often embraces and adopts technology in that traditional "early adopter" manner, but the department focused on not overwhelming everyone with some new tech gizmo every week and instead ensured that the technology available to all (like Canvas or Zoom) was utilized effectively. We found it was better to deeply understand the capabilities of one technology, like Zoom, rather than attempting to learn multiple technologies. In fact, as instructors began regularly using polls, breakout rooms, and other interactive features in Zoom, they found student engagement seemed to improve. Regular online meetings allowed us to engage in meaningful conversations, so together the faculty could stay on top of the technology's capabilities, share best practices, and prepare for any unforeseen issues before they arose—essentially staying afloat in the pandemic seas. The department took as a starting point the words of Emma Pettit (2021) who explains in her essay on helping faculty stay afloat in a pandemic that

> the year 2020 was not kind to the faculty. A frantic spring gave way to a grueling fall and winter. By December, as a global pandemic made confetti of the traditional academic calendar, professors were tapped out. In an October

survey conducted by *The Chronicle* and underwritten by Fidelity Investments, more than 75 percent of the 1,122 faculty respondents said their workload had increased since the start of the year. The majority said their work-life balance had deteriorated. (para. 5)

Pettit reviews several strategies for helping faculty in these times such as delaying the tenure clock, modifying tenure standards, reducing certain tasks such as holding events or program reviews, but she also points to the increased workload that remains uncompensated. While much of the increased workload for our public speaking coordinator and the chair of the department did remain uncompensated, the university at least provided a $500 stipend to all faculty, both full-time and adjunct, who completed the online training program focused on online teaching. This compensation was essential to the process of preparing our adjuncts to teach our public speaking course in a hyflex or fully online format, with the goal to not ask for any more additional time than what was necessary for our adjuncts, who are already historically undercompensated for the work they do.

Once we were comfortable in our technological shoes, we worked to build community among students and faculty. In normal circumstances, we see each other on campus; we interact in the café or coffee shop, and those interactions naturally build a sense of community and comradery—concepts that remained important, and perhaps became even more relevant, during the pandemic.

COMMUNITY BUILDING

Throughout the pandemic and transition to remote learning, we conducted community building exercises among our full-time and adjunct faculty and maintained community building exercises for our students, such as continuing our biannual speech competition for public speaking students via Zoom in the fall, and in a hybrid format in the spring—with both events livestreamed, giving students a chance to invite friends and family who in normal times might not have been able to attend. This is one of many forced adaptations to our regular routines that we experienced during the pandemic that led to innovative ways of doing things. For example, we will continue to livestream the speech competition in the future, even when we are back face-to-face, so students can include friends and family from afar. It was an ironic, unanticipated, and much-appreciated outcome that we were able to extend our community to include many who are only loosely connected to the university community, such as family and friends of students, in the midst of social distancing that kept so many separated. Truly, the pandemic taught us to appreciate the many nontraditional ways we embraced to stay connected.

Another one of these unexpected community-building lessons learned emerged when the need to transition to remote learning became apparent. We began holding a series of meetings via Zoom to map out a plan to create as smooth a transition as possible. What we discovered though was that bringing our faculty together fostered a sense of collaboration and comradery. Zoom made it convenient to bring everyone together to discuss logistics, assignments and safety protocols. Before the pandemic, pre-semester planning meetings were done in person, but rarely drew anywhere near 100 percent attendance. Zoom allows for more frequent meetings that support community-building among adjuncts and full-time faculty. Our department—full-time faculty and adjuncts alike—truly became a cohesive unit. We spent time together, trying to replicate those random hallway conversations on Zoom. We allowed for social time, characterized by one adjunct teasingly referring to another adjunct as "mom" because of her protective nature. Other faculty introduced their colleagues to their children and pets and shared personal hobbies and interests such as video projects, theatrical performances, volunteer work, and more.

Schwartzman (2020) eloquently argues for the importance of community building. He reports on a Facebook group he created titled, "Pandemic Pedagogy." The group became a clearinghouse for sharing information on all aspects of teaching in the pandemic, with topics ranging from various teaching strategies to sharing how various communities were responding to the pandemic, and what concerns faculty had regarding personal and student safety. Schwartzman also argues for the importance of resilience in the face of the challenges of teaching in a pandemic. He states, "Generally, resilience describes the ongoing processes of coping with trauma in positive ways. The deliberate invocation of trauma directs attention to the magnitude of the pandemic's impacts" (Schwartzman 2020, 510). Recognizing the magnitude of the pandemic on the personal and professional lives of instructors and students allows for the realization that personal agency needed to be encouraged through community building, and that we needed to encourage instructors in particular to be resilient, but to also accept the fact that sometimes the importance of self-care takes precedence over some particular task. Or, as Schwartzman states, "Resilience as endurance emerges in the capacity to acknowledge limitations, withstand adversity, and persevere" (Schwartzman 2020, 512). As our community of faculty persevered, our pandemic pedagogical abilities sharpened.

As the online teaching prowess of our faculty grew, and with the learning community infrastructure in place, we turned our attention to considering how we might develop blended learning experiences, as the possibility of some campus presence in the fall semester became evident. Those discussions also centered around thinking about what we might hold onto after the pandemic because it worked well in helping students achieve the particular learning goals set out for them.

BLENDED LEARNING EXPERIENCES

Our discussion of blended learning practices, combining online and face-to-face modes, was driven not only by the pandemic but also by the nature of our student body. Our students wear multiple hats, including employee, spouse, parent, and caretaker, and they face many obstacles in their educational journey ranging from unreliable technological access, to demands on their time coming from multiple directions, to transportation challenges, to the enormous burden of the cost of tuition, so we have learned that the flexibility afforded in the blended learning experience allows our students to achieve their learning goals while still meeting the demands of their daily lives. We discovered that many technology-based assignments (weekly video blogging in the public speaking course connected to that week's materials, for example) which we creatively developed out of necessity, have proven effective and not only allowed faculty to monitor the student's emotional responses to the pandemic (or any other stressor), but helped them develop stronger communication skills through regular practice in a low-stress environment. But even with the flexibility afforded by blended learning, our instructors still continually struggle with being adaptable to student needs and barriers to completing work on time while also maintaining course rigor.

Tatum and Frey (2020) review the many number of instructors who argued that during the pandemic, being a strict no-nonsense, deadline enforcing professor was not going to work. We found this to be true, particularly in our public speaking course. Transitioning to college is always a challenge, but it was exasperated by the pandemic and the sudden pivot to remote learning. With all the personal and technological challenges facing students, we simply had to be flexible with deadlines. What we weren't flexible with, as Tatum and Frey discuss, was our standards. One concern that remains to be seen is that as we return to a more "normal" environment, is whether these students who weren't held as accountable to strict deadlines will continue to expect that same degree of flexibility. The need to instill in students the importance of a habit of timeliness is essential for success upon graduation. It will likely be a challenge going forward but being aware of the challenge and being willing to creatively confront it, as we have demonstrated can be done with all the other challenges we faced, is the first step.

ENDURING LESSONS

As we now look forward to and plan for a fall 2021 back on campus, we are pondering what lessons from the quick pivot and a full year of hyflex and online learning has taught us. We seek to articulate which of the lessons we need to hold on to and which we can discard. We believe the lessons about technological inequalities and access, technological abilities, and the need to be flexible and open to change will endure. We've also developed an even stronger reflective focus on our own pedagogy and practice, as well as a stronger recognition of the crucial role community-building plays both in and out of the classroom, for faculty and students alike.

One lesson from our rapid pivot to fully online public speaking and instruction and the ensuing year of hyflex teaching and learning is that as instructors we need to focus on the core principles of what students need to learn to be effective communicators in today's world. We are heading Wallace's (2015) call that the basic communication course should focus on being outcome-driven to not only better serve the needs of a general education curriculum that connects the basic communication course to other GE courses but also help students understand the purpose of communication in their civic and professional lives. As such, we have discovered that what we have reenvisioned looks very different from our traditional views of public speaking with a performance focus—give three speeches in front of a face-to-face audience, make eye contact and avoid the fillers. We agree that the basic communication course has, for decades, remained focused on developing public speaking skills—emphasizing delivery as performance and platform as critical—meaning speaking in front of a live audience takes precedence (Upchurch 2014), but "Now, however, we have a mandate to prepare our students to communicate in this more virtual and digital world" (Prentiss 2021, 348).

What we've learned students need is experience in communicating in multiple modalities with an emphasis on adapting their message to their audience—whether that audience is right in front of them, virtual, or imagined. We've learned basically that we need to focus more on content and construction and less on delivery. Edwards (2021) argues that "digital communication can be public speaking, especially when it relies on the same core competencies as live oratory" (337). These core competencies, considering the communication channel, conducting audience analysis, understanding difference and otherness, adhering to ethical principles and practices, analytically analyzing messages, and influencing public discourse, connect the basic course to not only others in the students' general education curriculum and major but to skills and traits desired by potential future employers. Edwards continues by saying, "Online discussion forums, livestreaming monologues or dialogues, and asynchronous messages on platforms like TED and YouTube are public speaking when communicators develop intentional messages on topics of social or public consequence, even when interaction between speaker and audience may be mediated by time and technology" (337). Using assignments like the video blogs gave us an opportunity to advance many of these competencies while allowing instructors to continue to provide feedback on delivery in a less anxiety-producing manner, which students seemed to react to more positively.

Some research has shown that students had significantly lower trait-like public speaking anxiety after taking an online public speaking course (Westwick, Hunter, and Haleta 2015). James McCroskey (1970, 1978) first labeled communication anxiety (CA) communication apprehension and argued for the importance of addressing it in a variety of contexts and provided the first valid and reliable measurement tool, the Personal Report of Communication Apprehension (PRCA). Much research has been conducted on CA as Karen Foss (1982) discussed, laying out methods to treat CA and providing an extensive bibliography on the subject. However, more research on how these new and different delivery modalities impact the way students learn to manage CA will certainly be needed moving forward.

Another essential lesson we learned is that in the virtual world, we can build community, improve creativity, save students commuting time, and provide valuable technological skills that will be useful when they enter the labor force. According to Kasia Moreno (2021) in her article in *Forbes*, "Silver Linings: Key Lessons From How We Communicate In The New Normal," virtual communication is here to stay and has opened up many avenues to pursue various goals and achieve career and organizational success. *Forbes* surveyed 357 executives from around the globe and found "that videoconferencing has opened new avenues of communications, helped maintain productivity and spark creativity. It has helped strengthen and maintain important personal relationships and manage the work-life balance" (para. 3). Moreno discussed how remote work provides more free time for workers, making them more productive, creative, and satisfied. The same was true of our students.

Although the pandemic has proven stressful, and in many cases a cause of much personal grief, the ability to connect in multiple ways via technology allowed students to remain productive. We believe that we will continue to rely on building and strengthening these technological connections in the future. Reasons for this range from practical concerns such as moving class to an online format due to weather or other safety concerns, to scheduling periodic Zoom meetings to save students and instructors on commute time and expense, to making sure students continue to develop their technologically mediated presentation and communication skills and abilities because those abilities will be in high demand in the workforce they will enter and the world in which they will live. Ultimately, the communication discipline will lead the way in researching and providing practical support for developing this new communication ecosystem.

While we will continue to incorporate technologically based learning strategies in the classroom, we will also continue to utilize Zoom and other technologies to conduct departmental business for simple things. The chair intends to always provide a Zoom option for department meetings so faculty who may not be commuting to campus that day can participate while saving time, energy, and expense. Furthermore, we traditionally conduct on-campus meetings and training sessions for adjuncts, which is a significant time investment to ask of adjuncts who are often teaching at multiple institutions to make ends meet. All department training, meetings, and interactions will remain virtual in the future. Virtual training increased participation and built a community among our adjuncts that we had not witnessed before, hence that is a lesson-learned that we will definitely keep. Our adjuncts feel more connected to the department, and each other, which should translate to better outcomes in the classroom. Ultimately, it is better outcomes in the classroom that we strive for, not only in the midst of this pandemic but moving forward into our new normal—which hopefully will be a post-pandemic world soon.

Even post-pandemic, the idea that things will return to their pre-pandemic routine is naïve at best—for as we have seen after other major crisis situations, such as 9–11, many of the changes foisted upon us by the crisis will remain—and some changes we have already indicated will stick. One that we wish to stress is the incorporation of mediated speeches and group work into our public speaking course. With remote work poised to become the new norm, our students will emerge into a work force where they will be required to be able to present and collaborate in an online format. While we do not believe, as a liberal arts-based institution, that our only job is to prepare students for the workforce, but the ability to communicate in a virtual world will be important for our students when they leave us. Even though today's students are Digital Natives, the communication ecosphere has experienced a tremendous shift due to the pandemic that even they may not feel they are native to. Students will benefit from a continued effort to develop their mediated messaging skills and abilities, which begins with a focus on understanding their audience—which may prove even more challenging in our new normal, as the audience may no longer be geographically present but dispersed by space and time in ways we have not regularly seen before. We will also continue to explore creative ways, like our video blogging assignments, to help students practice their delivery and learn to manage their CA in various contexts so we can focus on helping them understand how to develop content to reach their particular audience, no matter where or how that audience may exist. One of the things that we need to address further is helping students navigate group collaboration virtually. That has typically been a challenging task even in a face-to-face classroom, but helping students learn to navigate group work in-person and in a virtual space will be relevant.

However, there are some shifts in practice that we should not allow to become the new normal. During the pandemic we were incredibly flexible with students on due dates, class attendance, and the like. This is one change that will not stick. Students need to relearn, or even perhaps learn, the importance of deadlines and the important role of active participation to their own learning. The flexibility was essential during the pandemic but post-pandemic we will return to a more traditional mode of enforcing deadlines and expecting active participation at all times. In the same way that K-12 educational institutions fully plan to return students to their regular in-classroom instructional routines, post-secondary classrooms must return to their pre-pandemic participation expectations in order to prepare students for their future careers and their role as civically engaged citizens.

We believe online and hyflex learning modalities are here to stay, and that students will experience these learning environments prior to entering college. The benefits of these online and hyflex models can help financially disadvantaged students who are often working multiple jobs or have added familial responsibilities, such as caring for younger siblings or older family members, to stay afloat. Having the option to take some classes online or in a hybrid format allows students to help support their families and balance work and going to school at the same time in a more reasonable manner. And although many students in the next several cohorts of college students will have experienced remote learning in some fashion during their K-12 educational journey, we must remain cognizant that not all of those experiences will be equal, based on their first- and second-level digital inequities, and we must continue to provide extended technological support both in terms or devices, access, and training.

Much of the benefits of the lessons learned we've discussed previously benefit students, but there have been benefits for faculty as well. Having the option to Zoom-in for department meetings allows faculty to save gas and commute time which will promote a healthier work-life balance. This also offers adjunct faculty the opportunity to become more engaged, not only in the business of the department, but with the institution, and most importantly with their colleagues. In addition, having to continuously think about how we incorporate new technology and new pedagogical strategies will keep professors engaged and focused on honing their craft. So, while it is challenging to predict exactly what a post-pandemic education landscape will look like, we are certain that professors and students alike will be happy when everyone can see each other's smiling faces. Even if some of the time those faces are on Zoom.

Finally, one strategy, taught to the department during the pandemic by one of our adjunct faculty, will remain: Music. One of our adjuncts adopted the practice of opening the Zoom call classroom five minutes early with music playing. It was always upbeat and fun music, and it clearly got the students excited for class. In the future, whether in person, or on Zoom, starting off with some music and a chance to informally chat with students should remain, or in some cases begin. It clearly improved teacher immediacy and helped start the class off on a dynamic footing. A simple, yet effective, strategy that took a pandemic to learn.

REFERENCES

Dwyer, Karen Kangas and Marlina M. Davidson. 2012. "Speech Center Support Services, the Basic Course, and Oral Communication Assessment." *Basic Communication Course Annual,* 24 article 9: 122–150. https://ecommons.udayton.edu/bcca/vol24/iss1/9

Edwards, Ashley A. Hanna. 2021. "From TED Talks to TikTok: Teaching Digital Communication to Match Student Skills with Employer Desires." *Basic Communication Course Annual,* 33, article 17: 336–341. https://ecommons.udayton.edu/bcca/vol33/iss1/17

Foss, Karen A. 1982. "Communication Apprehension: Resources for the Instructor." *Communication Education,* 33, no. 3: 195–203. doi: 10.1080/03634528209384683

Handel, Marion, Melanie Stephan, Michaela Gläser-Zikuda, Bärbel Kopp, Svenja Bedenlier and Albert Ziegler. 2020. "Digital Readiness and Its Effects on Higher Education Students' Socio-Emotional Perceptions in the context of the COVID-19 pandemic." *Journal of Research on Technology in Education* 1–13. doi: 10.1080/15391523.2020.1846147

Jones-Bodie, Ashley, Lindsey B. Anderson, and Jennifer Hall. 2020. "Where Do You Turn? Student-Identified Resources in the Basic Course Experience, Sources of Information, Feedback, and Help-Seeking Behaviors." *Basic Communication Course Annual,* 32, article 5: 30–54. https://ecommons.udayton.edu/bcca/vol32/iss1/5

Jones, Kiku, Bruce Saulnier, Bruce and Julia Fulick-Jagiela. 2020. "The Importance of Faculty/Staff Support During Times of Crisis. 2020 Proceedings of the EDSIG Conference." June 3 2021. http://proc.iscap.info; https://www.iscap.info

Katz, Vikki S., Amy B. Jordan, and Katherine Ognyanova. 2021. "Digital Inequity, Faculty Communication, and Remote Learning Experiences During the Covid-19 Pandemic: A Survey of U.S. Undergraduates." *Plos one,* 16, no. 2: e0246641. doi: 10.1371/journal.pone.0246641

Kim, Joshua. 2021. "Three Questions for Newly Minted Assistant Provost Derek Bruff." *Inside Higher Education.* May 26 2021. https://www.insidehighered.com/blogs/learning-innovation/3-questions-newly-minted-assistant-provost-derek-bruff, Accessed June 5, 2021.

Lischer, Suzanne, Netkey Safi, and Cheryl Dickson. 2021. "Remote Learning and Students' Mental Health During the Covid-19 Pandemic: A Mixed-Method Enquiry. Prospects." *Prospects* 1–11. doi: 10.1007/s11125-020-09530-w

McCroskey, James C. 1970 "Measures of Communication-Bound Anxiety." *Communication Monographs*, 37, no. 4: 269–277. doi: 10.1080/03637757009375677

McCroskey, James C. 1978. "Validity of the PRCA as An Index of Oral Communication Apprehension." *Communications Monographs*, 45, no. 3: 192–203. doi: 10.1080/03637757809375965

Miller, Ann Neville Miller, Deanna D. Sellnow and Michael G. Strawser. 2021. "Pandemic Pedagogy Challenges and Opportunities: Instruction Communication in Remote, HyFlex, and BlendFlex Courses." *Communication Education*, 70, no. 2: 202–204. doi: 10.1080/03634523.2020.1857418

Moreno, Kasia. 2020. "Silver Linings: Key Lessons From How We Communicate In The New Normal." *Forbes*. November 20 2020. Accessed April 14, 2021. https://www.forbes.com/sites/insights-zoom/2020/11/20/silver-linings-key-lessons-from-how-we-communicate-in-the-new-normal/?sh=2a7939a12784.

Pettit, Emma. 2021. "How to Help Your Faculty Stay Afloat During the Pandemic." In *Burned Out and Overburdened: How to Support the Faculty. The Chronicle of Higher Education.* https://chronicle.ca1.qualtrics.com/WRQualtricsControlPanel/File.php?F=F_ezjCrAD8ItYaw2W.

Prentiss, Suzy. 2021 "Our Basic Course and Communication Skills Training: The Time for Innovation is Now (Yes, Even in a Pandemic)." *Basic Communication Course Annual*, 33, article 19: 346–350. https://ecommons.udayton.edu/bcca/vol33/iss1/19

Preston, Marlene M., Matt J Giglio, and Kristin N. English. 2008. "Redesigning Public Speaking: A Case Study in the Use of Instructional Design to Create the Interchange Model." *Basic Communication Course Annual*, 20, article 10: 138–173. https://ecommons.udayton.edu/bcca/vol20/iss1/10

Schwartzman, Roy. 2020. "Performing Pandemic Pedagogy." *Communication Education*, 69, no. 4: 502–517. doi: 10.1080/03634523.2020.1804602

Tatum, Nicholas T., and T. Kody Frey. 2021. "(In)flexibility During Uncertainty? Conceptualizing Instructor Strictness During a Global Pandemic." *Communication Education*, 70, no. 2: 214–216. doi: 10.1080/03634523.2020.1857419

Upchurch, William R. 2014. "Public Address as the Basic Communication Course." *Basic Communication Course Annual*, 26, article 8: 25–33. https://ecommons.udayton.edu/bcca/vol26/iss1/8

Wallace, Samuel P. 2015. "A Model for the Development of a Sustainable Basic Course in Communication." *Basic Communication Course Annual*, 27, article 11: 78–101. https://ecommons.udayton.edu/bcca/vol27/iss1/11

Westwick, Joshua N., and Sherwyn P. Morreale. 2021. "Advancing an Agenda for Instructional Preparedness: Lessons Learned from the Transition to Remote Learning." *Communication Education*, 70, no. 2: 217–222. doi: 10.1080/03634523.2020.1857416

Westwick, Joshua N., Karla M. Hunter, and Laurie L. Haleta, 2015. "Shaking in Their Digital Boots: Anxiety and Competence in the Online Basic Public Speaking Course." *Basic Communication Course Annual*, 27, article 10: 43–77. https://ecommons.udayton.edu/bcca/vol27/iss1/10

Chapter 6

Networked Family Spirit

Paradox and Dialectical Tensions in Moving a Small, Liberal Arts University Online[1]

Katherine Hampsten and Amanda Hill

The COVID-19 pandemic created chaos among institutions of higher learning in early 2020. Universities and colleges nationwide sent students home for spring Break without knowledge of how or when it would be safe for them to return. This crisis presented a range of urgent concerns for academic communities, including health and safety, equity, academic rigor, and budgetary needs. The pandemic's effects continue to impact higher education on a large scale. Within a year of the pandemic's onset, 650,000 workers within higher education would lose their jobs (Bauman 2021), many of whom were among lower-wage workers (Douglas-Gabriel and Fowers 2020).

As students waited to return to their campuses, administrators and faculty patched together plans to ensure some degree of continuity in course instruction by moving face-to-face courses online. While some faculty were experienced in online learning, others faced the sudden transition with panic and/or a skill deficit (Westwick and Morreale 2021). Many faculty and students quickly became burned out and disenchanted with their hastily assembled online courses (Lang 2020). Not all students, however, fared equally well. The pandemic further revealed inequities and fissures in higher education, with lower income and students of color encountering greater difficulties in the transition (Garcia and Weiss 2020; Hampsten 2021).

While this abrupt shift in instruction strained all institutions, small, private universities faced unique challenges. In this chapter, we present a case study that examines how a small, faith-based, liberal arts university situated in a COVID-19 hotspot responded to the crisis. While the institution worked to ensure that consistent quality education would be available to all students, several challenges emerged. Not all faculty members were trained in online learning. Many students returned to homes that were not equipped with reliable internet service and/or technical devices (Garnham 2021). Further, as an institution focused on creating family spirit, consideration needed to be given to how the collegial and familial community that exists on campus might be replicated online. This case study provides a lens through which to explore how post-pandemic pedagogy will be marked by paradox and dialectical tension.

Specifically, St. Mary's University (St. Mary's) in San Antonio, Texas, experienced a host of unique concerns. As a small, private, Catholic and Marianist University with a Hispanic-Serving Institution designation (St. Mary's University 2020), St. Mary's culture embraces the Characteristics of Marianist Education (CMEs) ("Characteristics of a Marianist Education" 2021). This Marianist charism emphasizes specific values, including "educating in the family spirit," a commitment to an "integral, quality education," and embracing "adaptation and change." The importance of the CMEs proved critical for the transition to online learning. While the institution hoped to ensure that consistent quality education would be available to all students, several challenges emerged.

In this case study, we analyze data including university communications, institutional research data, and data from a faculty readiness program about online teaching that one of the authors (Hill) facilitated. Against this backdrop, multiple competing demands emerge. For example, the institution needed to educate in the family spirit, but students were forced off campus. Additionally, it strove to provide an integral, quality education, but a real digital divide exists for its students. Finally, faculty were tasked to educate for adaptation and change, but many were not prepared for such an extreme and rapid change. To make sense of this paradox (Tracy 2004), we employ a theoretical lens of dialectical tensions (Baxter and Montgomery 1996; Baxter 2011). We explore the dialectical tensions that emerged during the pandemic, including *integration/connection*, *stability/change*, and *short-/long-term orientation*.

This case study considers the ways in which this university adapted to meet the needs and demands of its students during the time of the COVID-19 pandemic. We examine the specific considerations of the university and its students as stakeholders to investigate how the teaching adaptations made by the university changed patterns of communication and education. While these changes were made rapidly in response to a worldwide crisis, it seems likely that the lingering effects of these changes will permanently alter the way in which faculty and the university prepares for instruction well into the future. As such, it is important to consider how the foundational values of institutions like St. Mary's grounded the adaptations that occurred and will occur moving forward. By considering the tensions that exist between the university's mission and identity in relation to the realities of the crisis, the authors open a conversation about larger dialectical tensions within the advancement of online learning schemas.

REVIEW OF LITERATURE

Pressures upon Small, Liberal Arts Institutions

While the COVID-19 crisis impacted all institutions of higher education, the effects on small, liberal arts universities and colleges were perhaps most critical. For decades, higher education experts have warned of these institutions' eventual demise (Bonvillian and Murphy 1996; Breneman 1994). These arguments suggest that, although a liberal arts education offers many benefits to students and society at large, it is "on the brink" of extinction (Ferrall, Jr. 2011). Indeed, recent years have seen declining enrollments in majors and degrees affiliated with liberal arts, in part due to the perception that these academic fail to prepare students for the current and future workforce (Marcus 2018), particularly jobs in the technical industries (Harris 2018). Consequently, experts advise small liberal arts colleges to take measures such as increasing enrollment for financial survival (Docking and Curton 2015), actively attracting students from higher-income backgrounds, and updating curriculum to teach skills perceived as necessary for the twenty-first century (Varlotta 2018) in order to survive.

Theories of Paradox and Dialectical Tensions

Clearly, liberal arts institutions are navigating a matrix of demands. Prior research has relied upon theories of paradox and dialectical tensions to approach the complexities in organizations. These theories both capture the ways that organizations experience competing demands and needs (Ashcraft and Tretheway 2004) within a range of complex contexts, such as organizational downsizing (Fairhurst et al. 2002), sexual harassment in a healthcare setting (McGuire et al. 2006), volunteer/manager communication within the nonprofit sector (McNamee and Peterson 2014), organizational change (Hoelscher 2019), and college students' perceptions of fear of missing out, or FOMO (Harrigan et al. 2021).

Researchers define and characterize paradoxes and dialectical tensions in different ways (Putnam 1986; Tracy 2004). Within communication, researchers have applied relational dialectics as developed by Baxter (with Montgomery 1996, 2011) to the common dialectical tensions within organizations. While researchers have identified multiple types of tensions, Baxter isolates tensions commonly experienced in relationships. These tensions include broad categories such as *integration/separation, stability/change*, and *expression/nonexpression*.

In this project, we adopt the approach of by prior researchers to take insight from both approaches to paradox and dialectical theory (Smith and Tracey 2016). Rather than viewing dialects as either/or constructs, we acknowledge the duality, or both/and nature, that reside within contradictions (Farjoun 2010). Furthermore, we take a constitutive approach that encompasses contradictions, dialectics, and paradoxes as inherent components of organizational life (Putnam et al. 2016).

This theoretical approach is particularly suited to studying organizational responses to the pandemic. Carmine et al. (2021) explored multiple facets of how paradox frames organizational tensions during the COVID-19 pandemic. These tensions include those of temporality, such as long-term versus short-term needs; knowledge sharing versus privacy; cooperation versus competition with other organizations; and survival versus innovation and change. Carmine et al. (2021) note that paradox research's focus on "the tensions that organizations experience during the pandemic and their responses," is uniquely situated as a lens through which to understand organizational experiences of COVID-19 (138).

Like Carmine et al. (2021), we agree this theoretical approach can "provide shards of clarity to this otherwise incomprehensible event" (138). In this project, we employ such an approach to identify and understand the complexities that are embedded within a university's response to COVID-19. By considering the tensions that exist between the university's mission and identity in relation to the realities of the crisis, the authors open a conversation about larger dialectical tensions within the advancement of online learning schemas. Therefore, we ask the following research question:

RQ: How did a small, faith-based liberal arts university manage paradoxical demands during the COVID-19 pandemic?

METHOD

Past research has employed the case study method as a way to understand organizational complexities, including organizational tensions (Mitra and Fyke 2017). This project uses a qualitative, descriptive case approach (Yin 2018) as a way to examine the phenomena of the COVID-19 response within the context of St. Mary's. Case study as a methodology acknowledges the interplay between a phenomenon and its context. Consequently, this method allows us to examine how the university's response to the COVID-19 pandemic was "influenced by the context within which it is situated" (Baxter and Jack 2008, 556).

As such, we first bound the case (Thomas 2015) to activities at St. Mary's between March 2020—September 2020. This time period represents the first six months of the pandemic. The time period also reflects the close of the spring 2020 semester, the summer season, and the start of the fall 2020 semester. We believe that these particular dates demonstrate a wide variety of pandemic responses, including the first initial responses in spring, the summer holidays in which faculty and administrators completed extensive planning and training, and the start of the "new normal" of a long semester during the pandemic.

Next, we collected a range of data, including mass email messages from administrators to faculty and students, institutional data including student demographics, student performance, and student/faculty survey responses, and multiple discussions about this project with university members, including our dean. We also actively reflected on our own experiences as faculty during this time, which included teaching virtually (Hill and Hampsten) and developing and leading a faculty instructional program over the summer (Hill). Throughout this data collection phase, we kept the following advice in mind regarding case study methods: "Each data source is one piece of the 'puzzle,' with each piece contributing to the researcher's understanding of the whole phenomenon. This convergence adds strength to the findings as the various strands of data are braided together to promote a greater understanding of the case" (Baxter and Jack 2008, 554).

Finally, we individually reviewed the data, making extensive notes. Collectively, we looked for emergent themes and points of tension within the data. We also frequently met to discuss our ongoing analysis, seeking points of convergence, and reconciling points of divergence.

DATA

Contextualizing St. Mary's

We collected and reviewed data regarding the university; its history, location, and faculty/student demographics; as well as institutional data the university collected during the pandemic. St. Mary's is a small, private, Catholic and Marianist university that sits on the Westside of San Antonio, Texas, United States, that was founded by the Brothers of the Society of Mary, or Marianists, in 1852. The university is one of three Marianist universities in the United States. St. Mary's currently serves approximately 3,500 students across undergraduate and graduate levels, including residential, doctoral and law degree-seeking students. The campus also hosts multiple residences for professed Marianists, several of whom visibly lead, teach and serve on campus.

Location as COVID-19 "Hotspot"

The university campus is located on San Antonio's historical Westside, minutes from the downtown center. The university's location is important when considering evidence that the rate of poverty in San Antonio directly corresponded to increased COVID-19 density within the city's population (Chen and Jiao 2020), which is further complicated by the shear spread of the virus across the city: San Antonio was named the 4th fastest growing "hotspot" for COVID19 in June 2020 (King 2020; Mendoza 2020). When the COVID-19 virus became prevalent in the spring of 2020, San Antonio responded by placing restrictions on large gatherings, enacting safety regulations on local businesses, and providing regular updates from city leaders ("COVID-19" 2021). Despite these efforts, COVID-19 infection and related hospitalization rates rose exponentially. Because many of the university's students are from San Antonio and other Texas regions, the community experienced the virus's effects.

Students' Hardships

These effects included the death of loved ones, reprioritized responsibilities, and financial hardships. Krogstad et al. (2020) suggest financial hardships, especially, were increasingly felt by Hispanic populations, which accounts for 64 percent of San Antonio's population ("COVD-19 in Numbers" 2021). Students' financial hardships are also a large consideration for the university's fiscal calculations, especially considering a significant portion comes from students' room and board fees. For the 2020–2021 academic year, St. Mary's tuition rates were $32,700 for courses and approximately an additional $10,000 for room, board, and fees ("Tuition" 2021).

St. Mary's was a founding member of the Hispanic Association of Colleges and Universities (HACU) and is a Hispanic-Serving Institution (HSI). 67.9 percent of the university's undergraduate students identify as Hispanic or Latino. While the demographics have fluctuated over time, Mexican American students have a long history with the institution and the Marianists. The former St. Mary's College served students of multiple ethnicities, including local Mexican American students and "a large Mexican and Tejano student body from the Mexican border region and interior" as early as the late nineteenth century (Flores 2019, quoting Gerald E. Poyo). Currently, almost half of St. Mary's students identify as first-generation college students. In 2019, 40 percent of the student body was classified as Pell Eligible ("St. Mary's Awarded $1.3 Million Grant to Help Underserved Students Finish College" 2020). Students who are eligible for these federal education grants "display exceptional financial need" ("Federal Pell Grants are Usually Awarded Only to Undergraduate Students" 2021). 51 percent of undergraduate students come from Bexar County, where San Antonio is located, and another 37 percent come from other counties within Texas. By contrast, only 14 percent of faculty identify as Hispanic origin. The majority of faculty (66 percent) identifies as white, non-Hispanic. In fall 2019, a total of 3,514 students were enrolled in undergraduate, graduate, and law programs, 2,270 of which were undergraduate students. 71.5 percent of undergraduate students were full-time and 1,158 undergraduate students were living on campus (Unpublished Raw Data, St. Mary's).

Mission and CMEs

According to the university's webpage, students at St. Mary's "experience a nurturing and vibrant community" that fosters a "holistic education in a faith-centered, family-spirit environment" ("About St. Mary's" 2021). As part of their educational experience, students "of all faiths, and of no faith," are invited to "join our community and search for truth together" ("About St. Mary's" 2021). The mission statement states that the university "fosters the formation of people in faith and educates leaders for the common good through community, integrated liberal arts and professional education, and academic excellence" ("About St. Mary's" 2021). This mission is grounded in the Characteristics of Marianist Education (CMEs), which guide all Marianist educational institutions. The CMES are as follows: (1) educate for formation in faith; (2) provide an integral quality education; (3) educate in the family spirit; (4) educate for service, justice and peace, and integrity of creation; and, (5) educate for adaptation and change ("Characteristics of a Marianist Education" 2021).

The CMEs form an active part of organizational life for multiple stakeholder groups across the university. For example, faculty and staff review and discuss them as part of their new employee orientation. New faculty may participate in the "Mentor for Mission Program" to learn how to integrate the spirit of the CMEs into their teaching and service at the university ("Mentor for Mission Program for New Faculty" 2021). Administrators cite them in their external communications (see, e.g., Roberts 2020). The CMEs inform the work of institutional groups such as the Center for Catholic Studies ("Center for Catholic Studies" 2021) and the Community for Teaching and Learning ("Community for Teaching and Learning" 2021). They inspire community events, such as the "Engaging the Mission Conversations" ("Engaging the Mission Conversations" 2021).

Students actively engage with the CMEs, as well. New students learn about the CMEs as part of their new student orientation. Resident hall programming is designed to teach students how to apply the CMEs "to their li[ves] and help them develop and grow" ("Student Staff" 2021). In sum, the CMEs animate life at

St. Mary's across multiple levels and stakeholder groups. These characteristics guide the university's practices. They played a key component in considering what elements of the university needed to be transitioned into the online learning environments and how these could be incorporated into a digital landscape.

Administrative and Faculty Responses to the Transition to Online Learning

In the summer of 2020, after an abrupt end to in-person learning during the spring semester, St. Mary's undertook significant new programming to develop faculty readiness for the summer and fall 2020 semesters. Educating for adaptation and change is particularly fitting for times of crisis, as we are in now, yet in their own ways, each of these characteristics manifested themselves within faculty's evolving curriculum. In order to help faculty prepare to undertake hybrid classes as well as synchronous and asynchronous online classes, the university encouraged all faculty members to complete a certificate in online training through the Academic Technology Services (ATS) and to participate in an online preparedness training webinars and brown-bag discussions through the Community for Teaching and Learning (CTL).

Online Teaching Program

The Online Teaching Certification Program (OTCP) has been in place since 2012 as a way to help faculty learn the processes and best practices of using digital infrastructures such as Canvas to teach online successfully and effectively. In the fall of 2019, less than a quarter (93 faculty) of full-time and part-time faculty were certified through the program. With the closure of campus in spring 2020 and the subsequent transition to online learning, the university pushed to certify as many faculty members as possible in online teaching. While this program was not necessary before faculty were allowed to teach online, there was a significant increase in faculty participation with the certification program. By the fall 2020 semester, 278 faculty members, out of approximately 220 full-time and 180 part-time faculty ("Consumer Information" 2021), had been certified through OTCP. This increase was made possible due to the ATS offering five additional sessions of the OTCP training between April and July 2020. Between February and July, 242 faculty members enrolled in the program, with 174 completing the program before September 2020 and 55 more participants were in the process of completing the program (Unpublished Raw Data, St. Mary's).

"Prepared to Pivot"

ATS's certification program was complemented by the "Prepared to Pivot" webinar series hosted by the CTL. The CTL hosted two webinar orientations for faculty moving to teaching online. These programs, titled "Prepared to

Pivot," were created in May 2020 and took place in June and July. They were designed to help faculty understand the spaces of hybrid learning that would take place during the fall semester: In-Person/Virtual (in-person and online synchronous) and Virtual (online asynchronous) as well as to help faculty transition their courses over to a digital format both in terms of course platform software (Canvas) and in terms of curriculum mapping and lesson design. The orientations consisted of six seminar sessions which took place over the course of three weeks. Once per week seminars were conducted to provide insight from campus organizations, faculty, and students to talk about best practices for online teaching and for moving courses online. The final three sessions were optional debrief sessions held at the end of each week to continue the conversations about the content learned earlier that week in the seminars.

In addition to the summer sessions, a Canvas course was set up for faculty to interact with one another on the topics discussed. 181 unique faculty members participated in at least one webinar session, with 107 attending all three seminar sessions of a single program virtually over Zoom. The sessions were additionally recorded for those who could not attend all of the seminars. Additionally, although the two programs were nearly identical in content, 22 faculty members attended seminars in both sessions, with 19 faculty members attending 4 or more seminars between the two programs. The ability to attend seminars across both programs and also to watch recordings of the webinars allowed an additional 32 faculty members to complete all 3 of the webinar sessions, meaning that a total of 139 faculty members attended all 3 webinars in some fashion (Unpublished Raw Data, St. Mary's). These faculty members were awarded a small technological device such a Logitech web camera, Bluetooth headphones, or a wireless slate and pen for their attendance.

Maintaining Community in Online Learning

On March 11, 2020, St. Mary's sent a formal notification to faculty, staff, and students, that they would be extending spring Break by an extra week. In a separate email sent that same day, the university encouraged its faculty to use the extra week to move all of its courses online in anticipation of a potential shift. Two days later, the university officially announced all coursework would be completed online for the remainder of the semester. As an institution, we were not alone. Universities across the world shuttered for (at that point) an undisclosed period of time as they waited to determine the severity and impact of the COVID-19 pandemic.

The importance of the CMEs proved critical for the transition to online learning. St. Mary's wanted to ensure that consistent quality education would be available to all students even in adapted technologically driven learning environments that many faculty members had not previously employed. Further, as a campus focused on creating family spirit, consideration was given to how the collegial and familial community that exists on campus, might be remediated online.

"Rattler Real Talk" Survey

To understand how students and faculty were coping with the transition in the fall 2020 semester, two students worked with the Rattler Student Success Center, an on-campus organization dedicated to advancing students' academic success, to survey faculty and first-year and transfer students about their experiences of learning during the pandemic. The students who responded came from three different colleges across campus: the College of Arts, Humanities, and Social Science (42.11 percent), the School of Science, Engineering, and Technology (36.84 percent), and the Greehey School of Business (21.05 percent). 71.05 percent of the students who responded self–identified as Latino or Hispanic. Based on the survey results, the Rattler Student Success Center partnered with the Counseling Center to develop workshops to address student concerns. 39 students and 56 faculty members engaged in the "Rattler Real Talk Survey" (Unpublished Raw Data, St. Mary's).

Although the survey is not an established instrument enabling us to report reliability/validity data for these research purposes, its findings are useful for this qualitative case study. While the number of respondents was relatively low, this survey provides a glimpse into the student/faculty perspective during fall 2020. Furthermore, the university acknowledged the survey and facilitated student workshops based on the needs the survey identified. We highlight the survey here as an important piece of our total data collection.

Student Perception of Connection

The students reported feeling "out of place/awkward/alone" (36.84 percent) "connected closely with one other student" (21.05 percent), "connected closely with more than one other student" (18.42 percent), "felt like a belonged immediately" (15.79 percent) during the first weeks of the fall 2020 semester. At the time the students were taking the survey, the students reported feeling "out of place/awkward/alone" (21.26 percent), "one friend I feel closely connected to" (16.22 percent), "more than one friend I feel closely connected to" (27.03 percent), "feel like I belong" (27.03 percent). Additionally, 16.22 percent of respondents said it was very difficult to make friends, 29.73 percent said it was difficult, 29.73 percent answered neutral, and 24.32 percent said it was easy. No students reported that making friends was very easy (Unpublished Raw Data, St. Mary's).

Only one student identified as feeling "connected closely with one professor/faculty member" during the first few weeks of college. At the time of survey completion, no students identified as having this connection. Two students selected that they feel "connected closely with more than one professor/faculty member" during the first few weeks of the semester, which jumped to three students by the time of the survey completion. This means that out of the 39 students who engaged in the survey, very few have created strong relationships with faculty members. This is important for the development and maintenance of the sense of community on which St. Mary's prides itself. However, unlike student responses to the difficulty in making friends, 5.41 percent of students said it was very easy to connect online with faculty or staff, 43.24 percent said it was easy, 27.03 percent answered neutral, 13.51 percent answered difficult, and 10.81 percent said it was very difficult. On average, then, students report that it is easier to connect with faculty members than it is to make friends; however, more students reported feeling closer to other students than they do to faculty members. Approximately half of the students (18) reported reaching out to professors and staff for support regarding academic concerns (Unpublished Raw Data, St. Mary's).

Student Perceptions of Academic Performance

36.23 percent of student respondents in the Rattler Real Talk survey reported concern about their current academic grades. The majority of students (56.76 percent) also felt that their academic performance has worsened as a result of a virtual learning environment. 35.14 percent were undetermined in response to this question and only 8.11% said the online environment probably or definitely did not affect their academic performance. Students additionally reported feeling concerned about their mental well-being (33.33 percent), and about financial, housing, food, and/or health insecurities (30.43 percent), factors which can impact a student's ability to succeed academically (Unpublished Raw Data, St. Mary's).

A sample of term GPAs from undergraduate students across the university also suggests student academic performance was significantly affected by the transition to online learning and the impact of the COVID-19. These GPAs were selected through a process of availability sampling. A sample of term GPAs from full-time and part-time students in fall 2019 (2,605 students) and a sample of term GPAs from full-time and part-time students in fall 2020 (2,110 students) shows a significant decline in student academic success. Table 6.1 shows a decrease in the percentage of students earning a term GPA of 2.5 or higher (although the percentage of students earning a term GPA between 3.5 and 3.9 remained the same). There is additionally an increase

Table 6.1 Comparison of Sample Student Term GPAs between Fall 2019 and Fall 2020

Term GPAs	Fall 2019	Fall 2020	Fall 2019 (%)	Fall 2020 (%)
4.0	290.0	187	11.13	8.86
3.5–3.9	830.0	673	31.86	31.90
3–3.4	578.0	376	22.19	17.82
2.5–2.9	293	193	11.25	9.15
2.0–2.4	126.0	103	4.84	4.88
1.5–1.9	39.0	50	1.50	2.37
0.5–0.9	16.0	32	0.61	1.52
0.1–0.4	7.0	10	0.27	0.47
0.0	30.0	52	1.15	2.46

of students earning a term GPA of 2.4 or below (Unpublished Raw Data, St. Mary's).

Additionally, while data are not yet available beyond the 2016 cohort, the 4-year graduation rate percentages demonstrate differences between Hispanics and non-Hispanics. For the 2016 cohort, who would have graduated in spring 2020 under a 4-year degree plan, Hispanic students dropped from a 47 percent graduation rate in the 2015 cohort (2019 graduation) to a 42 percent graduation rate. This drop is greater than the graduation rates for the previous two years, as the 2014 cohort had a 45 percent graduation rate and the 2013 cohort had a 47 percent graduation rate. Non-Hispanic students' graduations rates increased from the 2015 cohort (47 percent) to 2016 cohort (49 percent). This decrease in graduation rates among Hispanic students tracks with national averages, as this group tends to graduate from four-year institutions at a 12 percent lower rate than white students do (Fain 2020).

Faculty Perceptions of Student Engagement

Finally, faculty provided feedback about their perceptions of the transition to online learning. This feedback predominately centered around faculty's concerns about students being disengaged during classes delivered via Zoom. For example, in the Rattler Real Talk Survey, 69.2 percent of faculty noted that the majority of students did not turn their cameras on during class. Faculty connected the lack of on-camera presence to a perception of students' lack of engagement, building connections, and an instructor's ability to gauge understanding of course materials. One professor explained the tension in virtual learning and creating connection in the following way:

> Talking to a screen full of blank boxes in an empty room is the ultimate downer. If this became the norm, I'd resign. I was not trained for radio, nor do I believe that liberal education is the mere transmission of data. Everything about the

virtual format counteracts what should constitute genuine education: connection with others; accountability in the classroom as the time and place of education; dialogue; etc.

Another professor agreed: "Liberal education is more than instruction and requires genuine encounter. Nobody was meaningfully present this whole semester." Many professors additionally commented on the need for students to communicate with their instructors to create community, gain support, and get more information about coursework (Unpublished Raw Data, St. Mary's).

As faculty ourselves, we both self-reflexively observed the difficulty in moving classes online. For example, Hampsten observed that some of her classes were more easily adapted to online instruction than were other classes. In particular, she was teaching Research Methods in Communication when students abruptly returned home after spring Break. The research projects that the students had been developing suffered, with some students unable to access the data they needed to complete their research. Furthermore, due to the interruptions in face-to-face interaction, the professor's ability to supervise projects was hindered, as well. Ultimately, Hampsten chose to revise the original assignment requirements to measure student learning more equitably under these new circumstances. These sorts of issues and compromises were typical among the faculty we observed.

ANALYSIS

To answer our research question—*how did St. Mary's manage paradoxical demands during the COVID-19 pandemic*—we examine the tensions that emerged in our research. These data suggest that St. Mary's faced a complex range of pressures during the pandemic. Not only were administrators and faculty adjusting to the "new normal" of pandemic pedagogy, but the unique context of St. Mary's location and student population further complicated the response. Multiple tensions emerged within the data, particularly when examined against the embedded values of the CMEs. These tensions intersect and dovetail with each other, revealing a web of paradoxes.

Emergent Tensions

A prevalent tension that emerged was *integration/separation*. This tension connects to the CME to "educate in the family spirit." Prior to the pandemic, the "family spirit" was evident in the daily activities of the university community. However, campus life shifted dramatically when students were sent home after spring Break and in-person classes shifted to online learning.

As the faculty responses about online pedagogy imply (above), this sudden shift alarmed faculty, who noticed the dramatic difference in their students' behaviors.

These concerns around *integration/separation* intersect with the tension of *stability/change*. Obviously, the pandemic necessitated a cataclysmic shift in higher education. One shift was the physical separation of students from each other and faculty after March 2020, as noted above. University communications during this time revealed multiple uncertainties of the pandemic's duration. For example, students and faculty expected to have spring Break extended only by week. Administrators were unsure of how fall instruction would or could resume. Students and instructors who had avoided online instruction suddenly had to learn new modes of pedagogy. This change connects (and gives new meaning) to the CME of "educate for adaptation and change." Significantly, though, St. Mary's members yearned for the stability of pre-pandemic instruction and campus life.

Finally, we identify a third tension around *short-/long-term orientation*. This tension connects to the CME to "provide an integral, quality education." In the rush to respond to the pandemic, priorities shifted. The university community's health and safety rose to highest concern. Consequently, administrators and faculty grew concerned that their academic commitments to students were at risk of being compromised. Administrators and staff encouraged faculty to complete workshops in online instruction practices. As faculty members ourselves, we observed how allowances needed to be made for some students missing classes, not participating in class discussions in Zoom, submitting work late, or managing COVID-19's effects on themselves and/or families. Yet these classroom management decisions, which appeared necessary in the short term, would not be viable in the long term.

Furthermore, the data about academic success measures, as demonstrated in data about GPA and graduation rates, is also reflective of this tension. The downward trends during this time period, particularly for Hispanic students, may be attributed directly to the short-term stresses of the pandemic. However, the long-term effects of this pandemic upon students will not be known until well into the future.

Paradox Theory

A paradox theory approach is useful in making sense of these dialectical tensions and St. Mary's response to them. Through this lens, the contradictions inherent in the dialectal tensions are acknowledged. For example, it is *because of* the sense of connection and community that existed before the pandemic that we can understand the isolation that was felt sharply in its absence. Rather than managing the contradictions as *either/or* propositions, paradox acknowledges the *both/and* nature of how these tensions are enmeshed and inseparable.

Additionally, paradox theory brings to light the ways in which the tensions intersect and impact each other. For example, the loss of community (evident in *integration/separation*) impacted student learning as students became less interactive in class and scores decreased. Student learning intersects with the rapid shift to online instruction and, for many students, moving back home (evident in *stability/change*). Faculty responded by attending online learning workshops and adapting their classroom expectations but worry that these efforts are not sustainable (*short/long-term orientation*), that these teaching new methods degrade educational quality (*stability/change*) and sacrifice the type of learning the in-class professor/student relationship provides (*integration/separation*).

CONCLUSIONS AND IMPLICATIONS FOR POST-PANDEMIC PEDAGOGY

This case study demonstrates how a small, liberal arts university responded to multiple tensions related to the pandemic in 2020. At first glance, St. Mary's appeared to be at risk in multiple ways. Its location in a COVID-19 hotspot, the particular needs of its student body, and the seemingly already perilous position of small, liberal arts institutions suggested that St. Mary's would be primed for struggle. Furthermore, in this time of crisis, living up to the values inherent within the CMEs may seem unrealistic.

These factors, however, only reflect one side of the struggle. Through the lens of dialectics and paradox, we can acknowledge and embrace multiple dialectics in their full complexity. Rather than focusing only upon the strains, this lens invites a perspective that acknowledges how these strains could also be understood as opportunities. For example, *because* St. Mary's was small and private, it could respond to the chaos of the pandemic with a kind of creativity and agility that larger institutions, with their entrenched bureaucracies, may not have. Additionally, while the CMEs could seem restrictive, they provided an institutional touchstone that was invaluable in guiding the quick decisions administrators and faculty made. In sum, we understand this case as a *both/and* situation, in which the dialectics *both* enabled *and* constrained the actions of the university and its members.

We implore administrators and educators to apply this framework as they approach pedagogy in the current and future, post-pandemic world. While each institution has its unique cultures and concerns, understanding those variables as *both* opportunities *and* constraints opens up new possibilities for growth and adaptability. While post-pandemic pedagogy will look much different than it did before March 2020, embracing the dialectical tensions and paradoxes can help educators move forward.

NOTE

1. We would like to thank Leona Pallansch, Interim Dean of the College of Arts, Humanities, and Social Sciences at St. Mary's University, for her generous ideas and assistance with data collection for this project.

REFERENCES

"About St. Mary's." St. Mary's University. Accessed May 24, 2021. https://stmartyx.edu/about.
Ashcraft, Karen L. and Angela Tretheway. 2004. "Developing Tension: An Agenda for Applied Research on the Organization of Irrationality." *Journal of Applied Communication Research* 32, no. 2: 171–181. doi:10.1080/14795752.2004.10058565.
Bauman, Dan. 2021, April 19. "Here's Who Was Hit Hardest by Higher Ed's Pandemic-Driven Job Losses." *The Chronicle of Higher Education.* https://www.chronicle.com/article/heres-who-was-hit-hardest-by-higher-eds-pandemic-driven-job-losses.
Baxter, Leslie A. and Barbara. M. Montgomery. 1996. *Relating: Dialogues and Dialectics.* New York: The Guilford Press.
Baxter, Leslie A. 2011. *Voicing Relationships: A Dialogic Perspective.* Thousand Oaks, CA: Sage.
Baxter, Pamela and Susan Jack. 2008. "Qualitative Case Study Methodology: Study Design and Implementation for Novice Researchers." *The Qualitative Report* 13, no. 4: 544–559. doi:10.46743/2160-3715/2008.1573.
Bonvillian, Gary and Robert Murphy. 1996. *The Liberal Arts College Adapting to Change: The Survival of Small Schools.* New York: Routledge.
Breneman, David W. 1994. *Liberal Arts Colleges: Thriving, Surviving, or Endangered?* Washington, DC: Brookings Institution Press.
Carmine, Simone, Constaine Andriopoulos, Manto Gotsi, Charmine E. J. Hartel, Anna Krzeminska, Nkosana Mafico, Camille Pradies, Hassan Raza, Tatbeeq Raza-Ullah, Stephanie Schrage, Garima Sharma, Natalie Slawinski, Lea Stadtler, Andrea Tunarosa, Casper Winther-Hansen, and Joshua Keller. 2021. "A Paradox Approach to Organizational Tensions During the Pandemic Crisis." *Journal of Management Inquiry* 30, no. 2: 138–153. doi:10.1177%2F1056492620986863.
"Center for Catholic Studies." 2021. St. Mary's University. Accessed May 24, 2021. https://www.stmarytx.edu/academics/centers/catholic-studies/.
"Characteristics of Marianist Education." The Marianist Province of the United States. Accessed May 24, 2021. https://www.marianist.com/wp-content/uploads/2017/10/CME_09012016.pdf.

Chen, Yefu and Junfeng Jiao. 2020. "Relationship Between Socio-Demographics and COVID-19: A Case Study in Three Texas Regions." *SSRN Electronic Journal*. doi:10.2139/ssrn.3636484.

"Community for Teaching and Learning." 2021. St. Mary's University. Accessed May 24, 2021. https://www.stmarytx.edu/academics/centers/teaching-learning/.

"Consumer Information." 2021. St. Mary's University. Accessed May 24, 2021. https://www.stmarytx.edu/compliance/consumer-information/.

"COVID-19." 2021. City of San Antonio. Accessed May 24, 2021. https://covid19.sanantonio.gov.

"COVD-19 in Numbers." 2021. Data USA. https://datausa.io/profile/geo/san-antonio-tx/. Accessed May 24, 2021.

Docking, Jeffrey R. and Carman C. Curton. 2015. *Crisis in Higher Education: A Plan to Save Small Liberal Arts Colleges in America*. East Lansing, MI: Michigan State University Press.

Douglas-Gabriel, Danielle and Alyssa Fowers. 2020. "The Lowest-Paid Workers in Higher Education are Suffering the Highest Job Losses." *Washington Post*, November 17, 2020. https://www.washingtonpost.com/education/2020/11/17/higher-ed-job-loss/.

"Engaging the Mission Conversations." 2021. St. Mary's University. Accessed May 24, 2021. https://www.stmarytx.edu/academics/centers/catholic-studies/faculty-development/engaging-the-mission/

Fain, P. 2020. "Latinos' Degree Completion Increases; Equity Gaps Remain." *Inside Higher Ed*, August 12, 2020. https://www.insidehighered.com/quicktakes/2020/08/12/latinos-degree-completion-increases-equity-gaps-remain.

Fairhust, Gail T., Francois Cooren, and Daniel J. Cahill. 2002. "Discursiveness, Contradiction, and Unintended Consequences in Successive Downsizings." *Management Communication Quarterly* 15, no. 4. doi:10.1177/0893318902154001.

Farjoun, Moshe. 2010. "Beyond Dualism: Stability and Change as Duality." *The Academy of Management Review* 35, no. 2: 202–225. https://www.jstor.org/stable/25682409.

Ferrall, Jr., Victor E. 2011. *Liberal Arts at the Brink*. Boston, MA: Harvard University Press.

"Federal Pell Grants are Usually Awarded Only to Undergraduate Students." Federal Student Aid. Accessed May 24, 2021. https://studentaid.gov/understand-aid/types/grants/pell

Flores, Anndria. 2019. "Professor and Student Research St. Mary's Hispanic-Serving History." *St. Mary's University*, November 14, 2019. https://www.stmarytx.edu/2019/educational-pioneers/.

Garcia, Emma and Elaine Weiss. 2020. "COVID-19 and Student Performance, Equity, and U.S. Education Policy." *Economic Policy Institute*. September 10, 2020. https://www.epi.org/publication/the-consequences-of-the-covid-19-pandemic-for-education-performance-and-equity-in-the-united-states-what-can-we-learn-from-pre-pandemic-research-to-inform-relief-recovery-and-rebuilding/.

Garnham, Juan Pablo. 2021. "Millions of Texans Still Don't Have Broadband Access. Some Lawmakers are Trying to Change That." *Texas Tribune*, March 8, 2021. https://www.texastribune.org/2021/03/08/internet-broadband-texas/.

Hampsten, Katherine. 2021. "Embracing Discomfort and Resisting a Return to "The Good Old Days": A Call to Communication Educators." *Communication Education* 70, no. 2: 208–210. doi:10.1080/03634523.2020.1857413.

Harrigan, Meredith Marko, Iris Benz, Christopher Hauck, Emily LaRocca, Rachel Renders, and Stephanie Roney. 2021. "The Dialectical Experience of the Fear of Missing Out for U.S. American iGen Emerging Adult College Students." *Journal of Applied Communication Research* 1–17. doi:10.1080/00909882.2021.1898656.

Harris, Adam. 2018. "The Liberal Arts May Not Survive the 21st Century." *The Atlantic*, December 13, 2018. https://www.theatlantic.com/education/archive/2018/12/the-liberal-arts-may-not-survive-the-21st-century/577876/.

Hoelscher, Carissa S. 2019. "Collaboration for Strategic Change: Examining Dialectical Tensions in an Interorganizational Change Effort." *Management Communication Quarterly* 33, no. 3: 329–362. doi:10.1177/0893318919834340.

"How will the pandemic change higher education?" 2020. *The Chronicle of Higher Education*, April 10. https://www.chronicle.com/article/how-will-the-pandemic-change-higher-education/.

King, Cody. 2020. "San Antonio Metro Area Named COVID-19 Hotspot, CNBC Reports." *KSAT,* June 20, 2020. https://www.ksat.com/news/local/2020/06/20/san-antonio-metro-area-named-covid-19-hotspot-cnbc-reports/.

Krogstad, Jens Manuel, Ana Gonzalez-Barrera, and Luis Noe-Bustamante. 2020. "U.S. Latinos Among Hardest Hit by Pay Cuts, Job Losses Due to Coronavirus." *Pew Research Center*, April 3, 2020. https://www.pewresearch.org/fact-tank/2020/04/03/u-s-latinos-among-hardest-hit-by-pay-cuts-job-losses-due-to-coronavirus/.

Lang, James M. 2020. "On Not Drawing Conclusions About Online Teaching Now—or Next Fall." *Chronicle of Higher Education*, May 18, 2020. https://www.chronicle.com/article/on-not-drawing-conclusions-about-online-teaching-now-or-next-fall.

Marcus, Jon. 2018. "With Enrollment Sliding, Liberal Arts Colleges Struggle to Make a Case for Themselves." *The Hechinger Report,* May 18, 2018. https://hechingerreport.org/with-enrollment-sliding-liberal-arts-colleges-struggle-to-make-a-case-for-themselves/.

McGuire, Tammy, Debbie S. Dougherty, and Joshua Atkinson. 2006. "'Paradoxing the Dialectic': The Impact of Patients' Sexual Harassment in the Discursive Construction of Nurses' Caregiving Roles." *Management Communication Quarterly* 19, no. 3: 416–450. doi:10.1177/0893318905280879.

McNamee, Lacy G. and Brittany L. Peterson. 2014. "Reconciling 'Third Space/Place': Toward a Complementary Dialectical Understanding of Volunteer Management." *Management Communication Quarterly* 28, no. 2: 214–243. doi:10.1177/0893318914525472.

"Mentor for Mission Program for New Faculty." St. Mary's University. Accessed May 24, 2021. https://www.stmarytx.edu/academics/centers/catholic-studies/faculty-development/mission-program-for-new-faculty/

Mendoza, Madalyn. 2020. "CNBC: San Antonio Metro Area Ranks No. 4 in U.S. for Fastest Growth of COVID-19 in the Last Week." *My SA*, June 20, 2020. https://www.mysanantonio.com/news/local/article/CNBC-San-Antonio-ranks-No-4-in-U-S-for-fastest-15352481.php.

Mitra, Rahul and Jeremy Fyke. 2017. "Purpose-Driven Consultancies' Negotiation of Organizational Tensions." *Journal of Applied Communication Research* 45, no. 2: 140–159. doi:10.1080/00909882.2017.1288290.

Putnam, Linda L. 1986. "Contradictions and Paradoxes in Organizations." In *Organization-Communication: Emerging Perspectives,* edited by Lee Thayer, 151–167. Norwood, NJ: Ablex.

Putnam, Linda L., Gail T. Fairhurst, and Scott Banghart. 2016. "Contradictions, Dialectics, and Paradoxes in Organizations: A Constitutive Approach." *Academy of Management Annals* 10, no. 1: 65–171. doi:10.5465/19416520.2016.1162421.

Roberts, P. 2020. "St. Mary's Law Strives to Eliminate Inequities." St. Mary's University. June 3, 2020. https://www.stmarytx.edu/2020/eliminate-inequities/.

Smith, Wendy K. and Paul Tracey. 2016. "Institutional Complexity and Paradox Theory: Complementarities of Competing Demands." *Strategic Organization* 14, no. 4: 455–466. doi:10.1177/1476127016638565.

"St. Mary's Awarded $1.3 Million Grant to Help Underserved Students Finish College." 2020. St. Mary's University, October 7, 2020. https://www.stmarytx.edu/2020/trio-grant-2020/. St. Mary's University. https://stmarytx.edu.

"Student Staff." 2021. St. Mary's University. Accessed May 24, 2021. https://www.stmarytx.edu/campuslife/living-on-campus/student-staff/.

"Tuition." St. Mary's University. https://www.stmarytx.edu/admission/financial-aid/tuition/2020-2021/. Accessed May 24, 2021.

Thomas, Gary. 2015. *How to Do Your Case Study*, 2nd edition. Thousand Oaks, CA: SAGE.

Tracy, Sarah J. 2004. "Dialectic, Contradiction or Double Bind? Analyzing and Theorizing Employee Reactions to Organizational Tension." *Journal of Applied Communication Research* 32, no. 2: 119–146. doi:10.1080/0090988042000210025.

Varlotta, Lori. 2018. "Designing a Model for the New Liberal Arts." *Liberal Education* 104, no. 4. https://www.aacu.org/liberaleducation/2018/fall/varlotta.

Westwick, Joshua N. and Sherwyn P. Morreale. 2021. "Advancing an Agenda for Instructional Preparedness: Lessons Learned from the Transition to Remote Learning." *Communication Education* 70, no. 2: 217–222

Yin, Robert K. 2018. *Case Study Research and Applications: Design and Methods*, 6th edition. Thousand Oaks, CA: Sage.

Chapter 7

Post-Pandemic Anxiety

Teaching and Learning for Student Mental Wellness in Communication

Lori Blewett and Maureen Ebben

The COVID-19 pandemic was more than an infectious disease event. It was a mental health trigger with cascading consequences for the lives and learning of an estimated 26 million college students in the United States (Barry 2021). As a collective experience of trauma, the pandemic led to increased rates of anxiety, stress, grief, depression, and suicidality with long-term effects (Brooks et al. 2020; Jahnke 2020; Zhai and Du 2020). While awareness about student mental health has gained recognition across university campuses in recent years (House, Neal and Kolb 2020; Oswalt et al. 2020), the COVID-19 pandemic made student mental health visible in new ways with important implications for communication teaching and learning in the post-pandemic era.

Mental health matters in higher education because it has a significant effect on student success. Anxiety disorders may be exacerbated by stress and diminish student performance (Looi, Chan and Wu 2021). Depression can stymie motivation. Disparities in educational attainment attributable to socioeconomic status and race are acknowledged as key factors of student success, but the impact of mental health on student degree completion is less often recognized despite depression significantly contributing to the lack of persistence in college (Eisenberg et al. 2013). Further, intersectional differences compound students' experiences of mental wellness as students of color, socioeconomically disadvantaged students, and LGBTQI+ students experience depression at higher rates (Anderson 2020a,b; Czeisler et al. 2020; House, Neal and Kolb 2020; Smith and Applegate 2018). Currently, campus mental health resources are inadequate and will likely remain so in the post-pandemic future. Only 15.5 percent of colleges plan to increase their counseling and mental health staff, while the same percentage plan to reduce their mental health workforce and resources (Burke 2021; Hahn 2021; Zook 2021).

During the pandemic, college and university administrators encouraged faculty to pay attention to students' mental health in ways they never had before. Whether motivated by concerns about student well-being, academic success, or declining enrollment, mental health was suddenly relevant to everyone, not just the staff of campus counseling centers (LaBelle 2020). In this chapter, we identify dynamics related to student mental health and shifts in pedagogical practice that occurred during the COVID-19 pandemic. We discuss how these dynamics relate to the literature on student mental health and pedagogy, and we speculate about what may—or perhaps *should*—change for communication teaching and learning to support students' mental health and well-being in the post-pandemic era. Our discussion focuses on students' experiences of stress, anxiety, and depression because these conditions are most prevalent in higher education (Barry 2021; Huckins et al. 2020; Zhai and Du 2020). Other mental health problems were also exacerbated by the pandemic, but are beyond the scope of this chapter. Even within this delimited frame, students have a wide range of experiences with mental health challenges (from short term, to chronic, to life threatening), and they have multiple ways of conceptualizing their identities in relation to mental health. To reflect evolving and contested preferences in disability discourse, we use person-first language and identity-first language interchangeably in this chapter (e.g., "person with a mental health disorder" and "psychiatrized person").

POST-PANDEMIC COMMUNICATION PEDAGOGY FOR STUDENT MENTAL WELLNESS

Four lessons can be drawn from the intersection of communication pedagogy and student mental health during the pandemic. While each of these lessons is not wholly new, we believe that pandemic experiences of teaching and learning have served as a catalyst for the acceleration of changes already underway and will contribute to their adoption by communication faculty. First, student mental health will be understood as a matter of equity and more fully included in the diversity, equity, and inclusion (DEI) efforts of higher education institutions and communication departments. Second, the principles of Universal Design for Learning, as they apply to mental health, will be increasingly adopted for communication pedagogy. Third, the shared stress and anxiety experienced in the COVID-19 pandemic will galvanize the rise of trauma-informed teaching and critical grief pedagogy in communication education. Fourth, the growth and development of communication scholarship around disability will deepen faculty understandings about mental health and spur pedagogical challenges to ableist assumptions in the discipline. We conclude with a cautionary note about the disruptive potential of these changes and related cultural resistance. However, we believe that inclusive and equitable student learning experiences, born of pedagogical innovation and flexibility during the pandemic, will take root over time.

LESSON #1: STUDENT MENTAL HEALTH IS A MATTER OF EQUITY

In the midst of the pandemic, some interactional dynamics related to new instructional modalities rose to become pressing pedagogical questions with implications for student mental well-being. One significant question to emerge was whether students in synchronous videoconferencing (e.g., Zoom) "classrooms" should be required to turn on their cameras. Some faculty hoped that students' visual presence would more closely simulate normal conversation and decrease feelings of isolation (Aleman and Sommer 2020; Lin and Gao 2020). Other faculty assumed that low camera use by students signaled low levels of student engagement (Parkman-Williams 2021; Reed 2020). Yet students did not turn on their cameras for a variety of reasons—not only related to academic interests and motivation but also for emotional, psychological, and financial reasons.

For some students, being on camera triggered anxiety: social and communication anxiety, stereotype threat, anxiety about having one's appearance or environment judged, and academic anxiety related to low bandwidth and loss of instructional access (Castelli and Sarvary 2021). For many students, "the added anxiety [of being on camera] diminished their participation, as they felt a need to monitor their home, family members, and intimate spaces while attempting to attend classroom interactions" (Finders and Munoz 2021). Camera use illustrated students' attempts to mitigate stress and preserve agency as they negotiated complex situations. It was the anxiety triggered *by being on camera* that interfered with these students' engagement in class, not a lack of motivation (Castelli and Sarvary 2021; Jiang 2020).

Video concerns were disproportionately experienced by students of color, low-income students, and students with disabilities. Citing both mental health and economic equity issues, student leaders at one of our colleges asked that faculty not expect students to be on camera. For some pedagogical theorists the requirement that students have their cameras on during synchronous video instruction came to be understood not so much as an effort to foster student engagement, but rather as a faculty stance toward pedagogy that "positions students as docile bodies in need of surveillance" (Finders and Munoz 2021).

Students' varying experience with video classrooms highlighted to faculty how modalities of interaction can relate to mental health. These Zoom experiences "forced" faculty to recognize classroom interaction as an intersectional dimension of communication and mental health related to diversity, equity, and belonging. We predict this realization will stimulate faculty interest in learning about and using more equitable forms of pedagogy.

Many institutions of higher education were already doing serious work on DEI initiatives prior to the pandemic. Many were working toward becoming anti-racist institutions. Some sought to expand DEI to include student mental health, building upon calls by disability scholars, activist, educators, policy-makers, and others who have long advocated for equity-centered pedagogies (Casey 2020; Dunn and Schwallie Farmer 2020; Hughes 2016; Lehan, Hussey, and Babcock 2020). But student mental health is not yet fully integrated into DEI-inspired pedagogy at most colleges. For example, while many departments of communication routinely offer cultural and educational activities related to students' racial, ethnic, gender, or even religious identities, few offer courses or programming that involve intersectional discussions of mental health with other social identities.

The depth of disability exclusion runs deep. Researcher Lauren Shallish, at the College of New Jersey, challenges academic disciplines to confront their entrenched history around ability supremacy: "They've always prioritized the quote normal body or quote normal mind. Higher education is defined by who it excludes" (Burke 2020). As a group, communication faculty tend to be rather good at listening to students, empathizing with their challenges, and making good-faith efforts to accommodate students with special needs. But the merit-based guardrails that we call academic standards, and reliance on standardized instructional materials, often constrain our relationships with students and may limit our ability to treat students with mental health challenges not just equally, but differently in order to foster equitable outcomes.

When it comes to pedagogy, equal is not necessarily equitable. *Equality* approaches to pedagogy focus on equal access and equal treatment; everybody gets the same opportunity to learn and those with the greatest talent, motivation, and commitment achieve the greatest success (Solomon-Pryce 2015). *Equity* approaches to pedagogy focus on equality of outcomes; more resources go to communities or students with greater need and faculty adjust teaching practices as needed to help all students succeed (Great Schools Partnership 2015; Phuong et al. 2017). Equity approaches acknowledge that students have vastly different experiences prior to college; they face different barriers, opportunities, and experiences while on campus, and they have different learning styles and psycho-emotional needs. Our pandemic experiences brought these differences to the fore. We predict that the heightened awareness of student mental health needs brought on by the pandemic will accelerate the expansion of intersectional approaches to pedagogy that include considerations of the emotional and psychological diversity of students' experiences around learning. Communication faculty will increasingly center equity and access in our teaching, joining broader DEI efforts to put educational success within reach of all students.

LESSON #2: STUDENT MENTAL HEALTH BENEFITS FROM UNIVERSAL DESIGN PRACTICES

The pandemic challenged some of our most basic assumptions and pedagogical practices such as the reliance on verbal, face-to-face communication for lectures, discussions, and other forms of student engagement. Faculty and students adjusted to new modes of interacting: asynchronous student interactions, recorded lectures, simultaneous chat communication, and video conferences from home spaces. Out of a concern for "Zoom fatigue," faculty pre-recorded verbal presentations which made them accessible to more students. Rather than concentrate student work on major research papers and high-stakes tests, some departments encouraged use of low-stakes reflective exercises, online group projects, creative multimedia assignments, and self-paced learning with pre- and post-self-assessments. To make up for the lack of classroom engagement, faculty encouraged participation through online chat, instant polling, and asynchronous discussion, while simultaneously facilitating live conversation over Zoom.

Born of emergency as well as technological limits and opportunities, new practices in student-teacher interactions and assessment demonstrated that alternatives to conventional pedagogy were not only possible, but sometimes preferable for students' mental wellness. Although most students missed the interpersonal dynamics of in-person instruction, others found the changes beneficial (Winkie 2020). Students who were hesitant about voicing their perspectives out loud in the face-to-face classroom, especially those with social anxiety, were more comfortable writing comments on online discussion boards and chat forums. Access to recorded lectures eased student anxieties about missing information and were welcomed by many psychiatrized students and those whose lives were disrupted by physical health, work, or family needs. Students in the state of Washington considered access to archived lectures so important for equity that the Washington Student Association made a priority request for faculty in all of the state's public baccalaureate institutions to use lecture capture technology (WSA 2020).

During the pandemic, schools across the country also had to rethink conventional modes of assessment. Many colleges allowed students to convert letter grades to pass/fail grades late in the term and even after classes ended. They revised or abandoned expectations for time-limited, carefully monitored, individual testing. While high-stakes testing is often held to be the fairest and most accurate measure of student proficiency and future success especially in competitive disciplines, it was clear during the pandemic that students' collective knowledge (in the form of finding and sharing answers—a.k.a. cheating) made the presumptive best practices untenable (Steinberger, Eshet and Grinautsky 2021).

The turn to open-book exams, flexible testing hours, and greater use of group projects for assessment, marked a shift in expectations and practices for both faculty and students (Banki 2021; Juhary 2020). But the change turned out to be a boon to students who struggle with test anxiety. Prior to the pandemic, researchers had noted that collaborative-testing, open-book testing, and open-note testing reduced student stress and anxiety, and had either positive or neutral impacts on learning outcomes (Dallmer 2004; Hanshaw 2012). Such practices were already embraced in online courses where proctoring exams was not practical, but were less common in traditional educational settings (Corcoran 2020).

Pandemic teaching experiences also shed light on in-person practices that support mental health. Many came to realize that messy, spontaneous, synergistic, even uncomfortable, human interactions were a fundamental element of learning, not merely a spice to keep things interesting or a supplement to aid knowledge absorption. Such awareness resonates with pre-pandemic calls for greater attention to the development and assessment of collaborative communication skills (Dannels et al. 2014). Without emotionally connected, face-to-face communication there was concern for students' engagement and learning (Lee 2020; Petillion and McNeil 2020; Scott et al. 2021). K-12 students were the first to return to in-person school and the first to notice the difference in focus and learning connected to their emotional well-being. As 18-year-old senior Jzayla Sussmann reported, being around other students made her happy, and having teachers nearby increased her confidence. "I felt motivated, like I wanted to do more. I haven't felt that way in a while, and I got a lot of work done" (Durston et.a l. 2021). Diminishment of the fully embodied student-teacher relationship in online instruction during the pandemic reaffirmed its centrality for pedagogical effectiveness.

The new appreciation for the importance of multiple modes and modalities for instruction and the acceptance of a variety of forms of assessment seen during the pandemic is an expansion of Universal Design concepts that were already starting to gain ground. Universal Design for Learning (UDL) is a pedagogical strategy to achieve equity for all students, including those struggling with mental health issues. UDL asks faculty to take diverse student needs, learning styles, and abilities into account when planning and implementing a course, not just accommodate students with disabilities when required. The need for UDL is urgent:

> Eleven percent of undergraduates report some type of disability . . . the majority of disabilities are now non-apparent (e.g., mental, emotional, psychiatric condition/depression, ADHD, specific learning disabilities/dyslexia) . . . [and] between sixty and eighty percent of students with disabilities don't contact campus university services for "official" accommodation requests. (The Teaching Commons, n.d.)

The principles of UDL encourage faculty to create learning experiences that include multiple means of representation, multiple means of action and expression, and multiple means of engagement (Meyer et al. 2014). When UDL is used in course development, all students benefit. After more than a year of remote teaching, experimenting with new technologies and noticing their impact on student engagement and learning, communication faculty increased their capacity to design communication courses that follow UDL principles in ways that better meet the needs of students struggling with stress, anxiety, depression, and other mental health challenges. In the midst of the pandemic, communication Professor Taylor Hahn observed the pedagogical experimentation taking place, noted its limits, and suggested its effects on student mental health: "The ongoing COVID pandemic has not (yet) provoked revolutionary pedagogical innovations. Rather, it has spurred a more rapid and holistic adoption of multi-modal best practices that might otherwise have taken years, if not decades, for broad implementation. These rapid, sometimes chaotic transitions have had unforeseen mental health consequences" (Hahn 2021). In the post-pandemic world, a UDL approach to pedagogy will enable communication faculty to thoughtfully and intentionally incorporate new teaching modes in ways that expand access to higher education—not by replacing in-person classes with online teaching in a neoliberal race toward low-cost instruction, but rather by utilizing a variety of instructional modes that are more inclusive of students with diverse mental health needs.

There is, however, a potential dilemma that communication faculty face when trying to implement UDL principles with a mental health focus. Since a fundamental goal of our discipline is to improve students' communication skills, faculty may struggle to determine to what extent it is desirable to create modes of learning and expression that allow students with social anxiety to avoid engaging in verbal, face-to-face interactions or other forms of communication that are potentially distressing. Many communication faculty have experience teaching students with speech anxiety, and we know that with adequate training and support, the vast majority of these students can learn to manage their anxiety and become successful public communicators. UDL offers pathways for faculty to develop teaching strategies that can meet students' psychological needs while simultaneously creating an environment that challenges them to develop new skills and habits of mind that increase communication flexibility and foster resilience. UDL encourages us to think creatively and inclusively. It is not about creating accommodations that allow some students to "opt out," rather it is about using multiple teaching strategies and learning opportunities that allow more students to succeed, more of the time.

LESSON #3: COMMUNICATION STUDIES NEEDS TRAUMA-INFORMED TEACHING AND CRITICAL GRIEF PEDAGOGY

Pandemic teaching and learning occurred under conditions of existential uncertainty, trauma, and grief. Forced isolation, lack of clarity about the course of the pandemic, disconnection from peers and colleagues, fear of contagion, loss of income, illness, and sorrow from the death of loved ones characterized our pedagogical circumstances. Many faculty started their Zoom classes with student-centered emotional check-ins asking, "How are you feeling today? How are you doing?" To help students cope, some faculty offered stress breaks that included stretching, music, guided meditation, breathing exercises, and even dancing. There was explicit recognition that this was not "business as usual." It was not that we were working and studying from home; rather, we were *in a pandemic, and attempting* to work and study from home. In March 2020, the "Adjusted Syllabus" by University of North Carolina Professor Brandon Bayne went viral for its assertions about the pandemic conditions and their import for pedagogy: "Nobody signed up for this. Not for the sickness, not for the financial hardship, not for the social distancing. The humane option is the best option."

The pandemic precipitated appreciation for the fragility of the human psyche under strain. As disability scholar and activist Lydia X. Z. Brown (2021) observed, "we were all going through a collective crisis. None of us are okay." For students, "traumatic events bring about a whirlwind of emotions. Students often feel unsafe, anxious, and fearful" (Tulloch 2021). In the fall of 2020, 89 percent of college students reported that they experienced stress or anxiety as a result of COVID-19, and one in four students said that their depression increased significantly during the pandemic (ActiveMinds 2020). We might call our younger students members of "The Trauma Generation" as their experience of the COVID-19 ordeal must be contextualized within the cumulative upheaval endured by this cohort. Our students watched terrorist attacks on TV as children, lived through The Great Recession, experienced natural disasters and climate change, and then were confronted with a deadly pandemic.

We posit that these circumstances will foster the growth of communication pedagogy that includes trauma-informed perspectives. Such approaches presume that students "have a trauma history that impacts their learning [and] are critical because the social, economic, and health consequences of the pandemic will linger for years to come" (Tulloch 2021). Six principles comprise a trauma-informed approach to teaching: (1) safety, (2) trustworthiness and transparency, (3) peer support, (4) collaboration and mutuality, (5) empowerment and choice, and (6) cultural, historical, and gender issues (U.S. CDC 2020). But trauma-informed pedagogy is not achieved simply through checking items off a list. Emotions can be messy and complex. The opposite of anxiety is not calm; it is trust (Prizant and Fields-Meyer 2015). A central teaching strategy of a trauma-informed approach is to acknowledge the feelings of students with continual attention, compassionate awareness, and sensitivity. Not all students have the same level of comfort with the expression of emotions, so instructors need to plan carefully to preserve student autonomy with allowances for choice and the judicious use of content warnings. Communication faculty are not therapists, but we can go beyond disciplinary teachings about emotional intelligence and emotional message displays to deepen students' understanding of the impacts of trauma in our relationships and society.

Some trauma-informed strategies, such as trigger warnings and safe space agreements have become politicized in discourse that constructs them as pandering to "snowflakes" or infringing on the freedom of speech. Polarized "culture war" debates reflect a deep ambivalence about trauma-informed pedagogy. Yet such conflicts tend to dissipate when students see how trauma enters the classroom across the ideological spectrum: the veteran with PTSD, the survivor of sexual assault, the rural student who is unhoused, the victim of hate crime, the child of opioid addicts. Our students, either directly or through their connections with others, are rarely strangers to trauma.

Critical grief pedagogy is a focused strand of trauma-informed pedagogy that may be especially useful in the post-pandemic era. This approach draws on critical and feminist pedagogy to devise ways for both students and faculty to give voice to their experiences of personal loss. Erin Willer et al. (2021) write about a community-based group designed to support families who experienced the death of a baby. They describe critical grief pedagogy as a, "mad feminist response to the silencing of loss in academic spaces" (27). We believe this approach could be modified and used with students to help them understand and process the grief of the pandemic era. Critical grief pedagogy allows instructors to open conversations about loss in ways that help students develop critical thinking and communication skills. Student learning outcomes from this pedagogical technique include improved skills in compassionate communication, acceptance of "failure" as a mode of mourning, gaining empowerment to share one's and others' stories of loss, and the formation of a community of grievers (Willer et al. 2021).

We speculate that the development and practice of trauma-informed pedagogy, and perhaps even critical grief pedagogy, will accelerate in the post-pandemic era in ways that contribute to individual and community resilience. Pre-pandemic, attention to student resilience arose in the wake of young people's growing awareness of seemingly intractable problems like climate change, racism, and economic inequality. Faculty wanted students to be aware of these issues but not overwhelmed by their enormity and complexity. During the pandemic, the theme of resilience quickly entered discussions about communication pedagogy (Schwartzman 2020). Psychological resilience includes realistic acknowledgment of limitations and possibilities as well as the determination to persist and improve. Resilience is best understood as a social-psychological construct rather than as a characteristic of an individual person. Calls for "a collective culture of care" heard during the pandemic reflect the interdependent nature of resilience. Trauma-and-grief informed pedagogical practices can model relational forms of communication that support collective emotional and psychological resilience. Such an approach, though requiring new learning for faculty, would be a valuable contribution to health communication, interpersonal communication, family communication, and even organizational communication courses.

LESSON #4: COMMUNICATION PEDAGOGY SHOULD CHALLENGE ABLEIST ASSUMPTIONS

The toll pandemic life took on our mental health was widely acknowledged and openly shared. First-generation undergraduate students of the University of North Carolina at Chapel Hill, for example, freely expressed the ways in which their mental health suffered: "I was left without a sense of direction or purpose for an extended amount of time"; another reflected, "the pandemic made it incredibly difficult both mentally and physically. The fear of contracting it or other loved ones is a lot to handle"; and another disclosed, "it has negatively impacted me. I've had multiple panic attacks" (Davis 2021). Such pronouncements not only point to the deleterious effects of the pandemic on student mental health, but their open admission also demonstrates the broad acceptance of mental health distress as a central dynamic of the pandemic experience.

Mental health was understood as precious and essential. We were reminded repeatedly that we must be mindful of our mental health and take great care with it. We freely vented our mental anguish without fear of social ostracization or shaming backlash. Others shared our anxieties and were sympathetic. The pandemic normalization of psychological distress lies in stark contrast to its usual stigmatization which can inhibit students from seeking help (Turosak and Siwierka 2019). The normalization of mental health discourse during the pandemic suggests that attitudes and practices are shifting. Given the COVID-19 experience and the growth of scholarship and activism around mental health in our discipline, we expect the destigmatization of mental health to accelerate and shape communication pedagogy in the post-pandemic era. Communication scholarship like Crip theory and the "mad turn" explicate the cultural biases of compulsory able-bodiedness. Related activist efforts like disability justice and "mad justice" advocate for equity of all bodies and minds. These theoretical and activist movements have now coalesced with the pandemic normalization of mental health. We believe that the pandemic dynamics around the recognition of the importance of mental health coupled with the "mad turn" in communication means that our pedagogy will be transformed.

The mad turn emerged from disability communication studies and Crip theory. It refers to the effort to reframe understandings about mental health in ways that reduce its social deviance (Fredrick et al. 2020; Krebs 2019; McRuer 2006). Based on a strengths-approach to understanding psychiatry-involved people, the mad turn is a response to prior deficit-based conceptual frameworks that understood mental illness as a transgressive condition to be denied, controlled, or cured. In prior research about mental health, the voices and perspectives of people who lived with mental health challenges were typically left out. Scholarship and activism in the vein of the mad turn seek to reverse this practice by centering on those who possess first-hand experience with mental health problems. Mad justice research and action affords greater inclusivity of people with a breath of mental health experiences. These researchers note that even the concept of "health" can be limiting as it posits a false dichotomy between healthy and unhealthy that doesn't reflect the realities of human experience, particularly for those living with chronic physical and mental disabilities.

In the mad turn formulation, mental health is understood not so much as a problem, but rather as a social identity parallel to other identity groups such as the deaf community or the neurodivergent community. As a shared cultural identity, persons' experiences of mental health can forge connections to bridge interpersonal isolation and stigma. Individuals can reassert their agency through their distinctive ways of being in the world. An outcome of our pandemic experience and the mad turn is a new question about the kinds of accommodation and pedagogy of care that may be appropriate for student mental health. If mental illness is not necessarily a disease to be cured, a condition to be feared, or a problem to be solved, but, rather, a state of being to be understood, accommodated, and even accepted, what different responses may be needed from faculty? If we take the mad turn in communication seriously, what does that mean for our pedagogy?

Currently, the insights offered by the mad turn are largely absent in communication pedagogy. Practices to accommodate student mental health have been minor, mostly resulting from requirements spelled out in letters generated from a campus Disability Office—a problematic office title since lumping mental health into the frame of disability thwarts efforts to normalize mental wellness. Such letters typically call for extended test time, but faculty are still giving tests, or a class note-taker is recommended, but the "sage-on-the-stage" paradigm remains dominant. Mental health and its accommodation is regarded as an individual responsibility. But even gaining disability accommodation is often a fraught process. Krebs (2019) demonstrates the "intersectional issues of who has—or is barred from—access to such services with attention to social identities such as race, class, citizenship status, gender, and sexual orientation" (np) arguing that stigma persists as a central dynamic. The term "accommodation" itself functions rhetorically with a negative connotation for students with disabilities (Krebs 2019). Students are perceived by others, and even perceive themselves, as "less than" or "cheating the system" by "getting away with lower academic standards" through the use of disability accommodations (Krebs 2019). Although disability offices address student needs and educate faculty, instructional practices have only changed superficially. Universal Design for Learning, as a pedagogical strategy, supports destigmatization of mental health to the extent that it accomplishes greater accessibility without requiring students to self-identify, but UDL, on its own, does not accomplish the deeper cultural shift and social acceptance that the mad turn aims to achieve.

The pandemic demonstrated the situational nature of mental wellness. Mental health is not just an internal biochemical state; it can be precipitated by societal conditions. This acknowledgment was the great leveler of the pandemic. Student mental health could be understood as a collective experience that required a collective response. This view is consistent with previous research linking mental health in higher education to the benefits of engaged, collaborative learning, particularly for the prevention of depression and the mitigation of substance use disorders (Swaner 2007). Thinking of mental health as a public health issue does not take an individual off the hook from making thoughtful and responsible choices. Rather, it contextualizes student experiences of mental health within a larger set of social relationships and structural conditions. This perspective recognizes how social determinants of health (e.g., inequities based on race, class, gender, ability, etc.) shape the conditions within which people experience their psychological and emotional health. We speculate that, post-pandemic, the diversity of student experiences around mental health will be more widely recognized by faculty who will adjust their teaching styles to make space for mental health diversity. Mental health will be normalized as an essential component of health for all students. As such, it will transform communication pedagogy.

One way to encourage such transformation is to ask: How are the communicative experiences of stress, anxiety, and depression depicted in our course materials? Where is the role of mental health acknowledged in communication? How does our curricula work toward its destigmatization? Do psychiatrized and mad-identified people have presence, agency, and voice in our literature? Mental health is currently present in a limited way in some communication subfields. Outside of health communication, mental health concerns sometimes appear in gender communication (psychological impacts of sexism), public speaking (speech anxiety), and conflict studies (conflict avoidance, anger management), but they are remarkably absent in most other subfields. Even in interpersonal communication textbooks that fully embrace a diversity framework, mental health is only minimally present. For example, in Julia Wood's (2016) *Interpersonal Communication: Everyday Encounters*, one page offers "Guidelines for Confirming Communication with People with Disabilities" (230), and one page references anxiety in the context of rational-emotional approaches to feelings (210), but the topic of mental health and interpersonal communication is not explicitly addressed. Post-pandemic, we speculate that mental health will be an area of growth for research and teaching across the communication discipline and that courses and textbooks will be revised to include concepts and skills for mental wellness.

CONCLUSION

Within the classroom—whether online, face-to-face, or hybrid—pedagogical experiences afforded to students can support mental health or contribute to its worsening. Post-pandemic, we predict that communication faculty will increase their attention and sensitivity to the diverse mental health needs of students through at least four transformations: (1) a recognition of student mental health as a matter of equity, (2) increased use of UDL strategies, (3) the adoption of trauma-and-grief-informed pedagogical practices, and (4) the destigmatization of mental health through a critical examination of ableist assumptions. As a matter of post-pandemic equity, it seems probable that these more inclusive orientations toward student mental health will infuse our pedagogy.

Institutional and pedagogical change will likely happen, as it often does, through the efforts of individual faculty, staff, and students, inspired by social movements and issues of the day. Just as anti-racist efforts have entered the curriculum and started to create meaningful change on many college campuses, we see mental health advocacy engendering more inclusive forms of course design, classroom interactions, and learning assessment. This will likely be propelled by the efforts of DEI initiatives and faculty development where inclusivity is broadly conceptualized to encompass mental health.

While these trends were underway before the pandemic, our collective experience and experimentation during the pandemic have created new possibilities for pedagogical change. But such changes will not be uniformly adopted across institutions. Pedagogical practices that inclusively and overtly address student mental health needs may feel disruptive and scary to faculty who are anxious about maintaining professional boundaries around student health disclosures and relational expectations (Price 2020). For some faculty, "getting back to normal" may mean rejecting pedagogical practices that emerged during the pandemic. People who made it through the pandemic and its isolation with little mental health support may feel further justified in uncompromising "tough love" approaches to academic standards and traditional pedagogy. Where DEI initiatives are seen as an affront to free speech or discrimination against white culture, it is less likely that schools will move to normalize intersectional issues of mental health and adopt a culture of care in instructional curriculum and pedagogical practices. Despite the culture war discourse of our political moment, we predict that change will happen, particularly in departments of communication. The discipline of communication has been attending to issues of diversity, communication competence, and power inequities for decades. With new awareness and new skills emerging from the pandemic, communication faculty are well positioned to adopt and promote a variety of inclusive pedagogical approaches that foster equity and support student mental wellness.

REFERENCES

Active Minds. 2020. "Student Mental Health Survey (September2020)." Accessed April 10, 2021. https://www.activeminds.org/wp-content/uploads/2020/10/Student-Mental-Health-Data-Sheet-Fall-2020-1.pdf.

Anderson, Greta. 2020a. "Mental Health Needs Rise with Pandemic." *Inside Higher Ed*, September 11, 2020. https://www.insidehighered.com/news/2020/09/11/students-great-need-mental-health-support-during-pandemic.

Anderson, Greta. 2020b. "More Pandemic Consequences for Underrepresented Students." *Inside Higher Ed*, September 16, 2020. https://www.insidehighered.com/news/2020/09/16/low-income-and-students-color-greatest-need-pandemic-relief.

Banki, Susan R. 2021. "Learning Alone-a with Corona": Two Challenges and Four Principles of Tertiary Teaching. *Journal of Research in Innovative Teaching & Learning* 14, no. 1: 65–74. doi:10.1108/JRIT-12-2020-0081.

Barry, Ellen. 2021. "A College President Worried About the Risks of Dorm Isolation. So He Moved In." *The New York Times*, March 4, 2021. https://www.nytimes.com/2021/03/04/us/norwich-university-president-dormitory.html.

Bayne, Brandon (@brandonbayne). 2020. "Adjusted Syllabus." Twitter, March 15, 2020, 7:44 p.m. https://twitter.com/brandonbayne/status/1239336664176250880.

Brooks, Samantha K., Rebecca K. Webster, Louise E. Smith, Lisa Woodland, Simon Wessely, Niel Greenberg, and James G. Rubin, G. James. 2020. "The Psychological Impact of Quarantine and How to Reduce It: Rapid Review of the Evidence." *Lancet* 395 (10227): 912–920. doi:10.1016/S0140-6736(20)30460-8.

Brown, Lydia X. Z. 2021. "Weaving Crip, Mad, Queer, Trans Dreams: Disability Justice for our Futures and Our Freedom." Presentation at Beyond the Pandemic: How has COVID-19 Impacted Higher Education and Students with Disabilities? University of Southern Maine Virtual Conference, April 6, 2021.

Burke, Lilah. 2020. "Disability as Diversity." *Inside Higher Ed*, November 12, 2020. https://www.insidehighered.com/news/2020/11/12/could-disability-be-further-included-diversity-efforts.

Burke, Lilia. 2021. "Reopening, With Equity." *Inside Higher Ed*, March 15, 2021. https://www.insidehighered.com/news/2021/03/15/experts-consider-equity-and-college-reopening.

Casey, Caroline. 2020. "Do your D&I Efforts Include People with Disabilities?" *Harvard Business Review*, March 19, 2020. https://hbr.org/2020/03/do-your-di-efforts-include-people-with-disabilities.

Castelli, Frank R., and Mark A. Sarvary. 2021. "Why Students Do Not Turn On Their Video Cameras During Online Classes and an Equitable and Inclusive Plan to Encourage Them to Do So." *Ecology and Evolution* 1–12. doi:10.1002/ece3.7123.

Corcoran, Charles. 2020. "Should Notes Be Permitted During Testing?" *Journal of Instructional Pedagogies* 23: 1–9. https://www.aabri.com/manuscripts/193064.pdf.

Czeisler, Mark, Rashon Lane, Emiko Petrosky, Joshua Wiley, Aleta Christensen, Rashid Njai, Matthew Weaver, Rebecca Robbins, Elise Facer-Childs, Laura Barger, Charles Czeisler, Mark Howard, and Shantha Rajaratnam. 2020. "Mental Health, Substance Use, and Suicidal Ideation During the COVID-19 Pandemic--United States, June 24–30, 2020." *Morbidity and Mortality Weekly Report* 69: 1049–1057. doi:10.15585/mmwr.mm6932a1.

Dallmer, Denise. 2004. "Collaborative Test Taking With Adult Learners." *Adult Learning* 15, no. 3–4: 4–7. doi:10.1177/104515950401500301.

Dannels, Deanna P., Ann Darling, Deanna L. Fassett, Jeff Kerssen-Griep, Derek Lane, Timothy P. Mottet, Keith Nainby, and Deanna Sellnow. 2014. "Inception: Beginning a New Conversation about Communication Pedagogy and Scholarship."

Communication Education 63, no. 4: 366–382. doi:10.1080/03634523.2014 .934849.

Davis, Cassandra R. 2021. "COVID-19 and First-Generation Students in Higher Education." Presented at Elevating First-Generation Success in Higher Education, University of Southern Maine Virtual Conference, January 13, 2021.

Dunn, Maureen and Cathy Schwallie Farmer. 2020. "Neurodiversity: An Organizational Asset." *American Diversity Report*, October 18, 2020. https://americandiversityreport.com/neurodiversity-an-organizational-asset-by-maureen-dunne-cathy-schwallie-farmer.

Durston, Ellen, A., Dan Levin, and Juliana Kim. 2021. "'I Was So Nervous': Back to Class After a Year Online." *New York Times*, March 9, 2021. https://www.nytimes.com/2021/03/09/us/schools-reopen-covid.html.

Eisenberg, Daniel, Justin Hunt, and Nicole Speer. 2013. "Mental Health in American Colleges and Universities: Variation Across Student Subgroups and Across Campuses." *The Journal of Nervous and Mental Disease* 201, no.1: 60–67.

Finders, Margaret, and Joaquin Munoz. 2021. "Camera On: Surveillance in the Time of COVID -19." *Inside Higher Ed*, March 3, 2021. https://www.insidehighered.com/advice/2021/03/03/why-its-wrong-require-students-keep-their-cameras-online-classes-opinion.

Fredrick, Emma G., Sheri L. LaDuke, and Stacey L. Williams. 2020. "Sexual Minority Quality of Life: The Indirect Effect of Public Stigma Through Self-compassion, Authenticity, and Internalized Stigma." *Stigma and Health* 5, no.1: 79–82. doi:10.1037/sah0000176.

Great Schools Partnership. 2016. "Equity." *The Glossary of Education Reform*, April 21, 2016. https://www.edglossary.org/equity.

Hahn, Taylor. 2021. "Mental Health in Academia During the COVID Pandemic." *Spectra: The Online Magazine of the National Communication Association*, February 4, 2021. https://www.natcom.org/spectra/mental-health-academia-during-covid-pandemic.

Hanshaw, Larry. 2012. "Qualitative Aspects of Group-Only Testing." *College Student Journal* 46, no. 2: 419–426.

House, Lisa, Chelsea Neal, and Jason Kolb. 2020. "Supporting the Mental Health Needs of First Generation College Students." *Journal of College Student Psychotherapy* 34, no. 2: 157–167. doi:10.1080/87568225.2019.1578940.

Huckins, Jeremy F., Alex W. DaSilva, Weichen Wang, Elin Hedlund, Courtney Rogers, Subigya K. Nepal, Jialing Wu, Mikio Obuchi, Eilis I. Murphy, Meghan L. Meyer, et al. 2020. "Mental Health and Behavior of College Students During the Early Phases of the COVID-19 Pandemic: Longitudinal Smartphone and Ecological Momentary Assessment Study." *Journal of Medical Internet Research* 22, no. 6: e20185. https://www.jmir.org/2020/6/e20185.

Hughes, Jessica M.F. 2016. "Increasing Neurodiversity in Disability and Social Justice Advocacy Groups." Autistic Self Advocacy Network, June 2016. https://autisticadvocacy.org/wp-content/uploads/2016/06/whitepaper-Increasing-Neurodiversity-in-Disability-and-Social-Justice-Advocacy-Groups.pdf.

Jahnke, Art. 2020. "In College Students, COVID-19 Has Increased Depression Rates and Raised New Barriers to Mental Health Care." *The Brink: Pioneering Research from Boston University*, July 9, 2020. http://www.bu.edu/articles/2020/college-students-covid-19-increased-depression-rate-and-raised-barriers-to-mental-health care.

Jiang, Manyu. 2020, April 22. The Reason Zoom Calls Drain Your Energy. *BBC*. April 22, 2020. https://www.bbc.com/worklife/article/20200421-why-zoom-video-chats-are-so-exhausting

Juhary, Jowati. 2020. "COVID-19 Outbreak: A Critical Reflection on Teaching." In *10th International Conference, The Future of Education – Virtual Edition (Florence, Italy, 18–19 June 2020): Conference Proceedings*, edited by Pixel. Bologna: Filodiritto Editore.

Krebs, Emily. 2019. "Baccalaureates or Burdens? Complicating 'Reasonable Accommodations' for American College Students with Disabilities." *Disability Studies Quarterly* 39, no. 3. doi:10.18061/dsq.v39i3.6557.

LaBelle, Sara. 2020. "The Communicative Roles of Faculty in Students' Mental Health Management." *Spectra: The Magazine of the National Communication Association*, May 2020. https://www.natcom.org/sites/default/files/publications/NCA_SpectraMay2020.pdf.

Lee, K. 2020. "Coronavirus: Universities are Shifting Classes online—But It's Not as Easy as It Sounds." *The Conversation*, March 9, 2020. https://theconversation.com/coronavirus-universities-are-shifting-classes-online-but-its-not-as-easy-as-it-sounds-133030.

Lehan, Tara, Heather Hussey, and Ashley Babcock. 2020. "Mission Unaccomplished: Beyond 'Talk [ing] a Good Game' to Promote Diversity and Inclusion." *Journal of Educational Research and Practice* 10, no.1: 167–184. doi:10.5590/JERAP.2020.10.1.12.

Looi, Chee-Kit, Shiau-Wei Chan, and Longkai Wu. 2021. "Crisis and Opportunity: Transforming Teachers From Curriculum Deliverers to Designers of Learning." In *Radical Solutions for Education in a Crisis Context*, edited by Daniel Burgos, Ahmed Tlili, and Anita Tabacco, 131–145. Singapore: Springer.

McRuer, Robert. 2006. *Crip Theory: Cultural Signs of Queerness and Disability*. New York: NYU Press.

Meyer, Anne, David H. Rose, and David Gordon. 2014. *Universal Design for Learning: Theory and Practice*. Wakefield, MA: CAST.

Oswalt, Sara, Alyssa Lederer, Kimberly Chestnut-Steich, Carol Day, Ashlee Halbritter, and Dugeidy Ortiz. 2020. "Trends in College Students' Mental Health Diagnoses and Utilization of Services, 2009–2015." *Journal of American College Health* 68, no. 1: 41–51. doi:10.1080/07448481.2018.1515748.

Parkman-Williams, Elijah. 2021. "Survey Shows Having Video Conferencing Cameras Off Changes Student and Faculty Perception of Remote Learning." *The College Voice*, March 12, 2021. https://www.mcccvoice.org/cameras-on-cameras-off/

Petillion, Riley J., and W. Stephen McNeil. 2020. "Student Experiences of Emergency Remote Teaching: Impacts of Instructor Practice on Student Learning,

Engagement, and Well-Being." *Journal of Chemical Education* 97, no. 9: 2486–2493. doi:10.1021/acs.jchemed.0c00733.

Phuong, Andrew Estrada Judy Nguyenb, and Dena Mariea. 2017. "Evaluating an Adaptive Equity-Oriented Pedagogy: A Study of its Impacts in Higher Education." *Journal of Effective Teaching* 17, no. 2: 5–44.

Price, Sarah F., Heather J. Carmack, and Kequing Kuang. 2020. "Contradictions and Predicaments in Instructors' Boundary Negotiations of Students' Health Disclosures." *Health Communication* 1–9. doi:10.1080/10410236.2020.1712525.

Prizant, Barry M., and Tom Fields-Meyer. 2015. *Uniquely Human: A Different Way of Seeing Autism*. New York: Simon and Schuster.

Reed, Matt. 2020. "Should Showing Faces Be Mandatory?" *Confessions of a Community College Dean* (blog), *Inside Higher Ed*. May 13, 2020. https://www.insidehighered.com/blogs/confessions-community-college-dean/should-showing-faces-be-mandatory.

Schwartzman, Roy. 2020. "Performing Pandemic Pedagogy." *Communication Education* 69, no. 4: 502–517. doi:10.1080/03634523.2020.1804602.

Scott, Samantha R., Kenia M. Rivera, Ella Rushing, Erika M. Manczak, Christopher S. Rozek, and Jenalee R. Doom. 2021. "'I Hate This': A Qualitative Analysis of Adolescents' Self-Reported Challenges During the COVID-19 Pandemic." *Journal of Adolescent Health* 68, no. 2: 262–269. doi:10.1016/j.jadohealth.2020.11.010.

Smith, Rachel A., and Amanda Applegate. 2018. "Mental Health Stigma and Communication and Their Intersections with Education." *Communication Education* 67, no. 3: 382–393. doi:10.1080/03634523.2018.1465988.

Solomon-Pryce, Carolyn. 2015. "Is Equity the Same as Equality?" *Equity, Diversity and Inclusion* (blog), *London School of Economics*. December 9, 2015. https://blogs.lse.ac.uk/equityDiversityInclusion/2015/12/is-equity-the-same-as-equality.

Steinberger, Pnina, Yovav Eshet, and Keren Grinautsky. 2021. "No Anxious Student Is Left Behind: Statistics Anxiety, Personality Traits, and Academic Dishonesty—Lessons from COVID-19." *Sustainability* 13, no. 9: 4762. doi:10.3390/su13094762S.

Swaner, Lynn E. 2007. "Linking Engaged Learning, Student Mental Health and Well-Being, and Civic Development: A Review of the Literature." *Liberal Education* 951: 16–25.

The Teaching Commons. n.d. "Universal Design for Learning." Georgetown University (website). Accessed April 1, 2021. https://commons.georgetown.edu/teaching/design/universal-design.

Tulloch, Scott. 2021. "Trauma Informed Approaches to Media Studies: Reflections from an Epicenter." *Flow: A Critical Forum on Media and Culture*, March 15, 2021. https://www.flowjournal.org/2021/03/trauma-informed-approaches-to-media-studies/.

Turosak, Anna, and Siwierka, Julia. 2019. "Mental Health and Stigma on Campus: Insights from Students' Lived Experience." *Journal of Prevention & Intervention in the Community* 1–16. doi:10.1080/10852352.2019.1654264.

U.S. Centers for Disease Control and Prevention, 2020. "Infographic: 6 Guiding Principles to a Trauma-Informed Approach." Sep 17, 2020. https://www.cdc.gov/cpr/infographics/6_principles_trauma_info.htm.

WSA (Washington Student Association). 2020. "WSA 2021 Legislative Agenda." WSA. Accessed December 19, 2020. https://www.wastudents.org/our-work.
Willer, Erin K., Emily Krebs, Nivea Castaneda, and April Samaras. 2021. "Mad to the Bone: Learning Outcomes of Critical Grief Pedagogy." *Communication Education* 70, no. 1: 27–48. doi:10.1080/03634523.2020.1834118.
Winkie, Luke. 2020. "Meet the Students Thriving in Remote Learning." *Vox*, September 14, 2020. https://www.vox.com/first-person/21433095/coroanavirus-covid-19-school-reopening-online-learning-remote.
Wood, Julia T. 2016. *Interpersonal Communication: Everyday Encounters*, 8th edition. Boston, MA: Cengage Learning.
Zhai, Yusen, and Xue Du. 2020. "Addressing Collegiate Mental Health Amid COVID-19 Pandemic." *Psychiatry Research* 288: 113003. doi:10.1016/j.psychres.2020.113003.
Zook, Kristal Brent. 2021. "How Black Lives Matter Came to the Academy." *The New Yorker,* January 30, 2021. https://www.newyorker.com/news/the-political-scene/how-black-lives-matter-came-to-the-academy.

Chapter 8

The Pandemic and Disability Inclusive Pedagogy

Examining the Response to COVID-19 in Higher Education

Brittany N. Lash

Students with disabilities make up a growing number of students on college campuses (Scott, McGuire, and Foley 2003). This is a unique student population that faces obstacles in college environments different from those of able-bodied students. In an average higher education environment, students with disabilities may experience various barriers to learning, such as difficulty completing assignments, gaining accommodations, and accessing information in lectures (Macleod and Cebula 2009; Najarian 2008). With COVID-10 changing the structural and pedagogical landscape of higher education, students with disabilities experienced both additional challenges and increased accessibility in this learning environment. Overall, there is much to be learned from the changes to higher education during the pandemic and how those changes impacted students with disabilities.

This chapter will first briefly describe this student population. Then, I will highlight the common changes to pedagogy during the pandemic and outline how they impacted this population, in both challenging and beneficial ways. Finally, given some of the pedagogical lessons prompted by the COVID-19 response in higher education, this chapter will pose recommendations for best practices moving forward for accommodating students with disabilities.

STUDENTS WITH DISABILITIES

College environments are often quite diverse as institutions of higher education serve many unique student groups. Given these diverse student bodies, we must consider the inclusivity of our classroom design and policies as we strive to ensure that classroom material and structure is accessible to all students (Boothe et al. 2018; Scott, McGuire, and Foley 2003). Students with disabilities are one particular student population that needs to be considered as we work to make our campuses and learning environments inclusive and accessible (Joyce 2017), pre- and post-pandemic. Of the U.S. population in general, 13.1 % report having some form of disability (Houtenville and Boege 2020), a steadily growing number. Similarly, reports indicate this population's presence on campus is also growing as the number of students with disabilities on college campuses continues to steadily increase (Scott, McGuire, and Foley 2003). Despite this, students with disabilities have lower retention rates, are less likely to complete their degree, and, if they do complete their degree, they take longer to do so (Murray et al. 2000). In fact, pre-pandemic, the average retention rate for students with disabilities is only 12 percent (Rigler 2013).

Currently, about 19 % of undergraduate students report having a disability (National Center for Education Statistics 2019). Of those undergraduate students with disabilities, the most popularly reported disabilities include learning disabilities (31 %; e.g., dyslexia, dysgraphia, language processing disorders), ADHD (18 %), psychiatric disabilities (15 %; e.g., bipolar disorder, depression, anxiety, obsessive compulsive disorder), health/chronic disabilities (11 %; e.g., diabetes, multiple sclerosis, seizure disorders, migraines), and mobility disabilities (7 %) (National Center for College Students with Disabilities 2020). Other disabilities that are present in current undergraduate populations include deafness or hearing loss, visibility impairments, brain injuries (e.g., concussions, traumatic brain injury), and developmental disabilities (e.g., autism). Thus, students with disabilities are a diverse student group who experience higher education in unique ways. The rest of this chapter will examine those experiences during the COVID-19 pandemic as well as what we can learn from them.

STUDENTS WITH DISABILITIES AND THE RESPONSE TO COVID-19 IN HIGHER EDUCATION

With the advent of COVID-19 forcing college campuses around the world to rethink course delivery and campus life in general, we saw many notable changes to the structure of higher education. Some of these changes ended up benefiting students with disabilities, making classes and their materials more accessible. However, some of the pandemic adaptations only posed further barriers for this student population. I will start by discussing the initial response to the COVID-19 pandemic as that period was unique and characterized by quick, but often major, changes driven by uncertainty and shifting health recommendations. From there, the rest of this section will examine some of the more long-term adjustments made in higher education and how those alterations impacted students with disabilities.

Initial Response to Pandemic

In March of 2020, for most colleges and universities an increasing rate of COVID-19 infections forced administrations to make decisions to send students home and move classes to remote learning formats to slow the transmission of the disease and protect public safety. While students in general faced a wide variety of challenges as campuses rapidly transitioned to online learning, these challenges were particularly prescient for students with disabilities (Scott 2020). In comparison to the general student population, during this transition, students with disabilities reported increased difficulty accessing necessary technological equipment and devices for online learning, gaining access to network/Wi-Fi, accessing course materials and exams, and communicating with instructors. They also faced barriers to gaining necessary technology support and were more likely to report difficulty accessing the campus learning management system (i.e., blackboard, canvas, etc.) (Scott 2020).

To make things more challenging, gaining access to necessary accommodations also proved to be difficult during this rapid transition. Students with disabilities struggled to work with disability resource officers (DROs) as they scrambled to reassess and identify new barriers to access as well as solutions to those barriers in the changing environment (Scott 2020). Disability resource offices experienced an increased workload as the sudden shift to remote learning posed new, unexpected situations and an uptick in students needing accommodations. Simultaneously, DROs and campus ADA (Americans with Disability Act) coordinators reported difficulty with gaining support to necessary technology or software to support students with disabilities. These professionals also highlighted challenges in communicating with faculty about inclusive course design to ensure accessible remote course content (Scott 2020).

In that initial shift, students with disabilities encountered increased difficulties outside of the classroom as well. Students with disabilities were more likely to face financial strain, experience food and housing insecurity, and leave campus to unsafe living environments (Scott 2020; Soria et al. 2020). Additionally, students in general often rely on campus-based health services, which were interrupted or lost altogether during the transition to virtual learning environments. Students with disabilities require more regular healthcare visits and rely on services that cannot be translated into a virtual experience (Chugani and Houtrow 2020). Students with mental health needs reported additional barriers to accessing necessary mental health care, barriers that were compounded by privacy concerns online or at home, access to technology and Wi-Fi, and difficulty using virtual systems due to a physical disability (Chugani and Houtrow 2020).

After the initial frenzied transition to remote learning mid-semester in the spring of 2020, the summer of 2020 allowed an opportunity for administration, faculty, and staff to think through how to best approach classes and campus life for the 2020–2021 academic year. Thus, the increased use of technology, the changes we saw to classroom structure, and adjustments to campus life were a bit more methodical going into that next year. The rest of this section will examine these adjustments and how they impacted students with disabilities.

Increased Use of Technology

An increased reliance on technology was prompted by the COVID-19 pandemic as social-distancing requirements meant that fewer people could meet at once. Thus, many classes were moved to hybrid or hyflex structures, which required the use of technology to make class material or content readily available outside of the classroom in unprecedented ways. With this increased use of technology, students with disabilities experienced both increased access to materials as well as additional challenges in the learning environment. The integration of various forms of technology into the college classroom can "minimize students' disabilities, increase their motivation, engagement as well as performance" (Peng and Daud 2015, 50). However, it can also hinder learning if used in ineffective ways (Seale 2006). Traditionally, literature examining technology use for students with disabilities is divided into two categories: (1) assistive technology and (2) instructional technology. These categories will be used to guide the discussion of technology use during the COVID-19 pandemic.

Assistive Technology. Assistive technology (AT) is any technology that helps students meet any physical needs they may have (Al-Ibrahim 2019). This takes the form of hearing aids, note-takers, interpreters, screen readers, text-to-speech technology, real-time captioning, and mobility assistance (i.e., wheelchairs, crutches, etc.). Even lower-tech forms of technology can prove assistive. For example, the use of emails or announcements via a course learning management system before or after class or group meetings or the use of a working, shared computer document in-class can be helpful communication strategies that keep disabled students on track with course material (Elliot et al. 2016).

During the COVID-19 pandemic, many courses moved to updated formats (i.e., hybrid, hyflex, fully remote, etc.) to accommodate social-distancing requirements. As such, some forms of AT, such as regular emails or announcements, became regular practice for most faculty attempting to keep students up to date. However, we saw barriers to other forms of AT. Many college instructors are not trained in the use of assistive technologies (i.e., working with an interpreter, captioning videos, writing documents so they are accessible for text-to-speech technology, etc.). This lack of training can lead to the improper or inefficient use of these technologies in the classroom (Peng and Daud 2015), ultimately harming the learning opportunities of students who need them. With the changes required by COVID-19, not only were faculty asked to restructure their classes, integrating the use of AT in the process only added further challenges. Additionally, finding professionally trained interpreters, note-takers, and support staff is challenging for some institutions in pre-pandemic circumstances (Cawthon, Schoffstalll, and Garberoglio 2014). During COVID-19, access to interpreters, note-takers, and other support staff grew increasingly more difficult to navigate given social-distancing requirements and varied course formats (Scott 2020).

As an additional barrier, to access these assistive technologies, students must ultimately disclose about their disability, something they might not be accustomed to or comfortable doing as many students have not had to self-advocate prior to the transition to college (Cawthon, Schoffstalll, and Garberoglio 2014). As such, they are often hesitant to do so, leaving them without these accommodations. This was further complicated by the pandemic as communicating with DROs and disability resource offices became challenging, particularly while new procedures were being developed. Additionally, upon accessing these resources, students still faced barriers getting the needed technology for accommodations (Scott 2020). Due to these challenges to accessing and using AT, instructional technology is another option available (and one more closely aligned with Universal Design) to help make material accessible.

Instructional Technology. Instructional technology (IT) is technology that assists students with their instructional needs by allowing them to view lessons, using technology, independently and at a pace that accommodates their needs. This may take the form of videos, recorded presentations, simulations, and so on that a student can access outside of class (Al-Ibrahim 2019). This might also take the form of making class notes available online after class, providing outlines of lectures for students to download and print before class, or the use of discussion boards online to facilitate discussion in a way that is accessible to all, regardless of ability or even presence in the classroom (Johnson, Pliner, and Burkhart 2002; Schley and Stinson 2016).

The COVID-19 pandemic pushed many instructors to adopt various IT as material often had to be made available online or outside of the classroom. However, the ability to use IT can vary based on content of the class, motivation and attitude of the instructor, technical knowledge of the instructor, and student access to technology (Nilsson and Pareto 2010). While various forms of IT can help make educational content more accessible to a variety of students (Cawthon, Schoffstalll, and Garberoglio 2014), the use of such technology without a clear purpose or design can render it ineffective altogether (Peng and Daud 2015). As Peng and Daud (2015, 57–58) point out, "the success of integrating technologies in classrooms heavily relies on the teachers' ability to deploy them meaningfully" (Peng and Daud 2015, 57–58). While the use of these instructional technologies can benefit all students, but especially students with disabilities, variation in instructor knowledge or skill in using these technologies poses challenges.

Additionally, given the diversity of student disability, some IT strategies may be more or less accessible to certain students. For example, students who are suffering from concussions or who experience chronic migraines might struggle with course material that requires heavy screen use (Chugani and Houtrow 2020). Further, simply making recordings available online might help some students, but others, such as those with hearing loss might struggle to find these accessible without captioning or transcription services provided. Similarly, those who are visibly impaired might have difficulty accessing documents online (i.e., notes the instructor made available, assignments, instructions, etc.) if an instructor is unaware of how to format documents so that they are text-to-speech friendly. Further, including hyperlinks without meaningful labels or images without alt-text might also prevent visibly impaired students from accessing instructional materials (Behling 2017). Thus, while instructional technologies can certainly make classroom material more accessible, it must be used purposefully and with disability accessibility in mind when being designed.

Changes to Course Structure

In addition to increased technology use to make course material/content available, the COVID-19 pandemic also prompted many changes to course structure itself. Hybrid or hyflex course arrangements became popular ways to manage social-distancing requirements. For many faculty and instructors, this encouraged a move to a flipped classroom approach. This section will discuss these course structures and their impact on students with disabilities during the pandemic. This discussion will be prefaced by an overview of

Universal Design for Learning (UDL) as many of these changes to classroom structure are in line with UDL principles.

Universal Design for Learning. A strategy that can make classroom design more accessible to all students, regardless of diverse needs is UDL (Boothe et al. 2018; Scott, McGuire, and Foley 2003). UDL promotes flexibility in classroom and course design as we consider the "why," "how," and "what" of learning. By offering flexibility and variety in how material is presented/delivered, engaged with, and evaluated, we can help ensure that most of our students are able to access the course information in a way that works for them (Boothe et al. 2018). The Higher Education Opportunity Act (2008) defines UDL as course design that is flexible in how material is presented, how students engage with material, and how student knowledge or skills are evaluated. Universal Design is acknowledged as "good pedagogy" as it "does not privilege one particular modality over another or one kind of cognitive function over another. Rather, creating a universally inclusive curriculum requires actively engaging all students in learning regardless of the disability status" (Johnson, Pliner, and Burkhart 2002, 221). UDL allows for students to access course materials and complete class assignments in a manner that works best for them. It does so by promoting flexibility in how students learn course information as well as how they demonstrate mastery of that information. This often benefits all students and not just students with disabilities.

UDL includes multiple means of representation, multiple means of engagement, and multiple means of action and expression. First, UDL pushes for multiple means of representation, which is the ways in which students receive or acquire course information. Suggestions include using multiple formats, highlighting critical information, using an organized and easy-to-use learning management system, providing prompt feedback, and designing a syllabus with clear policies regarding disability accommodations as well as general course expectations (Boothe et al. 2018; Rao, Edelen-Smith, and Wailehua 2015; Scott, Temple, and Marshall 2015; Scott and Temple 2017; Smith 2012). UDL also emphasizes the need for multiple ways in which students can engage with course material (multiple means of engagement) by recommending collaborative learning opportunities (i.e., class or group discussions or online discussion boards), a variety of ways to access course materials (i.e., recorded lectures, transcripts, videos with captioning, online articles, textbook readings, etc.), the use of shared word documents to facilitate group work and discussion, scaffolding materials, and faculty accessibility to students via consistent email or office hour availability (Boothe et al. 2018; Gradel and Edson 2009; Schelly, Davies, and Spooner 2011; Schley and Stinson 2016; Smith 2012). Finally, UDL also advocates for multiple means of action and expression, or flexibility in how students demonstrate their understanding of course material. To meet this UDL goal, faculty should make sure assignment guidelines and expectations are clear, use discussion boards (even in person) to guide class discussion, provide choices regarding assignment formats (i.e., video vs. written), and collect summative assessments to highlight areas that need further instruction (Boothe et al. 2018; Gradel and Edson 2009; Rao, Edelen-Smith, and Wailehua 2015; Scott and Temple 2017; Smith 2012).

Given that UDL often relies on the use of technology in ways that are fully accessible to all students, much of the earlier discussion surrounding the use of assistive and IT is important to consider as instructors design and share class materials. Further, many of these UDL principles can be seen in hybrid, hyflex, and flipped classrooms. The next few sections will discuss these approaches to class formats as we saw them grow in popularity in response to the changes to higher education required by the pandemic.

Hybrid and Hyflex Classrooms. During the COVID-19 pandemic, many higher education classes switched to a hybrid or hyflex formats to meet social-distancing requirements while still maintaining some in-person engagement. Hybrid classes are classes that are taught by making some course content available online and some in face-to-face classroom settings. Hyflex classrooms allow students to choose between attending the class in person, attending the class virtually online, or doing some combination of the two. Because of the potential flexibility of both the hybrid and hyflex formats, which helps meet UDL principles, many students with disabilities are drawn to these class settings (Behling 2017). However, the true accessibility of a hybrid or hyflex class depends on the accessibility of the learning management system (e.g., Blackboard, Canvas, etc.), the publisher materials (e.g., online text materials, case study examples, notes, etc. provided by the publisher), and the instructor materials (e.g., documents, files, recordings, assignments, etc. produced by the instructor) used in the course. Thus, hybrid and hyflex courses have the potential to be more accessible to students with disabilities, but only if the technology utilized in those courses is designed with accessibility in mind (see sections on technology).

UDL considerations such as ensuring early access to course materials, making sure disability resources are listed in the syllabus, designing course sites and documents in ways that are accessible, and including captioning or transcripts for all recorded materials are some ways in which to safeguard the accessibility of a hybrid or hyflex course (Behling 2017). However, many faculty are either unaware of or untrained in how to make materials, particularly online materials (the learning management system used, course documents/assignments, recordings, etc.) fully accessible (Behling 2017; Wynants and Dennis 2017). Thus, inaccessible materials and course content often act as barriers to the accessibility of a hybrid or hyflex class that might otherwise be more accessible than a traditional class format.

Flipped Classrooms. Due to the increased hybrid and hyflex classrooms, many faculty moved to a flipped classroom approach during the pandemic. A flipped classroom moves all traditional lecture outside of the classroom environment through the use of web-based technology leaving class time for interactive activities and discussion, allowing for students to engage in more active learning of the concepts and material (Al-Ibrahim 2019). In general, the use of flipped classrooms has proven to be a helpful strategy for students with disabilities. The use of a flipped classroom allows for students to self-pace their learning outside of class, accommodating any extra time students with disabilities might need. Further, many recording programs also offer transcriptions or captioning, making recorded lectures or presentations more accessible than they may have been in the classroom. Thus, flipped classrooms are often more in line with UDL principles than a traditional class lecture format. Additionally, students have reported an increased sense of motivation in the class as well as an increased willingness to engage in active learning or collaborative in-class activities with the flipped class format (Al-Ibrahim 2019). Overall, if materials available online are accessible to students with disabilities (see sections on technology), a flipped classroom is naturally a more accommodating class structure than a traditional approach.

Campus Life and Student Health

In addition to changes in the classroom environment, the pandemic affected campus life and student health as well. In general, pre-pandemic, students with disabilities experienced various barriers to campus inclusion that remained present, or were even heightened, during COVID-19. Campus environments are not always readily accessible for students with disabilities. For example, disabled students might need visual signaling devices for various types of alarms/bells (e.g., doorbell, smoke/fire alarm, carbon dioxide alarm, tornado sirens, active shooter sirens/alarms, etc.). Additionally, they may need various types of communication accommodations (e.g., interpreters, text that can be screen read, braille, etc.) for extracurricular activities, sporting events, or programs outside of the classroom (Cawthon and Leppo 2013). Ensuring that areas and events beyond the classroom are accessible can go a long way in making campus social environments more welcoming to students with disabilities, and they also communicate a general openness toward these students (Cawthon, Schoffstalll, and Garberoglio 2014). In terms of structural accessibility, the buildings should utilize a universal design approach (i.e., ramps, elevators, open sightlines, sufficient lighting, etc.) that ensures students with disabilities are able to utilize campus environments as they attempt to interact with their peers and access various places on campus, helping these students feel like they have a place in the campus community (Cawthon, Schoffstalll, and Garberoglio 2014). Some of the environmental unique challenges students with disabilities faced during the pandemic included face masks (challenges for students with hearing loss), COVID-19 protocol signage or directional arrows to guide foot traffic (often not accessible for those with severe visual impairments), and easy access to buildings (limited entrances and exits posed challenges for those with mobility impairments).

During the pandemic, not only did they face some additional environmental barriers, feelings of being excluded from campus life for students with disabilities were also heightened. Students with disabilities reported they "were less likely to believe that they feel like they belong on campus and less likely to agree that the campus supported them during the pandemic" (Soria et al. 2020, 1). Nearly three-quarters of students without disabilities felt that the university supported them during COVID-19, but only 41–57 percent of students with disabilities (depending on the type of disability) felt supported. Similarly, while most (87 percent) students without disabilities felt as though they belonged on campus during the pandemic, only 60–76 percent of students with disabilities felt the same (depending again on the type of disability) (Soria et al. 2020). As a sense of belonging is linked to student success, retention, and graduation (Leake and Stodden 2014), making sure students with disabilities feel included is important to their academic achievement.

On top of feeling less a part of the campus community, students with disabilities experienced other impacts of the COVID-19 pandemic in ways that were often more intense than the general student population. Students with disabilities were more likely to experience financial hardships during this time due to unexpected increased technology needs/costs and increased living expenses in comparison to students without disabilities. This was compounded by the fact that students with disabilities were also more likely to report lost wages or employment (Soria et al. 2020). Further, students with disabilities were more likely to experience food insecurity and housing insecurity than students without disabilities during the pandemic. Finally, students with disabilities were less likely to have a place to live in which they felt safe (i.e., safe from emotional or physical abuse, safe from drug or alcohol abuse, or a place where their identity was respected) in comparison to students without disabilities (Soria et al. 2020). Thus, students with disabilities not only faced challenges with accessible material inside of the classroom, but had to navigate feeling unsupported on campus as well as financial, food, housing, and safety concerns.

Mental Health. In addition to, and because of, challenges to their general physical health (i.e., access to food, housing, and safe environments), students with disabilities faced struggles regarding mental health during the pandemic. Given the isolation caused by social distancing and quarantining protocols, many college students in general faced unexpected and unprecedented mental health concerns (Son et al. 2020; Wang et al. 2020). The number of students needing mental health care during the COVID-19 pandemic sharply increased. Research found that nearly three-quarters of the college students they surveyed reported increased stress levels (Wang et al. 2020). Increases in stress centered around academic performance in the new class formats, concerns about their health or the health of a loved one, experiences of social isolation, and uncertainty surrounding financial and living situations (Son et al. 2020; Wang et al. 2020). Further, college students reported higher rates of both depression and anxiety (Wang et al. 2020) as well as feelings of loneliness, hopelessness, and suicidal thoughts (Son et al. 2020). This is particularly problematic as, even pre-pandemic, student demand for mental health services on college campuses exceeded what many campuses could keep up with (Meleo-Erwin et al. 2021). The increasing need for mental health services in addition to the need to make these services available in remote formats during the pandemic further taxed campus mental health centers.

While college students in general experienced an increased need for mental health care, so did students with disabilities. Overall, students with physical, cognitive, or intellectual disabilities are more likely to experience mental disabilities (Chugani and Houtrow 2020; Soria et al. 2020). We saw mental health care needs increase even more sharply during the pandemic for this student population. During the pandemic, of students with physical, cognitive, or intellectual disabilities, 53–70 percent screened positive for major depressive disorder and 63–80 percent screened positive for generalized anxiety disorder, compared to 34 percent and 38 percent, respectively, of students without disabilities (Soria et al. 2020). As such, the need for mental health support also sharply increased for this student population during the pandemic.

Despite the increase in students, both with and without disabilities, needing mental health care, barriers to such care prevented students from accessing such care. In fact, 93 percent of the students who reported increased stress and anxiety did not seek out mental health care (Son et al. 2020). Barriers to mental health care for college students included stigma, lack of trust in services provided, and discomfort with telehealth options (Son et al. 2020). Other barriers to mental health care included a lack of information about the services provided and how to access them, limited access to services on campus, and concerns about cost (Wang et al. 2020). Overall, while we saw mental health concerns across college students increase exponentially during the COVID-19 pandemic, most students did not access the support services available to them.

RECOMMENDATIONS MOVING FORWARD

Given the observations and experiences of students with disability in higher education during the COVID-19 pandemic, there are several ways we can learn from and improve educational experiences for this population moving forward. First and foremost, faculty training and faculty development opportunities surrounding class accessibility, UDL, the use of technology, and working with this student population in general are a vital ingredient to making the campus environment more accommodating and supportive of students with disabilities (Scott 2020; Meleo-Erwin et al. 2021). Faculty who participate in this type of training feel more self-efficacious and prepared to help students who might need accommodations; they are also perceived to be more empathetic to the needs of students with disabilities (Joyce 2017).

Many faculty are resistant to UDL due to confusion, lack of technological knowledge, and concerns about time and resources. However, training in UDL can help make faculty feel more positively, knowledgeable, and confident about using UDL strategies (Wynants and Dennis 2017). Further, the pandemic prompted many faculty to adopt more flexible and varied approaches to how material in their courses was presented, delivered, and evaluated, something that should stick around post-pandemic given that it is in line with the principles of UDL. Workshops and training that emphasize UDL could help faculty improve upon the approaches they may have already taken in response to the pandemic, finding ways to utilize these strategies to continue to benefit an increasingly diverse student body.

Faculty would also benefit from professional development opportunities and support surrounding the use of technology that often accompanies UDL approaches as well as remote, hybrid, hyflex, or flipped classes. The use of assistive and IT has a learning curve for both students and faculty (Seale 2006), as demonstrated during the transition to remote classes. For example, many faculty members may not be aware of how to add captioning to online content or how to make online content screen-reader friendly (Scott 2020). Being trained in the use of such technology can help faculty feel more prepared to accommodate students with disabilities and can make these students feel more welcomed in the classroom. Any initiatives to design online materials in universally accessible ways can be supported by providing no-pressure, voluntary accessibility checks for faculty who might be interested in feedback (Scott 2020). Moreover, simply having access to information about accommodation resources and making classrooms accessible can ease the stress and anxiety faculty might experience when working with students with disabilities (Meleo-Erwin et al. 2021).

In addition to making sure faculty have access to training and support, students with disabilities themselves need to be able to easily access and navigate disability services available to them on campus. In general, there are many barriers for students with disabilities who may need accommodations on campus. These include discomfort disclosing about the disability (Luft 2014; Scott, McGuire, and Foley 2003), fear of discrimination or stigmatizing attitudes/treatment (Macleod and Cebula 2009; Najarian 2008), and uncertainty surrounding how to advocate for themselves (Palmer and Roessler 2000). In fact, some faculty doubt the disability status of their students and the need for accommodations, making these students feel even less safe asking for such accommodations (Leake and Stodden 2014). Research has noted an underutilization of accommodation services because of these barriers (Luft 2014). Students opt to "get by" without accommodations in order to pass as a "regular" student or to avoid "inconveniencing the system" (Cawthon and Leppo 2013, 445), often placing them at risk academically.

One way that higher education institutions can help is by making the process of finding and accessing disability resources as easy as possible. Research indicates that many students with disabilities on college campuses do not understand or are not aware of the processes required to get accommodations (Palmer and Roessler 2000). Prior to college, these students did not have to navigate the accommodation process themselves; their parents did it for them. College is often the first time they have to disclose about their disability or self-advocate for accommodations. This lack of awareness or uncertainty surrounding how to navigate this process, or even what they are entitled to, deters students with disabilities from seeking out disability support resources altogether. As such, these students might never get the accommodations they need to succeed in the classroom (Cawthon et al. 2015). Making sure that the disability services office is easily located, contact information for this office is available on the university website, and the process of gaining accommodations is straightforward are some steps higher education institutions can take to facilitate the use of these services.

In addition to making sure disability services are easily accessible, the pandemic highlighted the need to make information about and access to mental health support services easy to find as well. Staff and faculty should be well informed about the mental health services provided to students, how students can access these services, and be able to proactively share and disseminate information about these resources to students (Soria et al. 2020). Further, higher education institutions should ensure that mental health resources are easy to find and access on websites. The use of social media to promote and provide information about mental health services is another effective way to get this information to students (Son et al. 2020). Since students with disabilities are more likely to experience mental health concerns, mental health centers on campus should partner and communicate with disability support services in an effort to help promote and coordinate these two existing resources (Soria et al. 2020). Making sure that students know what resources are available and how to access those resources are key first steps in reducing barriers surrounding student uncertainty in these areas.

In order to help mitigate hesitancy to seek out mental health support due to social stigma, mental health services should also be available online through the use of telehealth or mobile apps. These remote or online ways of accessing mental health care can be less daunting to students and allow them to easily communicate with caregivers both on and off campus (Son et al. 2020). Students gravitate to mobile apps that aid students in self-care, such as apps that help with meditation, to help them cope with stress (Wang et al. 2020). These types of mental health support allow students to attend to their mental health needs without the fear of being seen at the campus mental health center (Wang et al. 2020). Given all this, there is still much research to be done regarding which approaches to mental health care are best suited to and most supportive of college student life.

Moving forward, it is also vital that disability support services, mental health and counseling centers, and the faculty and staff that operate these services have clear procedures and guidelines in place for future disruptions to "normal" class or campus operations. While "achieving educational equity for students with disabilities has long been a goal" for institutions of higher education, "the pandemic has highlighted how advances toward equity are often lost during crises" (Chugani and Houtrow 2020, 1722). In the initial response to COVID-19, there was no clear plan for students with disabilities, uncertainty surrounding accommodations in remote formats, and lack of communication to both this student population and the faculty that work with them (Scott 2020). This lack of a plan for this student population ultimately heightened their challenges in navigating the move to remote classes as well as threatened their general health and well-being. Clear guidelines and policies for future shifts to their learning environments can help prevent this student population from being lost in the shuffle again and eliminate uncertainty for faculty and staff working with them.

Most campuses' focus surrounding accessibility is aimed at students with disabilities in the classroom even though accessibility issues often extend beyond the classroom. There is very little research on campus climate or creating an inclusive social environment for students with disabilities (Leake and Stodden 2014). The research that is available emphasizes that colleges and universities should make sure that all campus facilities are physically accessible to create welcoming environments for this student population. Further, institutions should ensure that disability support services are available outside of the classroom as well (i.e., student research participation or assistance, social/recreational campus activities, or other nonacademic campus activities). These steps can help create more inclusive campus environments post-pandemic and support an active student life for students with disabilities (Leake and Stodden 2014).

Supporting students with disabilities also needs to include services that combat the higher risks of financial, housing, and food insecurity experienced by this population. This need was highlighted during the pandemic as students with disabilities were more likely to experience increased financial burdens, unsafe living environments, and food insecurity. Moving forward, campus initiatives to provide emergency housing for students with disabilities who do not have safe environments to live in might help mitigate some of the challenges surrounding financial and housing insecurity (Soria et al. 2020). Making sure that food delivery options are readily available on campus would support those with mobility impairments who might struggle to access healthy food options in the community. Additionally, positioning food pantries in areas that are easily accessible is vital to ensuring this student population can access them (Soria et al. 2020). All of these sorts of initiatives on campuses should be promoted at disability resource centers to be sure students with disabilities are aware of these resources available to them.

The challenges students with disabilities faced during the COVID-19 pandemic, particularly during the initial response to the pandemic, could have been mitigated with careful consideration of this student population. However, currently, many diversity initiatives and conversations often leave out disability. This lack of representation renders this student population invisible and accessibility becomes an afterthought. To further promote inclusion of this population in higher education, campuses should be sure to include disability in their diversity initiatives and discussions. It is also important that students with disabilities see themselves represented in faculty and staff. This not only provides these students with potential mentors, advocates, and role models but also communicates that they belong in all areas of campus (Leake and Stodden 2014). Finally, in terms of staffing, many disability resource centers and mental health centers are vastly understaffed and under supported, a fact that was particularly salient during the pandemic (Scott 2020; Soria et al. 2020). Making sure these services are fully staffed and have access to the resources they need will help ensure that students with disabilities and mental health needs can get the necessary support they need. Additionally, fully staffed disability resource centers could better support faculty in navigating classroom accommodations and building accessible course materials. These sorts of initiatives not only support students with disabilities and the faculty that work with them, but they also enrich the campus community at large, making learning and campus environments more accessible to all regardless of what might come our way in the future.

REFERENCES

Al-Ibrahim, Amal. 2019. "Deaf and Hard of Hearing Students' Perceptions of the Flipped Classroom Strategy in an Undergraduate Education Course." *European Journal of Educational Research* 8, no. 1: 325–336.

Behling, Kirsten. 2017. "Accessibility Considerations for Hybrid Courses." *New Directions for Teaching and Learning* 2017, no. 149: 89–101. doi:10.1002/tl.20230.

Boothe, Kathleen A., Marla J. Lohmann, Kimberly A. Donnell, and D. Dean Hall. 2018. "Applying the Principles of Universal Design for Learning (UDL) in the College Classroom." *Journal of Special Education Apprenticeship* 7, no. 3: 1–13. https://eric.ed.gov/?id=EJ1201588.

Cawthon, Stephanie W., and Rachel Leppo. 2013. "Accommodations Quality for Students Who Are d/Deaf or Hard of Hearing." *American Annals of the Deaf* 158, no. 4: 438–452.

Cawthon, Stephanie W., Rachel Leppo, Jin Jin Ge, and Mark Bond. 2015. "Accommodations Use Patterns in High School and Postsecondary Settings for Students Who Are d/Deaf or Hard of Hearing." *American Annals of the Deaf* 160, no. 1: 9–23.

Cawthon, Stephanie Washbourn, Sarah Joanna Schoffstalll, and Carrie Lou Garberoglio. 2014. "How Ready Are Postsecondary Institutions for Students Who Are d/Deaf or Hard-of-Hearing?" *Education Policy Analysis Archives* 22, no. 13: 1–25. doi:10.14507/epaa.v22n13.2014.

Chugani, Carla D., and Amy Houtrow. 2020. "Effect of the COVID-19 Pandemic on College Students With Disabilities." *American Journal of Public Health* 110, no. 12: 1722–1723. doi:10.2105/AJPH.2020.305983.

Elliot, Lisa, Michael Stinson, James Mallory, Donna Easton, and Matt Huenerfauth. 2016. "Deaf and Hard of Hearing Individuals' Perceptions of Communication with Hearing Colleagues in Small Groups." In *Proceedings of the 18th International ACM SIGACCESS Conference on Computers and Accessibility*, 271–272. ASSETS '16. New York, NY, USA: Association for Computing Machinery. doi:10.1145/2982142.2982198.

Gradel, Kathleen, and Alden J. Edson. 2009. "Putting Universal Design for Learning on the Higher Ed Agenda." *Journal of Educational Technology Systems* 38, no. 2: 111–121. doi:10.2190/ET.38.2.d.

Houtenville, A., and S. Boege. 2020. *2019 Annual Report on People with Disabilities in America. Institute on Disability, University of New Hampshire*. Institute on Disability, University of New Hampshire. https://eric.ed.gov/?id=ED605685.

Johnson, Julia, Susan Pliner, and Tom Burkhart. 2002. "D/Deafness and the Basic Course: A Case Study of Universal Instructional Design and Students Who Are d/Deaf in the (Aural) Communication Classroom." *Basic Communication Course Annual* 14, no. 1: 1–31. https://ecommons.udayton.edu/bcca/vol14/iss1/12.

Joyce, Jillian. 2017. "'I Didn't Even Think Of This': Examining The Influence Of Student Disability Accommodation Training On Basic Course Instructor Attitudes

And Self-Efficacy." MS Thesis, Illinois State University. doi:10.30707/ETD2017. Joyce.J.

Leake, David W., and Robert A. Stodden. 2014. "Higher Education and Disability: Past and Future of Underrepresented Populations." *Journal of Postsecondary Education and Disability* 27, no. 4: 399–408.

Luft, Pamela. 2014. "A National Survey of Transition Services for Deaf and Hard of Hearing Students." *Career Development and Transition for Exceptional Individuals* 37, no. 3: 177–192. doi:10.1177/2165143412469400.

Macleod, G., and K. R. Cebula. 2009. "Experiences of Disabled Students in Initial Teacher Education." *Cambridge Journal of Education* 39, no. 4: 457–472. doi:10.1080/03057640903352465.

Meleo-Erwin, Zoë, Betty Kollia, Joe Fera, Alyssa Jahren, and Corey Basch. 2021. "Online Support Information for Students with Disabilities in Colleges and Universities during the COVID-19 Pandemic." *Disability and Health Journal* 14, no. 1: 1–5. doi:10.1016/j.dhjo.2020.101013.

Murray, Christopher, Donald E. Goldstein, Steven Nourse, and Eugene Edgar. 2000. "The Postsecondary School Attendance and Completion Rates of High School Graduates With Learning Disabilities." *Learning Disabilities Research & Practice* 15, no. 3: 119–127. doi:10.1207/SLDRP1503_1.

Najarian, Cheryl G. 2008. "Deaf Women: Educational Experiences and Self-identity." *Disability & Society* 23, no. 2: 117–128. doi:10.1080/09687590701841141.

National Center for College Students with Disabilities (NCCSD). 2020. Accessed March 9, 2021. http://www.nccsdonline.org/.

National Center for Education Statistics. 2019. "Fast Facts: Students with Disabilities." Accessed March, 9, 2021. https://nces.ed.gov/fastfacts/display.asp?id=60.

Nilsson, Ann, and Lena Pareto. 2010. "The Complexity of Integrating Technology Enhanced Learning in Special Math Education – A Case Study." In *Sustaining TEL: From Innovation to Learning and Practice*, edited by Martin Wolpers, Paul A. Kirschner, Maren Scheffel, Stefanie Lindstaedt, and Vania Dimitrova, 638–643. Lecture Notes in Computer Science. Berlin, Heidelberg: Springer. doi:10.1007/978-3-642-16020-2_67.

Palmer, Charles, and Richard T. Roessler. 2000. "Requesting Classroom Accommodations: Self-Advocacy and Conflict Resolution Training for College Students with Disabilities." *Journal of Rehabilitation* 66, no. 3: 38–43.

Peng, Chong A., and Shafee Daud. 2015. "TPACK: A Missing Piece of the Technology Puzzle Among Special Education (Hearing Impairment) Teachers." In *Proceedings of the Graduate Research in Education Seminar: GREduc*, 57–65. Selangar, Malaysia: University of Putra Malaysia. http://spel3.upm.edu.my/max/dokumen/GREDUC_GREduc2015_E-proceedings.pdf#page=57

Rao, Kavita, Patricia Edelen-Smith, and Cat-Uyen Wailehua. 2015. "Universal Design for Online Courses: Applying Principles to Pedagogy." *Open Learning: The Journal of Open, Distance and e-Learning* 30, no. 1: 35–52. doi:10.1080/02680513.2014.991300.

Rigler, Michelle. 2013. "The Retention of College Students with Disabilities: What Encourages Them to Stay in College?" EdD diss., University of Tennessee at Chattanooga. https://scholar.utc.edu/theses/375.

Schelly, Catherine L., Patricia L. Davies, and Craig L. Spooner. 2011. "Student Perceptions of Faculty Implementation of Universal Design for Learning." *Journal of Postsecondary Education and Disability* 24, no. 1: 17–30.

Schley, Sara, and Michael A. Stinson. 2016. "Collaborative Writing in the Postsecondary Classroom: Online, In-Person, and Synchronous Group Work with Deaf, Hard-of-Hearing, and Hearing Students." *Journal of Postsecondary Education and Disability* 29, no. 2: 151–164.

Scott, LaRon A., Peter Temple, and David Marshall. 2015. "UDL in Online College Coursework: Insights of Infusion and Educator Preparedness." *Online Learning* 19, no. 5: 99–119.

Scott, LaRon, and Peter Temple. 2017. "A Conceptual Framework for Building UDL in a Special Education Distance Education Course." *Journal of Educators Online* 14, no. 1. https://eric.ed.gov/?id=EJ1133749.

Scott, Sally. 2020. "COVID-19 Transitions: Higher Education Professionals' Perspectives on Access Barriers, Services, and Solutions for Students with Disabilities." Association on Higher Education and Disability (AHEAD), 1–9.

Scott, Sally S., Joan M. McGuire, and Teresa E. Foley. 2003. "Universal Design for Instruction: A Framework for Anticipating and Responding to Disability and Other Diverse Learning Needs in the College Classroom." *Equity & Excellence in Education* 36, no. 1: 40–49. doi:10.1080/10665680303502.

Seale, Jane. 2006. "Disability, Technology and e-Learning: Challenging Conceptions." *ALT-J* 14, no. 1: 1–8. doi:10.1080/09687760500480025.

Smith, Frances G. 2012. "Analyzing a College Course That Adheres to the Universal Design for Learning (UDL) Framework." *Journal of the Scholarship of Teaching and Learning* 12, no. 3: 31–61.

Son, Changwon, Sudeep Hegde, Alec Smith, Xiaomei Wang, and Farzan Sasangohar. 2020. "Effects of COVID-19 on College Students' Mental Health in the United States: Interview Survey Study." *Journal of Medical Internet Research* 22, no. 9: e21279. doi:10.2196/21279.

Soria, Krista M., Bonnie Horgos, Igor Chirikov, and Daniel Jones-White. 2020. "The Experiences of Undergraduate Students with Physical, Learning, Neurodevelopmental, and Cognitive Disabilities During the Pandemic." Report. SERU Consortium, University of California - Berkeley and University of Minnesota. http://conservancy.umn.edu/handle/11299/216715.

Wang, Xiaomei, Sudeep Hegde, Changwon Son, Bruce Keller, Alec Smith, and Farzan Sasangohar. 2020. "Investigating Mental Health of US College Students During the COVID-19 Pandemic: Cross-Sectional Survey Study." *Journal of Medical Internet Research* 22, no. 9: e22817. doi:10.2196/22817.

Wynants, Shelli A., and Jessica M. Dennis. 2017. "Embracing Diversity and Accessibility: A Mixed Methods Study of the Impact of an Online Disability Awareness Program." *Journal of Postsecondary Education and Disability* 30, no. 1: 33–48.

Chapter 9

Landscape of Service Learning Courses

Post-Pandemic Evolution of Community Partnerships and Service Learning Projects

Sharon Storch

To understand the evolution of service learning before, during, and post-pandemic, this chapter takes a case-study approach to understanding the pandemic challenges and changes at the University of Nebraska at Omaha (UNO) and how the changes will shape post-pandemic service learning. The successes and lessons learned from UNO can be applied as a learning tool for other university service learning programs, faculty, and staff.

The chapter begins by unpacking what service learning means broadly by sampling information from the top-ranked service learning institutions. It continues by looking more specifically at UNO. Further, this chapter aims to understand the impacts of the global pandemic crisis on UNO stakeholders and their subsequent responses through adapting, improvising, and overcoming challenges specific to service learning. In order to understand those impacts, conversations over Zoom ensued with stakeholders to include students, graduate assistants (GAs), higher education instructors and professors, community partners, and SLA administrators and support staff. Their voices are strong in this chapter as they share their service learning experiences at UNO before and during COVID-19, as well as lessons learned and speculations on service learning's trajectory post-pandemic. While Institutional Review Board approval was deemed unnecessary by the Office of Regulatory Affairs, written permissions were sought and received for using all personal communication references throughout this chapter. However, the author assigned pseudonyms and removed titles to provide anonymity for the interviewees.

SERVICE LEARNING AT LARGE

Higher education researchers and academics posit that the roots of service learning evolved from the writings of John Dewey (Salam et al. 2019) in terms of learning by doing. Service learning is further described as an overarching experiential experience that encompasses community service, field education, volunteerism, and internships (Furco 1996). Each of those areas has a different function in higher education as the beneficiary, and the focus of each of those experiences is different (Furco 1996). For example, Furco's 1996 model exemplifies how the beneficiary of community service and volunteerism is the recipient, whereas with an internship and field education, the beneficiary is the provider of the service. Accordingly, the focus of community service and volunteerism is serving others where the focus of a field education or an internship is learning (Furco 1996). Furco posits that service learning is the intersection of the volunteerism and internships. Simply put, service learning links academic courses and their subsequent content to community partners to provide community service (Mitchell 2017). These collaborative experiences offer university students the opportunity to connect their learning to service projects that ultimately benefit both the students and the community.

However, service learning definitions vary throughout the different learning institutions. The connective tissue of the varied definitions includes three best practices to include in any service learning project: intentional learning goals, active reflections, and extension into the community (Association of American Colleges & Universities n.d.; Elon University n.d.a; Furco 1996; Mitchell 2017; Tulane n.d.a.). Various options for project interactions exist, such as direct (personal contact), indirect (behind the scenes), advocacy (public awareness, eliminate/solve problems), and research (collaboration for enacting business, community, or social change) (Chiva-Bartoll et al. 2018). In general, the direct option is most rewarding for students.

The top three ranked universities noted in the 2021 service learning college rankings from *U.S. News and World Report* were Berea College in Berea, Kentucky, Elon University in Elon, North Carolina, and Tulane University in New Orleans, Louisiana (Service Learning n.d.). The college websites offer a breadth of information, ideas, and resources that furthers our understanding of pre-pandemic frameworks, best practices, and experiences. Berea College highlighted fall 2019 projects that included an organizational communication class working with a nonprofit to research and implement rebranding and new communication strategies and a mentoring program with K-12 public school students (Berea College n.d.) thus enabling students to apply organizational communication and educational principles to each of their recipients. Next,

Elon University shared pre-pandemic face-to-face projects that included students from a Strategic Writing Course that provided client services with a local nonprofit agency (Kernoodle Center 2014). Similar to Berea, Elon students provided mentoring and tutoring to elementary-age students (Kernoodle Center 2014). Lastly, rather than project ideas, Tulane University promoted their planned service learning courses through the use of a spreadsheet that includes a brief project description and meetings days/times (Tulane University n.d.a.). They provide a valuable resource that allows students to consider project details when scheduling. Additionally, a provided reflection guide is on the Faculty Resource page to enable consistency and understanding with the important reflection component of service learning (Tulane University n.d.b.). While these examples allow for a picture of some university accomplishments, this is also a recommended springboard for universities to use when looking for tools and ideas to add to their service learning toolbox.

In addition to reflecting on the top ranked universities and their best practices in terms of framework, sample projects, available courses, and resources, it is important to consider the breadth of courses with potential for service learning experiences and partnerships. A simple Google Scholar search yields many articles written about higher education service learning experiences across varied disciplines including, but not limited to, teacher education, physical education, world languages, nursing, public health, business, arts, and sustainability (Beaman and Davidson 2020; Chive-Bartoll et al. 2019; Halberstadt et al. 2019; Palpacuer Lee, Curtis, and Curran 2017; Salam et al. 2019). Raising awareness of curricular areas with potential course connections can be beneficial as universities consider opportunities within their own programs.

Beyond the course connections and project work lies the value of acquiring and honing transferable skills that are applicable in future career and life experiences (Stolley et al. 2017). Stolley et al.'s qualitative study focused on community engagement and homelessness through interviewing college shelter managers in hopes of understanding more about the value of service learning experiences post-graduation. Noteworthy results from this qualitative research show the value of transferable skills gained from service learning engagement within skill sets that include interpersonal communication, leadership, and teamwork.

PRE-PANDEMIC SERVICE LEARNING AT UNIVERSITY OF NEBRASKA AT OMAHA

Definition and Framework

Prior to the pandemic, many UNO stakeholders described the UNO service learning experience primarily as an in-person, face-to-face modality. This section sheds light on pre-pandemic service learning insight from UNO faculty, staff, and stakeholders. To enable reflection on widespread university practices and service learning frameworks, it is important to understand UNO's definition and approach to service learning:

> Service learning is a method of teaching that combines classroom instruction with meaningful, community-identified service. This form of engaged teaching and learning emphasizes critical thinking by using reflection to connect course context with real-world experiences. Service learning instructors partner with community organizations as co-teachers and encourage a heightened sense of community, civic engagement, and personal responsibility for students while building capacity and contributing real community impact. (Service Learning Academy n.d.b.)

It is noteworthy to recognize that the three aforementioned best practices are included: combining classroom instruction, using reflection, and partnering with community organizations. Additionally, UNO includes the verbiage of real-world experiences which relate to research on transferable skills.

While universities structure their service learning definitions and approaches differently, Abril, a UNO service learning staff member, emphasized that service learning at UNO is beyond just logging in volunteer hours, it is about making connections with course work via project-based experiences where students partner with a community organization, agency, school, nonprofit, and so on. Additionally, Robin, a UNO service learning staff member, shared that "our emphasis was being in the community, meaning physically being out there." "Physically being out there" equates to in-person or face-to-face interaction. UNO GAs provided support in those physical spaces as Caroline, a service learning GA, articulated. The GAs role often focused on organizing logistics such as student transportation, food, paperwork, and the coordination of physical spaces. While face-to-face modalities had long been the structure and approach for partnerships, Abril mentioned that online service learning represented about 10–15 percent of pre-COVID-19 experiences. Vicky, a UNO service learning staff member, shared that those Pre-COVID-19 online projects were primarily focused on advocacy efforts. Elisa, a prior UNO student and a current service learning staff member, elaborated on her fall 2015 service learning project that offered electronic experiences with Podcasts or videos that she felt paved the way to later asynchronous work that occurred as a result of the pandemic.

Stakeholders of UNO service learning described pre-pandemic service learning as organized, supportive, and resourceful with experiences that provide transferable skills to students. Janine, an educational partner, expressed that UNO service learning has it "down to a science" with "topnotch" communication. As a result, she deemed service learning to be highly proficient at communication and organization (agendas provided, etc.), very comfortable and convenient for educational partners, and the overall experiences helped her grow as an educator. Mike, a nonprofit community partner, sees service learning as, "an opportunity to have access to university assets and resources in order to communicate with future leaders [university students] through a community engaged program." He elaborated that he wears "two hats," that of representing the community he serves, and the pedagogical side of helping facilitate the curriculum for the UNO course. Finally, service learning provides real-life experiences that Anthony, a UNO faculty member, believes his UNO students need and receive from SLA. Now with an understanding UNO's definition, pre-pandemic format (resources, support, modalities), and strengths, this next section highlights sample pre-pandemic projects and experiences.

Pre-Pandemic Projects

Projects at UNO primarily develop within undergraduate and graduate degree programs. Darcy, a UNO faculty member, expressed that her projects are such a "rich part of instruction" and a great way for undergraduate and graduate-level courses to integrate experiences with diverse cultures around the Omaha metropolitan area. Darcy's service projects were face-to-face and served children with, or who may be at risk for, communication disorders. Her undergraduate class worked with a community center project focusing on developmental milestones with young children ages 12 months to 4 years. The UNO students filled a gap in the program and provided early language coaching alongside the educational navigators from the community center. Her graduate class upheld a long-standing early intervention family literacy project (in effect since 2007) designed for preschool to school-age children.

Debbie, a UNO student and a GA, shared a project that partnered with an elderly community center where students were in-person serving meals and providing companionship. Interactions were plentiful, and included playing games such as dominoes and pool; the elderly community enjoyed interacting with, and teaching games to, the UNO students. According to Debbie, pre-pandemic service learning just "felt easy." She noted how if any elderly individual suffered from hearing loss, they had the opportunity to read lips—something that cannot be accomplished with masks on. Elisa shared the strength of the Senior Prom project, which combines English and Gerontology courses, was that UNO students had the opportunity to interact and gain multiple perspectives during a collaborative event.

In terms of educational partners, Anthony's UNO students work with fifth grade students in a face-to-face program where they extend the interpersonal communication skills coursework to activities intended to grow the skills of the elementary students. Debbie spoke about what face-to-face looked like pre-pandemic from both a student and graduate assistant perspective. In a project partnered with third grade students in an after-school program, UNO students were face-to-face where they built relationships, played games, and high-fived without concern. These two projects exemplified successful face-to-face in-school and after-school programming.

Brenda, a UNO faculty member, is part of a team delivering a unique grant-funded, nonprofit service learning experience. Brenda explained that the aim of the general education math course is to provide students an experience that feels less stressful, is fun, and affords the opportunity for students to gain transferable skills as they solve authentic problems and assist a nonprofit in making data-driven decisions. The grant funding was approved pre-COVID-19 with the intent to launch the face-to-face class in fall of 2020.

While this section offered a sampling of pre-pandemic projects at UNO, this next section unpacks how UNO service learning faced challenges, learned lessons, and moved forward through uncharted territories. These experiences serve as helpful information when considering ways that the pandemic impacted, and can change, service learning as a result of COVID-19.

PANDEMIC SERVICE LEARNING: ADAPT, IMPROVISE, OVERCOME

In March of 2020 the global pandemic of COVID-19 swept the world, forcing widespread closures and new guidelines for conducting business, teaching classes, and doing life emerged (Taylor 2021). In consideration of the abrupt and unsettling change that many faced in transitioning to remote learning, this section brings to light the impact it had on the service learning framework and/or experiences for Berea College, Elon University, and Tulane University, but more specifically, an in-depth look at UNO as the case used to explore pandemic service learning. These experiences, challenges, and subsequent adaptations may apply to any post-pandemic service learning structure and experience at a variety of universities.

To allow for a broad understanding of pandemic service learning, exploration continued with the top three service learning universities identified in 2021 *U.S. News and World Report* (Service Learning n.d.). Firstly, Berea's Health and Physical Education Department took an asynchronous approach to a pandemic service learning project by providing videos with physical movement content delivered in a fun and engaging manner (Berea College n.d.). The delivery of the videos to the community partner allowed for service learning engagement while adhering to COVID-19 safety protocols. Secondly, Elon developed and posted resources on their website to offer support to students, faculty, and partners in order to be informed and have a toolbox for managing pandemic service learning experiences (Elon University n.d.b). In approaching preparations for pandemic service learning, Tulane added a student information page to offer answers on conducting community projects (Tulane University n.d.c.) and on the spreadsheet of available courses, in spring of 2021, a column was added to inform students about whether the course would be remote or in-person (Tulane University n.d.a.). Highly ranked service learning universities reacted and made changes to projects and resources.

UNO also faced concerns and challenges along with its plans for reimagining the 2020 spring semester at the onset of COVID-19 (Service Learning Academy n.d.a.). Adapting to unknowns became a reality as the pandemic propelled a shift in teaching and service learning modalities. Mike described it as a "funky pandemic ride." When COVID-19 "hit the fan," there were two choices, "we are closing down and see you on the other side," or, "let's figure this out." To Darcy, the initial shift felt "traumatic" and stopped people in their tracks as they learned how to use different tools to creatively solve problems and move through this time. Caroline echoed that sentiment, "It was abrupt and scary for a lot of professors and they had to change everything with their class and concerns with time to make these adaptations to virtual." There were disappointments, cancellations, and reimagining experiences within a very short period of time. Although, as Jess, a UNO faculty member, articulated, there were also moments of realization on things that needed improving.

In taking an in-depth look at UNO service learning experience beginning with March 2020's shift to remote learning due to the pandemic, this section highlights data gleaned through interviews, UNO service learning newsletters, and UNO website information. Successes and lessons learned from UNO service learning affiliates provide opportunities for universities to use as a springboard for reflection and consideration for potential adaptations to their own service learning framework and experiences, as well as motivation. Themes derived from the data include mindfulness, support, flexibility, accessibility, and technological innovations.

Adapting: Mindfulness and Support

The first theme highlights adapting with mindfulness and finding new ways to be supportive. Universities and individuals can reflect upon their experiences to validate their approach and/or consider the mindset and ideas for further program growth.

At UNO, SLA fostered a "can-do" attitude and demeanor in order to embrace and make adaptations to each unique situation. Abril shared that when the pandemic hit, service learning didn't stop, but we adjusted, supported, and worked with faculty, students, and community partners to become creative in this new space. Further, she was "so unbelievably impressed with those individuals [UNO and/or community partners] that said 'yep I can do this,'" but she also exhibited mindfulness of the challenges that others [various UNO stakeholders] faced in terms of having the capacity for fast-paced change, or the vision of practical application in an online environment. Kathie, a UNO service learning staff member, worked to be mindful of individual situations and support partners who faced challenges in terms of energy and capacity to make so many changes in a short amount of time when, "pivoting between modes of delivery [face-to-face to online]," adhering to school district rules, and empty buildings. Robin remained mindful of relationships and how we consider the stress on the nonprofit community (doing more with less, COVID-19, social and political unrest, etc.). She took the approach of "people first and then the to-do list." She worked to create, maintain, and foster a positive culture with internal and external relationships in the absence of face-to-face interactions. Alongside mindfulness was the idea of support and what that looked like during this transition.

One of SLA's first levels of support was to ensure that everyone knew they were in the forefront of service learning's pandemic approach. Accordingly, Abril created and posted a motivating and informative video on the UNO SLA webpage. This adaptation served to spread the message to people in online spaces and helped people overcome and feel encouraged by seeing what is possible. As well, the video re-messaged what UNO worked so hard to institutionalize and showcased how service learning happened online. Elisa and Caroline shared that SLA wisely used this pandemic time to build up their website with transitioning resources. Previously, the website was primarily a conduit to contact individuals and evolved an in-depth hub of information. Elisa excitedly shared that currently, "you can drive your own journey of exploration and find your own resources on the website." As well, Robin communicated that video content was created for Canvas, UNO's Course learning management system, in order to make information readily available and accessible.

GAs provide a strong support network within SLA. However, at the onset of this pandemic, their roles changed significantly. The logistics of service learning evolved from transportation and physical scheduling of experiences to exploring technology options and virtual spaces. Caroline now spends considerable time with in-depth Zoom planning meetings focused on technology logistics. Face-to-face communication has evolved to phone calls and emails. Photo releases moved from hard copies to DocuSign. Small group discussions now were conducted in breakout rooms as technology attempts to humanize the experience and bring projects to life. Among the navigated changes and challenges for Caroline is the work with Omaha Public Schools

(OPS) and the technology differences; OPS uses Microsoft Teams and UNO uses Zoom. Without direct access to Microsoft Teams and Teams accounts, GAs couldn't provide the same level of support to OPS teachers and Caroline found it hard to watch someone struggle and not be able to help.

SLA also faced the cyclical challenge of how to best support the GAs in order to maintain valuable student experiences. This support looked different based on different virtual spaces with educational partners. While using the UNO Zoom platform, Vicky could send a private message to offer support to GAs, though she did not have that ability with educational partners that utilized Microsoft Teams. Thus, planning conversations occurred on how to alternatively communicate to offer support outside of that Teams environment via mobile devices or other means. While Vicky continued to regularly meet with graduate students via Zoom, mentoring looked completely different and, "this isn't something we had to deal with before being online." While she recognizes that flexibility was always a key component to her work, it is even more so during COVID-19 and requires thoughtful planning: "It may not look like we had planned—and that is okay." She shared that forgiveness and being able to go with the flow were characteristics valuable to this process of support. She strove to meet people where they are, which requires more creativity and advance planning now in order to see students shine and projects come together.

Project support looked different and SLA worked to adapt and individualize their support accordingly. Anthony discussed these adjustments in stating, "UNO has the absolute best service learning academy in the world." When COVID-19 hit, he wasn't sure how to continue, but felt SLA individuals at all levels provided amazing support: "They always have great ideas and they work to help you make things happen." Their can-do attitude was contagious as projects and professors struggled to recalibrate due to COVID-19. They assisted him in getting set up with asynchronous videos so his class could continue to work with the fifth grade students.

Overall, SLA stakeholders at all levels learned the lesson of being mindful of others and mindful of ways support looks different now in the pandemic. UNO learned through the challenges faced and experienced success as evidenced by the voices of interviewees. They also learned that being flexible to change at many levels enabled positive experiences.

Flexibility

While there are many success stories to share about COVID-19 transformations, there are some projects that simply had to change or shift to a new community partner. For SLA staff, professors, and students, this created feelings of disappointment, yet raised awareness to new opportunities they may not have realized without COVID-19 forcing this shift. For example, Darcy faced widespread library closures and experienced a long-standing program now placed on hold. By remaining flexible and open to finding a new community partner, she considered her professional network, which included previous graduates. Ultimately, the UNO students provided support to public school students with the added benefit of coaching by a field professional (her previous student), a quality the library program did not offer. Darcy confessed that she would not have altered this long-standing project unless her "hand was forced."

In a similar vein, Jess shifted a project to a digital campaign opportunity with a new nonprofit partner. Not only did her new project adapt seamlessly to various modalities (in-person, online, synchronous/asynchronous), but it also gave students a choice. It "shows even during a time where we have no choice over how we learn or how we work or what we do, we *can* still do something for the community. This is where service learning is even that much more powerful during COVID." With more brainstorming than even before, she experienced projects improving and developed new ways to make connections developed through flexibility and adaptations.

While Darcy and Jess experienced positive outcomes, Mike emotionally shared that "remote service learning is taking the legs out from under service learning projects." While the nonprofit organization and UNO made adjustments, he believed projects are best when students experience how chaos can evolve into community-based solutions. Pre-COVID-19, important discussions were a traditional circle time that became powerful and emotional. Breakout rooms simulate those experiences in the best possible way, but still remain, "pseudo community engagement at best." Change is not easy, as evidenced by Mike's nonprofit community perspective, but Mike's flexibility to adopt the breakout rooms allowed some level of his project to continue.

Planning and organization before, during, and after project implementation faced changes. Janine, having been involved with service learning pre- and during COVID-19, shared that flexibility, technology transitioning, and empathy topped her list of adaptations. The planning didn't feel very different for Janine, but flexibility in terms of modality, adjusting for school schedule changes, as well as getting students to interact in virtual settings posed new challenges. Similarly, Jess realized she needed to make some changes to the course and assignment timing. She realized the challenges students faced, and that doing things online meant connections and interview logistics take longer. In these examples, instructors and educational partners recognized the planning challenges and learned that being flexible to the tools and resources available enabled the projects to move forward.

These situations brought forth the notion of flexibility and adaptability as they realized that experiences looked and felt different. Elisa shared that the, "pandemic has made us more flexible and learned that life happens." The new mindset will be how we can make experiences accessible for students regardless of what is happening in life. While life happened for UNO stakeholders, as it did for universities at large, they also recognized the silver lining of increased accessibility.

Accessibility

In facing challenges and being mindful and flexible, SLA stakeholders realized the feasibility and accessibility benefits surfacing amid the changes and pandemic challenges. Debbie realized as a nontraditional student, and now as a GA, that "I have a home to maintain and kids here to look after. I feel like being able to not worry about driving places and being there in person and cutting out a lot of that time by logging on and doing things through Zoom, it's nice." She added, "Before this [COVID-19], we didn't really talk about synchronous/asynchronous." She elaborated that with a busy life, "any minute you can cut out is gold." This section highlights areas where pandemic improved accessibility by transforming planning and extending the local, statewide, and global reach.

Streamlined planning options improved the accessibility of overall experiences. For Janine's high school classes, it is much easier to meet and to manipulate schedules. Opting for virtual settings such as Zoom increased the accessibility of experiences and helped overcome the limitations of physical spaces. Similarly, Darcy described schedules as "the biggest bear in the room sometimes." Zoom meetings are a strong outcome from the shift to remote. With regard to her special event collaborative project with another Omaha university, using Zoom for planning removed barriers. While she admitted this festival project wasn't delivered seamlessly over Zoom as the success of this service learning modality is very project-dependent, the planning process was a positive change. She expressed the fall 2020 was so much easier to plan with the ability to collaborate over Zoom than pre-pandemic face-to-face planning sessions.

Planning and implementation changes overflowed into travel logistics. Travel for professors, students, and service learning staff could face substantial changes including for planning sessions, suggests Abril. Vicky shared that the benefit of meeting a teacher during their plan period over a videoconference equates to less travel around the city and a more efficient use of time: "Historically we would go to their place, their school." With COVID-19 adaptations, "many things are possible in ways we didn't ever anticipate," shared Vicky. The use of virtual meeting spaces also impact collaboration with community and educational partners.

Zoom has opened the door for greater engagement with service learning reflections and cumulative presentations. Community partners that may not have been able to attend campus presentations can now opt to join over Zoom or view recordings. Mike expressed a highlight with his food pantry project that students are now communicating with food pantries all over Nebraska, rather than Omaha. As a result, there are "some wonderful narratives about resilience and overcoming." These experiences broaden the reach of service learning in ways that weren't previously considered.

From a global perspective, pandemic service learning projects have opened our eyes to new experiences. Darcy discussed a career advocacy project with UNO students and high school students. UNO students from outside the Omaha area now have the ability to connect with their own high schools and make connections via Zoom, thus broadening our global footprint. While Mike believes in the strength of the face-to-face experience, he also recognized that with Zoom and Podcasts the reach extends to inviting guests or professors from another state. Overall, opportunities for different modalities post-pandemic are evident, and include the potential for growth in global partnerships, explained Abril. By exhibiting flexibility, new opportunities presented themselves and strengthened the future of service learning by expanding global opportunities.

Reusable resources extend the reach to the community at large. Anthony adapted his face-to-face project work with a fifth grade class to providing asynchronous videos. In doing so, he learned the value of the video to the community partner and the students. Ultimately, students now love the video and when fifth graders were unable to be present, "the video gives ability to show multiple times and to share with colleagues [community partner colleagues]." The community organizations love the flexibility the video offers. UNO students are using platforms they are very familiar with and incorporated movie clips or TikTok—things they would not have done in a face-to-face environment. Projects are posted on a YouTube Channel and submitted as a URL to the community partner. Similarly, Caroline worked with two classes that provided reusable resources via a YouTube Channel. In considering the technology side of reusable resources, other adaptations included developing strong technological options for students and educational and community partners.

Technology Innovations

In light of the aforementioned lessons learned, Abril stated that figuring out technology solutions and "gaps we didn't even know we had" were at the forefront of challenges on "how to support folks in the format they want and can do it." While there was some fear in using Zoom, Brenda was surprised with the positive outcomes and community engagement with her project and breakout rooms within a new math class. Elisa discussed the challenges to sync not only technology but also times with OPS, the largest P12 partner, due to safety and vetting for preparing experiences in online spaces. Though UNO worked through these challenges to be flexible in finding new creative ways to technologically work around the idea that "we can't go there and you can't come here." This section on technology innovations shares UNO solutions and success stories for universities to apply to their own programs.

UNO professors revisited service learning plans and considered alternate modalities. Jess shared that in her Public Speaking Class, COVID-19 transformed an interview process moved from in-person to online; thus collaborations and final presentations were accomplished remotely via Zoom. Another project focused on building and sharing fundraising ideas for a local nonprofit. With some creativity, this project moved to online and students worked to provide an electronic-only fundraising handbook, previously shared in hardcopy. This led to being creative and flexible with available software. Brenda and Jess faced challenges with software that was available only on campus versus on student's own computers, especially for math and graphic design. According to Jess, students learned how to use Canva and Publisher to work through the process to adapt and overcome. Stakeholders at all levels faced varying situations that required flexibility. With instructors and partners being mindful and patient through these challenges, it sets the tone for how students manage the changes.

According to Robin, SLA are all "learning and finding new technology to make decisions." She explained that working to make this world more 3D and additions of Padlet and Google Earth aided in transforming experiences in addition to the previously used Kahoot. An *IT for Development* course, which pre-COVID-19 required a bus tour of the Omaha metro area, transformed into a virtual tour using Google Earth (Al-Ghaithi 2020). Kathie talked about the innovation in determining what type of service, or output (end points), should look like. Students learned new ways to communicate, such as a project communicating a video exchange using FlipGrid. Alongside Padlet, FlipGrid, and Google Earth, Elisa shared that end points (projects or presentations) might include a Podcast, a 30-second TikTok, Instagram advocacy posts, or other creative choices. She shared that it is, "really exciting to think out of the box." Creativity and thoughtful consideration were given to actualize an output, "in ways that she wouldn't have thought of if weren't in virtual inclusive communities." The technology is critical and the reach is greater as a result. Universities can value the ideas and lessons learned/implemented to maintain interest and engagement.

With that said, SLA staff shared that there needs to be mindfulness of Zoom fatigue. For example, in terms of trainings and collaborative experiences, such as the summer Service Learning Academy, there needs to be intentional thought on the time spent in a virtual space, shared Kathie. SLA provided their annual training virtually for the first time in spring 2020 and worked together to discuss new ways to engage students while making community connections and sharing a toolbox of technology resources with participants (Nelson 2020).

While UNO, like many universities across the globe, faced a scary and unsettling change, we also embraced the challenges through mindfulness, supportiveness, flexibility, and recognizing the value of increased accessibility and technological innovations. Abril stated that while she believes that face-to-face will be back as that level of interaction is so valuable, but our "technology muscle is strengthened," we also now realize the possibilities of online and virtual spaces.

POST-PANDEMIC SPECULATIONS

This section of the chapter focuses on extrapolating what we learned and experienced from pandemic service learning, and speculates about how what we learned may alter the landscape of service learning post-pandemic. Building community through mindfulness, support, flexibility, and technology innovations is a strong start to reimagining service learning post-pandemic. I will share challenges to best practices, suggest new mindsets, and propose potential elimination of practices. Faculty must consider the lessons learned and use them to reimagine service learning post-pandemic in your classes, in your community, and at your universities.

First of all, I challenge everyone to consider what the framework will look like overall. One of our stakeholders, Debbie, believes that post-pandemic service learning will surface as a new mix of in-person (when we are ready), but also that Zoom and virtual programming, "is going to stick." With the increase in online classes overall, options are seemingly endless with the ability to join synchronously in a virtual space or asynchronously with service learning assignments and tasks that can be completed on one's own schedule. While UNO only had 10–15 percent of online service learning pre-pandemic, opportunities exist for that number to increase post-pandemic. Professors and students now have greater options and they are more creative and resilient having been through this change. As UNO learned, some key rewards are greater accessibility, streamlined planning, and growth in technology innovativeness.

With the flexibility, adaptability, creativity, and innovation of students, staff, faculty, and community partners, post-pandemic projects invite the dynamic interplay between in-person and virtual modalities. Faculty should consider their long-standing projects and be flexible to change, perhaps with alternating semesters to broaden experiences. UNO learned that with change brought growth and awareness to new opportunities they didn't know existed.

Accessibility benefits encompass both local and global reach to increase the ability to be involved with and view student final projects and build community with partners outside of the Omaha area. That accessibility also affords the opportunity for efficient planning meetings in virtual spaces in order to use time and resources wisely. Additionally, community engagement changed with partners joining remotely to strengthen the experiences. The opportunity now exists for faculty to efficiently use their time and maximize engagement by using virtual spaces rather than face-to-face to planning and presentations.

A key improvement and lesson learned by UNO was the power of technology to create engaging experiences. Options are plentiful and with some creativity and flexibility, technological innovations and virtual spaces can pave a new road with which to travel in remote and online service learning modalities. Schools, units, and faculty who employ service learning can now explore how best to support and apply technological programs to augment service learning ideas. Perhaps a staff member or graduate assistant(s) could lead this effort and promote and train others. As course instructors, faculty must continue to confront their fears and reluctance toward technology, and embrace new ideas to infuse into face-to-face or virtual experiences. The technology tools and platforms available for immediate engagement or creating reusable resources starts with the open-mindedness and bravery of stakeholders to try new ideas and accept change that has the potential to make experiences more widely accessible.

CONCLUSION

The aim of this chapter was to explore the evolution of pandemic (COVID-19) service learning projects and partnerships in terms of challenges faced, adaptations made, and how COVID-19 adaptations might shape post-pandemic service learning experiences. Using the UNO Service Learning Academy as a conduit, individuals, departments, colleges, community partners, and etc. have the opportunity to gain an understanding of this phenomenon and how to apply it to their situations. Vicky reflected on her experience, "Now being in this space [COVID-19 service learning], I think many things are possible." Key findings included mindfulness, support, flexibility, accessibility, and technological innovations.

Limitations to this chapter include, but are not limited to, the unknowns of how we can holistically extrapolate what we learned and apply it to post-pandemic service learning. Moreover, a second limitation could be that the conversations that occurred did not represent the realm of possible projects and partnerships because they were focused on one Midwest university. Although, as we transition to post-pandemic service learning, stronger understandings of what we learned and what adaptations will move with us in this new space will become evident. Even when the light is bright at the end of the pandemic tunnel and we have face-to-face options, it is evident that virtual service learning offers valuable and viable options post-pandemic. We have filled our pedagogical toolbox with new resources and fresh outlooks as we move into post-pandemic service learning. It is my hope that faculty sees this new horizon as an opportunity to find motivation, ideas, and tools to add to their personal, university, and service learning toolbox so we can continue tov better influence and increase student learning.

REFERENCES

Al-Ghaithi, Ali. 2020. "Virtual Tour of Omaha." *University of Nebraska at Omaha Service Learning Newsletter* 11, no. 1 (Fall): 3. https://www.unomaha.edu/service-learning-academy/_docs/newsletters/2020-fall-sla-newsletter.pdf

Association of American Colleges & Universities. n.d. "High Impact Educational Practices." https://www.aacu.org/node/4084

Beaman, Adam, and Patricia M. Davidson. 2020. "Global Service-Learning and COVID-19-What the Future Might Look Like." *Journal of Clinical Nursing* 29, no. 19–20: 3607–3608. doi: 10.1111/jocn.15369

Berea College n.d. "Service Learning Stories." Accessed May 31, 2021. https://www.berea.edu/celts/service-learning/service-learning-stories-2/

Chiva-Bartoll, Oscar, Pedro Jesús Ruiz-Montero, Ricardo Martín Moya, Isaac Pérez López, Javier Giles Girela, Jonatan García-Suárez, and Enrique Rivera-García. 2019. "University Service-Learning in Physical Education and Sport Sciences: A systematic review." *Revista Complutense de Educación* 30, no. 4: 1147–1164. doi:10.5209/rced.60191

Elon University n.d.a "Academic Service-Learning for Students." Accessed May 31, 2021. https://www.elon.edu/u/service-learning/current-students/academic-service-learning/

Elon University n.d.b "COVID-19: Campus & Community Resources." Accessed May 31, 2021. https://www.elon.edu/u/service-learning/volunteer-toolkit/virtual-resource-bank/

Furco, Andrew. 1996. "Service-Learning: A Balanced Approach to Experiential Education." In *Expanding Boundaries: Serving and Learning*, 2–6. Washington, DC: Corporation for National Service.

Halberstadt, Jantje, Christoph Schank, Mark Euler, and Rainer Harms. 2019. "Learning Sustainability Entrepreneurship by Doing: Providing a Lecture-Oriented Service Learning Framework." *Sustainability* 11, no 1287: 1–22. doi:10.3390/su11051217

Kernoodle Center. 2014. "Academic Service Learning." *YouTube* video, 04:04. January 2, 2014. https://youtu.be/ECuwK8SbuFk

Mitchell, Tania D. 2017. "Teaching Community On and Off Campus: An Intersectional Approach to Community Engagement." *New Directions for Student Services 2017*, no. 157: 35–44.

Nelson, Grace. 2020. "Virtual Service Learning Seminar." *University of Nebraska at Omaha Service Learning Newsletter* 11, no. 1 (Fall): 7. https://www.unomaha.edu/service-learning-academy/_docs/newsletters/2020-fall-sla-newsletter.pdf

Palpacuer Lee, Christelle, Jessie H. Curtis, and Mary E. Curran. 2017. "Shaping the Vision for Service-Learning in Language Education." *Foreign Language Annals* 51: 169–184. doi:10.1111/flan.12329

Salam, Maimoona, Dayang Nurfatimah Awang Iskandar, Dayang Hanani Abang Ibrahim, and Muhammad Shoaib Farooq. 2019. "Service Learning in Higher Education: A Systematic Literature Review." *Asia Pacific Education Review* 20: 573–593. doi:10.1007/s12564-019-09580-6

Service Learning Academy. n.d.a. "Service Learning Covid-19 Response." University of Nebraska at Omaha. Accessed October 20, 2020. https://www.unomaha.edu/service-learning-academy/covid-19/students.php

Service Learning Academy. n.d.b. "What is Service Learning?" University of Nebraska at Omaha. Accessed March 3, 2021. https://www.unomaha.edu/service-learning-academy/index.php

"Service Learning." n.d. *U.S. News and World Report.* Accessed May 28, 2021. https://www.usnews.com/best-colleges/rankings/service-learning-programs

Stolley, Kathy Shepherd, Takeyra Collins, Patty Clark, Diane E. Hotaling, and Robin Cote Takacs. 2017. "Taking the Learning from Service Learning into the Postcollege World." *Journal of Applied Social Science* 11, no. 2: 109–126. doi:10.1177/1936724417722579

Taylor, Derrick B. 2021. *"A Timelines of the Coronavirus Pandemic."* March 17, 2021. *The New York Times.* https://www.nytimes.com/article/coronavirus-timeline.html?smid=url-share

Tulane University. n.d.a. "Service Learning Course." Accessed May 31, 2021. https://cps.tulane.edu/academics/service-learning-course

Tulane University. n.d.b. "Faculty Resources." Accessed May 31, 2021. https://cps.tulane.edu/info-for-faculty/faculty-resources

Tulane University n.d.c "Student COVID-19 Information." Accessed May 31, 2021. https://cps.tulane.edu/content/student-covid-19-information

Chapter 10

Navigating Uncertainty Together

Pandemic Lessons Learned from Training New GTAs in Teaching Public Speaking

Anne C. Kretsinger-Harries, Elizabeth Helmick, Kate Challis, and Ali Garib

Amid the ongoing, uncertain, and evolving context of the COVID-19 pandemic, a new generation of scholars is learning to teach. Broeckelman-Post and Ruiz-Mesa (2018) argue that for communication studies, "high quality GTA training is a solid investment in the quality of undergraduate education, in the quality of faculty teaching done, and in the future sustainability of the discipline" (93). Likewise, Valenzano, et al. (2014) remind us that "many faculty members in communication departments found their instructional start in the basic course, and learned to hone their pedagogy there before moving on to teach upper-division courses and seminars" (363). Notably, a GTA's first years of teaching are crucial for cultivating a sense of "teacher efficacy," the confidence in one's ability to help students learn (Hoy and Spero 2005, 343–344). Yet, as Joyce, et al. (2019) have noted, more research on GTA training is needed, given the crucial role that GTAs play in the success of basic communication course programs (27). As such, it is important to reflect on the experiences of this cohort of GTAs who taught for the first time amid the pandemic to account for what can be learned from this unique experience and how these lessons might impact future practices of pedagogical training.

The fall 2020 semester unfolded amid the evolving global COVID-19 pandemic, which altered life as we knew it, forcing widespread changes on college campuses. Higher education was confronted with budget strains, changes in teaching modalities, campus safety concerns, and general uncertainty. These challenges tested the limits of conventional wisdom on pedagogical training, as basic communication courses moved online on a large scale and instructors and students alike navigated new modalities and unprecedented teaching scenarios. In many cases new GTA training also moved online or took a modified form, which presented challenges for course directors tasked with helping new GTAs through this unique situation while also navigating it themselves. Furthermore, the impacts of the pandemic will have a ripple effect as these new GTAs eventually transition into more traditional face-to-face environments, in many cases without the applicable pedagogical training they typically would have received as first-time teachers.

This chapter examines the teaching and training challenges experienced by one "pandemic cohort" of graduate students and their basic course director, to determine what enduring lessons might be gleaned for the future of GTA pedagogical training. Responding to Broeckelman-Post and Simonds' (2020) call to involve graduate student in instructional communication research (171) and to Hennings' (2011) observation of "a lack of GTA voice in the research about GTAs" (128–129), this project is both: (1) a collaboration between a basic communication course director and three GTAs who taught public speaking for the first time amid the pandemic, and (2) a collection of the experiences of one pandemic cohort. We agree with McRae (2010) who asserts that "the GTA subject position offers important insights about what it means to teach the foundational course in communication, and it also can reflect the constraints of the ways the foundational course is conceptualized" (175–176). Accordingly, in this chapter we hold up GTA experiences as important evidence of what teachers and scholars are learning about themselves, their teaching, and the discipline from the experience of teaching for the first time amid the pandemic. As such, this chapter makes space for GTA voices by allowing their experiences and reflections to guide our insights.

Together, the authors of this chapter navigated the pandemic's ongoing challenges in fall 2020 and then worked together in the months afterward to examine and reflect on this experience. Working collaboratively, we surveyed our full cohort of twelve new public speaking GTAs to examine the most pressing challenges they faced. We generated a set of survey questions to probe themes that emerged during our fall graduate pedagogy seminar discussions, including building cohort community, developing instructor credibility, facilitating community in online classrooms, supporting students amid the pandemic, using technology, and developing professionally. We distributed this survey anonymously through Qualtrics after the fall 2020 semester had finished and then reviewed the survey responses to identify common themes.

In what follows, we weave together the survey responses from the pandemic cohort with our own reflections. We begin by describing how graduate pedagogy training changed amid the pandemic. We then explore the most substantial challenges faced by the GTAs, including navigating cohort community, building instructor ethos, developing communication skills, and performing empathy for students. By exploring these themes we build an archive of the unique experiences of GTAs who taught public speaking for the first time amid the pandemic, while also highlighting how the pandemic context has revealed new opportunities to strengthen new GTA training. We conclude with advice for basic course directors on how future iterations of graduate pedagogy training could evolve to reflect what we have learned during this challenging time.

NAVIGATING THE SHIFT ONLINE: EARLY PANDEMIC DECISIONS

When classes first moved online at the start of the pandemic in March 2020, every aspect of the upcoming fall semester was thrown into uncertainty. The course director spent the spring and early summer months weighing possibilities while navigating emerging information about the pandemic and evolving messages from university administration concerning modalities for the fall semester. When it was finally determined that online learning would be a necessity for the months ahead, the course director worked with faculty to convert the existing web-blended version of the course to a fully realized, asynchronous online version, including pre-made lecture videos, assignments, and grading rubrics.

This transition to an online format was an exercise in what Morreale, Thorpe, and Westwick (2020) call "crisis pedagogy" (117). While the development of the online course was informed by scholarship on best practices of teaching public speaking online, it was created in the crisis context of the pandemic with minimal opportunities to pilot and revise the course before rolling it out to hundreds of undergraduate students in the fall semester. The course director settled on an asynchronous format to allow flexibility for a student body that, due to the pandemic, suddenly had to grapple with a host of learning and lifestyle variables such as limited internet access, inconvenient living situations, a variety of learning modalities, and ongoing COVID challenges ranging from personal risk and illness to family health crises.

At the same time, however, this population of students was largely unequipped to move online. After all, as Easton (2003) has argued, online learning is best suited to students who not only have opted into this modality, but who are older, highly motivated, self-disciplined, and comfortable communicating openly with their instructors (88–89). In contrast, our largely traditional undergraduate student body was predominantly accustomed to face-to-face, on-campus learning, which was important to keep in mind when designing a course that would "support students' self-management of learning, self-monitoring of their learning, and motivation to engage in learning"

(Miller 2010, 161). As Vallade and Kaufmann (2018) learned from surveying online learners, "unclear, inconsistent, or confusing course structure or organization prohibit[s] students from learning" (373). Accordingly, the course director focused on the development of a clear, well-structured course with ample infrastructure to guide students through the new terrain of online learning, including a user-friendly navigation, detailed yet concise instructions, regular weekly deadlines for readings and assignments, and ample built-in reminders.

The asynchronous online format was also intended to support the more than twenty instructors—primarily GTAs—who would teach the course. Broeckelman-Post, et al. (2019) argue, "It is better to have the disciplinary experts build and assess the effectiveness of online courses" to ensure a quality and consistent experience for students (145). This was especially relevant at our institution, where roughly half of our instructors were new graduate students and the rest were largely inexperienced with online teaching. On top of this, the vast majority of our instructors came from disciplines beyond communication, with limited subject-matter expertise. The fully-formed, standardized, asynchronous course allowed these instructors to hit the ground running at the start of a chaotic semester. As one GTA expressed in their survey response, "Having a course shell already written and tested made a huge difference in my confidence instructing this class."

With this new modality and ongoing COVID safety concerns, pedagogy training for new GTAs needed to be overhauled as well. In a "normal" year at our institution, new GTA training begins with a weeklong face-to-face orientation week and continues throughout the semester as a three-credit graduate pedagogy seminar. In line with recommendations from scholars like Broeckelman-Post and Ruiz-Mesa (2018) and Fassett and Warren (2012), training topics include mastery of public speaking course objectives and curriculum, classroom management and facilitation, discussion of relevant pedagogy literature, practice speech grading and writing feedback, and use of course learning management systems (LMS).

Scholarship on best practices of new GTA training typically focuses on this kind of face-to-face training for new instructors teaching in face-to-face environments. For instance, Fassett and Warren (2012) recommend that training include practice lesson planning, microteaching practice lessons, simulation and discussion of difficult classroom moments, practice grading, and discussion of assigned pedagogy readings, offering advice for how to accomplish these activities in a physical classroom. While many of these topics were still relevant in the pandemic year, they took on new and different dimensions in the online teaching context. For instance, lesson planning was not an immediately pressing skill for new GTAs teaching asynchronous online classes, nor was simulation of difficult classroom moments, since the online teaching context afforded GTAs more time to seek advice when challenging issues arose in the online space. More crucial, however, was familiarizing GTAs with the asynchronous online course materials and technologies.

To convert the training to an online modality, the course director created a series of prerecorded orientation videos introducing new GTAs to the online public speaking course they would teach, instructions for setting up and customizing their course LMS, and basic online teaching tips. Instructors were asked to review these materials asynchronously in preparation for synchronous Zoom one-on-one conferences and group meetings scheduled for the week prior to the semester. Following this orientation week, the semester-long pedagogy seminar downplayed face-to-face teaching simulations, lesson planning approaches, and discussion of classroom management, in favor of ensuring familiarity with the course LMS, technology tools, and strategies for communicating with students and fostering engagement online. Emphasis was still placed on public speaking course learning objectives, curriculum, assignments, and grading, but overviews of these topics came through guided explorations of the course LMS, viewing and grading recorded student speeches, and other online exercises.

While the online training provided necessary support, under the unique circumstances it was undoubtedly an entirely different first-semester teaching and learning experience from what new public speaking GTAs typically receive. These unique experiences, compounded by additional layers of uncertainty, led new GTAs to experience both challenges and opportunities fueled by the pandemic context. In the following sections, we discuss the main themes that emerged.

NAVIGATING GTA COHORT COMMUNITY

Basic communication course directors play an instrumental role in fostering a sense of community among instructors that supports the course as a whole. As Hershberger (2021) asserts, "establish[ing] the course as a unified front committed to student learning" and providing space for instructors to "empathize with each other as they share similar experiences" can, in turn, "have a positive impact on the health of the course overall as GTAs feel support from both their peers and the [course director]" (328). This role is especially important for new GTA cohorts as their experience teaching becomes for them an early "point of connection and common ground" (Huber 2019, 178). Additionally, as Myers (1998) highlights, "supportive communication relationships with peers" is a "primary socialization" mechanism for new GTAs who rely substantially on their peers for "sense-making, direction, and most importantly, comfort" (66). In the typical year, part of this sense of community forms in the fall graduate pedagogy seminar through in-class discussions, shared readings, assignments, and projects assigned by the course director. It also arises organically through unstructured activities such as informal conversations that occur before and after class, during office hours, and in the hallways where GTA and course director offices are located. In the context of the pandemic, many of these unstructured opportunities vanished as instructors worked from home and both training and teaching occurred online.

The substantial negative effects of graduate school on mental health have been well established, even pre-pandemic, so much so that these impacts have been labeled a mental health "crisis" (Wedemeyer-Strombel 2019). The stressors of graduate school are uniquely challenging for students balancing the demands of higher learning with first-time teaching responsibilities and faced with "insecurity regarding their teaching capability, time/role conflicts, and uncertainty regarding their department status" (Hendrix 2000, 161). Because of this, mental health services and other campus resources are always shared with new GTAs during orientation and across the fall semester. However, the COVID-19 pandemic further compounded the personal challenges that students typically face upon entering graduate school. Survey responses demonstrate that the first impacts of these challenges were felt during the early stages of online orientation and training. As one GTA reflected, "I had moved halfway across the country to start a graduate school program in a new city where I didn't know a single person. In addition to this, the pandemic made it unsafe to get out and meet new people. The social isolation affected my self-esteem and general happiness."[1]

Notably, within the new GTA training context, the lack of in-person interaction inhibited rapport and bonding among the cohort, particularly at the start of the semester:

> I felt particularly disconnected the first few weeks of the course. The dreaded self-introductions sounded extra cringe-y as I watched my tiny digitized reflection within my Zoom square. I think I attempted to tell a joke, but if anyone laughed, I couldn't hear it, because everyone was muted. I couldn't decide what was worse: the blank faces or the blacked out Zoom squares. I felt like a lonely fraud. What was I doing here?

A second GTA reflected on how the online training modality limited the cohort's ability to build community: "Rapport is often built in the 'between times'—the snippets of conversation before and after class. Due to the online nature of the [fall pedagogy seminar], there was much less opportunity for chit-chat. And most chit-chat was broadcasted for the group. This is a detriment for introverts like me who experience anxiety during group interactions." Another new GTA added, "Zoom was really difficult for me to navigate. In the best of times, I already struggle with major social anxiety. Without the immediate nonverbal feedback of my peers' body language (Are they listening to me? Do they understand me?), I tend to assume that my peers think the worst of me." As these reflections illustrate, the online modality of graduate teaching training contributed to feelings of isolation, social anxiety, an imbalance in GTA participation, and a delayed sense of community at the start of the semester.

The synchronous component of the fall graduate pedagogy seminar was instrumental to community building as a space where the cohort and director exchanged experiences and bounced ideas off each other in real time. The course director worked to facilitate a stronger sense of community among new GTAs by incorporating breakout discussion sessions that allowed them to connect with their peers and with more experienced GTA peer mentors who occasionally joined the meetings. While the peers discussed questions and swapped experiences, the basic course director hopped from one virtual pod to the next to check on progress. This intimate, small-group dynamic offered quieter GTAs more time and security to speak and offered everyone a chance to bond. One GTA noted, "[Our instructor] made extensive use of Zoom breakout groups, which was really important because it made sure that everybody got a chance to talk." Another shared, "Breakout groups were great. Being able to talk in small groups with multiple different people helped me get to know my cohort much better than being in a large group." Other GTAs stated that small-group breakout sessions functioned to build rapport among peers, while others noted that they would log into Zoom early to interact informally with the course director.

Ultimately, then, the first theme that emerged from our survey was the substantial impact the online learning environment had on the new GTAs. It created significant hurdles socially, academically, and pedagogically. The online format of training compounded the uncertainty of the students' first-semester teaching, making the formation of meaningful community more difficult. However, because all GTAs in our cohort attended class regularly and made participation a priority, the synchronous format worked for the graduate seminar in a way not necessarily transferable to all learning contexts. Virtual classroom strategies such as synchronous meetings, small-group breakout rooms, and facilitated connections with experienced peer GTA mentors proved effective for overcoming the myriad challenges of the pandemic context.

NAVIGATING INSTRUCTOR ETHOS

A second theme that emerged from the new GTA surveys was the issue of instructor credibility. As Dannels (2015) argues, this credibility "is a complex, communicative process that involves your behavior and the students' perceptions of your behavior" (23). The establishment of instructor credibility is important both for instructor confidence and for student learning, as students who perceive their instructor as credible typically are more motivated to learn, hold greater respect for their instructor, communicate more openly inside and outside of class, and demonstrate increased learning (Dannels 2015).

Scholarship on credibility in the classroom typically focuses on face-to-face instruction. Dannels (2014), for instance, notes that when GTAs attempt to "manage their students perceptions of them," they experience a sense of imposter syndrome, with concerns relating to age and setting themselves apart from the undergraduate student body (94). She also notes that instructors may worry about not having all the answers, giving wrong answers, being challenged about subject matter, lacking adequate expertise, or encountering students with superior expertise (Dannels 2015). However, many of these concerns were not relevant in the asynchronous, online context. Age was rendered mostly invisible, and instructors had ample time to answer questions and challenges via email, even seeking advice for difficult scenarios before responding.

As instructor credibility took on a different form amid the pandemic, so did the imposter syndrome experienced by the new GTAs. For instance, one GTA stated:

> I definitely felt that I was a bit of an imposter. I was learning how to implement technical pieces of the class (how to use Studio in Canvas, how to hide grades from students, how to navigate the rubrics, etc.) but I was supposed to be the reliable instructor. Many of my students called me "Professor" in their emails . . . I didn't want to tell them, "This is my first time teaching this class!"

As this student notes, the online learning management system (Canvas) was preloaded with everything from the assignments, rubrics, lecture videos, and resources. All new GTAs recorded "meet your instructor" and "course overview" videos which undergraduate students were assigned to watch in the first week of the semester. Beyond this, instructors were provided with opportunities to customize their courses through the addition of supplementary instructor-created videos, the posting of weekly course announcements and reminders, assignment feedback, and customization of smaller mini-speech assignments.

Due to the time constraints of being a new graduate student and the learning curve that comes along with teaching a course for the first time, most new instructors focused their customization efforts on their weekly Canvas announcements and their assignment feedback. As a result, the new GTAs were administering a course that, on the whole, someone else had created and handed to them. As one GTA noted, "I worried that students would see me as under-qualified since the lecture videos were recorded and added to the online Canvas [course template] by another instructor." This new form of imposter syndrome stemmed not from a lack of expertise, but from a lack of creative agency.

Yet, unlike an in-person teaching scenario wherein instructors create and lead face-to-face lesson plans, asynchronous online teaching allowed unique opportunities to perform instructor credibility by leaning into the technology tools provided. Essentially, the Canvas templates enacted a level of credibility on behalf of the instructor. One GTA illustrated this phenomenon when they reflected, "Having a complete and well structured online class helped build my credibility as an instructor. This was later confirmed with the student [teaching evaluation] survey results." Another described how the complete course template helped them master the curriculum: "I put the work in to thoroughly understand the content of the course, as well as utilizing the language within the [Canvas] course [template when communicating with students]." Other GTAs noted how the complete course template and asynchronous online format made space for them to focus on other essential skills such as grading and providing meaningful feedback.

Survey results also demonstrate that GTAs saw a relationship between instructor credibility and instructor immediacy. This is not surprising, because even in the face-to-face environment new GTAs are attuned to the dynamics of "negotiating relationships" and "managing identities" (Dannels 2014, 99–100). In the context of online instruction, GTAs had to find different ways of creating this sense of immediacy. "My synchronous virtual meetings with my students helped me establish my knowledge and credibility by providing them with recommendations and or clarifications. Also, my email communication with the students helped establish my presence as their instructor," described one GTA. Another GTA viewed their email interactions as a form of humanization: "[My emails give] students a chance to feel that I am not simply a profile on Canvas or a TA who was told to grade their work. I want them to know that I pay close attention to the work they put in." As these reflections illustrate, GTAs turned to email correspondence and synchronous online office hours to foster immediacy with students.

These forms of online immediacy, however, significantly compounded existing stressors for GTAs. The pandemic dynamic blurred the boundaries between home life and work life. Since GTAs were steps away from their computers at all times, working hours became hyper-flexible to the point of being ubiquitous. This sometimes led to potentially untenable conceptions about how readily available an effective instructor needs to be. For instance, one GTA's reflection shows a tendency to become overly available to students:

> I also learned that I need to monitor my email at all times because students could need help at any moment and in a situation like the pandemic, I think it was very important to be available to my students at all times even though that would take more effort and time on my side, but it guaranteed that I supported them in every way possible during the semester.

Another echoed this tendency toward over-availability: "I was very careful to respond to my students' email inquiries instantly and sometimes I responded one or two minutes after receiving their emails. I think this [encouraged] them to send more inquiries as they would not have to wait long for a response." GTAs were not required or instructed to be available to their students to this extent, but some over-extended themselves as a way to establish goodwill and community with their students. GTAs were required to hold two office hours per week per course and to clearly communicate a reasonable response time for student-instructor email communication. Time management can be a challenge even in a "normal" semester, as GTAs juggle the roles of instructor and student simultaneously (Dannels 2015). In the online context, however, striking a balance proved even more difficult for GTAs, particularly given that so much of their own teaching, coursework, and socializing happened in the same online spaces.

NAVIGATING INSTRUCTOR COMMUNICATION SKILLS

A third theme that emerged from the survey of new GTAs was growth in their own communication skills and understanding of public speaking. As one GTA reflected in their survey response, "Teaching public speaking is also a great opportunity to improve a teacher's communication skills and not just the students." At the authors' institution, the introductory public speaking course is housed in a large English department that includes several graduate programs. As such, GTAs who teach the introductory public speaking course come from a variety of disciplines, including applied linguistics, creative writing, literature, English education, and rhetoric and professional communication. Thus, the majority of GTAs who teach public speaking are new to the discipline of communication studies. In the basic course director's experience, she observes that new GTAs who teach the public speaking course grow alongside their students in their own understanding of public speaking as a discipline and in their own public speaking and communication skills. GTAs commonly share that they observe an evolution in their own ability to craft well-organized, engaging, and effectively-delivered presentations both in teaching scenarios and in their own graduate courses. These same phenomena occurred in the fall 2020 pandemic scenario, but in different ways.

The online pandemic teaching and learning context heightened GTA attunement to different aspects of the public speaking skillset within synchronous contexts. Survey responses indicate that GTAs noted the importance of nonverbal communication behaviors such as posture, body language, and gestures, which one GTA described as "all the more important" in the online context when attempting to build a sense of immediacy with virtual audiences. GTAs also demonstrated growth in their understanding of the technological dimensions of professional online communication such as how to "make eye contact" by looking directly at the webcam, how to angle the camera and set up lighting so that the speaker can be clearly seen, and how to navigate audio- and video-recording technologies. Additionally, GTA survey responses display attunement to critical listening skills. When reflecting on their experience with the graduate training seminar, some GTAs found it difficult to interact virtually with colleagues fearing that their participation might interrupt others. As one GTA noted, "It is difficult, at times, to read people's reactions in an online format. So I had to be more observant." Ultimately, then, the skills that the pandemic cohort developed were those that the online pandemic teaching context highlighted and necessitated. These skills—though different than those cultivated in normal times—are ones that will serve GTAs in both online and face-to-face communication contexts.

In the online teaching context, GTAs also gained more extensive practice in written communication skills than they typically receive in face-to-face teaching contexts. One GTA noted the difficulty of striking a balance between brevity, clarity, and detail: "I . . . had to be wary in my feedback both in emails and assignments to ensure that students were getting the right amount of information in a concise manner." This reflection illustrates Vallade and Kaufmann's (2018) contention that in the online classroom, "the lack of opportunity for online students to ask questions or follow up with an instructor during FtF class time makes the use of email even more important to student learning in online classes, particularly when they are confused or need help" (372). Accordingly, GTAs also expressed frustration with how easy it is to miscommunicate information in the written, online context. Students' difficulty or failure to follow written instructions for using technology added a significant workload burden for the GTAs, in many cases requiring them to address panic and frustration from struggling students. In response to some of these communication challenges, however, GTAs developed an ability to translate complex ideas or instructions into simplified language. These GTAs focused on using clear and concise language in their email communication and assignment feedback to create shared meaning between students and their instructor.

NAVIGATING INSTRUCTOR EMPATHY

Finally, as one GTA aptly noted, "Teaching is as much about the relationships and support of a classroom as it is about the content." The stressors of the pandemic greatly influenced the types of support undergraduate students needed throughout the semester. COVID-19 swept through the student body, with many students ill or quarantined at any given moment. Students also grappled with illness and deaths among their families and friends across the country. On top of this, many students navigated online coursework for the first time, overcoming technological barriers and time-management challenges without the social support typical of university life. Students who were unaccustomed to self-directed time management struggled to meet deadlines. As a result, GTAs of the pandemic cohort gained extensive experience navigating the gray areas of student support.

Across the fall semester, discussion of how to balance course policies with students' extenuating circumstances was a constant agenda item in our seminar class. GTAs expressed concern over how to uphold course policies regarding the timely submission of coursework and keep students on track in the course, while still demonstrating grace and empathy when their students were struggling. The extra effort of sending reminder emails proved effective for many GTAs; however, it stirred up feelings of insecurity about "pushing" students to complete their tasks. This type of labor was viewed as "hand-holding" or micromanaging by some instructors. One GTA admitted to waiving all late penalties in an effort to extend grace in their class sections but later felt self-conscious in light of how their peers handled late work. The complexities of these experiences are evident in the following GTA reflection:

> The main way that I helped support my students was by being extremely lax on my due date policies. Turning in an assignment by a specific deadline is, of course, a valuable skill. But I wanted to evaluate their ability to give and analyze speeches more than their ability to be punctual and follow directions, especially because there were many issues with internet connectivity, students with coronavirus (I was informed every time a student was not allowed to come to my class due to health reasons, even though I was teaching online and asynchronously), and just general stress.

This GTA's reflection exhibits empathy in balancing the rigidity of course policies with desired student learning outcomes, a crucial skill that new instructors learned by necessity across the stressful, unpredictable semester.

These gray areas were further complicated by the degree of emotional vulnerability expressed by students. One GTA offered an illustrative example:

> One student emailed me at around 9 pm, mere hours before the first major speech video recording was due, desperately asking for an extension. Despite the late hour, I felt obligated to respond and granted her a 24-hour extension. She asked to meet with me on a video call the next day and arrived in tears. She expressed that she was stressed out by the sheer amount of coursework due in all her classes, the stress of the job fair going on that week, and the overall chaotic nature of the semester. I was able to talk her through the assignment and she left much calmer. She sent me an email the next day apologizing for her emotional outburst and expressed deep embarrassment over the situation.

The vignette above illuminates the emotional toll the pandemic inflicted upon the student-teacher relationship. For some GTAs, upholding strict guidelines meant denying the pandemic's impact on a student's life. As students themselves, the GTAs understood the overwhelming combination of pandemic fatigue and school-related pressures. As a result, the GTAs got a crash course in referral skills by introducing their students to student counseling services, stress management resources, and crisis hotlines. Multiple GTAs related stories about students disclosing personal details related to their health and home life when asking for extensions. Other GTAs found that reaching out to the students who were missing work led these students to confide in them.

Student support is never one-size-fits-all. By the end of the semester, most GTAs felt called to be more gracious and empathetic to students amid and post-pandemic. One GTA summed up this impulse well:

> My experience teaching amid a pandemic shaped my teaching philosophy regarding flexibility and compassion. I granted far more extensions than I anticipated because nearly a dozen students reached out for accommodations. Moving forward, I anticipate that I will continue to model grace and understanding when students take initiative to communicate their struggles and verbalize their need for extensions. I will also continue to proactively email students who are falling behind as a way of checking in with them.

This reflection demonstrates how first-time GTAs navigated their students' need for emotional and academic support through compassion. Amid the pandemic, empathy and flexibility became part of the teaching ethos—a part that will stay with them as they continue to teach and grow as instructors.

CONCLUSION AND TRAINING RECOMMENDATIONS

All in all, this cohort of GTAs confronted a difficult situation that was challenging on multiple levels, but in so doing they learned invaluable lessons that will inform the future of their teaching and professional careers. As we move out of the pandemic and toward a "new normal," it is clear that online learning is here to stay. "Increasingly, departments are urged to develop courses online, to meet the needs of a variety of populations and improve the bottom line of universities who are facing enrollment issues," notes Chatham-Carpenter (2017, 492). In fact, as recently as 2018, one-third of all U.S. college students enrolled in at least one online course (Lederman 2019). In this context, basic course directors should be attuned to the lessons learned from the pandemic year as they plan future training for new GTAs and ongoing mentoring for the pandemic cohorts that they advise. While the COVID-19 pandemic is recent enough that we do not yet have all the answers, we have identified a few key recommendations for the consideration of basic course directors.

First, we must be careful not to forget the pandemic cohort of graduate students who learned to teach in this unique context. As these instructors transition into new teaching situations, additional mentorship will be needed on topics and skills such as lesson planning, classroom management, and facilitation of live discussion, which were minimized in their training due to the demands of the pandemic. At our institution, for instance, GTAs gained only minimal experience with lesson planning for face-to-face classes through a seminar project that required each GTA to model a sample lesson plan synchronously online. Our survey found that almost all instructors indicated apprehension about the transition into the physical classroom, so course directors should be ready to provide appropriate support.

Conversely, for future cohorts of new GTAs, graduate pedagogy must take on a dimension of multimodality to prepare instructors for the various teaching contexts they may encounter. This could take the form of synchronous and asynchronous online modules in otherwise face-to-face orientation or graduate training to familiarize students with these formats. Such models would also provide a space to include readings and discussions on best practices and particular challenges of online teaching. Course directors should also invite critical thinking about online teaching modalities by assigning the work of scholars like Huber (2020), who brings a critical pedagogy lens to online teaching, arguing that "online education structurally compels teachers into 'help desk' positions" to the effect of "limiting instructor dynamism and foreclosing opportunities for relationship building, problem posing, and collaboration" (464–465).

Additionally, basic course directors should consider including assignments that ask new GTAs to create video lessons for online classes, to practice online teaching, and to develop and hone online communication skills. Formal GTA training programs can promote increased instructor self-efficacy and confidence by requiring practice in multiple modes of performance-based aspects of teaching (Young and Bippus 2008, 124–125). When GTAs were asked in our survey about what things they would do differently when teaching online in the future, several responded that they would like to incorporate more multimodal materials in their courses. One GTA noted that they would "create more video announcements, instead of written announcements." Another GTA reflected: "I plan to use video or audio feedback on major assignments. I feel like putting a voice to my feedback instead of simply typing out my responses will give the students a chance to feel that I am not simply a profile on Canvas or a TA who was told to grade their work." Drawing on these ideas, we advise that course directors should create opportunities for GTAs to feel ownership and agency over the online course they teach. For instance, course directors should build more required customization projects into GTA training, perhaps including introductory videos for major speech assignments or mini video lectures on specific course concepts. These videos could be included in online courses or posted to the course LMS for face-to-face learners to review as supplementary course materials.

At a more basic level, communication pedagogy courses should provide some training in written communication, to prepare GTAs both for online teaching scenarios as well as for the vast amounts of email and assignment writing that come with face-to-face teaching. As the survey results show, our GTAs spent much of their time on email communication, course announcements, and written feedback, and miscommunications in these contexts were rampant. As Miller (2010) writes, "Rather than relying on the face-to-face communication characteristic of the traditional classroom, online communication relies on the ambiguity of text based communication where fine communication nuances may not be as evident" (163). Thus, pedagogy courses should provide models and practice opportunities for students to cultivate these skills and to receive instructor and peer feedback.

This pandemic experience also points to at least two areas of needed research within the field of basic communication pedagogy. First, we know from Hennings (2011) that GTAs feel pressure to be "perfect" teachers, and we saw this take on a new and different form as so much of the student-teacher relationship took place in online spaces. Additional research is needed to examine this "perfect teacher" fallacy in terms of workload, email responsiveness, and instructor availability, particularly in online contexts.

Second and finally, basic course directors need to develop new and innovative ways to train graduate students to negotiate the stressful "gray areas" of teaching and to balance expectations with grace. One possibility is to turn to the work in composition studies on "emotional labor," to contemplate how this scholarship can enrich our thinking on the graduate pedagogy training experience (Micciche 2007). While gray areas and emotional labor have always been parts of teaching, the pandemic made this explicit as instructors and students alike navigated new levels of stress and uncertainty together.

While we all look forward to a "return to normal," the changes to teaching and learning that have taken place amid the pandemic will undoubtedly have some lasting institutional effects. We must remember that, moving forward, basic course directors will be training new GTAs to teach in this changed environment, and new approaches will be needed to account for the multitude of teaching contexts and corresponding challenges that future generations of graduate teaching assistants will face. But of equal importance, we must continue to incorporate graduate students into our research and thinking on communication pedagogy and to allow their experiences to inform the future of introductory communication courses and pedagogical training.

NOTE

1. The survey we conducted went through the IRB approval process and was declared exempt. All names and identifying information have been removed.

REFERENCES

Broeckelman-Post, Melissa A. and Kristina Ruiz-Mesa. 2018. "Best Practices for Training New Communication Graduate Teaching Assistants." *Journal of Communication Pedagogy* 1, no. 1: 93–100.

Broeckelman-Post, Melissa A., Katherine E. Hyatt Hawkins, Anthony R. Arciero, and Andie S. Malterud. 2019. "Online versus Face-to-Face Public Speaking Outcomes: A Comprehensive Assessment." *Basic Communication Course Annual* 31: 144–170.

Broeckelman-Post, Melissa A. and Cheri J. Simonds. 2020. "Recruiting and Nurturing a Pipeline of Future Basic Course Directors." *Basic Communication Course Annual* 32: 170–178.

Chatham-Carpenter, April. 2017. "The Future Online: Instructional Communication Scholars Take the Lead." *Communication Education* 66, no. 4: 492–494.

Dannels, Deanna P. 2014. "Teacher Communication Concerns Revisited: Calling into Question the Gnawing Pull Towards Equilibrium." *Communication Education* 64, no. 1: 83–106.

Dannels, Deanna P. 2015. *Eight Essential Questions Teachers Ask: A Guidebook for Communicating with Students*. New York: Oxford University Press.

Easton, Susan S. 2003. "Clarifying the Instructor's Role in Online Distance Learning." *Communication Education* 52, no. 2: 87–105.

Fassett, Deanna L. and John T. Warren. 2012. *Coordinating the Communication Course: A Guidebook*. Boston, MA: Bedford/St. Martin's.

Hendrix, Katherine. 2000. "Peer Mentoring for Graduate Teaching Assistants: Training and Utilizing a Valuable Resource." *Basic Communication Course Annual* 12: 161–192.

Hennings, Jennifer M. 2011. "Tales of Teaching: Exploring the Dialectical Tensions of the GTA Experience." *Basic Communication Course Annual* 23: 127–171.

Hershberger, Michelle. 2021. "Managing Graduate Teaching Assistant Misbehaviors: Perspectives of Basic Course Directors from the Front Porch." *Basic Communication Course Annual* 33: 308–334.

Hoy, Anita Woolfolk and Rhonda Burke Spero. 2005. "Changes in Teacher Efficacy During the Early Years of Teaching: A Comparison of Four Measures." *Teaching and Teacher Education* 21: 343–356.

Huber, Aubrey A. 2019. "Celebrating Community in the Basic Course." *Basic Communication Course Annual* 31: 177–180.

Huber, Aubrey A. 2020. "Failing at the Help Desk: Performing Online Teacher." *Communication Education* 69, no. 4: 464–479.

Joyce, Jillian, Alex Kritselis, Samantha Dunn, Cheri J. Simonds, and Ben Lynn. 2019. "Synthesizing the Current State of the Basic Communication Course Annual: Furthering the Research of Effective Pedagogy." *Basic Communication Course Annual* 31: 2–43.

Lederman, Doug. 2019. "Online Enrollments Grow, but Pace Slows." *Inside Higher Ed*, December 11, 2019. https://www.insidehighered.com/digital-learning/article/2019/12/11/more-students-study-online-rate-growth-slowed-2018.

McRae, Chris. 2010. "Repetition and Possibilities: Foundational Communication Course, Graduate Teaching Assistants, etc." *Basic Communication Course Annual* 22: 172–200.

Micciche, Laura R. 2007. *Doing Emotion: Rhetoric, Writing, Teaching*. Portsmouth, NH: Boynton/Cook Publishers.

Miller, John J. 2010. "Student Evaluations for the Online Public Speaking Course." *Basic Communication Course Annual* 22: 153–171.

Morreale, Sherwyn P., Janice Thorpe, and Joshua N. Westwick. 2020. "Online Teaching: Challenge or Opportunity for Communication Education Scholars." *Communication Education* 70, no. 1: 117–119.

Myers, Scott A. 1998. "GTAs as Organizational Newcomers: The Association Between Supportive Communication Relationships and Information Seeking." *Western Journal of Communication* 62, no. 1: 54–73.

Valenzano, Joseph M., III, Samuel P. Wallace, and Sherwyn P. Morreale. 2014. "Consistency and Change: The (R)Evolution of the Basic Communication Course." *Communication Education* 63, no. 4: 355–365.

Vallade, Jessalyn I. and Renee Kaufmann. 2018. "Investigating Instructor Misbehaviors in the Online Classroom." *Communication Education* 67, no. 3: 363–381.

Wedemeyer-Strombel, Kathryn R. 2019. "Why We Need to Talk More About Mental Health in Graduate School." *The Chronicle of Higher Education*, August 27, 2019.

https://www.chronicle.com/article/why-we-need-to-talk-more-about-mental-health-in-graduate-school/.

Young, Stacy L. and Amy M. Bippus. 2008. "Assessment of Graduate Teaching Assistant (GTA) Training: A Case Study of a Training Program and Its Impact on GTAs." *Communication Teacher* 22, no. 4: 116–129.

Chapter 11

A Case for Teaching Public Speaking without Live Audiences

Matt McGarrity

Public speaking remains the most common form of the introductory communication course (Morreale et al. 2016). Prior to the pandemic, online versions of the course struggled for acceptance. The most recent basic course survey showed that only around one-third of four-year schools offered a speech course completely online (Morreale et al. 2016). Half of the respondents in Ward's survey of public speaking instructors strongly disagreed with the statement "Public speaking should be offered online" (2016). The online public speaking courses that did exist usually required speakers to assemble live audiences for their assignments. Around 80 % of the public speaking instructors surveyed by Ward (2016) favored speakers assembling their own audiences, with many requiring it.

COVID-19 demanded that public speaking instruction move online; quarantining and social distancing eliminated, or dramatically curtailed, most in-person audiences. If Ward's (2016) survey numbers held true, that meant potentially half of the online public speaking courses offered in 2020 were taught by reluctant teachers who doubted the medium's ability to provide a suitable pedagogical experience. Even if a teacher was teaching an online version of the course, social distancing eliminated the preferred method of having speakers assemble audiences to address. This seemingly left public speaking instructors in the worst possible position: forced to teach online without copresent audiences.

Post-pandemic, in-person public-speaking classes will probably be among the last to return to campus. Singing, or speaking loudly, increases the emission of respiratory droplets, which makes them more likely to be superspreader events, where one person infects many others. Such events "have played an oversized role in the transmission of the virus that causes the disease" (Aschwanden 2020). COVID thus impacted public speaking classes more than perhaps any other in the communication curriculum. Such a massive disruption to the course, though, presents us with an opportunity to expand our understanding of public speaking skills and audiences.

In this chapter, I argue against the assumption that live, copresent audiences are a necessary precondition for effective public speaking education. My argument proceeds through a few steps. First, by examining CRTNET discussions about online public speaking, I trace how physically copresent audiences were framed as the *sine qua non* of public speaking education, thus requiring speakers to assemble their own audiences and avoid rerecording their speeches. The remainder of the chapter refutes each contention. I argue that, while valuable, our in-class audiences are limited. If we assume that the chief benefit of the course is skill development,[1] the loss of an in-class audience is not significantly harmful to the goals of the course. Adopting a skills perspective highlights that rerecording speeches should be encouraged rather than discouraged. Finally, I claim that the requirement for speakers to assemble their own audiences is unnecessary, burdensome, and should probably be abandoned. Reducing the dominance of audiences in public speaking education was possible before the pandemic, but I argue it will be more necessary in the post-pandemic landscape given increased student and faculty demand for more flexibility in classes and assignments.

DEFENSES OF COPRESENT AUDIENCES

A literature search for online public speaking reveals quite a few articles about how speech apprehension or peer review work in online classes, but one doesn't get the sense that there is much controversy around teaching speech online. Before the pandemic, there was entrenched opposition to moving the public speaking course online, but it rarely made its way into publication. A notable exception would be Hunt's (2012) article, "Why I am not going to teach public speaking online." Hunt opposes online public speaking teaching because live teaching works well, he is called to work with students in person, and that public speaking calls for embodied teaching. Hunt's article is one published instance of a prevalent opposition to online public speaking. The absence of publishing doesn't mean that the issue is unimportant to the discipline; these conversations simply happen elsewhere.

Tracking attitudes about teaching practice often requires looking at more informal disciplinary spaces. Stephen North was interested in how the common pedagogy for teaching English Composition had emerged with such consistency across departments. His study tracked Composition's teaching lore, the "accumulated body of traditions, practices, and beliefs" for teaching (North 1987, 22). This lore, he argues, is developed through teachers reflecting on their positive and negative teaching experiences and then sharing them communally. Textbooks offer insights into these disciplinary discursive practices. For example, Makkawy and Moreman (2019) examine textbooks in order to trace non-disableist assumptions in the communication field. William Keith (2016) takes an ecological approach to understanding the public speaking course, which includes examining the role that textbooks play in reflecting and shaping teaching practice. Textbooks don't really help with the teaching lore around online public speaking though, since most remain primarily focused on traditional classrooms. The most common place for arguments for and against online teaching and public speaking audiences is, ironically, online.

The Communication Research and Theory Network (CRTNET) was founded in 1985 by Thomas Benson. Until it was discontinued in May of 2020, it served as a major public space for the communication discipline to post job searches, request information, and debate ideas. In research articles, CRTNET is often mentioned as a space for recruiting study participants, but it hasn't been featured as a discursive field meriting analysis. Kathleen McConnell (2018) briefly turns to CRTNET, in addition to journal articles, in her discussion of scholarly attitudes about research productivity. CRTNET is however an ideal space to trace how communication teachers think about audience and online public speaking. This message board gives us a way to study the types of pedagogical conversations that would otherwise ephemerally exist only in departmental hallways and early morning conference panels.

I performed a search for "online public speaking" in the CRTNET archives that yielded 85 posts between 1998 and 2020. Some of the posts in this sample linked to previous ones that dealt with online public speaking and/ or online audiences missed in the initial search; I added these to the sample. Some posts simply included job announcements; I excluded these. I was left with a sample of 78 posts about teaching public speaking online. The conversations were sporadic. Usually, an initial post generated a flurry of responses for about a week and then the issue faded away. Examining these posts helps clarify opinions and practices about online public speaking and copresent audiences. Three interlocking themes stand out in this sample. First, copresent audiences are framed as the *sine qua non* of public speaking education. Second, instructors worry that the absence of copresent audiences allows students to "cheat" by rerecording their speeches. Third, in order to prevent rerecording and provide the benefits of a live audience, instructors require that students in online classes assemble audiences for their speech assignments.

One of the first flurries of activity in the sample was in 1998 dealing with the arguments about distance learning classes with videotaped speeches. Even before public speaking courses started to be offered more regularly online, there was opposition to moving the class out of the classroom and reducing the role of copresent audiences. Reffue (1998) writes, "While I realize perfection is not the goal in a classroom setting, I demand that my students understand the 'live' nature of a speech and appreciate their 'one shot.'" Wendt (1998) notes, "The live-ness, the simultaneity, of public speaking is its defining feature-what separates it, categorically, from writing an essay or reading a poem aloud." Corman (1998), who was teaching a class online adds, "But I don't see how students can become good public speakers without experience speaking before large, live audiences." Even before discussions of MOOCs or online platforms, there was an established opposition to pedagogy that might reduce the role of the live in-class audience.

The early 2000s had a few small flare-ups, including a comment by Gore (2003) that an "essential part of public speaking is the immediacy of a live audience." There wasn't another major discussion of online public speaking until 2005. The first entry in this discussion was a defense of the live, in-class audience. "Speech communication is a performing art. Like music, theatre, dance, and athletics, you have to 'be there for the game' to truly show what you know" (King 2005). Six of the eight posts in this 2005 discussion focused on requiring assembled audiences for online speakers, a theme that returns later.

The longest exchange on the topic happened in 2016. Steinfatt (2016) generated a series of exchanges by posing this proposition, "It is absurd to believe that public speaking classes taught via the internet involve public speaking. 'Public speaking' refers to speaking in public. Standing alone in a bedroom talking to a camera is not public speaking." Sarapin (2016) agrees, "I think that teaching students public speaking online is the communication field's most obvious oxymoron. If it weren't so counterintuitive and unhelpful, it would be laughable. I am ashamed that educators think this is acceptable and give credit for it." Honeycutt (2016) classifies online classes as "Skype speaking in pajamas" because "Immediate audience feedback is extinct." King (2016) concludes, "I have run the idea of online public speaking by several of my colleagues in other disciplines and their reaction is always laughter. I do worry about our credibility." Horan (2016) adds, "It's UNREAL that this is considered an appropriate modality for Public Speaking, when the biggest challenge students face is a FEAR of speaking to a live audience."

This is a small sampling of the support for live audiences in these CRTNET discussions. Certainly, they are not the only voices; many argue for online teaching. Most supporters of online public speaking in these exchanges require students to assemble audiences to replicate the in-class experience. What is notable is that these CRTNET conversations become longer and more pitched as nontraditional public speaking classes take root. In 1998, videotaped distance education courses were a minor feature of the discipline. By 2016, online education was in full swing. The discussions also shift in tone from 1998 to 2016. Part of this might stem from the increased presence of online courses (there are simply more); part of this might stem from the fact that there are more defenders of online education by 2016 (a good debate needs adversaries). Nevertheless, we end 2016 with multiple teachers in the discipline framing online public speaking education without live, copresent audiences as "absurd," "shameful," "laughable," and "unreal."

Much of this concern for a live speech encounter seems to be linked to the persistent concern that students will rerecord their speeches. In 1998, Newman argued, "In the 'real world' there really is a specific time during which the speaker must speak, and that speaker cannot 'do it over' if the speech does not meet with the speaker's expectations." Edwards (2005) worries that "some students (those who send in videotapes) can retape the speech until he or she 'gets it right.'" Years later, Sarapin (2016) continues to echo these concerns, "Although our in-class students are expected to practice before delivering their speeches, the online students can videotape each practice run-through, and when one looks particularly good, that's the one that's submitted." Turpin (2019) writes, "The limitation I see with just letting students turn in a selfie-video is that there will be a strong temptation to, um, curate themselves, which is to say edit themselves in the best possible light. While I do think that is a valuable skill, I consider it media production rather than public speaking." Instructors seem worried that, given the chance, students will not replicate the conditions of the live in-class audience and rerecord their speeches until they are satisfied.

In response to these concerns about a lack of a live audience and the ability to rerecord, many, if not most, online public speaking classes require speakers to assemble live audiences on their own. Wignall (1998) demonstrates this concern in his post, "The importance of audience." He demands that his students pan the audience "from time to time in order that I get a sense of audience engagement/involvement, a view of the setting, the incorporation of speech aids . . . in short, the only thing different from the classroom setting is that I am not there in person." This explanation of institutional practices is a common theme in the various CRTNET discussions. Not surprising since roughly 80 % of surveyed public speaking instructors favored speakers assembling their own audiences (Ward 2016). In pushing for assembled audiences, these posts seem to embrace the need for a copresent audience while trying to avoid the dangers of student rerecording.

It's unclear how these positions evolved during the pandemic since CRTNET ended just as the pandemic was getting into full swing. It's doubtful that such strong pessimism about online public speaking instruction will return given the broad acceptance of online pedagogy during the pandemic.

Despite consistent reports of low motivation (Means and Neisler 2020), surveys have shown both students and faculty are more receptive to online instruction. A report by Bay View Analytics and Cengage Learning (Seaman and Johnson 2021) showed over half of the 1,469 students surveyed felt more positive about online learning than they did pre-pandemic, with almost half reporting that they wanted to take another fully online course again post-pandemic. Results were similar for faculty, with over half reporting feeling more optimistic about online learning than they did before the pandemic. Less than 10 % of faculty surveyed planned on returning to their pre-pandemic pedagogy without any changes. Over half said that they would make moderate or substantial changes to their pedagogy. This aligns with *The Chronicle of Higher Education*'s study "Online 2.0: Managing a Large-Scale Move to Online Learning," in which roughly 66 % of faculty surveyed reported that their initial foray into online teaching was positive (June 2020). The pandemic forced students and faculty online, normalizing some expectations about what can be taught remotely and without synchronous class meetings. The next section argues that speech assignments can fit into this category.

SKILL DEVELOPMENT DOESN'T REQUIRE COPRESENT AUDIENCES

Despite instructors leaning heavily on the term *public* in their defenses of copresent audiences, our actual in-class audiences are rarely robust publics. This isn't necessarily bad; it's simply a feature of *in-class* audiences. Our duty as teachers calls for us to impose conditions that sand down the pointier edges of audiences (rudeness, apathy, etc.) so that students can speak under the best possible conditions. This is justified since the primary benefit of the class is skill development, not providing practice audiences. The skills that our rubrics point to can be taught well, even in the absence of copresent audiences, as the pandemic year has tested.

To begin with, the *public* in public speaking groans under the weight it is often asked to carry. Valenzano (2020) interrogates the discipline's understanding of the term, arguing that the communication discipline has "lost sight of what the phrase 'public speaking' actually means and erroneously and dangerously equated it with simply delivering formal presentations" (106). This presentational understanding of public is neither the only nor the best. Valenzano (2020) shows that Dewey provides a broader notion of publicity: "If public is understood as an audience which has time to develop, and could be either broad or targeted in nature, or if it is understood as a way of identifying topics of communal importance, then it opens the door to new ways of implementing the course without changing its name" (115). This topical and community aspect is key to Warner's (2002) understanding of a public as called into being by discourse, not by virtue of having a group of people in a room together. Warner writes, "A public is a space of discourse organized by nothing other than discourse itself. . . . It exists by virtue of being addressed" (67). This might be a counter public (Asen 2009; Fraser 1990) that defines itself in opposition to the larger public; it might be a parasitic public (Larsen and McHendry 2019) that exists in relationship to a larger discourse. These publics might manifest as physical audiences, but they often don't. Arguing that students have to address copresent audiences because the course title is *public speaking*, is cherry-picking a single, narrow definition of public not reflected in the literature.

When viewed as topical publics, in-class audiences suffer since the group assembled has little in common beyond the fact that they attend the same university and signed up for the same class. Outside of the public speaking class, there are external reasons for why the audience and the speaker might meet. A manager needs to give a safety briefing to the office; a project supervisor needs to provide a budget update to their team. The rhetorical situation presented to the speaker who is outlining new safety protocols for their staff at an industrial processing plant might sound prosaic, but it's fraught with opportunities and challenges. The audience has a shared history; the speaker has subject matter topoi to draw upon. That sort of rich rhetorical situation requires time and topic. It is rare to achieve these sorts of publics in a ten- or fifteen-week course. The classroom audience has little shared background with the topic, the speaker, or one another.

Over the years, there have been efforts to make audiences more like publics. McGarrity and Crosby (2012) examine how textbook advice on invention limits classroom audiences before they identify some strategies for making classrooms proto-public spaces. Recently, composition courses have explored corequisite status. Students enroll in one topical course (in religious studies, for example) and a colisted composition course where the writing assignments deal with the content from the linked course. *Composition Studies* (Shepard, Sturman, and Estrem 2020) recently devoted a special edition to the corequisite course system. Corequisite public speaking courses could challenge speakers and improve the quality of the student experience and are worth exploring. That said, changes to the course doesn't alter the fact that in-class audiences are students in a college course.

Pedagogical necessity demands that we sanitize in-class speaking situations. We force the audience into being there with participation or attendance points. We design activities for audience members in order to encourage more critical engagement with the speaker. We take a hundred different policy actions to ensure that the audience exists for the development of speaker skills. Let's say that a student gives a solid speech, but the in-class audience is visibly bored. That speech would still be graded well, with maybe a few comments about engaging the audience, or we might simply ignore audience reactions altogether. Such actions aren't bad; they're part of our pedagogical duty to help speakers develop as speech writers and performers.

Physical audiences are valuable in the service of helping students develop their speaking skills, but they are of secondary importance and not a precondition for those benefits. Pre-pandemic opponents to online public speaking invert this and frame physical audiences as necessary for any public instruction to occur. Steinfatt (2016) argued on CRTNET, "'Public speaking' refers to speaking in public. Standing alone in a bedroom talking to a camera is not public speaking." Is standing in front of an unenthusiastic classroom audience of strangers who have little background or interest in the speech topic, delivering a speech reflecting a clear grading rubric for the sole purpose of securing a grade really that much better? Such defenses seem to frame in-class audiences at their best: engaged, enthusiastic students who present challenges and rewards to invested speakers. Audiences, however, exist on a continuum: some are great, many are fine, and some are just bad. We shouldn't rest the reputation of the public speaking course on the quality of the audiences generated.

If in-class audiences were so essential to the survival of the course, one could assume that they would be the focus of scholarship. While *Communication Teacher* offers a number of great ideas for fostering in-class audiences, there's no scholarship for evaluating their quality. The opposite is true for public speaking skills. The discipline has devoted considerable scholarly attention to speech rubrics. Broeckelman-Post et al. (2020) recently classified dozens of existing evaluation measurements according to the six essential public speaking competencies outlined by the Social Science Research Council, in partnership with NCA, which include: (1) create messages appropriate to the audience, purpose, and context, (2) critically analyze messages, (3) apply ethical communication principles and practices, (4) utilize communication to embrace difference, (5) demonstrate self-efficacy, and (6) influence public discourse (3). None of these competencies require copresent audiences.

Since our grading standards seem unconcerned with in-class audiences, it should come as no surprise that there are few differences separating online and face-to-face courses. In their comprehensive comparison of online and in-person classes, Broeckelman-Post et al. (2019) conclude, "there was no difference between the two formats in public speaking performance, final exam performance, course grades, public speaking anxiety, communication competence, or interpersonal communication competence" (158). The years to come will provide a more complete picture of what the pandemic instruction looked like. Ongoing research at UC-Irvine indicates that students were working harder on their classes and achieving higher grades during the pandemic (McMurtie 2021). If this is true, then the pandemic year wasn't a lost year of public speaking instruction; students were achieving more or less the same outcomes while online. This isn't to say that no differences exist between online and in-person formats. My point here is that our efforts have historically been focused on our greatest educational value: speech skill development. Live audiences might aid skill development, but they are not a prerequisite.

ENCOURAGING RERECORDING AND ENDING REQUIREMENTS FOR ASSEMBLED AUDIENCES

The CRTNET posts defending physical audiences never seemed to praise their robustness; rather, live audiences make sure that students get "one-shot" at the graded speech. In the absence of a classroom audience, students must assemble proxy audiences in order to prevent rerecording speeches. However, taking a skills perspective on the course leads to an opposite position: encouraging the rerecording of speeches and eliminating the requirement of speakers to assemble their own live audiences.

As a practical matter, assembled audiences don't really prevent rerecording since an audience made of friends or family would be willing to sit through multiple versions of the same speech. Failing that, a student could rerecord the speech in front of a different assembled audience, if they knew enough people to muster. The situation with assembled audiences seems similar to that of any recorded speech; students can choose which recording to submit. The policy seems to reward students with the most time and largest circle of friends, who can run different speeches in front of different audiences. At best, this requirement for assembled audiences is a nuisance for those who want to record the speech multiple times. More to the point, we should actually encourage rerecording since it allows students to experience high-quality rehearsals before performing a speech for a grade.

The quality of a speech rehearsal matters. For example, Smith and Frymier (2006) showed students performing better on their graded speeches when practicing in front of live audiences. This had a stronger effect than simply reading the speech silently or aloud to oneself. Performing the speech in front of a mirror also improved rehearsals and had a positive effect on speech grades. The issue is whether rehearsal is as realistic as possible. Rehearsal realism can happen even in the absence of physical audiences. Choi, Honeycutt, and Bodie (2015) show that imagined interactions in a rehearsal can improve performance over simply visualization alone. We want speakers to practice as they will perform, but getting students to engage in enough quality rehearsals can be challenging.

Submitted video speeches might generate more quality rehearsals by virtue of their form. Let's say a student rehearses a speech twice before recording it for a grade. After recording, they review the video and decide that the submission isn't great and so they rerecord once more. That first recording transforms from a submitted speech to a high-quality rehearsal. It was a "full dress rehearsal," but the student didn't know it at the time. In evaluating a speech for submission, the student is also engaging in another sound pedagogical practice: video review. LeFebvre et al. (2015) explored how students review videos of their performances. They showed that students varied in how accurately they viewed their performances when compared with a grader; some overestimated their abilities, others underestimated. Regardless, the authors conclude by reaffirming the pedagogical value of video review. In their comparative assessment of online and offline public speaking courses, Broeckelman-Post et al. (2019) also argue that rerecording and rewatching is a positive, not a negative, aspect of online courses.

Additionally, rerecording allows for much greater flexibility around when and how students prepare their assignments. Flexibility was forced on us by the pandemic, but it is something that students report appreciating. Teachers and students had to remain flexible about classes and assignments as we combated concerns about infection and dealt with changing expectations. As student obligations increase so does this preference for flexibility. Students who are married, employed, and/or have children all report a greater preference for taking classes offered fully online (Seaman and Johnson 2021). Post-pandemic, students will continue to expect this higher level of flexibility. Video submission allows for this type of flexibility while aligning student motivations for higher grades with good pedagogical practice (reviewing video and putting the time into high-quality rehearsals).

If skills can be taught without physical audiences and we want to encourage rerecording, we can also dispense with the common online class requirement of requiring speakers to assemble their own audiences. To begin with, these assembled audiences are poor proxies since they are both smaller and more charitable than the in-class audience. In Ward's (2016) study of online public speaking, most respondents required audiences of between five and seven members. This smaller audience doesn't seem to demand much in terms of projection or delivery. Moreover, the audience often emerges from a preexisting interpersonal relationship with the speaker. While some students might speak to their work colleagues, most are picking family and friends. This isn't inherently bad, but it moves the speech out of the public mode and into a private mode of communication. If the desire for an assembled audience is to make the speech "more real," then speaking to a handful of family members in a living room doesn't seem to achieve that.

But even if the assembled audiences were great rhetorical situations (they're often not) and they provided students quality spaces for refining their speech skills (they typically don't), we should still not require them since it is an intrusive burden on teachers and students. The requirement for assembled audiences demands that students have easy access to a relatively large social circle; successful completion of the course requires that students have seven friends that they can call on multiple times in the semester. Assuming that students perform two or three speech assignments, that's a fair bit of logistical work involving multiple people who have no relationship to the class itself. This requirement was challenging in the best of times; it was impossible for some during COVID lockdowns. Additionally, international students, working students, socially anxious students are all potentially starting with a difficulty not faced by their classmates. In essence, this requirement demands a type social relationship that has nothing to do with the course content. This is similar to Wood's (1996) discussion of participation requirements. She noted that such a requirement isn't necessarily bad, but it becomes so when we grade students without explaining what they're being held accountable for. Wood suggests teaching how to participate in class in order to grade participation. We shouldn't grade based on assembled audiences, if we don't teach how to build them.

Finally, assembled audiences require intrusive policing. In the 2016 CRTNET discussion, Webster outlines the rigor of their demands for assembled audiences.

> a minimum of eight adult audience members with a fixed camera above and behind them so that the speaker is in focus as well as all members of the audience at all times. This has allowed us to capture 'fake' audience members from time to time because it's quite obvious when there is no panning. Speeches must be given with a single take and the time stamp must show this.

Such intrusive practices aren't outliers; they're built into the very requirement for assembled audiences. If you ask for seven audience members, you have to confirm seven people. We've created a layer of intrusive rules that we then must enforce through rigorous oversight. In this sense, proctoring services like Proctorio, which gained notoriety during the pandemic, would be ideal for ensuring assembled audiences. They monitor the space for other humans and posted notes, track eye movements, monitor voices to ensure that speakers aren't being fed their lines (Mangan 2021). Modern technology for surveilling students seems to have caught up with what some online speech teachers have been doing for decades.

Moving toward more efficient surveillance would be going in the wrong direction. These services have rightly been critiqued as a disturbing foray into student surveillance, using problematic algorithms to invade students' private space (Harwell 2020; Kelley 2020; Ongweso 2020). The services are not always great at distinguishing test-related stress from cheating-related stress;

facial recognition software doesn't work well for all races. More importantly, this CCTV approach to teaching seems at odds with Calloway-Thomas's (2018) call for a pedagogy of empathy. She notes, "goodwill lies at the very core of a pedagogy of empathy. It is made possible when we give people the benefit of the perceptual doubt" (498). Intrusive surveillance policies designed to catch "fake audiences" begin with an assumption of doubt; these practices eat time and corrode trust. The benefits of assembled audiences are simply not worth the cost to students and teachers.

CONCLUSION: TINKERING OUR FUTURE

In *The Charisma Machine* (2019), Morgan Ames charts the techno-utopianism of the One Laptop Per Child movement. The OLPC promised revolutionary changes in education once children had access to new technology. Such a promise isn't new. Moran writes, "Educational reform efforts have often been techno-utopian, and charismatic technologies from radio to the internet have been hailed as saviors for an educational system that appears perpetually on the brink of failure" (187). Justin Reich (2020) points out that the pandemic has allowed techno-utopianism to return. Arizona State University, long an online education leader, has themed their 2021 ed-tech summit "The Dawn of the Age of Digital Learning." Their website highlights how we can mark time as B.C. (before coronavirus) and A.D. (after disease) when thinking about education technology. Reich, like Ames, avoids the overblown utopianism of Silicon Valley's promises to education and the pessimism of modern luddites. Rather they look to the concept of technological tinkering. Tyack and Cuban (2009) write, "Tinkering is one way of preserving what is valuable and reworking what is not" (5). Tinkering with educational technology is pragmatic, but not terribly revolutionary. Reich notes, "If you see the pandemic as a moment for a disjunctive break with the past, you're setting yourself up for disappointment."

An asynchronous online speech assignment is a good tool for tinkering with. Such assignments can teach skills for digital environments (Edwards 2021; Gerbensky-Kerber 2017; Kirkwood et al. 2011; Lind 2012). Public speaking classes have always faced a scheduling challenge; we must devote at least a third of the class to student performances. An online speech allows teachers to ask for more performances without costing class meeting time. Tinkering with the assignment means that we keep in its proper role: a tool for teaching speech skills. We certainly shouldn't rely on existing arguments against asynchronous speech assignments and discard the assignment once the pandemic ends. What will the public speaking course look like after the pandemic? A lot like it did before the pandemic, except now we have more experience with more tools to help students refine their skills.

NOTE

1. While some might disagree that the public speaking course should aim primarily at skills, this is a common approach. For example, the NCA/Social Science Research Council document on assessing public speaking learning is defined by a skills approach (Broeckelman-Post and Ruiz-Mesa 2018).

REFERENCES

Ames, Morgan G. 2019. *The Charisma Machine: The Life, Death, and Legacy of One Laptop Per Child.* Cambridge, MA: The MIT Press.

Aschwanden, Christie. 2020. "How 'Superspreading' Events Drive Most COVID-19 Spread." *Scientific American*, June 23, 2020. https://www.scientificamerican.com/article/how-superspreading-events-drive-most-covid-19-spread1/

Asen, Robert. 2009. "Ideology, Materiality, and Counterpublicity: William E. Simon and the Rise of a Conservative Counterintelligentsia." *Quarterly Journal of Speech* 95, no. 3: 263–88. doi:10.1080/00335630903140630.

Broeckelman-Post, Melissa A., and Kristina Ruiz-Mesa, 2018. Measuring College Learning in Public Speaking. *Learning in Higher Education.* Social Science Research Council. http://highered.ssrc.org/wp-content/uploads/2018.10-MCL-in-Public-Speaking-Report.pdf

Broeckelman-Post, Melissa A., Katherine E. Hyatt Hawkins, Anthony R. Arciero, and Andie S. Malterud. 2019. "Online versus Face-to-Face Public Speaking Outcomes: A Comprehensive Assessment." *Basic Communication Course Annual* 31: 144–170.

Broeckelman-Post, Melissa A., Karla M. Hunter, Joshua N. Westwick, Angela Hosek, Kristina Ruiz-Mesa, John Hooker, and Lindsey B. Anderson. 2020. "Measuring Essential Learning Outcomes for Public Speaking." *Basic Communication Course Annual* 32: 2–29.

Calloway-Thomas, Carolyn. 2018. "A Call for a Pedagogy of Empathy." *Communication Education* 67 no. 4: 495–499. doi:10.1080/03634523.2018.1504977.

Choi, Charles W., James M. Honeycutt, and Graham D. Bodie. 2015. "Effects of Imagined Interactions and Rehearsal on Speaking Performance." *Communication Education* 64, no. 1: 25–44. doi:10.1080/03634523.2014.978795.

Corman, Steven. 1998. "Unsure about Distance Public Speaking." *CRTNET Archives*, July 31, 1998. https://lists.psu.edu/cgi-bin/wa?A2=ind9807&L=CRTNET&P=R15749&X=O2792D11D4F498EF960&Y.

Edwards, Ashley A. Hannah. 2021. "From TED Talks to TikTok: Teaching Digital Communication to Match Student Skills with Employer Desires." *Basic Communication Course* Annual 33: 336–341.

Edwards III, John W. 2005. "Re: query #8852." *CRTNET Archives*, August 25, 2005. https://lists.psu.edu/cgi-bin/wa?A2=ind0508&L=CRTNET&P=R3590&X=OA5E20205FEBE032749&Y.

Fraser, Nancy. 1990. "Rethinking the Public Sphere: A Contribution to the Critique of Actually Existing Democracy." *Social Text* 25–26: 56–80. doi:10.2307/466240.

Gerbensky-Kerber, Anne. 2017. "Creating a Structured Practice Space with Online Mini-Speeches." *Communication Teacher* 31, no. 2: 70–73. doi:10.1080/1740462 2.2017.1285409.

Gore, John. 2003. "Public Speaking on the Internet." *CRTNET Archives*, August 8, 2003. https://lists.psu.edu/cgi-bin/wa?A2=ind0308&L=CRTNET&P=R1089&X =O2792D11D4F498EF960&Y.

Harwell, Drew. 2020. "Cheating-Detection Companies Made Millions During the Pandemic. Now Students Are Fighting Back." *The Washington Post*, November 12, 2020. https://www.washingtonpost.com/technology/2020/11/12/test-monitor ing-student-revolt/.

Honeycutt, James. 2016. "RE: Public Speaking Courses via the Internet (Thomas M. Steinfatt, CRTNET #15215)." *CRTNET Archives*, June 1, 2016. https://lists.psu.ed u/cgi-bin/wa?A2=ind1606A&L=CRTNET&P=R110&X=O2792D11D4F498EF9 60&Y.

Horan, Virginia. 2016. "RE: Public Speaking Courses via the Internet (Thomas M. Steinfatt, CRTNET #15215)." *CRTNET Archives*, June 6, 2016. https://lists.psu.ed u/cgi-bin/wa?A2=ind1606A&L=CRTNET&P=R1218&X=OA5E20205FEBE032 749&Y.

Hunt III, Arthur W. 2012. "Why I Am Not Going to Teach Public Speaking Online." *Explorations in Media Ecology* 11, no. 2: 163–176. doi:10.1386/eme.11.2.163_1.

June, Audrey Williams. 2020. "Did the Scramble to Remote Learning Work? Here's What Higher Ed Thinks." *The Chronicle of Higher Education*, June 8, 2020. https ://www.chronicle.com/article/did-the-scramble-to-remote-learning-work-heres-wh at-higher-ed-thinks

Keith, William. 2016. "Understanding the Ecology of the Public Speaking Course." *The Review of Communication* 16, no. 2–3: 114–124. doi:10.1080/15358593.201 6.1187451.

Kelley, Jason. 2020. "Students Are Pushing Back Against Proctoring Surveillance Apps." *Electronic Frontier Foundation*, September 25, 2020. https://www.eff .org/deeplinks/2020/09/students-are-pushing-back-against-proctoring-surveillance -apps.

King, Corwin. 2005. "Re: Announcements and queries #8852." *CRTNET Archives*, August 23, 2005. https://lists.psu.edu/cgi-bin/wa?A2=ind0508&L=CRTNET&P= R3083&X=O2792D11D4F498EF960&Y.

King, Paul E. 2016. "RE: Public Speaking Courses via the Internet (Thomas M. Steinfatt, CRTNET #15215)." *CRTNET Archives*, June 2, 2016. https://lists.psu.ed u/cgi-bin/wa?A2=ind1606A&L=CRTNET&P=R1042&X=O2792D11D4F498EF 960&Y.

Kirkwood, Jessica, Nichola D. Gutgold, and Destiny Manley. 2011. "Hello World, It's Me: Bringing the Basic Speech Communication Course into the Digital Age." *Communication Teacher* 25 no. 3: 150–153. doi:10.1080/17404622.2011.579905.

Larson, Kyle R., and George F. McHendry. 2019. "Parasitic Publics." *Rhetoric Society Quarterly* 49, no. 5: 517–541. doi:10.1080/02773945.2019.1671986.

LeFebvre, Luke, Leah LeFebvre, Kate Blackburn, and Ryan Boyd. 2015. "Student Estimates of Public Speaking Competency: The Meaning Extraction Helper and Video Self-Evaluation." *Communication Education* 64, no. 3: 261–279. doi:10.10 80/03634523.2015.1014384.

Lind, Stephen J. 2012. "Teaching Digital Oratory: Public Speaking 2.0." *Communication Teacher* 26, no. 3: 163–169. doi:10.1080/17404622.2012.65919.

Makkawy, Amin, and Shane T. Moreman. 2019. "Putting Crip in the Script: A Critical Communication Pedagogical Study of Communication Theory Textbooks." *Communication Education* 68, no. 4: 401–416. doi:10.1080/03634523.2019.164 3898.

Mangan, Katherine. 2021. "The Surveilled Student." *The Chronicle of Higher Education*, February 15, 2021. https://www.chronicle.com/article/the-surveilled-s tudent

McConnell, Kathleen F. 2018. "Fear of Etiolation in the Age of Professional Passion." *Text and Performance Quarterly* 38, no. 3: 153–169. doi:10.1080/1046 2937.2018.1461918.

McGarrity, Matt, and Richard Benjamin Crosby. 2012. "Rhetorical Invention in Public Speaking Textbooks and Classrooms." *Rhetoric Society Quarterly* 42, no. 2: 164–186. doi:10.1080/02773945.2012.659322.

McMurtie, Beth. 2021. "Good Grades, Stressed Students." *The Chronicle of Higher Education*, March 17, 2021. https://www.chronicle.com/article/good-grades-stre ssed-students

Means, Barbara, and Julie Neisler, with Langer Research Associates. 2020. *Suddenly Online: A National Survey of Undergraduates During the COVID-19 Pandemic*. San Mateo, CA: Digital Promise. https://www.everylearnereverywhere.org/wp-con tent/uploads/Suddenly-Online_DP_FINAL.pdf.

Morreale, Sherwyn P, Scott A. Myers, Philip M. Backlund, and Cheri J. Simonds. 2016. "Study IX of the Basic Communication Course at Two- and Four-Year U.S. Colleges and Universities: A Re-Examination of Our Discipline's 'Front Porch'." *Communication Education* 65, no. 3: 338–355. doi:10.1080/03634523.2015.1073 339.

Newman, Marc. 1998. "Distance ed. and Focus." *CRTNET Archives*, July 28, 1998. https://lists.psu.edu/cgi-bin/wa?A2=ind9807&L=CRTNET&P=R14509&X=O A5E20205FEBE032749&Y.

North, Stephen M. 1987. *The Making of Knowledge in Composition: Portrait of an Emerging Field*. Upper Montclair, NJ: Boynton/Cook Publishers.

Ongweso Jr., Edward. 2020. "2,000 Parents Demand Major Academic Publisher Drop Proctorio Surveillance Tech." *Vice*, December 21, 2020. https://www.vice.com/en /article/88am8k/2000-parents-demand-major-academic-publisher-drop-proctorio-s urveillance-tech.

Reffue, John. 1998. "The Flag's Still Red." *CRTNET Archives*, July 28, 1998, https ://lists.psu.edu/cgi-bin/wa?A2=ind9807&L=CRTNET&P=R14509&X=OF7A8B D694FB3BA65D3&Y.

Reich, Justin. 2020. "Ed-Tech Mania is Back." *The Chronicle of Higher Education*, September 14, 2020. https://www.chronicle.com/article/ed-tech-mania-is-back.

Sarapin, Susan H. 2016. "RE: Public Speaking courses via the Internet (Thomas M. Steinfatt, CRTNET #15215)." *CRTNET Archives*, June 1, 2016. https://lists.psu.edu/cgi-bin/wa?A2=ind1606A&L=CRTNET&P=R110&X=O2792D11D4F498EF960&Y.

Seaman, Jeff and Nicole Johnson. 2021. *Pandemic-Era Report Card: Students, Faculty, and Administrators Reflect Upon the Academic Year*. Oakland, CA: Bay View Analytics. http://www.bayviewanalytics.com/.

Shepard, Dawn, Samantha Sturman, and Heidi Estrem. 2020. "From the Guest Editors-Corequisite Writing Courses: Equity and Access." *Composition Studies* 48, no. 2: 9–17.

Smith, Tony E., and Ann Bainbridge Frymier. 2006. "'Get 'Real': Does Practicing Speeches Before an Audience Improve Performance?" *Communication Quarterly* 54, no. 1: 111–125. doi:10.1080/01463370500270538.

Steinfatt, Thomas M. 2016. "Discussion: Public Speaking courses via the internet." *CRTNET Archives*, May 31, 2016. https://lists.psu.edu/cgi-bin/wa?A2=ind1605E&L=CRTNET&P=R2&X=O2792D11D4F498EF960&Y.

Turpin, Paul. 2019. "Re: The Live Audience in Online Public Speaking Courses." *CRTNET Archives*, February 19, 2019. https://lists.psu.edu/cgi-bin/wa?A2=ind1902C&L=CRTNET&P=R1216&X=OA5E20205FEBE032749&Y.

Tyack, David B., and Larry Cuban. 2009. *Tinkering Toward Utopia: A Century of Public School Reform*. Harvard University Press.

Valenzano, Joseph M. III. 2020. "What's in a Name? Exploring the Definitions of 'Public' and 'Speaking.'" *Basic Communication Course Annual* 32: 106–123.

Ward, Susan. 2016. "It's Not the Same Thing: Considering a Path Forward for Teaching Public Speaking Online." *The Review of Communication* 16, no. 2–3: 222–235. doi:10.1080/15358593.2016.1187458.

Warner, Michael. 2002. *Publics and Counterpublics*. Cambridge, MA: Zone Books.

Webster, Linda J. 2016. "RE: Public Speaking Courses via the Internet (Thomas M. Steinfatt, CRTNET #15215)." *CRTNET Archives*, June 7, 2016. https://lists.psu.edu/cgi-bin/wa?A2=ind1606A&L=CRTNET&P=R1915&X=OCD9F77A74C0A6EFC7E&Y.

Wendt, Ted. 1998. "The Macduff Dialogues: A Meditation on Mediation." *CRTNET Archives*, July 31, 1998. https://lists.psu.edu/cgi-bin/wa?A2=ind9807&L=CRTNET&P=R15749&X=O2792D11D4F498EF960&Y.

Wignall, Dennis. 1998. "The Importance of Audience." *CRTNET Archives*, July 31, 1998. https://lists.psu.edu/cgi-bin/wa?A2=ind9807&L=CRTNET&P=R15749&X=O9178CD8F7E9ACA39DB&Y.

Wood, Jennifer. 1996. "Should Class Participation Be Required in the Basic Communication Course?" *Basic Communication Course Annual* 8: 108–124.

Chapter 12

Progressing through Tuckman's Phases in a Virtual College Classroom

Using Online Tools to Support Student Group Development

Angela M. McGowan-Kirsch and Amanda Lohiser

As state governments issued stay-at-home orders in 2020, offices and workplaces shifted to remote work. In fact, 71 percent of workers reported that they did their jobs from home all or most of the time during lockdowns (Parker, Menasce Horowitz, and Minkin 2020). Remote work was on the rise even before the pandemic (Mak and Kozlowski 2019; National Association of Colleges and Employers 2016; Orlando 2017). The transition to telework requires employees to interact with organization stakeholders virtually while completing collaborative projects. Despite being an integral part of workplace success, 36 percent of managers reported that new college graduates lacked interpersonal and teamwork skills (PayScale, 2016). With the goal of developing this soft skill, group assignments are a useful addition to college curricula, as they teach students about cooperating, communicating, and depending on others to accomplish tasks.

Completing an assignment as a group exposes students to divergent opinions (Freeman 1996) and helps students develop time management, problem solving, cooperation, and critical thinking skills(Hammar Chiriac 2014; Kilgo, Ezell Shcets, and Pascarella 2015). Despite these benefits, conducting group projects in a college classroom can be challenging during a normal semester, let alone a term encumbered with a global crisis like the COVD-19 pandemic. Social-distancing guidelines, remote-course scheduling, and changing from in-person to a virtual work environment caused a dramatic shift in the way group work occurred at institutions of higher learning. Researchers have identified challenges that arose during the pandemic that made engaging in effective group work problematic, including outside influences, geographical differences, and team member performance issues (Wildman et al. 2021).

The COVID-19 pandemic had a tremendous effect on collaborative educational settings (Wildman et al. 2021), but reticence toward group assignments existed before obstacles imposed by the recent global pandemic. While initiating group work, instructors are often met with resistance from students as they expressed perceptions of grouphate. *Grouphate* refers to a feeling of dread that arises when someone faces the possibility of working in a group (Sorensen 1981). When asked why they dislike group work, students claimed that working in groups compounded their confusion over material and expressed concern for potentially working with someone they disliked (Taylor 2011). Additionally, students have cited a lack of cohesion and consensus (Myers and Goodboy 2005), a concern that some group members are unmotivated to contribute to the group task (Espey 2010; Payne and Monk-Turner 2006), and previous experience with perceptions of group members' social loafing (Burtis and Turman 2006). Moreover, many of the problems groups have with poor performance are an end result of faulty decision-making resulting from groupthink (Janis 1971). A jarring global crisis only exacerbated these complex challenges.

Students' feelings of grouphate is troubling, for when students maintain a negative attitude toward working in groups, they are less likely to succeed in academics and report less learning, less relational satisfaction, and fewer positive attitudes about group work (Keyton, Harmon, and Frey 1996; Myers and Goodboy 2005). Faculty oversight helps determine whether students find value in group work (Livingstone and Lynch 2000). When used deliberately and effectively, Pear Deck, MURAL, Google Docs, and Google Forms can engage students in authentic ways and position them to effectively and actively participate in collaborative groups.

In light of the shift to virtual collaborative settings, instructors need tools that enable them to facilitate productive group work remotely. This chapter proposes that Tuckman and Jensen's (1977) phasic model is a useful tool for guiding an instructor's efforts to support students' group development in a distance-learning environment. Tuckman (1965) originally developed a four-stage model as a result of reviewing studies pertaining to group formation that described behaviors within two "realms": the social (or "group structure") realm and the task-related realm. The resulting four-stage linear model of group development includes forming, storming, norming, and performing (Tuckman 1965). Tuckman and Jensen (1977) later revised the model to include a fifth stage: adjourning. Group development scholars have applied Tuckman's phasic model to the development process in face-to-face groups, and, as the Internet evolved, the model has also been applied to the study of online groups (Glowacki-Dudka and Barnett 2007; Gresch, Saunders, and Rawls 2020; Gunawardena et al. 2001; Kaur et al. 2021).

As colleges and universities return to face-to-face instruction, it is critical to recognize that online teams and remote work will continue in a post-pandemic world (Orlando 2017). To help students engage in virtual teamwork, educators need access to online tools that develop students' virtual group communication skills as well as reinforce their abilities to use these collaborative tools. Therefore, the chapter begins with an overview of four online tools that can be used to guide virtual group work. Intentional methods for implementing four digital tools are explored to highlight Tuckman's model while simultaneously addressing and controlling for potential student concerns. The chapter concludes with a discussion of lessons learned and ideas for application of the online tools in a post-pandemic classroom.

USING ONLINE TOOLS TO GUIDE GROUP WORK

Researchers point out that "the effectiveness, accessibility, and enjoyability of diverse instructional strategies and digital tools will vary depending on how each strategy is implemented" (Gillis and Krull 2020, 296). Instructors who want to help students improve their teamwork skills, enrich their communication, and build relationships should identify projects that lend themselves to collaboration. Furthermore, fostering group interaction in a distance-learning course helps offset the effects of isolation that were purported to have negatively impacted students' mental health during the COVID-19 pandemic. Findings from a study by Hamza et al. (2021) suggest that increased social isolation during the recent pandemic coincided with declining mental health among students. Combined with appropriate instructor-learner communication, the online tools outlined below enable students to form relationships and can mitigate frustrations and negative attitudes that cause students to loathe group work.

Pear Deck

Pear Deck is a distance-learning interactive presentation tool that instructors can use to virtually facilitate classroom conversations. Pear Deck, free at the basic level, offers instructor-led synchronous and student-paced asynchronous presentation options. After installing Pear Deck as a Google Slides add-on, instructors build a Google Slides presentation and use Pear Deck to integrate interactive questions (Pear Deck, 2020c). By incorporating a Pear Deck interactive question template or custom question, instructors build formative assessments into the presentation that provide real-time insight into student understanding (Pear Deck 2020a).

In a synchronous class, instructors start the slideshow presentation, and then give students a hyperlink that enables them to join the Pear Deck from any device with a web browser. After clicking on the hyperlink, students are prompted to log in to Pear Deck using their Gmail account. This step lets instructors see the names of students who have joined the Pear Deck and view students' answers to questions in real time. When using Pear Deck synchronously, the instructor advances the students through the slides, prompting students to answer questions along the way. Students' answers can be displayed anonymously to the rest of the class.

MURAL

MURAL is an interactive whiteboard tool that enables students to work on collaborative assignments in much the same way they would use a whiteboard or sticky notes in a classroom. MURAL, which is free to students and educators, allows instructors to create their own activities or customize ready-made templates to engage students. MURAL can be used to help student groups discover common interests, engage in brainstorming sessions, and participate in a myriad of other "hands-on" activities from a remote setting. MURAL can be used synchronously or asynchronously, making it a flexible learning tool that promotes self-paced learning.

Once students create their free MURAL account by going to https://www.mural.com/, they can access designated MURAL rooms set up by the instructor. There they can both participate in MURAL activities built by the instructor or create their own MURAL for their group's collaborative needs. In a classroom setting, students can attend virtual meetings using videoconferencing software and use MURAL on their split-screen or secondary device. Breakout rooms on web-conferencing platforms, such as Zoom, assist in creating the feeling of a distraction-free student group experience.

Google Forms and Google Docs

Similar to MURAL, Google Forms and Google Docs are tools that enable students to communicate and collaborate. Google Docs, in particular, permits virtual groups to contribute to a single document and comment on each other's contributions. The "chat" sidebar allows for groups to dialogue in a relay-chat style while working. When an instructor creates folders for student groups and invites students to join the folder, the instructor becomes the owner of the content found inside the folder. Thus the instructor can monitor student progress by examining version histories that identify students' work and restrict student access to the documents. Google Forms can be used for assessing student progress as well as their group experience through ongoing assessments, peer evaluations, and end-of-semester surveys.

In sum, although requiring group assignments is a beneficial learning experience (Kelly 2012), researchers urge instructors not to assign group projects in a distance-learning course noting that students are experiencing illness, unreliable Internet connection, and inadequate work environments (Davidson and Katopodis 2020). Yet the number of employees working remotely due to the COVID-19 pandemic caused Davidson and Katopodis (2020) to advocate, "Now is *exactly* the time to be helping students learn how to collaborate online" (para. 4). Instructors can use tools for engagement, including Pear Deck, MURAL, Google Docs, and Google Forms, to support their efforts to encourage student interaction.

GROUP DEVELOPMENT PHASE ONE: FORMING

Facilitating group work during synchronous virtual class meetings became challenging as in-person classes were forced to move online. Even under normal circumstances, students are often unaware of the benefits of group work (Vittrup 2015) and how to work productively with others. Prior to assigning group work, an instructor can use Pear Deck to facilitate class discussions that (*a*) educate students as to why the assignment is being completed as a group; (*b*) permit students to express their concerns with group work; and (*c*) propose useful strategies for collaboration. This conversation enables students to see what they gain by being part of a group, including improved communication, critical-thinking skills, and reciprocal learning. This exercise also offers a platform for students to express grouphate and recognize if the attitudes pertain to membership in a particular group (e.g., a prior group project) or classroom groups in general. After this exercise, students enter the first group development phase.

Tuckman (1965) proposes that as groups form, they observe their peers' reactions to discover what interpersonal behaviors are accepted by group members. They also look to a leader or existing norms for guidance about proper group behavior. Additionally, in this phase, group members will clarify the task, identify what information is needed, and determine the way(s) in which the group might tackle the work. This stage, referred to as the *forming* phase, establishes relationships with group members and leaders along with implicit and explicit norms (Tuckman 1965). During this time, groups test social and task-oriented boundaries. Previous group experiences that resulted in grouphate might negatively influence students' preconceptions of one another; thus, organization, orientation, and effective icebreakers are useful ways for alleviating students' negative beliefs about group work.

Whether maintaining a face-to-face teaching schedule or planning for a potential disruption to in-person learning, instructors need best practices for organizing student groups. Research recommends that student groups be created by the instructor to ensure optimum learning conditions (Michaelson and Sweet 2008; Synnott 2016). When engaging in distance learning or in-person learning, MURAL enables educators to form groups and facilitate icebreaker activities. For instance, instructors can use MURAL to create a deck of "ID cards." The 3×5 card, available through MURAL, should have a designated space for students to add a personal photo and respond to questions provided on the card. The instructor uses the cards to sort students into groups based on the prompts the instructor puts on the cards (e.g., sorting by personality inventory results or common areas of academic interest). If groups have already been randomly assigned, or if groups have been formed using MURAL, the cards may then be sorted by group so that group members have a readily available photo and biographic card for each person. This activity complements the forming phase in that its objective is to help group members find their places within the group, learn about one another, and engage in "getting-to-know-you" discussions. As a result, students who are feeling socially isolated and lonely get to know their peers while creating open channels of communication.

Once the groups are formed, instructors should orient students to the online tools that will be used to execute the group project. For example, instructors can create and invite students to join a group Google Drive folder that contains assignment templates. This action enables the instructor to observe group member participation as students collaboratively organize research, contribute to a Google Sheet used to store group member contact information and meeting times, and take meeting notes on a Google Doc. Furthermore, the Google Drive folder permits instructors to monitor students' motivations and assess their technological literacy.

Next, students should collaboratively arrive at a consensus on the group's ground rules, called *explicit norms*. The establishment of explicit group norms aids in eventual evaluation of the group experience and facilitates the functionality of "leaderless" groups (Spich and Keleman 1985) while also increasing trust and performance among members of virtual groups (Moser and Axtell 2013). Establishing ground rules helps group members answer the question "What is expected of me?" Using a Google Doc, each group creates a code of conduct that supports group efforts to make the workload reasonable, establishes expectations, and considers group member roles. Question prompts include: (*a*) What will your group do to encourage high group cohesion? (*b*) Who will fulfill certain group roles? (*c*) What disciplinary action will be taken for missing a deadline? and (*d*) How will the group make decisions so as to avoid groupthink? To give the students a sense of ownership and to establish the document's importance, students should sign off on the ground rules before formally adopting the code of conduct. Instructors may also use a

MURAL to assist groups as they create lists of explicit group norms including brainstorming, organization, and synthesis using sticky notes. The purpose of these exercises is to help group members navigate anticipated issues.

Finally, group members often get to know one another during the forming stage through finding common ground. Relationship-building aids with improving student learning (Webb and Obrycki Barrett 2014). By working with others, students develop social skills, learn about multicultural issues, feel less isolated, and assign meaning to their peers' actions. Even in the best of circumstances, students may experience unanticipated technological problems such as unreliable Internet connectivity. To offset potential tech issues, instructors can permit that work be done asynchronously. One such asynchronous team-building exercise involves discovering group members' strengths. For example, an instructor can create a MURAL prompting students to conduct a strengths inventory. By recognizing the strengths that they bring to the group, students feel more confident and empowered as they discover the value of combining diverse assets. The exploratory nature of this task helps group members form positive perceptions of one another.

In general, instructors overseeing virtual group work should help students clarify group goals and support the same level of communication richness that is available during face-to-face encounters. As the forming phase begins, group members tend not to trust one another and discussion takes on a preparatory quality. The activities discussed in this section can assist instructors seeking to support students' efforts to uncover interpersonal behaviors that are accepted by group members. Once groups have formed and the cautious, superficial communication style inherent to the forming stage wears off, students focus on the task at hand. A combination of personality dynamics and differing work styles can lead to conflict as groups progress to the storming stage.

GROUP DEVELOPMENT PHASE TWO: STORMING

Groups enter the next stage as they begin to form opinions about one another. Students express their individuality through hostility and nonconformity within the group structure. This phase is characterized by an overall lack of unity. Group members react to the disparity between their expectations of their roles in the task and what the task actually requires of them. This stage, where interpersonal issues create conflict and pose challenges toward moving forward on task completion, is called *storming* (Tuckman 1965). It is likely that many grouphate-inducing events might occur at this stage, so at this time, instructors should teach conflict resolution strategies and take deliberate measures to protect against early perceptions of social loafing. This is particularly important when overseeing virtual teamwork as group issues, such as coordination and conflict, can escalate especially quickly in an online context (Mortensen and Hinds 2001).

As group members start sharing ideas and talents, primary and second tensions may arise. Groups anticipate handling conflict at some point (Wall and Nolan 1986) with resolving conflict being an important part of the storming stage. As compatibility issues appear, instructors can use Pear Deck to teach students how to identify problems and develop solutions that position the group to achieve its educational goals. For instance, an instructor can create a slideshow that overviews types of small group conflict, conflict-handling styles, and communication-based conflict resolution strategies. Using Pear Deck, the instructor incorporates an interactive question set that includes questions: (*a*) keeping in mind a recent conflict your group experienced, how did you respond emotionally, behaviorally, and cognitively; (*b*) what conflict-handling style does your group prefer; and (*c*) what are some long-term and short-term benefits of group conflict. In responding to these prompts and the subsequent class discussion, participants learn conflict-management strategies. This effort offers students an opportunity to connect with peers and hone their use of soft skills, including creative thinking, conflict resolution, and teamwork. Moreover, as disagreement arises post-discussion, students are equipped with the knowledge and skills they need to resolve differences in how to approach a task and divergent personality traits.

When people merge their contributions into group work, they sometimes accomplish less than might be expected based on the sum of their individual capabilities (Karau and Williams 1993). Using Pear Deck, instructors can prompt students to complete an individual reflection that raises questions about the division of labor within the group. This exercise might include multiple-choice questions (e.g., "do you feel the division of labor within your group is fair") or open-ended questions (e.g., "describe your group experience this week by paying particular attention to group members' contributions to the project"). The open-ended responses can also launch a dialogue about impediments students face while enrolled in a distance-learning course like a lack of a dedicated work-space, time zone differences, and feeling unmotivated. After seeing students' answers, the instructor shows responses anonymously on the Projector View and leads a class discussion about group frustrations, such as instances of social loafing.

Social loafing is defined as "a decrease in individual effort due to the social presence of other persons" (Latané, Williams, and Harkins 1979, 823). Social loafing, which occurs when people make less effort when they work collectively than when they work alone or coactively (Karau and Williams 1993; Latané, Williams, and Harkins 1979), can hinder a group from achieving its goals (Latané, Williams, and Harkins 1979). Group members' motivation can be negatively affected by their perceptions of the presence of social loafing (Williams, Harkins, and Latané 1981). When the COVID-19 pandemic caused instructors to shift their mode of instruction from in-person to remote, students admitted to feeling unmotivated and distracted (Gillis and Krull 2020). Online tools, such as Pear Deck, could lessen such barriers that might otherwise lead to perceptions of social loafing. The open-ended responses available through Pear Deck help an instructor address such experiences directly and position the groups to combat issues stemming from social loafing.

Similar to Pear Deck, Google Forms can be used to mitigate conflicting points of view, fault lines, and frustrations concerning task allocation. For instance, instructors can require that students submit a project journal for each stage of the assignment or at the end of a week that the group worked toward its goal. The project journal, constructed as a Google Form, can be set up using a linear scale with these statements: (*a*) participated in writing content for the presentation's slideshow; (*b*) consistently and actively contributed knowledge, opinions, and skills without prompting or reminding; (*c*) did work that was accurate and complete. When used this way, the project journal serves as a check-in that offers the instructor a space to see what is or is not working and barriers to accessibility and effectiveness that a virtual group might be experiencing. Students' responses also elucidate who may be engaging in social loafing and identify potential causes for dysfunctional behavior. After reviewing each person's assignment, the instructor can model communication tactics that students could implement with their group members. In this way, not only are students encouraged to consider their own participation but they are given actionable steps to improve (or maintain) their group's communication.

Since some universities do not anticipate a return to "fully normal" on-campus instruction until fall 2023 (Kaiser Health News 2021), educators must consider practices that alleviate ongoing obstacles caused by the COVID-19 pandemic. Such proactivity includes incorporating interactive tools that assist students' efforts to develop relationships and open lines of communication. Once this occurs, groups begin to naturally flow into the norming and performing stages in which the group becomes an instrument of collaboration rather than a source of discontent.

GROUP DEVELOPMENT PHASES THREE AND FOUR: NORMING AND PERFORMING

Eventually, groups establish norms for their interactions while accepting both the group and group members' unique characteristics. At this point, the group becomes a "whole" rather than a sum of parts and conflicts are avoided or effectively resolved in order to preserve harmony. This stage, in which group members begin feeling comfortable sharing personal opinions, the group feels cohesive, and standards and roles are established, is called *norming* (Tuckman 1965). As the pandemic caused in-person classes to move online, students lost opportunities typically afforded groups at this stage. In-person groups create "traditions" that foster relationship-building (e.g., regularly meeting at a university library, dining together, and inviting one another into their living spaces). When meeting at a distance, instructors can assign structured activities that mimic these in-person experiences.

The established standards strengthened in the norming stage are called *implicit group norms*. As opposed to explicit standards discussed in the forming stage, the implicit norms are understood as implied rules that govern group members' behaviors. Group norms help members understand and predict what behaviors will be seen as acceptable or unacceptable and serve to express central values of the group (Feldman 1984). The creation of these norms is critical to group development, as the norms influence a group's productivity levels while developing trust and acceptance. The fostering of these feelings is key to resolving past grouphate and moving forward into what is hopefully a more productive, positive group experience. Given that remote students value peer and instructor interaction (Gillis and Krull 2020), activities occurring during this phase should be made available both synchronously and asynchronously. This provision enables students experiencing technological barriers to remain active group participants.

Unwritten group norms can be difficult for group members to express, so the instructor may determine that the best route for discussion is a Pear Deck multiple choice interactive response type. The instructor supplies students with a question on the slide (e.g., "What are your group's unspoken norms?"). Then, using students' project journals as a guide, the instructor constructs multiple answers. When students join the session, the slide prompts participants to respond to the multiple choice question. In doing so, students and the instructor are able to see points of commonality among groups' implicit norms. After showing students' responses, the instructor leads a conversation using the text-based response option that encourages students to discuss: (*a*) when they realized behavior was an implicit norm; (*b*) ways in which the norm helped the group function smoothly especially when facing conflict; and (*c*) how the norm promoted positive interactions. In an effort to improve group interaction, the conversation concludes by developing solutions for coping with group members who are not following the implicit norms. The instructor should encourage solutions that foster a psychologically safe discussion space and promote prosocial behaviors among virtual group members.

One solution may be requiring groups to use Google Docs in a shared folder. This enables students to work collaboratively while also monitoring others' contributions. As they see the work that others are producing, acceptance and cohesiveness may emerge. When groups experience unity, they remain committed to working on the task as a unit (Tuckman 1965). This fosters group dialogue about role-taking. To support norming and cohesion, MURAL templates can also be used to monitor task progression, such as Gantt charts and Kanban. By tracking tasks and deadlines, members demonstrate a commitment to the group and a willingness to cooperate.

Next, when groups become more comfortable, cohesive, and are ready to embrace the performing stage, the group becomes "a problem-solving instrument" (Tuckman 1965, 387). Group members take constructive action to achieve positive change and complete the task at hand. This stage is called performing, because "interpersonal structure becomes the tool of task activities" (Tuckman 1965, 396). The performing stage positions students to produce the most work (Chidambaram and Bostrom 1996), while focusing energy on accomplishing tasks (Wheelan and Hochberger 2003). Additionally, group members are provided an evaluation by someone from outside the group.

Groupthink can occur when a group becomes so cohesive that the members begin to prize unanimity above all else and become conflict-avoidant. Groupthink is defined as "a rationalized conformity—an open, articulate philosophy which holds that group values are not only expedient but right and good as well" (Whyte 1952, 114). This phenomenon results in self-censure, castigation of dissenters, disinterest in critically evaluating alternative courses of action, and demonizing out-group members (Janis 1971). Fear of being marginalized may cause a group member to remain in line with the majority. Groupthink has the potential to lead to poor group decision-making during the performing phase, thus laying the groundwork for future grouphate.

Using MURAL, instructors can guide students through complex issues that may otherwise result in groupthink, for instance, using hands-on virtual activities to lead students through a four-step Creative Problem Solving (CPS) Process. During this time students work together to clarify a problem, come up with ideas to solve it, develop said ideas into workable solutions, and create an action plan for implementation (Grivas and Puccio 2012). Enacting this process helps mitigate symptoms of groupthink by which groups blindly forge ahead with a solution without evaluating it or considering other workable solutions. Problem-solving processes, like the CPS Process, encourage participants to methodically brainstorm ideas and develop solutions. As grouphate may be caused by a group experience in which poor decision-making led to an unfortunate end result (e.g., unsuccessful presentation, poor grade, or in-group conflict), a methodological system can help prevent negative outcomes and deter groupthink.

Additionally, groups that did not go through the storming stage early in its lifespan will often return to the storming phase toward the end of the group process (Karriker 2005). The emergence of group members feeling defensive or argumentative may be the result of group members paying attention to if and how group members are contributing to the group goal. Frustrations concerning perceptions of fairness may arise if group members perceive someone as putting in less effort. Although the relationship structure of the group permits students to resolve conflict on their own, it is helpful for the instructor to guide their efforts. Each time students submit an assignment that is part of the project, they complete a Google Form that prompts them to reflect on people's contributions. The feedback forms permit the instructor to gauge participation and progress and offer feedback. The Google Form can include short answer questions: (a) identify all the tasks you contributed to this week; (b) what is something you need to do better next week; (c) if applicable, identify the name(s) of people who you perceive as not contributing to the group project; and (d) explain what the group can do to motivate this person. Questions like these hold students accountable and offset concern that a group member's lack of effort will harm the group's goal.

After compiling students' responses into a single document, the instructor holds virtual conversations with groups to provide insight into how students can increase performance and decrease ineffective behaviors. This is especially important as Synnott (2016) found that social loafers often perceive themselves as contributing just as much as their group members. The conversation morphs into a peer feedback exercise that helps students gain a richer understanding of their tasks and monitor their work. Moreover, these instructor-led conversions provide a safe space for sharing hardships students may be enduring during a time of crisis such as those caused by a pandemic. The supportive dialogue leads to empathetic understanding and an increased sense of collaboration. As the group performs the task output, they may experience a sense of accomplishment in taking necessary steps toward goal attainment. Once groups submit their final project, they begin transitioning into the adjourning stage.

GROUP DEVELOPMENT PHASE FIVE: ADJOURNING

A later review of Tuckman's work determined that the model needed to account for the group members departing from the group (Tuckman and Jensen 1977). As a result, the researchers identified adjourning as the final stage. Adjourning represents a sort of death, or dissolution, of the group. This stage can be fraught with a sense of organizational and emotional upheaval; therefore, the final stage of a group's life cycle can evoke sadness, self-evaluation, disengagement, positive feelings toward the leader, anxiety about separation, and high levels of affection (Tuckman and Jensen 1977). The assessment strategies overviewed in this section prompt students to actively reflect on their experiences and catalogue their collective and individual strengths and weaknesses. It is at this final stage that reflecting on a negative group experience may build future grouphate, but reflection on a positive group experience can promote an outgoing outlook toward future group work.

First, during the adjourning stage, groups enter this phase when the time frame that the instructor established ends and/or the task is complete. To assist students with processing emotions tied to the dissolution of the group and assess their contributions to the finished task, instructors can require that students use a Google Form to complete a self-assessment. *Self-assessment* refers to the involvement of learners in making judgments about their own learning (Boud and Falchikov 1989). With this definition in mind, the instructor constructs a Google Form that asks students to rate their perceptions, opinions, or behaviors. When designing the questionnaire, the instructor's goal is to foster students' reflection on their own learning process thus making students active participants in their own learning (Boud 1995). The Google Form can include short answer questions: (*a*) what was the most significant strength you brought to this group; (*b*) describe your overall involvement in the group; and (*c*) how did you contribute to the formation of interpersonal relationships in your group. This self-assessment tool enables students to express how they felt about the group ending, assess the group's cohesiveness, and reflect upon feelings concerning the formation of interpersonal relationships.

Second, instructors can create a second Google Form that serves as a peer assessment instrument in which students evaluate peers' performances in the group. *Peer assessment* occurs when "groups of individuals rate their peers" (Falchikov 1995, 175). Using a linear scale, students assess group members' performance by responding to questions about each person's activity level, task functions (e.g., task performance), and maintenance functions (e.g., cooperation). With directions stating, "using the following linear scale, where 1 is strongly disagree and 5 is strongly agree, indicate the rating you would give this group member," assessment statements might include: (*a*) showed sensitivity to others' feelings and learning needs; (*b*) valued the knowledge, opinion, and skills of all group members; and (*c*) willingly accepted assigned tasks and participated positively during group discussions. Students also provide qualitative feedback as a means for supporting the quantitative ratings by responding to questions: (*a*) identify the unique perspective this person brought to the group; (*b*) identify the person's strengths and skills that were most useful for the group; and (c) what information did this person require to work productively. The questionnaire, in conjunction with the self-assessment, serves to give groups a sense of accomplishment and ideas of who to work with the next time students are asked to collaborate.

Third, instructors can modify the "celebrating students" Pear Deck template to give group members the opportunity to "compliment each other and recognize unique perspectives" (Pear Deck 2020b). The template encourages creativity and critical thinking by incorporating interactive slides that include free response. For instance, an interactive prompt asks students to identify a group member who was helpful during the group project and what the person did. Another question requests that students identify their favorite trait that a particular group member possessed. During the presentation session, the instructor can monitor student responses and then show comments so that everyone can see the text field. Likewise, an interactive question such as "what is something you have done during this project that you are proud of" prompts students to consider their own contributions to the group project and, in turn, celebrate their own achievements. The goal of this exercise is to offer groups an opportunity to recognize accomplishments, celebrate achievements, and say goodbye. These considerations are especially critical in a pandemic-afflicted world. In 2020, university students reported a lack of social connectedness and sense of belonging, which adversely affected their mental health (Lederer et al. 2020). With this in mind, instructors should handle the adjourning phase of the group's life cycle with particular care.

CONCLUDING THOUGHTS AND LESSONS LEARNED

Instructors teaching distance-learning courses must give careful thought to the presentation of content and assignments while also selecting appropriate instructional tools that assist in executing course learning objectives (Gillis and Krull 2020). The online tools outlined in this chapter aid instructors who want to develop students' sense of responsibility and accountability to a group. Specifically, Pear Deck, MURAL, Google Forms, and Google Docs can be used asynchronously or synchronously to assist instructors wanting to help student groups progress through the phases of group formation. In the following section, suggestions are offered to help instructors anticipate and alleviate potential pitfalls of group projects.

First, collaborative group work promotes student learning and academic achievement (Gillies and Boyle 2011) along with instilling teamwork skills and insight about a topic (Payne et al. 2006). Despite reporting that group work is a satisfying and productive learning experience (Espey 2010), issues such as distribution and completion of work on assignments and time management may arise (Gottschall and Garcia-Bayonas 2008). These challenges should be addressed during the performing stage. Positive group experiences require communication, frequent interaction, trust, and respect (Espey 2010). To help students have a favorable group experience, it is recommended that students remain in the same group throughout the semester and while completing short- and/or long-term class assignments. Instructors can use the online tools detailed in this chapter to facilitate social connections that support mental health and offset feelings of loneliness.

Second, if the storming phase is too conflict-ridden, groups may not be able to progress to the norming phase. Students requesting for their instructor to serve as a third-party mediator in conflict resolution, to join another group, or to work solo are usually indicators of a group that is working through the storming stage. Open communication between students and the instructor is important, as some groups may need help overcoming issues that might otherwise lead to insurmountable conflicts that can hinder the group's progression and further grouphate. Regular implementation of self- and peer-assessment Google Forms and class discussion using Pear Deck are resourceful ways to hold group members accountable and articulate feelings. Despite efforts to mitigate strife, when a group does not appear to be able to move beyond the conflict, the instructor should step in as a third-party mediator. Communicating virtually often coincides with reduced nonverbal cues which can cause misunderstanding. Therefore, instructors should use a web-conferencing platform to meet with group members to help de-escalate conflict. Instructors helping students navigate their group conflict during a crisis, such as one brought on by a global pandemic, should offer a mix of optimism and realism regarding students' obligations outside of class.

Third, during the norming and performing stages, students may experience personal or group challenges that they do not directly bring to the attention of their group members or the instructor. To this end, it is important to hold regular virtual check-ins either with groups or one-on-one conversations. The latter can occur over a web-conferencing platform whereas the former can occur through Pear Deck, MURAL, or Google Forms. An instructor can draft short answer questions, such as "what is working" and "what is not working," that help them be in touch with their students. This exercise is particularly useful in a distance-learning class since the instructor is unable to directly monitor group encounters in a physical classroom. As an example, when groups are in the performing stage, students may express issues with reliable Internet, lack of childcare, or inadequate work-space and technology. A class discussion enables participants to recognize challenges that are compounding students' inabilities to contribute to group efforts. Making these challenges known enables the instructor to modify requirements such as using Google Docs or MURAL to complete work asynchronously. Despite working at separate times, these tools enable groups to maintain a feeling of collaboration. Students report appreciating an instructor's engagement with a course (Price et al. 2016); therefore, it is crucial that instructors communicate regularly with students.

In closing, online education was already on the rise before the COVID-19 pandemic forced schools to remote instruction (Gillis and Krull 2020). The pandemic accelerated colleges' and universities' obligations to reflect on how they will contribute to a new era in which "digital, online, career-focused learning became the fulcrum of competition between institutions" (Gallagher and Palmer 2020, para. 3). While it might be tempting to retire online collaborative methods once institutions of higher learning return to face-to-face instruction, such an action would be a disservice to students. After all, students must be prepared to enter a workforce in which remote collaboration is becoming the norm and will likely continue to rise in the future (Orlando 2017). Research points to the need for deliberate and organized course design, communication between instructor and students, and institutional support as instructors design distance-learning courses (Price et al. 2016; Woodley et al. 2017). Using Tuckman's Model of Group Development as a framework, instructors can use Pear Deck, MURAL, Google Docs, and Google Forms to support students' efforts to critically examine the implications of effective group processes and reinforce stages of the group process model. Whether supporting students' efforts to work collaboratively in a face-to-face or virtual setting, instructors should incorporate online tools such as those described here to provide faculty oversight and an active learning experience.

REFERENCES

Boud, David. 1995. *Enhancing Learning Through Self-assessment*. New York: Routledge.

Boud, David, and Nancy Falchikov. 1989. "Quantitative Studies of Student Self-assessment in Higher Education: A Critical Analysis of Findings." *Higher Education* 18, no. 5: 529–549. doi:10.1007/BF00138746.

Burtis, John O., and Paul D. Turman. 2006. *Group Communication Pitfalls: Overcoming Barriers to an Effective Group Experience*. Thousand Oaks, CA: SAGE.

Chidambaram, Laku, and Robert P. Bostrom. 1996. "Group development (I): A Review and Synthesis of Development Models. *Group Decision and Negotiations* 6, no. 2: 159–187. doi:10.1023/A:1008603328241.

Davidson, Cathay N., and Christina Katopodis. 2020. "8 Ways to Improve Group Work Online." *Inside Higher Ed*, October 28, 2020. https://www.insidehighered.com/advice/2020/10/28/advice-how-successfully-guide-students-group-work-online-opinion

Espey, Molly. 2010. "Valuing Teams: What Influences Student Attitudes?" *NACTA Journal* 54: 31–40. https://www.nactateachers.org/attachments/article/110/Espey_NACTA%20Journal%20March%202010-5.pdf

Falchikov, Nancy. 1995. "Peer Feedback Marking: Developing Peer Assessment." *Innovations in Education and Training International* 32, no. 2: 175–187. doi:10.1080/1355800950320212.

Feldman, Daniel C. 1984. "The Development and Enforcement of Group Norms." *Academy of Management Review* 9, no. 1: 47–53. doi:10.5465/AMR.1984.4277934.

Freeman, Kimberly A. 1996. "Attitudes Toward Work In Project Groups as Predictors of Academic Performance." *Small Group Research* 27, no. 2: 265–282. doi:10.1177/1046496496272004.

Gallagher, Sean and Jason Palmer. 2020. "The Pandemic Pushed Universities Online. The change was Long Overdue." *Harvard Business Review*, September 29, 2020. https://hbr.org/2020/09/the-pandemic-pushed-universities-online-the-change-was-long-overdue

Gillies, Roybn M., and Michael Boyle. 2011. "Teachers' Reflections on Cooperative Learning (CL): A Two-Year Follow-Up." *Teacher Education* 22, no. 1: 63–78. doi:10.1080/10476210.2010.538045.

Gillis, Alanna, and Laura M. Krull. 2020. "COVID-19 Remote Learning Transition in Spring 2020: Class Structures, Student Perceptions, and Inequality in College Courses. *Teaching Sociology* 48, no. 4: 283–299. doi: 10.1177/0092055X20954263.

Glowacki-Dudka, Michelle, and Nicole Barnett. 2007. "Connecting Critical Reflection and Group Development in Online Adult Education Classrooms." *International Journal of Teaching and Learning in Higher Education* 19, no. 1: 43–52. https://www.learntechlib.org/p/55033/.

Gottschall, Holli, and Mariche García-Bayonas. 2008. "Student Attitudes Towards Group Work Among Undergraduates in Business Administration, Education and Mathematics." *Educational Research Quarterly* 32, no. 1: 3–29.

Gresch, Eric, Mary Saunders, and Janita Rawls. 2020. "Are We Bonding Yet? Using a Mixed Methods Survey Design to Evaluate Team-Building Exercise Outcomes." *Business Education Innovation Journal* 12, no. 1: 83–91. Retrieved from http://www.beijournal.com/v122020/v12n1fulltextfinal.html

Grivas, Chris and Gerard J. Puccio. 2012. The Innovative Team. San Francisco, CA: Jossey-Bass.

Gunawardena, Charlotte N., Ana C. Nolla, Penne L. Wilson, Jose R. Lopez-Islas, Noemi Ramirez-Angel, and Rosa M. Megchun-Alpizar. 2001. "A Cross-Cultural Study of Group Process and Development in Online Conferences." *Distance Education* 22, no.1: 85–121. doi:10.1080/0158791010220106.

Hammar Chiriac, Eva. 2014. "Group Work as an Incentive for Learning— Students' Experiences of Group Work." *Frontiers in Psychology* 5: 1–10. doi:10.3389/fpsyg.2014.00558.

Hamza, Chloe A., Lexi Ewing, Nancy L. Heath, and Abby L. Goldstein. 2021. "When Social Isolation Is Nothing New: A Longitudinal Study on Psychological Distress During COVID-19 Among University Students With and Without Preexisting

Mental Health Concerns." *Canadian Psychology/Psychologie canadienne* 62, no. 1: 20–30. doi:10.1037/cap0000255.supp.

Janis, Irving L. 1971. "Groupthink." *Psychology Today Magazine*, November 1971, 84–90. http://agcommtheory.pbworks.com/f/GroupThink.pdf

Kaiser Health News, "Colleges and Universities Plan for Normal-ish Campus Life in the Fall," USNews.com, March 29, 2021. https://www.usnews.com/news/health-news/articles/2021-03-29/colleges-and-universities-plan-for-partially-normal-campus-life-in-the-fall

Karau, Steven J., and Kipling D. Williams. 1993. "Social Loafing: A Meta-analytic Review and Theoretical Integration." *Journal of Personality and Social Psychology* 65, no. 4: 681–706. doi:10.1037/0022-3514.65.4.681.

Karriker, Joy H. 2005. "Cyclical Group Development and Interaction-based Leadership Emergence in Autonomous Teams: An Integrated Model." *Journal of Leadership and Organizational Studies* 11, no. 4: 54–64. doi:10.1177/107179190501100405.

Kaur, Simran, Megha Bir, Dinu S. Chandran, and Kishore Kumar Deepak. 2021. "Adaptive Strategies to Conduct Participant-Centric Structured Virtual Group Discussions for Postgraduate Students in the Wake of the COVID-19 Pandemic." *Advances in Physiology Education* 45, no. 1: 37–43. doi:10.1152/advan.00136.2020.

Kelly, Rob. 2012. "Group Work, Discussion Strategies to Manage Online Instructor Workload." *Faculty Focus*, June 7, 2012. https://www.facultyfocus.com/articles/online-education/online-course-design-and-preparation/group-work-discussion-strategies-to-manage-online-instructor-workload/

Keyton, Joann, Nicole Harmon, and Lawrence R. Frey. 1996. "Grouphate: Its Impact on Teaching Group Communication." Paper presented at *Speech Communication Association,* San Diego, 1996.

Kilgo, Cindy, Jessica K. Ezell Sheets, and Ernest T. Pascarella. 2015. "The Link Between High-Impact Practices and Student Learning: Some Longitudinal Evidence." *Higher Education* 69, no. 4: 509–525. doi:10.1007/S10734-014-9788-Z.

Latané, Bib, Kipling Williams, and Stephen Harkins. 1979. "Many Hands Make Light the Work: The Causes and Consequences of Social Loafing." *Journal of Personality and Social Psychology* 37, no. 6: 822–832. doi:10.1037/0022-3514.37.6.822.

Lederer, Alyssa M., Mary T. Hoban, Sarah K. Lipson, Sasha Zhou, and Daniel Eisenberg. 2020. "More Than Inconvenienced: The Unique Needs of U.S. College Students During the COVID-19 Pandemic." *Health Education & Behavior* 48, no. 1: 14–19. doi:10.1177/1090198120969372.

Livingstone, David, and Kenneth Lynch. 2000. "Group Project Work and Student Centered Active Learning." *Studies in Higher Education* 25, no. 3: 325–345. doi:10.1080/03098260220144748.

Mak, Stanton, and Steve W. J. Kozlowski. 2019. "Virtual Teams: Conceptualization, Integrative Review, and Research Recommendations." In *The Cambridge Handbook of Technology and Employee Behavior*, edited by Richard N. Landers, 441–479. Cambridge, United Kingdom: Cambridge University Press. doi:10.1017/9781108649636.018.

Michaelsen, Larry K., and Michael Sweet. 2008. "The Essential Elements of Team-based Learning." *New Directions for Teaching and Learning* 116: 7–27. doi:10.1002/tl.330.

Mortensen, Mark and Pamela J. Hinds. 2001. "Conflict and Shared Identity in Geographically Distributed Teams." *International Journal of Conflict Management* 12, no. 3: 212–238. doi:10.1108/eb022856.

Moser, Karin S., and Carolyn M. Axtell. 2013. "The Role of Norms in Virtual Work: A Review and Agenda for Future Research." *Journal of Personnel Psychology* 12, no. 1: 1–6. doi:10.1027/1866-5888/a000079.

Myers, Scott A., and Alan K. Goodboy. 2005. "A Study of Grouphate in a Course on Small Group Communication." *Psychological Reports* 97, no. 2: 381–386. doi:10.2466/pr0.97.2.381-386.

National Association of Colleges and Employers. 2016. "Job Outlook 2016: Attributes Employers Want to See on New College Graduates' Resumes." Trends and Predictions. http://www.naceweb.org/s11182015/employers-look-for-in-new-hires.aspx

Orlando, J. 2017. "Tips for Addressing Social Loafing in Group Projects." *Faculty Focus*, October 6, 2017. https://www.facultyfocus.com/articles/teaching-with-technology-articles/tips-addressing-loafing-group-projects/

Parker, Kim, Juliana Menasce Horowitz, and Rachel Minkin. 2020. "How the Coronavirus Outbreak has - and hasn't - Changed the Way Americans Work." December 9. *Pew Research Reports*. December 9, 2020. https://www.pewresearch.org/social-trends/2020/12/09/how-the-coronavirus-outbreak-has-and-hasnt-changed-the-way-americans-work/

Payne, Brian, K., and Elizabeth Monk-Turner. 2006. "Students' Perceptions of Group Projects: The Role of Race, Age, and Slacking." *College Student Journal* 40, no. 1: 132–139.

Payne, Brian K., Elizabeth Monk-Turner, Donald Smith, and Melvina Sumter. 2006. "Improving Group Work: Voices of Students." *Education* 126, no. 3: 441–448. https://digitalcommons.odu.edu/cgi/viewcontent.cgi?article=1023&context=sociology_criminaljustice_fac_pubs

PayScale. 2016. "2016 Workforce-Skills Preparedness Report." https://www.payscale.com/data-packages/job-skills

Pear Deck. 2020a. "Pear Deck Logic Model." The Learning Science Behind Pear Deck. https://www.peardeck.com/efficacy

Pear Deck. 2020b. "Celebrating Students." Pear Deck Templates. https://www.peardeck.com/templates

Pear Deck. 2020c. "The Fastest Way to Transform Presentation into Classroom Conversations." Pear Deck for Google Slides. https://www.peardeck.com/googleslides

Price, Jill M., Joy Whitlatch, Cecilia Jane Maier, Melissa Burdi, and James Peacock. 2016. "Improving Online Teaching by Using Established Best Classroom Teaching Practices." *Journal of Continuing Education in Nursing* 47, no. 5: 222–227. doi:10.3928/00220124-20160419-08.

Sorensen, Susan M. 1981. "Grouphate: A Negative Reaction to Group Work." Paper presented at *International Communication Association*, Minneapolis, 1981.

Spich, Robert S., and Kenneth Keleman. 1985. "Explicit Norm Structuring Process: A Strategy for Increasing Task-Group Effectiveness." *Group & Organization Studies* 10, no. 1: 37–59. doi:10.1177/105960118501000103.

Synnott, Kevin. 2016. "Guides to Reducing Social Loafing in Group Projects: Faculty Development." *Journal of Higher Education Management* 31, no. 1: 211–221. doi:10.33902/JPR.2020465073.

Taylor, Ann. 2011. "Top 10 Reasons Students Dislike Working in Small Groups . . . and Why I Do it Anyway." *Biochemistry and Molecular Biology* 39, no. 3: 219–220. doi:10.1002/bmb.20511.

Tuckman, Bruce W. 1965. "Developmental Sequence in Small Groups." *Psychological Bulletin* 63, no. 6: 384–399. doi:10.1037/h0022100.

Tuckman, Bruce W., and Mary Ann C. Jensen. 1977. "Stages of Small Group Development Revisited." *Group & Organization Studies* 2, no. 4: 419–427. doi:10.1177/105960117700200404

Vittrup, Brigitte. (2015). "How to Improve Group Work: Perspectives from Students." *Faculty Focus*, November 19, 2015. https://www.facultyfocus.com/articles/teaching-and-learning/how-to-improve-group-work-perspectives-from-students/

Wall, Victor D., Jr., and Linda L. Nolan. 1986. "Perceptions of Inequity, Satisfaction, and Conflict in Task-oriented Groups." *Human Relations* 39, no. 11: 1033–1052. doi:10.1177/001872678603901106.

Webb, Nathan, & Laura Obrycki Barrett. 2014. "Student Views of Instructor-Student Rapport in the College Classroom." *Journal of the Scholarship of Teaching and Learning* 14, no. 2: 15–28. doi:10.14434/josotl.v14i2.4259.

Wheelan, Susan A., and Judith M. Hochberger. 1996. "Validation Studies of the Group Development Questionnaire." *Small Group Research* 27, no. 1: 143–170. doi:10.1177/1046496496271007.

Whyte, William. H., Jr. (1952). "Groupthink." *Fortune*, March 1952, 114–117, 142, 146.

Wildman, Jessica L., Daniel M. Nguyen, Ngoc S. Duong, and Catherine Warren. (2021). Student Teamwork During COVID-19: Challenges, Changes, and Consequences. *Small Group Research* 52, no. 2: 119–134. doi:10.1177/1046496420985185.

Williams, Kipling D., Stephen Harkins, and Bib Latané. 1981. "Identifiability as a Deterrent to Social Loafing: Two Cheering Experiments." *Journal of Personality and Social Psychology* 40, no. 2: 303–311. doi:10.1037/0022-3514.40.2.303.

Woodley, Xeturah, Cecilia Hernandez, Julia Parra, and Beyan Negash. 2017. "Celebrating Difference: Best Practices in Culturally Responsive Teaching Online." *TechTrends,* 61, no. 2: 470–478. doi:10.1007/s11528-017-0207-z.

Chapter 13

Post-Pandemic Pedagogy in Intercollegiate Academic Debate

Performing Civic Life in Hybrid, Virtual, and In-Person Environments

John J. Rief

As the COVID-19 pandemic has continued to transform the landscape of higher education, significant attention has been paid to the demise of the classroom and the rise of online course delivery.[1] Less attention has been given to co-curricular activities. One such activity, intercollegiate academic debate (IAD), has long been an important communication pedagogy aimed at training students in the habits and practices of public advocacy, community dialogue, and civic deliberation (Bartanen and Littlefield 2014; Greene and Hicks 2005; Hogan et al. 2017; Keith 2010; Mitchell 1998b; Rief 2018). Throughout its history, IAD has pierced the boundaries between the classroom and the wider world, offering students opportunities both to travel in search of competition at tournaments and host exhibition debates for community stakeholders.

With on-campus life and university-sponsored travel largely on hiatus over the past year, IAD practitioners realized they would have to make use of socially distanced environments enabled by platforms for synchronous and asynchronous audiovisual interaction, recording, and document sharing to maintain the activity throughout the public health emergency. In some ways, the very fact that IAD is one of the few intercollegiate activities that can be conducted virtually has been a major advantage. Competitions continued throughout the past year; however, the technological solutions adopted by numerous debate communities to maintain their activities raise questions about the necessary and sufficient conditions of *valuable* (as opposed to *mere*) participation in events.

Indeed, for many debate practitioners and scholars, IAD and argumentation pedagogy are humanizing endeavors rooted in mutual engagement, critical listening, and respect for the other (Ehninger 1970; Habineza, Rief, and Wilson 2018; Mitchell 2011). The technological adaptations necessitated by the pandemic referenced previously have fostered numerous debate events at which the other is not immediately present, or is made present through a device's screen, with consequences for the educational value, not to mention the ethical context, of the activity. This dilemma surrounding the highly technologized modes of debate practice that emerged over the past year suggests the value of critical reflection and open deliberation about the sustainability of IAD's more human and humane elements as it pushes into new electronic frontiers. In this vein, Carly Woods et al. (2006) argue that debate practitioners should learn from the Amish tradition of careful deliberation about technological innovation: "The Amish example shows how human communities can use collective deliberation to make considered decisions regarding their relationship to technology" which is important because "choices about technology carry political implications, because patterns of sociality are embedded within technical tools" (82).[2]

Taking Woods et al.'s perspective seriously means raising questions about how far IAD should go in its adventures beyond the direct human-to-human encounter. As we move past the emergency conditions of the past year that forced certain decisions upon us, we are in a position to actively deliberate about our choices and create flexible approaches to debate that retain what has worked in the past, capitalize on opportunities presented by our *brave new world*, and cultivate resilience in the face of unpredictable future interruptions. What's more, such a reflective stance may reveal the value of creatively remixing in-person and virtual applications in response to the new historical, social, cultural, and political conditions we are experiencing. In short, we cannot go back to February 2020. But we also need not push forward as if the pedagogical approaches of the past are simply irrelevant.

The rest of this chapter maps prospective contours of post-pandemic IAD pedagogy and practice with careful attention to the concerns introduced in the previous paragraphs. In the next section, I offer a review of pre-pandemic technological innovation in debate and argumentation pedagogy. This review leads into a conversation about radical interruptions in IAD practice over the past year that have opened avenues for cultivating what I call "virtual *paideia*" (Rief 2012), a mode of instruction and practice inspired by our recent technological revolution and the classical Greek rhetorical tradition that emphasizes hybrid (i.e., overlapping virtual and in-person) approaches to student preparation, tournament participation, and hosting exhibition events.

PRE-PANDEMIC DEVELOPMENTS
IN VIRTUAL DEBATING

Since its invention in the late nineteenth century, IAD practitioners have experimented with technological innovations to augment the pedagogy and practice of the activity. In the first half of the twentieth century, IAD programs used radio to engage in mass mediation of debates, turning to television in the 1960s (Bartanen and Littlefield 2014, 228–229; Rief 2018). During the 1960s, debate programs were also trading "tapes" to engage in "remote debates" with each other (Snider 2006, 140). More recently, many practitioners have assiduously pursued the integration of both digital (i.e., data retrieval and management) and virtual (i.e., online human interaction) technologies. We have even seen the rise of virtual reality (Michaels 2020) and artificially intelligent (AI) debating systems (Reed 2021; Slonim 2021), though these remain novelties. Technological experimentation and innovation in IAD have often followed different trajectories depending on the specific debate community in question. For example, evidence-based programs have been among the most enthusiastic adopters of digital approaches to research, organizing materials, writing speeches, and note-taking (Edwards 1998; Voth 2005). However, most if not all debate communities are now using some form of digital tournament management system for online entry, pairings, judge preferences, and/or results tabulation (see e.g., Voth 2005). Until recently, virtual debate competitions have been rare, but both scholarly dialogue and conversation among practitioners about the pedagogical anxieties and technophilic dreams they engender has been ongoing for some time.

In an early account of technological change in IAD, Rich Edwards (1998) ruminates on the possibilities and perils of virtual competition from a position of pedagogical anxiety: "This is another of those potential futures which should be consciously rejected. It is the promise of rich intellectual interaction in an intensive community environment that makes tournament competition special" (Edwards 1998, 401). Writing several years later, Ben Voth (2005) describes the rise of "a virtual community of debate" (420) made possible through LISTSERV, digital tournament registration, and online aggregation of tournament results, a kind of precursor to, and adjunct for, virtual tournaments. Despite these developments, he notes that fully remote debating had so far experienced "limited success" (Voth 2005, 419), though he clearly values its potential to promote student skills in the use of new communication technologies. In 2006, growing awareness of accelerating digital and virtual changes in IAD yielded a forum in *Contemporary Argumentation and Debate* (*CAD*). In his introduction to the forum, Allan Louden (2006) points out: "There are real questions if tournament debate will survive when multiple ways to communicate are easier and cheaper than getting past airport security" (71) which is among the potential changes in the activity he argues is both "exhilarating *and* disquieting" (72, emphasis in original). What Edwards viewed as a possibility to be avoided was quickly becoming an inevitability to be managed.

Several essays in the *CAD* forum directly address the newly visible horizon of virtual debating at the time, mostly with optimism. For example, Timothy M. O'Donnell (2006) argues "Multi-User Virtual Environments" offer opportunities "for radical experimentation" involving "collaboration, communication, teaching, and research" (78). His technophilic vision imagines the possibility that debaters might eventually compete in "3-D virtual worlds" (O'Donnell 2006, 78). He also notes the potential value of disseminating videos of debates online to cultivate wider awareness of the activity and its benefits but suggests care be taken in this regard given the diverse audiences that would potentially have access to their content (O'Donnell 2006, 79; Morris 2006). Rae Lynn Schwartz-DuPre (2006) offers an analysis of recent social media use by women to "cultivate a sense of agency and community" (108) as they continue work to gain recognition and inclusion in IAD, a project that has been ongoing since the nineteenth century (Bartanen and Littlefield 2014; Woods 2018). Alfred C. Snider (2006) describes the value of recording debates for training purposes (see also Morris 2006; Voth 2005). He reminds his readers that "internet distance debates" have been happening since 1999 when Cornell debated the University of Vermont, but they had failed to become the norm given technical limitations (Snider 2006, 141). To address these limitations, he offers the alternative of asynchronous "videoblogging" (Snider 2006, 143) in which students iteratively post recorded speeches. Snider (2006) concludes by admitting virtual debate does not offer the same "interpersonal contact" (145) as traditional tournaments, but defends it as a way to "dissolve the tyranny of distance and time" (145) and enshrine a new "Global Debate Community" (146). Overall, the 2006 *CAD* forum offers a vision of an as yet not fully realized virtual environment for debate encompassing preparation, competition, community building, and public exhibition.[3]

Six years after the *CAD* forum, Josh Compton (2012) edited *The Forensic's* special issue on "Forensics and the Net Generation" (1–2). Many of the contributors address the challenges facing debate educators working with students who have become inextricably intertwined with their virtual worlds. In this regard, Tomeka M. Robinson and Ben Reese (2012) describe their creative deployments of "Facebook, Skype, and Google+" (5) to promote online practice debates. Robinson and Reese (2012) report that their students benefited from these engagements, especially those that were audiovisual (Skype and Google+) as opposed to written (Facebook). While they admit to some "technical difficulties" (Robinson and Reese 2012, 8), their overall experience was positive, especially the fact that they could now reach students outside the spatiotemporal constraints of in-person meetings. Ryan Louis (2012) echoes this sentiment, arguing that new communication technologies may allow "underserved communities" including "those in rural areas" (47) to take part in online debate events. Kevin Doss (2012) notes the potential rise of "electronic forensic tournaments" (41) as does David Bailey (2012). Furthermore, many contributors argue debate pedagogy should be responsive to student needs and interests including their increasing use of online tools for interpersonal, pedagogical, and professional purposes (e.g., Holm 2012).

That IAD would undergo a necessary and even inevitable *virtualization* cuts across many of the materials previously cited. Echoing this theme in their history of IAD, Michael D. Bartanen and Robert S. Littlefield (2014) opine that while virtual debating has been rare in the past, its inexorable ascent has been clear for some time (304). They also note its multiple benefits including not only avoiding the costs and carbon footprint of travel but also adapting to the rising use of social media and other online platforms by students (Bartanen and Littlefield 2014, 304). Indeed, scholars have started to acknowledge online competitions as critical exemplars of experimentation and innovation (Mabrey and Richards 2017, 21–22). Moreover, evidence is beginning to accumulate showing that online debate and argument training can be a catalyst for robust learning and may enhance offline modes of engagement. For example, Kalypso Iordanou (2013) has shown that argumentation skills are portable between communicative modes (e.g., online written communications and in-person encounters) and that students can cultivate "metalevel awareness" (317) of their practices when given opportunities to evaluate the digital texts of their arguments. Blaine E. Smith, Carita Kiili, and Merja Kauppinen (2016) investigate the value of "multimodal transmediation" (145, Figure 2) of student arguments, that is, the movement of argumentation between written and virtual modes. Their research suggests that "the malleability of working with multiple modes allowed students to foreground and background visuals, sound, movement, and text in unique ways to build their argument" which gives them "skills that will become increasingly important in their personal and professional futures" (Smith, Kiili, and Kauppinen 2016, 149). Finally, Jessica A. Kurr and Paul E. Mabrey (2020) have recently discussed design issues related to debate in HyFlex classrooms. They advise that asynchronous models (with content posted iteratively and over time) can help students develop "research and critical thinking" skills while synchronous models are better at promoting "listening and dialogue" (Kurr and Mabrey 2020, 63). In sum, recent research and experience suggests dynamic pedagogical designs involving various modes of argumentative engagement may yield major benefits for instructors and students. In line with Woods et al.'s (2006) advice, past prognostications and novel experiments have been replaced with evidence-based deliberation about cutting-edge practices.

In sum, IAD practitioners have developed many applications for online practice, competition, exhibition, and community building. While all these applications have faced both technical and human problems, recent breakthroughs, like increasingly more stable synchronous interactions possible on Zoom and Microsoft Teams, offer some solutions. But the deeper pedagogical questions raised by virtuality remain both alive and ever more salient. A dialectic of anxiety and technophilia has undergirded ongoing discussions about virtual debating, especially as it has grown to become the only mode of competition available during the past year. Crucially, our previous imaginings and experiments occurred against the backdrop of the physical environments of classroom, podium, stage, and auditorium. Over the past year, this backdrop evaporated, creating an opportunity to test whether remote debating could be a *complete* replacement for its in-person predecessor. As we wait to learn about the actual outcomes of this test, I argue in the next section that we should build on recent research findings about the value of modal hybridity adumbrated earlier to promote the interplay of the in-person and virtual worlds of debate.

DEVELOPING A VIRTUAL *PAIDEIA* FOR POST-PANDEMIC IAD

In-person IAD tournament competition ground to halt in March 2020. Despite the shock of such a precipitous change, it did not take long for virtual tournaments to become operational. However, many practitioners see virtual debating as a short-term adaptation rather than a longer-term evolution of the activity. On his blog, *New York City Sophist*, Steven M. Llano (2020b) has argued that online learning is not merely an "emergency measure" but a key feature of educational life that is here to stay. He has also offered advice to debate practitioners seeking to make the best of the newly emergent virtual worlds of debating. In line with some of the research cited previously, Llano (2020a) avers: "Online pedagogy seems to be in agreement that the best online assignments are both multimodal and asynchronous." What's more, he suggests, "The vitality and energy from an in class debate is related to the physical presence, but that is not a necessary cause of good debating. Good debating is based on reasoned responses and engagement between the sides" (Llano 2020a). While I agree with Llano that in-person and virtual pedagogy require different approaches and that powerful learning experiences can occur without "physical presence," I am not so certain that "good debating" is purely a matter of reasoning and clash. As Tim Michaels (2020) notes, his inclusion of synchronous engagement in a debate assignment during the pandemic promoted "a sense of normalcy in an otherwise trying time" (102), in part by "replicat[ing] the interactivity amongst peers that had since become elusive" (102). His words hint at the relational elements of what some might call a *good* debate that can be lost in an asynchronous environment.

Ultimately, Llano and Michaels invite us to engage in creatively rethinking COVID-19's imposition into our pedagogical universe not as an unmitigated disaster, but as an opportunity to innovate. At the same time, we cannot ignore the anecdotal evidence suggesting the loss of physical learning environments has had negative consequences. While there will be no return to some halcyon pre-pandemic pedagogical paradise of purely in-person interactivity, we should take seriously the long-term evidence in support of in-person learning. Indeed, peering back across the two and a half millennia of rhetorical instruction in the Western tradition, the presence of other human beings has been a central feature. Moreover, it also has a demonstrated track record, whether at Isocrates' school, Aristotle's Lyceum, the many *gymnasia* of the fifth and fourth centuries BCE (Hawhee 2004; Walker 2011), or the classrooms of twentieth-century college life.

In what follows, I argue that IAD pedagogy in the post-pandemic context should embrace both continuities and discontinuities with this past without falling into the traps of either unreflective nostalgia or unwarranted idealism. To frame my analysis, I apply a hybrid concept, "virtual *paideia*" (Rief 2012), that forges a connection between a term central to our technological era—"virtual"—which refers to online spaces of human interactivity—with a term that looks back to the ancient Greek world—"*paideia*"— which captures a form of education that involves the whole sociocultural and political context of the individual's life (Jaeger 1945; Nussbaum 1994; Walker 2011).[4] As such, *paideia* encompasses not only the classroom but also the civic and professional environments of engaged learning. It is thus capacious enough to apply in the curricular, co-curricular, extra-curricular, experiential, and applied learning contexts that make up contemporary higher education.

Furthermore, because the notion of *paideia* was developed in the context of in-person learning, it offers us a way to consider what is lost when we migrate online. We have recently experienced a significant circumscription of person-to-person contact. Our bodies have been trapped within the rectangular borders of the digital camera frame and in spaces such as our home offices. This lack of immediate presence to and with others would have constituted a major problem for the Greek practitioners of *paideia*. As Debra Hawhee (2004) notes, the central feature of their educational approach was the "*agōn*" (15) which she describes as "the contestive encounter" (16), one that yields opportunities for constitutive acts of self-creation and transformation. The sophists would commonly relate their particular form of the *agōn*, rhetorical education, to *wrestling* (Hawhee 2004, 37–39), thus articulating it as an approach deeply informed by, and dependent upon, embodied entanglement. In other words, rhetorical *paideia* represented an encounter between bodies. Our modern experiment with virtual education implicates this conception of *paideia* to the degree that it disembodies or at least redefines the role of the body in the learning process (Hawhee 2004, 195). Therefore, virtual *paideia* both encompasses the central tension of our era, and points to the value of maintaining in-person connections while pursuing new modes of online interactivity.

Pursuing virtual *paideia* also invites reflection about what Hawhee (2004) calls "associative pedagogy" (150) or the learning that takes place through the relationships students develop in their educational environments. Tapping into the works of Isocrates, Hawhee (2004) argues the encounter at the heart of learning inspires "imitation" (148) through "association" (149): "What Isocrates pinpoints here is a pedagogy of association—a cultivation of habits and practices achieved by placing oneself in close relation to those who practice the arts one is pursuing" (149). While Hawhee primarily imagines the teacher-student relationship, there is ample evidence to suggest that debaters often learn from one another (Bartanen and Littlefield 2014). The application of "associative pedagogy" in the current context suggests that the rich connections developed between debaters at in-person events might be powerfully expanded in virtual spaces, a possibility I investigate throughout the rest of this chapter.

The following sections detail how the modal hybridity of an emergent virtual *paideia* that makes room for both in-person and online interactivity may help us accomplish numerous goals in the post-pandemic era including: (1) making IAD more resilient to unexpected interruptions like COVID-19; (2) managing anxieties about the loss of embodied interactivity; and, (3) augmenting the relational contexts in which debate is practiced, performed (at tournaments), and made public (at exhibition debates).[5] Ultimately, decisions about how to accomplish such hybridity should draw not only on evidence (requiring ongoing research and assessment), but also on careful deliberation rooted in shared goals and aspirations (Voth 2005; Woods et al. 2006).

EXPANDING PEDAGOGY ACROSS SPACE AND TIME: VIRTUAL *PAIDEIA* AND THE PRACTICE ROOM

In this section, I consider how virtual *paideia* might help us to reconceptualize debate practice or preparation for competitions and public events. According to Hawhee (2004), the ancient Greeks *practiced* at the *gymnasium*, an intentionally designed space meant to promote the merging of bodies and minds so as to constitute a "citizen *ēthos*" (111), a way of being in the *polis* that involved all the attributes the Greeks valued including physical prowess, mental acuity, and verbal dexterity: "From this spatial intermingling of practices there emerged a specific syncretism between athletics and rhetoric . . . a crossover that contributed to the development of rhetoric as a bodily art: an art learned, practiced, and performed by and with the body as well as the mind" (111). These spaces were designed to facilitate not only "peripatetic" philosophical and rhetorical training but also wrestling, activities which took place alongside one another (Hawhee 2004, 117–122). For contemporary debaters, the *gymnasium* has been transformed into what is often called the "squad room." Some debate programs may not have squad rooms, and such rooms are often not so intentionally designed as the Greek *gymnasium*. Still, physical practice spaces, whether they are squad rooms, classrooms, or living rooms, facilitate collaborative work (e.g., writing speeches, giving practice speeches, using dry erase boards or paper to map out arguments) that simply cannot be imitated online.

Expanding the squad room through felicitous virtual pathways, on the other hand, presents valuable opportunities, especially the inclusion of students who might not otherwise be able to participate (Louis 2012; Robinson and Reese 2012). For example, in fall 2020, MSU Denver Debate members used virtual meetings to prepare for a major competition. In a paper forthcoming in *Orbis: A Journal of World Affairs*, these students note that while many challenges arose, virtual collaboration allowed them to overcome their otherwise divergent work and school schedules (Flores, Hitchcock, and Wicks, forthcoming). What's more, virtual meetings can be recorded so those who cannot attend may still benefit. In all, these methods allow for a spatiotemporal realignment of the pre-virtual squad room that expands opportunities for students to associate with and thus learn from one another.

Virtual practice also presents opportunities to build ties between debate organizations. For example, remote scrimmages involving teams from around the region, nation, and world could bring students into contact who might otherwise never encounter each other, thus broadening the associative network available to students. Indeed, despite his skepticism about online competitions noted earlier, Edwards (1998) concedes: "It is, of course, conceivable that Internet-mediated debates could provide the means for stimulating practice debating for those debate squads too small to find competition within the squad" (401). Using online platforms like Discord, Zoom, or MS Teams, small programs could begin to host full practice sessions. This would be especially helpful in formats like British Parliamentary Debate that require eight debaters and up to three judges to accomplish the rehearsal of contest round conditions. What's more, all of the methods described here for connecting students with each other could be used to connect them with other teachers, experts, and even public audiences who could assess their performances and provide feedback ahead of competitions and/or exhibition debates.

In sum, the preceding analysis suggests potentially major dividends for practitioners willing to embrace a trans-modal practice space. There is no platform that can replace the physical practice room populated with the bodies of other participants working together at the same time. Without the dynamics of embodied rhetorical performance, which tend to exceed the capabilities of any screen to adequately represent, the virtual environment lacks the pedagogical alchemy necessary for debate training. However, as the pandemic recedes, we may benefit from maintaining some elements of remote preparation as we return to our campuses, especially to create wider associative networks for our students that simultaneously facilitate skills development relevant to their heavily technologized professional and civic environments. In this way, the practice room of the post-pandemic era could mirror key elements of the ancient *gymnasia*, especially when it combines a central physical location for embodied practice with a series of virtual pathways circling around it through which spatially and temporally distanced participants can enter to observe others, interact with them, and develop their skills.

HYBRIDIZING VIRTUAL AND IN-PERSON TOURNAMENT PARTICIPATION

Since the invention of the art, rhetorical educators have trained students not only how to write powerful arguments but also how to deliver them in particular places and for specific audiences. Christopher Lyle Johnstone (1996, 2001) describes how the acoustics of locations like the outdoor Pnyx (a hill on which Athenian citizens engaged in open deliberation), various stoas, and other enclosed spaces impacted speaking pedagogy, especially in the area of delivery. Virtual *paideia* attunes us to the newly emergent oratorical sites of the twentieth century. In order to serve the needs of our students, we should offer them opportunities to learn how video cameras, microphones, platforms, and screens influence their ability to share information, engage in persuasive advocacy, use their voices in creative combination with text and images, and even remix portions of different performances together. All of these are skills rooted in the socially mediated world our students must navigate to be successful in life. Thus, twenty-first-century debate programs have a responsibility to train students about not only traditional methods of in-person delivery, but also how to leverage technology to address wider audiences in the vast array of mediated contexts that make up our communicative environment (Errera and Rief, forthcoming).

Online tournaments represent a powerful crucible for the development of such skills while offering several other benefits for post-pandemic debate educators. First among these is their ability to break through access barriers that have limited participation, engagement, and competitive equity in the past. As they are delinked from any particular place, their costs are much lower than physical tournaments that demand travel and hotel rooms (Bartanen and Littlefield 2014). Programs with smaller (or even nonexistent) budgets may now be able to participate in tournaments that were far beyond their reach previously, thus expanding their associational networks and enhancing the diversity and quality of their competitive opponents. Such tournaments also offer opportunities to address problems with IAD's accessibility. New collaborative platforms will allow for transcription and closed captioning in real time. Moreover, access through the screen eliminates concerns about getting around unfamiliar and potentially inaccessible campuses. In sum, online tournaments may address barriers that have made in-person tournaments unwelcoming or inaccessible places for many students in the past. Of course, all of these potential benefits will require sustained efforts to address ongoing problems related to the "digital divide" including student and program ability to finance necessary—and often expensive—hardware and software (Voth 2005, 420).

Despite these benefits, practitioners will need to address problems that arise when participants do not inhabit the same physical space. Most importantly is the issue of networking and community-building. Platforms for virtual interactivity are not good at promoting one-on-one exchanges and informal dialogue at events. In-person tournaments feature large rooms or outdoor spaces where everyone congregates to receive pairings for the next round and learn about results. In such places, students and coaches informally interact, sometimes for hours. In addition, debating on campus requires movement between various classrooms for different rounds of competition. Such movement creates time for conversation, not only about debate, but also the many topics that tend to build relationships and even friendships over time. To replicate these opportunities for community building, more time will need to be spent developing spaces for dialogue outside the video lounge or breakout rooms crafted specifically for distanced competition.

Modal hybridity addresses some of these problems by emphasizing the combination of asynchronous, synchronous, and/or in-person elements. Such combinations would yield numerous advantages including promoting public health and wellness, reducing access barriers, and allowing for networking and cultural outings at tournaments no longer over-burdened by the compressed timeframe of a single weekend. Such competitions could begin with asynchronous rounds in which students iteratively respond to recorded speeches (Snider 2006), a strategy that has been used previously (Michaels

2020, 97). Alternatively, students could engage in several synchronous rounds of competition. Either way, at the end of the remote rounds, a smaller slate of teams would, based on their performance, attend an in-person championship competition.

Given the smaller number of in-person competitors, the costs of hosting would decrease or could be diverted for use in providing scholarships to championship participants to cover travel costs. In-person championship competitions would be smaller and more intimate, would not require students to engage in large numbers of debates over the course of a weekend, and might give visiting programs time to experience the cultural life of the cities to which they travel. To avoid only rewarding top-performing programs with travel opportunities, sanctioning organizations could offer tournaments in all the modes—hybrid, virtual, and in-person—throughout the semester. This would still decrease costs overall, promote learning about both in-person and virtual modes of communication, and offer opportunities to think about how these events might be designed differently. For example, virtual tournaments could feature more rounds of competition, whereas in-person tournaments could offer fewer rounds with more opportunities for cultural outings and community-building activities.

In short, there are many ways to imagine hybridizing debate tournament designs and schedules. The point would be to carefully balance the financial, logistical, and health benefits so that students optimize the elements each mode of interaction facilitates. Crucially, the hybrid approach imagined here would help educators frame different modes as opportunities to practice different skills. Remote rounds of competition could emphasize the invention of strong arguments and facility with the use of online tools for collaboration, interaction, and mediated delivery of information. In-person rounds could feature oratorical skills, the use of the body and gestures, and adaptation to audience feedback. With fewer rounds in the in-person setting, students could also commit themselves to interpersonal interaction, tourism, and other educational opportunities afforded by the universities, cities, and regions to which they travel. In sum, hybrid tournament experiences rooted in a conception of virtual *paideia* could promote learning that spans the gulf between traditional oratory and online advocacy, thus paving the way for our students to become skilled professionals and civic leaders in our technological era.

VIRTUAL EXHIBITION DEBATING: EXPANDING THE CIVIC AND PUBLIC IMPACT OF IAD

Isocrates' choice to focus his rhetorical *paideia* on writing as opposed to the spoken word demonstrates how embracing new communication technologies can augment one's message and expand one's audience (Mitchell 2011; Walker 2011). As we turn to the civic and public spaces of exhibition debating, we should keep in mind that practitioners of the ancient *paideia* imagined students eventually moving beyond the practice space and into their wider public and civic environments (Walker 2011). Just as Isocrates realized that "writing [had] freed oratory from the water clock" (Mitchell 2011, 68) as well as any particular place, so we must acknowledge that online video production and interactivity can do the same and more for message invention and dissemination in the present. Failing to realize this opportunity risks allowing debate to remain locked in the "hermetically sealed" (Mitchell 1998a, 20; Mitchell 1998b) space of the contest round within the "specialized kind of environment" (Wenzel 1971, 253) at tournaments rather than reconnecting the activity to the public square. Indeed, remote debating may facilitate a connection between the sundered spaces of tournaments and public exhibition events by easing the process of inviting and granting access to audience members (Rief 2018).

Crucially, just as with practice/preparation and tournament competition, virtual public events could be a site for expanding access to students who might otherwise be excluded by distance, resources, time, and similar barriers. This would be especially important in the context of traditionally marginalized populations for whom debate has been hard to access but who would potentially garner numerous benefits from participation (Bartanen and Littlefield 2014; Louis, 2012; Mitchell, 1998b). While access to technology might remain a barrier, it may be easier to manage than securing money for travel and other expenses related to in-person engagements. In addition, the use of virtual exhibition debates would augment the recruitment of new students and catalyze the creation of new programs, especially in underserved areas where there may not be any existing infrastructure for debate. For these areas and communities, public online events that are simultaneously developed into freely accessible videos for training purposes could make a major pedagogical contribution.

Furthermore, one of the great challenges of exhibition debate planning is securing audiences composed of experts, members of the public, or both (Broda-Bahm, Kempf, and Driscoll 2004; Rief 2018). Just as with virtual squad rooms and tournaments, delinking exhibition events from specific places and times provides a potential solution to this problem. However, live and in-person designs promote an electric atmosphere at many exhibition debates that is hard to replicate online. Hybrid public debates provide a way to accomplish both feats, especially when they offer options for synchronous and asynchronous engagement. Events with these features are also resilient when confronted by unexpected disturbances like weather and illness. MSU Denver Debate experienced just this sort of disturbance while planning a public debate in fall 2019, the audience for which was diminished by a snowstorm and late start. However, plans for the event called for a Facebook Live video that eventually received over five hundred views.

Moreover, there are many ways for practitioners to hybridize public debate events. Recording and/or live streaming could be combined with, for example, the use of social media for audience feedback, a strategy that has been used at in-person events in the past (Eckstein and Mitchell 2020 504). Global or national level virtual events could be used to inspire local opportunities for in-person dialogue. The main point is to use these combinations to enhance the associational possibilities for students, faculty, and stakeholders. A great example of this is using online platforms to connect public debaters with experts who, because of their distance, would be unable to attend and provide feedback. Of course, there are risks to this approach. Perhaps the most important is having less control over the audiences one might reach. Depending on the sorts of arguments being advanced and the style of their performance, event planners may want to exert some control over who has access to view and manipulate recordings, post comments, and get in contact with participants directly (O'Donnell 2006; Morris 2006).

Despite these risks, there is every reason to believe hybrid exhibition debating offers major potential benefits to practitioners. Using the methods described above to reach ever larger audiences for public exhibition debates, IAD may refurbish its role in constituting democratic culture by performatively reimagining the deliberative practices of our real and virtual worlds. Debate programs would do well to design exhibition events that intentionally promote practices (e.g., use of evidence, inclusion of experts, opportunities for all sides to speak and engage with each other) we would like to see in use at public deliberations (Rief and Schrader 2020). Doing so would put IAD in a position to address the persistent problems of extremism, polarization, and the epidemic of misinformation that undermine effective democratic deliberation (Eckstein and Mitchell 2020; Mitchell 2011; Errera and Rief, forthcoming). In this way, the associational networks of debate reimagined through the lens of virtual *paideia* could work bidirectionally, not only putting debaters in contact with experts and public audiences but also giving them a platform to influence democracy in progress.

CONCLUSION: HYBRIDITY AS A
POST-PANDEMIC FRONTIER FOR IAD

In this chapter, I have reviewed the history of IAD's technological developments, revealing it to be an activity firmly committed to innovations that advance its many pedagogical and practical goals. In the face of restrictions imposed due to the COVID-19 pandemic, this commitment facilitated swift and, at least at times, quite successful adaptations. However, these very same innovations may facilitate a loss of *humanness* in an activity that has roots going back as far as the ancient Greeks for whom the body and its entanglement with others was a cornerstone of excellent pedagogy. Rather than resolving this tension, we might instead use it to frame a more productive approach to the post-pandemic pedagogical universe. Specifically, allowing both optimism and anxiety to coexist in our thinking about virtual debating may help to maintain healthy deliberation and ongoing reflection about IAD, thus allowing it to remain a vital, effective, and humane training platform for future professionals and civic leaders.

Moreover, I advanced the notion of virtual *paideia* to make sense of the creative tensions and potential connections between the virtual frontiers of IAD and the ancient embodied/associative aspects of in-person rhetorical education (Hawhee 2004). As we have seen, the ancient teachers of rhetoric highlighted context, delivery, and new communication technologies as critical components for shaping responsive and relevant approaches to pedagogy. Their insights about the importance of embodied interaction as a necessary component of rhetorical instruction raise the stakes for reconfiguring the conversation about virtuality. Instead of asking about the limits of our virtual frontiers, we should instead seek ways to cultivate *hybrid frontiers* rooted in the accumulated knowledge of rhetorical practitioners, communication scholars, and debate coaches over the past 2,500 years.

In sum, rather than mistaking our adaptations over the past year as short-term interruptions (Llano 2020b) or imperatives for future action, we should instead deliberate about their value (Woods et al. 2006) and refurbish them for the world to come. Whether we consider virtual practice, online competitions, or distanced exhibition events, the growth of remote debating during the pandemic has allowed us time and space to redesign IAD for the post-pandemic world in ways that will make the activity more resilient, enhance pedagogical outcomes, reduce access barriers, decrease costs, and promote public dialogue. Put differently, the pandemic has radically expanded the conversation about virtual debating in ways we could never have predicted. It has thus granted us an unexpected opportunity to innovate in ways that are responsive not only to our past but also to the challenges of our present as we anticipate and plan for a pedagogically robust future for IAD.

NOTES

1. Thank you to the editor of this volume, Joseph Valenzano, for his guidance while bringing this chapter to completion. Thanks as well to Matthew Brigham, Kevin

Cummings, and Brian Schrader for their comments on the manuscript. Special thanks to Shara Merrill, Ben Voth, Paul Mabrey, and Tim Michaels for sharing numerous helpful materials on virtual debating with me.

2. In making this observation, they draw on the work of Richard E. Sclove (1995) who offers a rich description of this model of deliberation in the Amish tradition.

3. Woods et al. (2006) appears in this forum but focuses on digital rather than virtual technologies.

4. In my dissertation (Rief 2012), virtual *paideia* refers to online patient education in the chronic care environment. In this chapter, I emphasize the *tensions* embedded in the term as a way to bridge virtual and in-person approaches to IAD pedagogy and practice.

5. My discussion of modal hybridity here builds on Michael Gilbert's (1994) conceptualization of argument as a "multi-modal" activity, recent discussions about virtual debating (Kurr and Mabrey 2020; Llano 2020a; Michaels 2020), and materials cited in the previous section on trans-modal argumentation pedagogy (Iordanou 2013; Smith, Kiili, and Kauppinen 2016). My primary innovation is to feature the relationship between in-person and virtual modes of debating.

REFERENCES

Bailey, David. 2012. Review of *From Digital Natives to Digital Wisdom: Hopeful Essays for 21st Century Learning*, by M. Prensky. *The Forensic of Pi Kappa Delta* 97: 39–40.

Bartanen, Michael D., and Robert S. Littlefield. 2014. *Forensics in America: A History*. Lanham, MD: Rowman & Littlefield. Kindle.

Broda-Bahm, Ken, Daniela Kempf, and William Driscoll. 2004. *Argument and Audience: Presenting Debates in Public Settings*. New York, NY: International Debate Education Association.

Compton, Josh. 2012. "Introduction to *The Forensic* Special Issue: Forensics and the NetGeneration." *The Forensic of Pi Kappa Delta* 97: 1–2.

Doss, Kevin. 2012. Review of *From Digital Natives to Digital Wisdom: Hopeful Essays for 21st Century Learning*, by M. Prensky. *The Forensic of Pi Kappa Delta* 97: 40–42.

Eckstein, Justin, and Gordon R. Mitchell. 2020. "Designing Public Debates to Facilitate Dynamic Updating in a Network Society." In *Networking Argument*, edited by Carol Winkler, 499–506. New York, NY: Routledge.

Edwards, Rich. 1998. "Technological Requirements of the Debate Director in the 21st Century." In *Argument in a Time of Change: Definitions, Frameworks, and Critiques*, edited by James F. Klumpp, 399–403. Annandale, VA: National Communication Association.

Ehninger, Douglas. 1970. "Argument a Method: Its Nature, Its Limitations and Its Uses." *Speech Monographs* 37, no. 2: 101–110.

Errera, David, and John J. Rief. Forthcoming. "Featuring Performance in Intercollegiate Academic Debate Pedagogy and Practice." In *Local Theories of Argument*, edited by Dale Hample, 433–438. Taylor & Francis.

Flores, José, Samantha Hitchcock, and Matthew Wicks. Forthcoming. "Using the Transatlantic Partnership to Hold China Accountable: A Three-Tiered Approach to the Uyghur Genocide (An Undergraduate Research Note)." *Orbis: A Journal of World Affairs*. https://www.fpri.org/orbis/.

Gilbert, Michael A. 1994. "Multi-Modal Argumentation." *Philosophy of the Social Sciences* 24, no. 2: 159–177.

Greene, Ronald Walter, and Darrin Hicks. 2005. "Lost Convictions: Debating Both Sides and the Ethical Self-Fashioning of Liberal Citizens." *Cultural Studies* 19, no. 1: 100–126.

Habineza, Jean Michel, John J. Rief, and Rachel Wilson. 2018. "The iDebate Rwanda Tour of the U.S.: Cross-Cultural Perspectives on Debate, Memory, and Social Justice." Paper presented at the National Communication Association's 104th Annual Convention, Salt Lake City, UT, November 2018.

Hawhee, Debra. 2004. *Bodily Arts: Rhetoric and Athletics in Ancient Greece*. Austin, TX: University of Texas Press.

Hogan, J. Michael, Jessica A. Kurr, Michael J. Bergmaier, and Jeremy D. Johnson, editors. 2017. *Speech and Debate as Civic Education*. University Park, PA: The Pennsylvania State University Press. Kindle.

Holm, Todd T. 2012. "Managing Millennials: Coaching the Next Generation." *The Forensic of Pi Kappa Delta* 97: 25–38.

Iordanou, Kalypso. 2013. "Developing Face-to-Face Argumentation Skills: Does Arguing on the Computer Help?" *Journal of Cognition and Development* 14, no. 2: 292–320.

Jaeger, Werner. 1945. *Paideia: The Ideals of Greek Culture, Volumes I-III, Second Edition*. Translated by Gilbert Highet. New York, NY: Oxford University Press.

Johnstone, Christopher Lyle. 1996. "Greek Oratorical Settings and the Problem of the Pnyx: Rethinking the Athenian Political Process." In *Theory, Text, Context: Issues in Greek Rhetoric and Oratory*, edited by Christopher Lyle Johnstone, 97–127. Albany, NY: State University of New York Press.

———. 2001. "Communicating in Classical Contexts: The Centrality of Delivery." *Quarterly Journal of Speech* 87, no. 2: 121–143.

Keith, William. 2010. "Keynote Address: A New Golden Age — Intercollegiate Debate in the Twenty- First Century." In *Navigating Opportunity: Policy Debate in the 21st Century*, edited by Allan D. Louden, 11–26. New York, NY: International Debate Education Association.

Kurr, Jessica A., and Paul E. Mabrey. 2020. "Structured Debates." *The Journal of Faculty Development* 34, no. 3: 62–63.

Llano, Steven M. 2020a. "Holding Debates in Online Classes." *New York City Sophist* (blog). March 11, 2020. https://stephen-llano-klbp.squarespace.com/?offset=1590463602402.

———. 2020b. "Public Speaking Will Not Bend. Why?" *New York City Sophist* (blog). August 10, 2020. https://stephen-llano-klbp.squp.arespace.com/.

Louden, Allan. 2006. "*CAD Forum*—Technology and Debate: An Assessment." *Contemporary Argumentation and Debate* 27: 71–74.

Louis, Ryan. 2012. Review of *Rethinking Education in the Age of Technology: The Digital Revolution and Schooling in America*, by A. Collins and R. Halverson. *The Forensic of Pi Kappa Delta* 97: 46–47.

Mabrey, Paul E., and Keith Richards. 2017. "Evidence Based Decision Making and Assessment for the Cross Examination Debate Association." *Contemporary Argumentation and Debate* 36: 1–31.

Michaels, Tim. 2020. "Seeking Civility in Cyberspace: A Tetradic Analysis of Public Forum Debate for Distance Learning." In *Pandemic University: Teaching and Learning in a Global Crisis*, edited by Danette DiMarco, Jason T. Hilton, and Timothy Ruppert, 94–103. Slipper Rock, PA: Slippery Rock University of Pennsylvania.

Mitchell, Gordon. 1998a. "Reflexive Fiat: Incorporating the Outward Activist Turn into Contest Strategy." *The Rostrum* 72: 11–21.

———. 1998b. "Pedagogical Possibilities for Argumentative Agency in Academic Debate." *Argumentation and Advocacy* 35, no. 2: 41–60.

———. 2011. "iSocrates: Student-led Public Debate as Cultural Technology. *Controversia* 7, no. 2: 54–75.

Morris, Eric. 2006. "Argue into the Camera, Please: An Exploration of Comprehensive Digital Recording in Debate." *Contemporary Argumentation and Debate* 27: 148–156.

Nussbaum, Martha C. 1994. *The Therapy of Desire: Theory and Practice in Hellenistic Ethics*. Princeton, NJ: Princeton University Press.

O'Donnell, Timothy M. 2006. "On Further Integrating Information Technology or Academic Debate." *Contemporary Argumentation and Debate* 27: 75–80.

Reed, Chris. "Argument Technology for Debating with Humans." *Nature*, March 17, 2021. https://www.nature.com/articles/d41586-021-00539-5.

Rief, John J. 2012. "Searching for the Good Life: Rhetoric, Medicine, and the Shaping of Lifestyle." PhD diss. University of Pittsburgh.

———. 2018. "(Re)Designing the Debate Tournament for Civic Life." *Speaker & Gavel* 55, no. 1: 36–58.

Rief, John J., and Brian J. Schrader. 2020. "Reconciling Playing the Game with Civic Education in Intercollegiate Academic Debate." Paper presented at the 6th Tokyo Conference on Argumentation: Argumentation and Education, E-Conference, August 10–31, 2020.

Robinson, Tomeka M., and Ben Reese. 2012. "Digitizing Forensics: Coaching the Net Generation." *The Forensic of Pi Kappa Delta* 97: 3–13.

Schwartz-DuPre, Rae Lynn. 2006. "Women in Debate: From Virtual to Material." *Contemporary Argumentation and Debate* 27: 106–120.

Sclove, Richard E. 1995. *Democracy and Technology*. New York, NY: The Guilford Press.

Slonim, Noam, Yonatan Bilu, Carlos Alzate et al. 2021. "An Autonomous Debating System." *Nature* 591: 379–385.
Smith, Blaine E., Carita Kiili, and Merja Kauppinen. 2016. "Transmediating Argumentation: Students Composing Across Written Essays and Digital Videos in Higher Education." *Computers & Education* 102: 138–151.
Snider, Alfred C. 2006. "Internet Debating: Technical Solutions for the 21st Century." *Contemporary Argumentation and Debate* 27: 140–147.
Voth, Ben. 2005. "State of the Art: A Survey of Technology and Debate Practice in the 21st Century." In *Critical Problems in Argumentation*, edited by Charles Arthur Willard, 416–421. Washington, DC: National Communication Association.
Walker, Jeffrey. 2011. *The Genuine Teachers of This Art: Rhetorical Education in Antiquity*. Columbia, SC: The University of South Carolina Press.
Wenzel, Joseph W. 1971. "Campus and Community Programs in Forensics: Needs and Opportunities." *The Journal of the American Forensic Association* 7, no. 5: 253–259.
Woods, Carly S. 2018. *Debating Women: Gender, Education, and Spaces for Argument, 1835-1945*. East Lansing, MI: Michigan State University Press. Kindle.
Woods, Carly, Matthew Brigham, Brent Heavner, Takuzo Konishi, John Rief, Brent Saindon, and Gordon R. Mitchell. 2006. "Deliberating Debate's Digital Futures." *Contemporary Argumentation and Debate* 27: 81–105.

Conclusion

Predicting the New Pedagogical Paradigm

Joseph M. Valenzano III

Writing in his book *The Time Machine*, H.G. Wells (1895/2002) proposed that people need to embrace change and challenges, for without them growth is not possible. Such an approach sounds simple, especially when the challenges we encounter are relatively mundane; but, when confronted with a situation that simultaneously tests us all, the idea of embracing the difficult can seem impossible. Rare moments in history change the paradigm for human interaction and behavior, and even rarer moments do so for higher education. The ivory tower has long seen itself as impermeable to the events that happen outside its walls. The COVID-19 pandemic, however, changed that way of thinking.

Change in education can seem glacial at times. Scholars like to think deeply and for long periods of time before taking action. When the pandemic began and lockdowns commenced they did not have that luxury, and needed to adapt on a comparative moment's notice. Within weeks, in-person instruction disappeared; whiteboards to help diagram problems were replaced with screens you could draw on; small group assignments became difficult to pull off without new digital tools to connect people; hand marking essays became almost impossible, replaced instead with track changes and comment boxes; cocurricular events were canceled, or moved online; and, all under the added stress of fiscal uncertainty and austerity measures which replaced the joy of welcoming students back to campus. Though some faculty who had either taught online before or studied how to do it were better prepared for the sudden switch in pedagogical style, the overwhelming majority were not so lucky.

In the days, weeks, months, and semesters since the move to online or hybrid teaching formats faculty have risen to the challenge. They innovated solutions both big and small. From using new tools to facilitate group work, to embracing more elements within course management platforms than ever before, to appreciating the importance of care and compassion, instructional methods dramatically changed. Not all of the changes will be permanent, but a good number will. New questions will emerge going forward regarding the work/life balance of faculty and staff, the feasibility of online-only degrees, and the importance of brick and mortar schools with a residential focus. The answers to these will differ from school to school, but it is certain that when things return to "normal," it will not be the "normal" that existed before the invisible scourge of COVID-19 upended our routines, changed the way in which we conduct our work, and altered the way in which students learn.

THE COVID EFFECT AND HIGHER EDUCATION

The contributors to this volume build the case that the pandemic forced meaningful and important changes to pedagogy. They further suggest that the adaptations faculty made result in a new set of best practices and suggestions for enhancing teaching for all students going forward. This is the very definition of what Kuhn (1962) called a paradigm shift. To paraphrase Kuhn, a paradigm shift does not necessarily mean the world has changed, but rather that the way the scholar sees that world changes. The pandemic may have actually done both: change the world, and change the way we see it. It is definitely true for instruction, where the world of teaching changed in ways that will not go quietly, and it also changed the nature of the questions we ask about instruction as scholars, practitioners, and students. The writers in this volume focus their efforts on three key areas of pandemic-induced shifts: instructional design, in-class interaction and effectiveness, and technology.

One of the consistent themes throughout several chapters in the volume is the increased importance of universal design for learning in a course. Pre-pandemic this was a concept faculty often relegated only to accommodating students with special needs. The strategies for UDL that once were perceived as helping those who needed accommodations, suddenly were needed to help almost all students. In a sense, universal design for learning became the universal style of good teaching during the pandemic. Moving forward the idea of presenting material in multiple ways for students, recording and posting lectures and encouraging collaborative assignments, among other things, will remain post-pandemic. Faculty who went to extraordinary efforts to learn this approach and develop courses consistent with it should, as a matter of good pedagogy, continue to use things they did that work, and as a practical matter will not want to ditch things they spent time to create. Students, for their part, will go forward expecting some of these teaching practices to continue even after the pandemic ends. Nevertheless, we all should realize that just because we shifted online and survived the pandemic does not mean we all shifted our teaching equally or well.

The instructional toolkit expanded as a result of COVID-19 course preparation and delivery, and just like any mechanic, faculty will not throw away good tools in case they are needed again. The obvious tool faculty can now deploy videoconferencing software. On one extreme end, their presence and utility in delivery classes virtually could spell the end to the traditionally coveted "snow days." Now, if inclement weather hits a university such that they would normally shut down, faculty could instead offer remote classes for that day through videoconferencing software. On the other end, faculty could hold virtual office hours, and these may very well prove more popular than the posted office hours as students may be more inclined to have a video call than trek to an office. Other tools include software like GoogleDocs, Pear Deck, and MURAL, which allow for a stronger degree of collaborative work by students and between faculty. Whether it is videoconferencing tools, or document sharing software, each of these technological tools comes with both advantages and challenges and faculty and scholars will need to continue to explore and examine how best they are deployed. After all, just because they are available does not mean they need to be used. Pedagogy drives technology choices, technology choices do not drive pedagogy.

In this volume, Carozza and Gennaro noted one specific area of technology that faculty and administrators alike should think more critically about. The notion of surveillance technology, or test/presentation proctoring software, is rife with ethical and pragmatic questions that must be explored. It is true, these tools can help ensure academic honesty, at least to a certain degree, but they also may send a message that diminishes trust between faculty and students. Is such a loss of trust worth the test security? Or, should we consider different ways to evaluate student work that encourages them to produce their best work, and not just reward performance under pressure? How efficacious are the surveillance tools? These are just a sampling of questions this new technological tool raises that scholars need to explore further in coming years for it will impact the degree of comfort, as well as the course design, for online courses in the future.

In addition to the technological adaptations now available to faculty, courses themselves may be reimagined in the wake of the pandemic. Public speaking, long a class focused on in-person instruction and performance, moved to fully online or hybrid modalities during the pandemic. Even before the pandemic online versions of this course existed and were studied by scholars, but the courses bread and butter remained in-person. This may change on a large scale after the pandemic with more fully online versions of the course delivered by faculty, as McGarrity explores in this volume. It also may change on a more micro-level where faculty become much more open to having students do recorded speeches and uploading them for view. This would add actual instructional time to class, and more importantly, perhaps better mimic the ways in which students would need to communicate post-graduation.

COVID-19, and the damage it inflicted on people, families and friends, resulted in a major shift in the appreciation students have for their faculty, and that faculty have for their students. In addition to the deadly nature of the disease, the lockdowns isolated people from one another causing a mental health epidemic that did not differentiate between students and faculty. With everyone confronting these strains pedagogy became infused with a level of care for wellness never seen before. This is not to say faculty never cared for their students' well-being, or vice versa, but rather the pandemic brought that element of the instructional relationship to the fore. Going forward, the deep understanding of mental health challenges by faculty for students will not dissipate, and course policies will continue to show empathy and care for students at a higher degree than before the pandemic.

Lest we not forget, pedagogy also includes co-curricular enterprises and they changed just as much during the pandemic and are not immune from more lasting impacts as well. From debate to student clubs and preprofessional organizations, cocurricular elements of the college experience needed to adapt to remain relevant during the pandemic just as much as instruction needed to change. In the case of debate, one of the more popular co-curricular enterprises in the communication discipline, the changes forced by the pandemic may open more access to both viewers and potential participants in the activity. It also may lower institutional costs by diminishing the need for travel and tournament hosting in-person, thus making the expansion of debate programs a distinct possibility in an era of budget-conscious planning.

As the authors in this volume illustrate, there are many lessons to be gleaned from the pandemic teaching experience. Some of those lessons tell us what not to do, but a great many point the way to improved pedagogy and student learning. The shift faculty across the world made to digital instruction came with tremendous work, and that work created many unanticipated benefits. Faculty would do well to embrace the pedagogical paradigm shift thrust upon them and look to ways we can improve our teaching and student learning. Change to pedagogy and institutional structures in the past has often been slow to take root; this time, however, the change was not gradual, but sudden.

WHAT WILL THE FUTURE BRING?

The adjustments forced by the pandemic will not all be so swiftly discarded for a return to the higher education of a now bygone era. Thus, the core question for the coming years is not whether things will change in the classroom after the pandemic, but rather *how much* will they change? There will be new data threads to track, new practices to test, new policies to develop. Students, faculty, and administrators alike will not return to the carefree study abroad, course prep, and budgeting of summers past. It will take time to determine what the new rhythm will be, and how each group operates within it—but it will be different. Some of these differences will be slight, while others more apparent.

Data collection will be imperative as we chart the new future for pedagogy. It will be interesting to see how many courses begin to trend more online than in-person as the pandemic wanes. Will the trend to go online be grounded simply in large public universities, or will private residential schools also change their approach over time to adopt more online pedagogy? How will student enrollment be impacted by such turns at schools? Or perhaps, schools will move to a more hybrid format, with some in-person interaction. Will flipped learning spread like wildfire across academia? On a more microscale, will course readings and textbooks accelerate their shift to a digital rather than printed platform? What will that mean for open-source texts for classes? There are numerous questions that remain about how the pandemic has changed our pedagogical approach, and only time, observation, trial, and error will provide an answer to that question.

One thing we did discover during the pandemic is the public perception of the relationship between cost and course modality. In a survey by the College Savings Foundation in summer 2020, 51 % of parents stated they would not pay full price for online courses. Additionally, 89 % of respondents said that traditional in-person universities should lower tuition costs if the school moved all its classes online. For them, the on-campus student experience and in-person instruction were significant value adds. Clearly, the move of classes online during the pandemic, and the instructional quality delivered after the shift, is not a bellwether of a wholesale move online for college courses in the future. That said, and as the contributors in this volume point out, there are some significant lessons and pedagogical advancements that can and should come from the experience of moving online or hybrid.

Instructional communication scholars would do well to reorient their efforts, in part, toward comparing what we thought we knew about instruction and student learning before the pandemic, to what we discover we learned during it in examining how to employ the best post-pandemic teaching. Hopefully, we discard the things that no longer work and embrace new ways of teaching that enhance learning, and do not simply choose the convenient or the familiar because they are convenient and familiar. Whether in-person, online, or hybrid, the core focus should always be improving our teaching to enhance student learning. In that sense, the paradigm has not changed, but how we see the best ways to achieve that outcome may very well be different in the wake of the pandemic. Only time will tell.

REFERENCES

"College Savings Foundation Survey of High School Students Finds COVID-19 Changes Higher Education Plans and Financing." 2020. *College Savings Foundation.* June 3, 2020. https://www.collegesavingsfoundation.org/press-releases/college-savings-foundation-survey-of-high-school-students-finds-covid-changes-higher-education-plans-and-financing/

Kuhn, Thomas. 1970. *The Structure of Scientific Revolutions.* Chicago, IL: University of Chicago Press.

Wells, H.G. 1895/2002. *The Time Machine.* New York: Signet Classic.

Index

Page numbers followed with "n" refer to endnotes.

academic integrity, 41
Academic Technology Services (ATS), 116
access to technology, 50
active learning, 75–78
ADA coordinators. *See* Americans with Disability Act (ADA) coordinators
adjourning of groups, 230–32
administration-instructor interactions, 75
affinity seeking, 20
aggressive communication, 21
Algorithms of Oppression (Noble), 59
Althusser, Louis: ideology, 50, 58, 59
Americans with Disability Act (ADA) coordinators, 151
Ames, Morgan, 214
Anderson, Lindsey B., 9, 97
anxiety, 95, 96, 131, 135–37, 139
argumentation skills, 243
argumentativeness, 21–22
artificial intelligence, 60
assembled audiences, online class requirement for, 211–14
assertive instructors, 21
assertiveness, 21
assignment and test deadlines policies, 66–68

assignment deadline policy, 67–68, 70
assistive technology (AT), 152–53, 156, 160
associative pedagogy, 11, 246
Astin, Alexander W., 74
asynchronous online format, 188, 193
asynchronous online speech assignment, 214
AT. *See* assistive technology (AT)
ATS. *See* Academic Technology Services (ATS)
attendance policies, 6
authentic self, 29

Bailey, David, 243
banking method of education, 58, 64
Bartanen, Michael D., 243
basic communication course, 103
BATs. *See* behavior alteration techniques (BATs)
Bayne, Brandon, 136
Bayne, Siân, 60
behavior alteration techniques (BATs), 23
Bejamin, Ruha, 59
benefits of online and hyflex models, 106
Benson, Thomas, 205

266   *Index*

Berea College, 168; Health and Physical Education Department, 172
Bjorn-Andersen, Niels, 45
Black Girls Code, 59–60
blended learning experiences, 102
Blewett, Lori, 9
Bodie, Graham D., 211
Bolkan, San, 27
Brinkley, J., 82
broadband access, 62
Broeckelman-Post, Melissa A., 185, 186, 188, 210, 212
Brown, Lydia X. Z., 136

CA. *See* communication anxiety (CA)
Calloway-Thomas, Carolyn: pedagogy of empathy, 213
care ethics, 65–66
Carmine, Simone, 112
Carozza, Linda, 8, 261
cataclysmic shift in higher education, 122
celebrating students, 232
Center for Instructional Design and Academic Technology, 97
Challis, Kate, 10
Characteristics of Marianist Education (CMEs), 110, 115–17, 121, 123
The Charisma Machine (Ames), 214
Chatham-Carpenter, April, 198
China, 1
Choi, Charles W., 211
civic online reasoning, 44
clarity, 19
Clark-Gordon, Cathlin V., 28
CMC. *See* computer-mediated communication (CMC)
CMEs. *See* Characteristics of Marianist Education (CMEs)
collaborative consistency, 81, 86
collaborative educational settings, 220
collaborative group work, 232
College Student Experience Questionnaire (CSEQ), 74
communication anxiety (CA), 104, 105
communication apprehension, 104
communication model, 43
communication pedagogy: critical grief and trauma-informed, 136–38; mental health and, 138–41; post-pandemic, 130–31
communication pedagogy courses, 199
communication processing time, 45–46
Communication Research and Theory Network (CRTNET), 205–7, 210, 211, 213
communication skills, 44, 104; of GTAs, 194–96; of instructor, 194–96
Communication Teacher, 210
communication technologies: advantages of, 46–47
communicator style, 21
community building, 100–102
Community for Teaching and Learning (CTL), 115, 116
community service, 168
compassion, pedagogy of, 61–64
compassionate and caring course curriculum, 68–70
Compton, Josh, 242
computer-mediated communication (CMC), 38, 43, 46–47, 49
confirmation, 20
conflict resolution strategies, 225–26, 233
Contemporary Argumentation and Debate (CAD), 241–42
"the contestive encounter," 245
conversation hours, 82
copresent audiences, defenses of, 204–5
Corman, Steven, 206
course assignments, 3, 5, 19, 23, 27, 28, 58, 61, 63, 64, 66–70, 78, 79, 84, 93, 95, 97, 101, 104, 105, 133, 149, 154–56, 180, 187–90, 192, 195, 198–99, 209, 212–14, 220, 222–24, 227, 230, 232, 244, 245, 259, 260
COVID-19 pandemic, 1–4, 129; assignment deadlines in, 68; emergency remote teaching (ERT) in, 38, 40–42, 44, 46, 50n3; and

higher education, 260–62; impact on small, liberal arts institutions, 111; integrating technology into pedagogy, 42–45(recommendations for, 45–50); and mental health in pedagogy. *See* mental health; online pedagogy and critical theory, 58–61; online teaching recommendations, 26–29; organizational tensions during, 112 (St. Mary's University. *See* St. Mary's University, COVID-19 impact on); response to, students with disabilities, 151–52; service learning, 172–75 (accessibility of students, 177–78, 180–81; flexibility of students, 175–77, 180–81; technology innovations of students, 178–81; University of Nebraska at Omaha (UNO), 173–76, 178–80); teaching effectiveness, 23–25; technology as necessary, 40–42; trauma and critical grief pedagogy, 136–38
Creative Problem Solving (CPS) process, 229
Crip theory, 139
critical grief pedagogy, 136–38. *See also* trauma-informed pedagogy
critical pedagogy, 61, 198
critical theory, 58–61
Crosby, Richard Benjamin, 209
CRTNET. *See* Communication Research and Theory Network (CRTNET)
CSEQ. *See* College Student Experience Questionnaire (CSEQ)
CTL. *See* Community for Teaching and Learning (CTL)
Cuban, Larry, 214

Dannels, Deanna P., 191–92
Darby, Flower, 69
data collection, 263
Daud, Shafee, 154
Davidson, Cathay N., 223
debates: exhibition, 250–52; intercollegiate academic. *See* intercollegiate academic debate (IAD); internet distance, 242; online, 241–44, 247; post-pandemic intercollegiate academic, 244–46; virtual, 241–44
debate tournament, hybridizing, 250
defenses of copresent audiences, 204–5
DEI. *See* diversity, equity, and inclusion (DEI)
department meetings, 105
depoliticization of ideology, 60
destigmatization of mental health, 139–41
Dewey, John, 168, 208
dialectical tensions, St. Mary's University, 111–12, 122–23
Dickson, Cheryl, 96
digital, 57, 61–63, 116, 117, 214, 234, 243, 263; communication, 43, 50, 103; inequalities, 91, 92, 94–95; inequities, 106; literacy, 62; pedagogy, 58, 66, 69; technology, 49; tools, 221; tournament, 241
"digital divide", 80, 92, 110, 249
digital natives, 105
digital surveillance policy, 48
disabilities, students with. *See* students with disabilities
disability communication studies, 139
disability exclusion, 132
disability resource centers, 163
disability resource officers (DROs), 151, 153
disability resource offices, 151
disability services, 161
diversity, equity, and inclusion (DEI), 130, 132, 133, 142
Doss, Kevin, 243
DROs. *See* disability resource officers (DROs)

early pandemic decisions, 187–89
Easton, Susan S., 187
Ebben, Maureen, 9
educational reform, 214
Edwards, Ashley A. Hanna, 8, 103

Edwards, Rich, 241, 242, 247
Edwards III, John W., 207
electronic forensic tournaments, 243
Elon University, 169; pandemic service learning, 173
emergency remote teaching (ERT), 38, 40–42, 44, 46, 51n3, 187
emotional resilience, 138
emotions, 137
empathy of instructor, 196–97
engagement, 6, 9, 73–75, 97; active learning for, 75–76; communicative dimensions of, 75; in the future, 85–86; multi-level. *See* multilevel engagement; traditional conceptualizations of, 75, 77, 84
enrollment, 3
equality, 132
equity, 59, 131–33, 141
ERT. *See* emergency remote teaching (ERT)
ethics of care, 8
ethos of instructor, 191–94
Evans, Peter, 60
exhibition debating, 250–52
explicit group norms, 223–25
explicit ideology, 59
expression/nonexpression, 112

Facebook, 242
fake audiences, 213–14
Fassett, Deanna L., 188
feedback, 23, 120
financial insecurity, 95
flexibility, 106
flipped classrooms, 157, 160
flipped learning, 6–7
"Forensics and the Net Generation" (Compton), 242
formal training, 81, 86
forming of groups, 223–25, 232
Foss, Karen, 104
Foucault, Michel, 60
Freire, Paulo: "banking method of education," 58, 64

Frey, T. Kody, 102
Frisby, Brandi N., 75
Frymier, Ann Bainbridge, 20, 211
Furco, Andrew, 169

Galvin, Kathleen M., 22
Garib, Ali, 10
GAs. *See* graduate assistants (GAs)
Gennaro, Steve, 261
Gilbert, Michael, 254n5
Gilligan, Carol: ethics of care, 65
Girls Who Code, 59–60
Giroux, Henry, 61
Goldman, Zachary W., 25
Goodboy, Alan K., 27
good debating, 244, 245
Google+, 242
Google Docs, 223, 224, 229, 233
Google Drive folder, 224
Google Forms, 223, 227, 230, 231, 233
Gore, John, 206
GPAs, 119–20, 122
graduate assistants (GAs), 170, 174, 175
graduate pedagogy, 198
graduate teaching assistants (GTAs), 198–200; building instructor ethos, 191–94; developing communication skills, 194–96; navigating cohort community, 189–91; of pandemic cohort, 195, 196, 198; pandemic cohort of, 10; performing empathy for students, 196–97; teaching public speaking, 186–89, 194–95; training, 185–86, 188–90, 199
Gramcian definition of ideology, 59
Greene, Jody, 84
Grobmeier, Cyndi, 9
group conflict, 226
group development phases, 11, 220; adjourning, 230–32; forming, 223–25, 232; norming, 227–29, 233; performing, 229–30, 233; storming, 225–27, 230, 233
group explicit norms, 223
grouphate, 220, 228, 229, 231

group implicit norms, 223
group norms, 228
groupthink, 229
group work, 219–20, 232; online tools for, 221–23
GTAs. *See* graduate teaching assistants (GTAs)
gymnasium, 246–48

Hahn, Taylor, 135
Hall, Jennifer, 97
Hampsten, Katherine, 9, 121
Hamza, Chloe A., 221
Handel, Marion, 92
Harries, Anne C. Kretsinger, 10
Hawhee, Debra, 245; associative pedagogy, 246
Helmick, Elizabeth, 10
Hennings, Jennifer M., 186, 199
Hershberger, Michelle, 189
higher education, 4–5; cataclysmic shift in, 122; COVID and, 260–62; integration of technology into, 39; obviousnesses in, 58, 60, 64; technology also threats to, 39
higher education institutions, 161; of students with disabilities. *See* students with disabilities
Hill, Amanda, 9
History of Sexuality (Foucault), 60–61
Honeycutt, James M., 206, 211
Horan, Virginia, 206
Huber, Aubrey A., 198
humor, 19
Hunt III, Arthur W., 204
hybrid classrooms, 156, 160
hybrid public debates, 251–52
hyflex classrooms, 156, 160
hyflex models, 98–99, 103, 106

ideology, 58–60
immediacy, 6, 19–20
implicit group norms, 228
implicit ideology, 59
implicit norms, 223, 228

imposter syndrome, 192, 193
in-class audiences, 204, 208–10
inclusive pedagogy, 149–63
incorporate technology into your pedagogy, 45–50
inequities, 67
Infante, Dominic A., 20; aggressive communication model, 21
inflexible assignment deadlines, 70
informal conversations, 82–83, 86
in-person instruction, 6
in-person learning, 245
in-person pedagogy, 244
in-person tournament participation, 248–50
institutional change, 142
instructional communication, 8, 18–20, 26, 186
instructional communication scholars/ scholarship, 43, 75, 263
instructional feedback, 23
instructional inoculations, 26; recommendation, 26–29
instructional resilience, 26, 29
instructional technology (IT), 153–54, 156, 160
instructor: behaviors, 25; clarity, 26–27; communication skills, 194–96; confirmation, 28, 29; credibility, 191–93; empathy, 196–97; ethos, 191–94; feedback, 27–28; immediacy, 193; misbehaviors, 22
instructor resource site (IRS), 80–81
instructor-student engagement, 75, 84
integration/separation, 112, 121–23
interactional dynamics, 131–33
intercollegiate academic debate (IAD), 239–40; civic and public impact of, 252–53; hybridity as a post-pandemic frontier for, 252–53; innovation in, 241; technology in, 241; virtual, 241–44; virtual *paideia* for, 244–46
internet connectivity, 62
internet distance debates, 242

Interpersonal Communication: Everyday Encounters (Wood), 141
intersectional issues, 140, 142
intrusive surveillance policies, 213–14
Iordanou, Kalypso, 243
IRS. *See* instructor resource site (IRS)
Isocrates, 246, 250, 251
IT. *See* instructional technology (IT)
Italy, 2–3

Jensen, Mary Ann C., 220
Johnstone, Christopher Lyle, 248
Jones-Bodie, Ashley, 97
Jordan, Amy B., 91, 92, 94–96
Joyce, Jillian, 185
justice, 19, 59

kairotic moment, 8, 42–45
Katopodis, Christina, 223
Katz, Vikki S., 91, 92, 94–96
Kaufmann, Renee, 75, 188, 195
Kauppinen, Merja, 243
Keith, William, 205
Kelsey, Dawn M., 27
Kiili, Carita, 243
Kim, Joshua, 98
King, Corwin, 206
Knoster, Kevin C., 25
Kohlberg, Lawrence: moral development theory, 65
Krebs, Emily, 140
Krogstad, Jens Manuel, 114
Kuhn, Thomas, 6; paradigm shift, 261
Kurr, Jessica A., 243

Lang, James M., 69
Lash, Brittany, 10
learning, 6
learning management system (LMS), 79, 93, 96, 188, 189
LeFebvre, Luke, 212
liberal arts education, 111
liberal arts institutions, 111; theories of paradox and dialectical tensions, 111–12

liberal education, 121
Lischer, Suzanne, 96
Littlefield, Robert S., 243
Lizzio, Alf, 23
Llano, Steven M., 244–45
LMS. *See* learning management system (LMS)
Lohiser, Amanda, 11
Louden, Allan, 241
Louis, Ryan, 243
Lucas, Melissa A., 9

Mabrey, Paul E., 243
maintenance communication, 82, 83
Makkawy, Amin, 205
managerial teaching, 22–23
managing identities, 193
Marcuse, Herbert, 65, 66
massive online open courses (MOOCs), 68
Mazzone, Raphael, 9
McConnell, Kathleen, 205
McCroskey, James C., 28, 104
McGarrity, Matt, 10–11, 209, 261
McGowan-Kirsch, Angela, 11
McGrew, Sarah, 44
McMillan, Jill J., 82
McRae, Chris, 186
media literacy, 44
Meisenbach, Rebecca J., 82
Mello, Brad, 9
mental health, 9–10, 129–30, 140–41; and accommodation, 140; benefits, 133–36; challenges, 139; and communication pedagogy, 138–41; crisis, 190; destigmatization of, 139–41; as a matter of equity, 131–33, 141; pandemic normalization of, 139
mental wellness, 130–31, 133, 140
"Mentor for Mission Program," 115
metalevel awareness, 243
Michaels, Tim, 244–45
mid-semester evaluation assignment, 84
Mid-Semester Evaluation of College Teaching, 84

Miller, Ann Neville Miller, 84, 98–99
Miller, John J., 199
modal hybridity, 249, 254n5
MOOCs. *See* massive online open courses (MOOCs)
moral development theory, 65
Moreman, Shane T., 205
Moreno, Kasia, 104
Morreale, Sherwyn P., 91–92, 99, 187
motivation, 27
MSU Denver Debate, 251–52
multilevel engagement, 74–77; principles, 77–85 (formal training, 81; informal conversations, 82–83; online engagement strategies, 83–86; robust virtual space for instructors, 80–81, 86; teaching standards, 77–80, 86)
multimodal transmediation, 243
multi-section presentational speaking course, 74–75
Multi-User Virtual Environments, 242
MURAL, 222, 224, 225, 229, 233. *See also* Google Docs; Google Forms
music playing, 107
Myers, Scott A., 8, 17, 22, 30n2, 189

negotiating relationships, 193
Newman, Marc, 207
New York City Sophist (Llano), 244
Noble, Safiya, 59
Noddings, Nel: ethics of care, 65
nonaggressive teaching, 21–22
nonverbal immediacy behaviors, 20
norming of groups, 227–29, 233
North, Stephen, 204
Norton, Robert: communicator style, 21
Nussbaum, Jon F., 8

obviousnesses of pandemic teaching, 58, 60, 64
O'Donnell, Timothy M., 242
Ognyanova, Katherine, 91, 92, 94–96
OLPC. *See* Laptop Per Child movement (OLPC)

Omaha Public Schools (OPS), 174–75
One Laptop Per Child movement (OLPC), 214
online audiences, 205
online class requirement for assembled audiences, 211–14
online course teaching, 25–26; recommendations, 26–29
online debate, 241–44, 247
online education, 207, 234; advantages of, 42; caring pedagogy in, 65–66; concerns, 41
online engagement strategies, 83–86
online immediacy, 193
online learning, 3; feedback, 120; modalities, 106, 189–91
online learning management system, 192
online pedagogy, 58–61, 244
online proctoring technology, 59–61
online public speaking, 103, 204–7, 212; audience and, 205; classes, 206, 207, 214; courses, 203, 205, 209
online public speaking pedagogy, 10–11
online teaching, 69
Online Teaching Certification Program (OTCP), 116
online tools for group work, 221–23
online tournaments, 249
online training, 187–89; transition to, 187–89
open office hours, 83
OPS. *See* Omaha Public Schools (OPS)
Orbis: A Journal of World Affairs, 247
organizational tensions during the COVID-19, 112
OTCP. *See* Online Teaching Certification Program (OTCP)

pandemic cohort of graduate students, 195, 196, 198
pandemic induced paradigmatic moment, 4–7
"Pandemic Pedagogy" Facebook group, 80, 85, 101

pandemic service learning, 172–75; accessibility of students, 177–78, 180–81; flexibility of students, 175–77, 180–81; projects, 178, 180; technology innovations of students, 178–81; University of Nebraska at Omaha (UNO), 173–76, 178–81
pandemic teaching under trauma and grief, 136–38
paradigm shift, 261
paradox theory, St. Mary's University, 111–12, 122–23
Pear Deck, 221–23, 226–28, 232, 233
pedagogical change, 142
pedagogical practices, 142
pedagogy: care ethics in, 65–66; of compassion, 61–64; critical grief, 136–38; of empathy, 213; equality approaches to, 132; equity approaches to, 131–33; flexible, 47–48; inequality, 67; integrating technology into, 43–45 (recommendations for, 45–50); online, and critical theory, 58–61; space and time, 246–48; trauma-informed perspectives, 136–38; UDL approach to, 134–36
Pedagogy of the Oppressed (Freire), 64
pedagogy paradigm shift, 8
peer assessment instrument, 231–32
Peng, Chong A., 154
performing of groups, 229–30, 233
Personal Report of Communication Apprehension (PRCA), 104
Pettit, Emma, 99–100
physical audiences, 210
plan for academic year in 2020–2021, 98–100
positive learning environment, 28–29
post-hoc Spearman's Rho correlation coefficient, 26
post-pandemic communication pedagogy, 130–31
post-pandemic intercollegiate academic debate (IAD), 244–46

post-pandemic online learning, 208
post-pandemic pedagogical paradigm prediction, 8–11
post-pandemic speculations, 180–81
Pottinger, Matthew, 3
power of instructors, 22–23
PRCA. *See* Personal Report of Communication Apprehension (PRCA)
pre-COVID-19, assignment deadlines in, 67
pre-pandemic developments in virtual debate, 241–44
pre-pandemic online learning, 208
pre-pandemic service learning at UNO, 169–72
"Prepared to Pivot" program, 116
presentational teaching, 20–21, 28
problem-posing method of education, 64
professional development, 96
psychological resilience, 138
public, 209
public speaking, 10–11, 203, 208; competencies, 210; defined, 206, 210; skill development, 208–11; teaching, 186–89, 194–95
public speaking anxiety, 104

quality rehearsals, 211–12

Race, Politics, and Pandemic Pedagogy: Education in a Time of Crisis (Giroux), 61
Race After Technology (Bejamin), 59
racial disparities, 51n3
racial profiling, 59
radical communication, 62–64
Rancer, Andrew S., 20
"Rattler Real Talk" Survey, 118, 120
Reese, Ben, 242
Reffue, John, 206
rehearsal realism, 211
Reich, Justin, 214
Reif, John, 11
relational teaching, 19–20, 28

Remote Learning Proficiency (RLP), 96
remote work, 219
representation, 59
rerecording of speeches, 211–14
resilience, 101, 138
responsive instructors, 21
responsiveness, 21
responsive teaching behaviors, 28, 29
rhetorical *paideia*, 245, 250
rhetorical situation, 209
rhetorical teaching, 18–19
RLP. *See* Remote Learning Proficiency (RLP)
Robinson, Tomeka M., 242
robust virtual space for instructors, 80–81, 86
Ruiz-Mesa, Kristina, 185, 188

Safi, Netkey, 96
San Antonio, 114–15
Sarapin, Susan H., 206, 207
Schrodt, Paul, 23
Schwartz-DuPre, Rae Lynn, 242
Schwartzman, Roy, 78, 80, 101
Scott, Michael D., 8
self-assessment, 231, 232
self-disclosure, 19
Sell, A. J., 82
Sellnow, Deanna D., 75, 84, 98–99
service learning, 10, 168–69; COVID-19 pandemic. *See* COVID-19 pandemic: service learning; UNO's definition and approach to, 170–71
Shallish, Lauren, 132
Shannon–Weaver Model, 43
Shel, Tammy, 65, 67
short-/long-term orientation, 122
SIDE. *See* social identity model of deindividuation effects (SIDE)
"Silver Linings: Key Lessons From How We Communicate In The New Normal" (Moreno), 104
Simonds, Cheri J., 186
skill development for public speaking, 208–11

Skype, 242
SLA, 171, 173–75, 179–80; stakeholders, 175, 177
Smith, Blaine E., 243
Smith, Tony E., 211
Snider, Alfred C., 242
social identity model of deindividuation effects (SIDE), 47
social information processing theory, 45–46
social loafing, 226–27
social media, 50
socio-communicative style, 21
socio-emotional well-being, 92–96
speech communication, 206
speech rehearsal quality, 211–12
squad room, 247, 251
stability/change, 112, 122, 123
Steinfatt, Thomas M., 206, 210
St. Mary's University, COVID-19 impact on: case study, 110 (as COVID-19 "hotspot," 114; data collection and review, 113; faculty perceptions of student engagement, 120–21; GPAs, 119–20, 122; graduation rate, 120, 122; maintaining community in online learning, 117–18; methodology, 112–13; mission and CMEs, 115–16; "prepared to pivot," 116–17; "Rattler Real Talk" Survey, 118–20; student perception of connection, 118–19; student perceptions of academic performance, 119–20; students' financial hardships, 114–15); dialectical tensions, 122–23; emergent tensions, 121–22; paradox theory, 122–23
Stolley, Kathy Shepherd, 169
Storch, Sharon, 10
storming of groups, 225–27, 230, 233
Stratton, Casey M., 8
Strawser, Michael G., 84, 98–99
student: population, 10, 149–51, 158–60, 162, 163; support, 197; uncertainty, 48–49; video blogs, 96

student engagement. *See* engagement
student learning, 6, 8, 17–22, 38–40, 49, 74, 75, 85, 99, 121, 123, 131, 138, 189, 192, 195, 196, 225, 232, 262, 263
student retention or "ghosting" policy, 48–49
students with disabilities, 10, 140, 149–50; access to mental health support services, 161–62; accommodations, 151, 161; campus life, barriers to, 157–58, 161; challenges, 151–52, 163; changes to course structure, 154–57; COVID-19 response and, 150–51; depression, stress and anxiety, 159; diversity initiatives, 163; educational equity, 162; increased use of technology, 152–54; mental health centers for, 161–63; mental health concerns, 158–59; mental health support for, 161–62; supporting the, 163
surveillance, 41; of students' online activities, 59; technology, 261
survey questions, 84
Swauger, Shea, 61
synchronous online classes, 78
Synnott, Kevin, 230

Tatum, Nicholas T., 102
teacher-student relationship, 246
teaching authenticity, 29
teaching effectiveness: COVID-19, 23–25; frames, 17–18; as managerial frame, 22–23; as nonaggressive frame, 21–22; as presentational frame, 20–21; as relational frame, 19–20; as rhetorical frame, 18–19
teaching public speaking, 186–89, 194–95
teaching standards, 77–80, 86
technological ability, 96
technological access: and abilities, 92–96; issues, 93–95
technological challenges, 93
technological surveillance tools, 60

technological tinkering, 214
technology: access issues, 50; during COVID-19 pandemic, 40–42; to enhance communication skills, 44–45; to enhance diversity, equity, and inclusion of courses, 44; failures, 50; integrating in classroom, 38–40, 43; integrating into pedagogy, 43–45 (recommendations for, 45–50); limitations, 49–50; model thoughtful criticism of, 49–50; as necessary during COVID-19 pandemic, 40–42; as novel and dangerous, 38–40; as part of communication model, 43; as pedagogical necessity, 42–45; pervasiveness, 43; in pre-pandemic, 38–40; threat of, 39; use in higher education, 38–40
technology infrastructure issues, 94
Teven, Jason J., 28
textbooks, 205
Thorpe, Janice, 187
time, 7
tinkering, 214
Todorova, Nelly, 45
transition to online format, 187–89
transition to online learning, 116, 117, 119, 120
trauma-informed pedagogy, 136–38
Tuckman's phasic model. *See* group development phases
Tulane University, 169; pandemic service learning, 173
Turman, Paul D., 23
Turpin, Paul D., 207
Tyack, David B., 214
Tyler, Ralph, 74

UDL. *See* Universal Design for Learning (UDL)
uncertainty, 48–49, 187, 189
underserved communities, 243
United States, 1, 2
Universal Design for Learning (UDL), 66, 68, 130, 134–36, 140, 155–56, 160, 261

University of Nebraska at Omaha (UNO), 167; graduate assistants (GAs), 170, 174, 175; pandemic service learning, 173–76, 178–81; pre-pandemic projects, 171–72; pre-pandemic service learning at, 169–72

Valenzano, Joseph M., 185, 208
Vallade, Jessalyn I., 22, 188, 195
verbal aggressiveness, 21–22
verbal immediacy behaviors, 20
video blogs, 104, 242; assignments, 95
video conferencing, 40, 46, 104, 131; software, 6, 222, 261
video submission, 212
virtual communication, 104
virtual debate, 11, 241–44
virtual exhibition debating, 250–52
virtual office hours, 83, 85–86
virtual *paideia,* 244–48, 250, 253; defined, 254n4
virtual spaces, 80–81, 86
virtual tournament participation, 248–50
virtual training, 105
volunteerism, 168
Voth, Ben, 241

Wallace, Samuel P., 103
Wanzer, Melissa Bekelja, 20
Ward, Susan, 203, 212
Warner, Michael, 209
Warren, John T., 188
well-being, 9
Wendt, Ted, 206, 207
Westwick, Joshua N., 91–92, 99, 187
WHO. *See* World Health Organization (WHO)
Willer, Erin, 137
Wilson, Keithia, 23
Wineburg, Sam, 44
Witt, Paul L., 23
Womack, Deanna F., 20
Wood, Jennifer: participation requirements, 213
Wood, Julia, 141
Woods, Carly, 240, 243–44
World Health Organization (WHO), 2, 3
Wuhan, 1

Zoom, 5–7, 94, 96–101, 104–7, 117, 120, 122, 132, 133, 136, 167, 174, 175, 177–80, 189–91, 222, 247
Zoom fatigue, 133

About the Contributors

Lindsey B. Anderson (PhD, Purdue University) is an associate professor in the Department of Communication at the University of Maryland and the executive director of the oral communication program. She is a qualitative researcher whose communicate education-based research has appeared in outlets such as *Communication Teacher*, the *Basic Communication Course Annual*, and *Qualitative Research Reports in Communication*.

Lori Blewett (PhD, University of Illinois) is a professor of communication studies at The Evergreen State College in Olympia, WA. She is a faculty fellow for the office of Inclusive Excellence and Student Success and Evergreen's faculty representative to the Washington State Legislature.

Linda Carozza (PhD, York University) teaches within the discipline of philosophy at York University in Toronto, Canada. She has been developing and delivering both blended and fully online courses for the last decade. Dr. Carozza founded an e-learning community of practice at York University in which both authors are members.

Kate Challis (BA, Brigham Young University) is a first-year MA student in the teaching English as a second language/applied linguistics program in the Department of English at Iowa State University. She holds a BA in French teaching and a minor in teaching English as a second language. She taught public speaking for the first time amid the COVID-19 pandemic as a graduate teaching assistant in Iowa State's speech communication program.

Maureen Ebben (PhD, University of Illinois at Urbana-Champagn) is an associate professor in the Department of Communication and Media Studies at the University of Southern Maine, Portland. An award-winning teacher and scholar, her work appears in the volumes *Coding Pedagogy*, and *Teaching, Learning and the Net Generation: Concepts and Tools for Reaching Digital Learners*, as well as journals such as *Learning, Media, and Technology*.

Ali Garib (MA, Arizona State University and M., University of Manchester) is a PhD student in applied linguistics and technology in the Department of English at Iowa State University. He holds MA degrees in linguistics, teaching English as a second language, and educational technology and is a Fulbright and Chevening alumnus. He taught public speaking for the first time amid the COVID-19 pandemic as a graduate teaching assistant in Iowa State's speech communication program.

Steve Gennaro (PhD, McGill University) is one of the founding faculty members of York University's children, childhood, and youth studies program. In addition to his own teaching, he works as the learning designer for the Office of the Dean in the Faculty of Liberal Arts and Professional Studies at York University.

Cyndi Grobmeier (MA, Governors State University) serves as the introductory course in communication director at Saint Xavier University (SXU). She is currently nearing completion of her doctorate in educational technology at Norther Illinois University. Her work at SXU involves managing adjuncts for the introductory course and developing new technology courses focused on effective communication in a social media space.

Katherine Hampsten (PhD, Texas A&M University) is an associate professor of communication studies at St. Mary's University. Her scholarship and teaching focus on intersections of communication, gender, and work. Hampsten has authored multiple edited chapters and articles about work/life issues, pedagogy, and qualitative research in publications such as the *Journal of Applied Communication Research* and the *International Encyclopedia of Communication Research Methods*. She has received top paper and panel recognition from the National Communication Association and Central States Communication Association. In 2016, the Alumni Association of St. Mary's University awarded her the Distinguished Faculty Award for Excellence in Teaching.

Ashley A. Hanna Edwards (PhD, Michigan State University) is an assistant professor of communication studies at the University of Wisconsin–La Crosse who regularly teaches in the basic communication course. She is an interpersonal communication scholar, with special interests in social support, technology-mediated communication, and culture, as well as the pedagogy of teaching students about communication.

Elizabeth Helmick (BA, University of Nevada, Las Vegas) is a first-year MA student in English with literature specialization at Iowa State University. She holds a BA in journalism and media studies with an emphasis in integrated marketing communications and a minor in English. She taught public speaking for the first time amid the COVID-19 pandemic as a graduate teaching assistant in Iowa State's speech communication program.

Amanda Hill (PhD, University of Central Florida) is an assistant professor of communication studies at St. Mary's University specializing in storytelling and media production. She has presented internationally and has published in a diverse range of journals including *Media Education Research Journal*; *Storytelling, Self, Society*; *Visual Ethnography*; *Community Literacy Journal*; *Florida Studies*; and the *IAFOR Journal of Psychology & the Behavioral Sciences*.

Anne C. Kretsinger-Harries (PhD, The Pennsylvania State University) is an assistant professor of rhetoric and professional communication and director of public speaking in the Department of English at Iowa State University. Her research examines rhetoric and pedagogy and has appeared in *Rhetoric & Public Affairs* and *Communication Teacher*.

Brittany N. Lash (PhD, University of Kentucky) is an assistant professor of communication at the University of Dayton. Having earned her PhD in communication with an emphasis on health communication from the University of Kentucky, her primary research interests focus on the intersections between health and interpersonal communication. A particular passion in disability studies and the communication issues surrounding individuals with disabilities has driven much of her research as she strives to give a voice to individuals within this population.

Amanda Lohiser (PhD, SUNY Buffalo) has over ten years of experience teaching in higher education. She has taught undergraduate and graduate students in the United States, Singapore, and Denmark. She brings a unique perspective to the classroom through her educational background in communication studies (BA and PhD), public relations (MS), creativity and change leadership (graduate certification and pending MS), and face coding (three certifications). She has published in the fields of pedagogy, communication, and creativity.

Melissa A. Lucas (PhD, University of Maryland) is a professional track faculty member of the Department of Communication at the University of Maryland and the comanaging director of the oral communication program. She developed and currently teaches a specialized version of the oral communication course as well as the rhetoric of gender activism.

Raphael Mazzone (PhD, George Mason University) is a professional track faculty member of the Department of Communication at the University of Maryland and the comanaging director of the oral communication program. He teaches a variety of courses including foundations of oral communication, organizational communication, intercultural communication, and peer-mentoring.

Matt McGarrity (PhD, Indiana University) is a teaching professor and founder of the University of Washington Speaking Center. His research and teaching focuses on public speaking, argumentation, and the history of rhetoric. He founded, and continues to direct, the University of Washington Speaking Center. His free online public speaking classes have reached a million students in over 170 countries.

Angela M. McGowan-Kirsch (PhD, University of Southern Mississippi) has fifteen years of experience teaching undergraduate courses, such as mass media and society, rhetoric and criticism, persuasion, and presidential campaign communication, both online and face-to-face. She holds a certificate in training and development. In 2019, she was named SUNY Fredonia's Open SUNY Online Teaching Ambassador. She has published in the fields of political communication and communication pedagogy.

Brad Mello (PhD, University of Oklahoma) is professor and chair at St. Xavier University. He spent thirteen years teaching and serving as chair of the Department of Communication at Trinity Washington University followed by six years as the associate director for Academic and Professional Affairs at The National Communication Association (NCA) where he acquired a nearly $600,000 grant from Lumina foundation to support NCA's student learning outcomes in communication project. He is also a featured speaker for the National Institute of Student Learning Outcomes and an HLC peer reviewer.

Scott A. Myers (PhD, Kent State University) is a professor and Peggy Rardin McConnell Endowed Teaching Chair of Communication Studies in the Department of Communication Studies at West Virginia University and an instructional communication researcher whose projects focus primarily on the role communication plays in the instructor-student relationship, both in and out of the classroom, using experimental, survey, and content analytic research methods.

John J. Rief (PhD, University of Pittsburgh) is an assistant professor of rhetoric and debate and Director of Debate at Metropolitan State University of Denver. He has been actively involved in intercollegiate academic debate as a coach, consultant, and mentor for nearly fifteen years. His coauthored scholarship on argumentation theory and debate pedagogy and practice has appeared in such venues as *Communication and Critical/Cultural Studies*, *Argumentation & Advocacy*, *Contemporary Argumentation and Debate*, and the selected works volumes of the *Alta Argumentation Conference*.

Sharon Storch (PhD, Indiana University of Pennsylvania), is an assistant professor of organizational communication in the School of Communication at the University of Nebraska, Omaha. Her research interests qualitatively examine mobile devices and their subsequent influences on professional and familial dynamics. Sharon teaches undergraduate and graduate communication classes with a focus on providing real-life learning experiences in the classroom.

Casey M. Stratton (M.A., Missouri State University) is a PhD graduate student in the Department of Communication Studies at West Virginia University. He is an instructional and organizational communication enthusiast, with professional experience in organizational learning and instructional design. He recently led an organizational learning redesign strategy to embrace virtual pedagogical methods, due to COVID-19.

Joseph M. Valenzano III (PhD, Georgia State University, 2006) is professor and chair of the Department of Communication at the University of Dayton. He is a two-time winner of the NCA Basic Course Division Program of Excellence Award, and is the lead author of three national communication textbooks. A former editor of the *Basic Communication Course Annual*, he has authored or coauthored over twenty peer-reviewed publications (appeared in *Communication Education*, *Communication Monographs*, and *Basic Communication Course Annual*, among other outlets), two monographs and co-edited one book. His expertise is in communication pedagogy, as well as the intersection of religious communication, political communication, and popular culture.

www.ingramcontent.com/pod-product-compliance
Lightning Source LLC
Chambersburg PA
CBHW020111010526
44115CB00008B/788